THE ROAD TO COMMUNISM

**D O C U M E N T S
OF THE 22nd CONGRESS
OF THE COMMUNIST PARTY
OF THE SOVIET UNION**

October 17-31, 1961

FOREIGN LANGUAGES PUBLISHING HOUSE
MOSCOW

ПУТЬ К КОММУНИЗМУ

СБОРНИК МАТЕРИАЛОВ XXII СЪЕЗДА КОММУНИСТИЧЕСКОЙ ПАРТИИ СОВЕТСКОГО СОЮЗА

17—31 октября 1961 года

Printed in the Union of Soviet Socialist Republics

CONTENTS

N. S. KHRUSHCHOV

REPORT
OF THE CENTRAL COMMITTEE
OF THE COMMUNIST PARTY
OF THE SOVIET UNION
TO THE 22nd CONGRESS OF THE C.P.S.U.

October 17, 1961

Comrades, some six years have elapsed since the Twentieth Congress of the Communist Party of the Soviet Union, years that have had exceptional, we may well say historic, significance for our Party, for the Soviet people and for all mankind.

Our Soviet homeland has entered the period of the full-scale construction of communism along the entire broad front of giant undertakings. The economy and culture of the Soviet Union are making rapid progress. The Seven-Year Plan, the plan for a tremendous development of our country's productive forces, is being successfully implemented. Throughout the country the creative forces of the people gush forth as from thousands of fountainheads. The triumphant flights of Soviet men into space, the first in human history, may be said to crown our wonderful achievements, to be the banner of communist construction raised on high.

Socialism has been firmly established throughout the world socialist community. The major events of the past years have been an expression of the chief law of the day —the tempestuous growth and strengthening of the vital forces of the world socialist system.

Our Party and our state have been functioning in a complicated international situation. On a number of occasions the imperialists have attempted to bring the world to the brink of war and to probe the strength of the Soviet Union and the courage of its peoples. Many bourgeois politicians have sought comfort in the illusion that our plans might fail and the socialist camp disintegrate. They have undertaken more than a few acts of provocation and sabotage against us. The Party and the entire Soviet people have exposed the intrigues of our enemies and have emerged from all trials with honour. The Soviet Union is today stronger and more powerful than ever before! (*Prolonged applause.*)

Now that the Land of Soviets is in the prime of its creative strength and we are reviewing the victorious path we have travelled, there may be some people who think that that path has been an easy and simple one. But it has not; the period since the Twentieth Congress has been neither easy nor simple, it has required of our Party and of all the peoples of the Soviet Union tremendous effort and devotion. *It has fallen to the lot of the Soviet people, of the Party of Communists of the Soviet Union, to be pioneers in the great mission of communist construction, and advance to the victory of communism over uncharted paths.*

History does not develop in a straight line, it has its zigzags and abrupt turns. To be a political leader, a party must possess truly great qualities and not lose sight of the overall perspective under conditions of swift advance and sharp turns in the development of society, must see clearly the road to communism. These qualities are possessed in full by the Party of Communists of the Soviet Union, the party created by the great Lenin. To find the correct solution to the chief problems, evolve the general line in home and foreign policy and put it firmly into effect, the Party and its Central Committee needed a profound understanding of events, revolutionary boldness and determination.

Events have fully borne out the Party's theoretical conclusions and political course, its general line. The ten-million-strong Party of Communists of the Soviet Union has come to its Twenty-Second Congress united and solid, linked up with the Soviet people by unseverable bonds. (*Stormy applause.*) The five thousand delegates to our

Congress, the finest sons and daughters of the great Party of Lenin, personify the unity of the Party and the people, their will and thoughts. (*Applause.*)

The course adopted by our Party has been of tremendous significance in strengthening the unity of the socialist countries, the unity of the international Communist and working-class movement, and in preserving the peace and preventing a new world war. The Soviet state has gained still greater authority and prestige in world affairs. Meetings of representatives of Communist and Workers' parties have assessed highly the role of the C.P.S.U. in the international Communist and working-class movement.

Permit me, on behalf of this Congress, on behalf of all Communists of the Soviet Union, to express our heartfelt gratitude to the fraternal parties for their confidence in our Party. (*Prolonged applause.*) Permit me to assure our dear guests here, the delegates from the fraternal parties, that the Communist Party of the Soviet Union will continue to fulfil its internationalist duty to the working people of all countries, to all progressive mankind. (*Stormy applause.*)

I

THE PRESENT WORLD SITUATION AND THE INTERNATIONAL POSITION OF THE SOVIET UNION

Comrades, the chief content of the period following the Twentieth Congress of the C.P.S.U. is the competition between the two world social systems—the socialist and capitalist systems. It has become the pivot, the main feature of world development in the present historical period. Two lines, two historical tendencies in social development, have been more and more evident. One of them is the line of social progress, of peace and creative activity. The other is the line of reaction, oppression and war.

If we imagine the whole globe to be the scene of this competition, we see that socialism has been wresting one position after another from the old world. In the first place, capitalism has been seriously cramped by socialism in a decisive sphere of human activity, that of material production. The socialist system's share in world production has increased and its rates of development greatly exceed those of the most advanced capitalist countries. It is obvious to everyone that the socialist countries are able to develop colossal productive forces and create a real abundance of material and spiritual values.

While conducting an unswerving policy of peace we have not forgotten the threat of war on the part of the imperialists. We have done everything necessary to ensure the superiority of our country in defence. The achievements of socialist production and of Soviet science and technology have enabled us to effect a veritable revolution in matters military. Our country and the entire socialist camp now possess vast power, ample to provide a reliable defence for the great gains of socialism against the inroads of imperialist aggressors. (*Applause.*) The growing defence might of the Soviet Union and the other socialist countries and the world peace forces have not allowed the imperialists to divert the competition between the two systems from the path of peace on to that of armed conflicts, of war. The Soviet Union, while pursuing the Leninist policy of peaceful coexistence, has resolutely exposed and checked imperialist provocations.

The fact that it has been possible to prevent war and that Soviet people and the peoples of other countries have been able to enjoy the benefits of peaceful life must be regarded as the chief result of the activities of our Party and its Central Committee in increasing the might of the Soviet state and in implementing a Leninist foreign policy, as a result of the work of the fraternal parties in the socialist states and of greater activity by the peace forces in all countries. (Prolonged applause.)

During recent years, as we know, the imperialists have made a number of attempts to start a new war and test the strength of the socialist system. During the past five years the U.S.A. and its closest allies have repeatedly resorted to brutal force, have rattled the sabre. But on each occasion the Soviet Union and the other socialist countries have checked the aggressor in good time. Of particular, fundamental importance were the actions of the socialist countries in defence of the peoples struggling for their liberty and independence. The masses are getting to realise more and more that the Soviet Union and all the socialist countries are a reliable support in the struggle the peoples are waging for their liberty and independence, for progress and peace. (*Applause.*)

In the course of the peaceful competition between the two systems capitalism has suffered a crushing moral defeat in the eyes of all peoples. Ordinary people are becoming daily convinced that capitalism cannot solve any of the urgent problems facing mankind. It is becoming ever more obvious that these problems can be solved only through socialism. Faith in the capitalist system and the capitalist path of development is dwindling. Monopoly capital is losing influence and resorting more frequently to the intimidation and suppression of the people, to methods of open dictatorship to implement its home policy and to acts of aggression against other countries. The masses, however, are offering increasing resistance to reaction.

It is no secret that intimidation and threats are not a sign of strength but are evidence of the weakening of capitalism and the deepening of its general crisis. As the saying goes, "If you couldn't hang on by the mane, you won't hold on by the tail!" (*Laughter.*) The reactionaries in some countries are still able, in defiance of constitutions, to dissolve parliaments, cast the best representatives of the people into prison and dispatch cruisers and marines to subdue the "unruly". Such measures of repression may put off for a time the fatal hour of capitalist rule, but they expose, to a still greater extent, the predatory nature of imperialism. The imperialists are cutting off the branch on which they are sitting. There are no forces in the world that can stem mankind's advance along the road of progress. (*Stormy applause.*)

Events show that our Party's policy, elaborated by the Twentieth Congress, was a correct and true one; the Congress noted that the main feature of our epoch was the emergence of socialism beyond the bounds of one country and its conversion into a world system. In the period since that Congress there has been further important progress—the world socialist system is becoming the decisive factor in the development of society.

The Party drew the conclusion that the collapse of colonialism is inevitable. Under the powerful blows of the national-liberation movement the colonial system has, to all intents and purposes, fallen to pieces.

The Party propounded the important thesis that wars between states are not inevitable in the present epoch, that they can be prevented. Events of the past years serve to confirm this, too. They show that the mighty forces standing watch over the peace have today effective means of preventing the imperialists from launching a world war. The superiority of the forces of peace and socialism over those of imperialism and war has become more evident.

To put it briefly, comrades, for us those six years have been good years on a world scale. (*Stormy applause.*)

1. The Further Growth of the Might of the Socialist System and Its Conversion into the Decisive Factor in World Development. Strengthening of the International Brotherhood of the Socialist Countries

In the period under review an important stage in the development of the world socialist system has been completed. Its specific features are these:

The Soviet Union has launched the full-scale construction of communism; the majority of the People's Democracies have abolished multiformity in their economies and are now completing the building of socialism; fraternal co-operation and mutual aid between the socialist countries have been developed in every way. Not only in the Soviet Union, but in all socialist countries, social and economic possibilities for the restoration of capitalism have now been eliminated. The growing might of the new world system guarantees the permanence of the political and socio-economic gains of the socialist countries. The complete victory of socialism within the framework of the community of genuinely free peoples is certain.

The economy of the world socialist system continues to develop at incomparably higher rates than capitalist economy. Here are some figures showing the growth of industrial production in the socialist and capitalist countries (for a comparable area, in %% of 1937):

Years	Socialist countries	Capitalist countries
1937	100	100
1955	362	199
1956	404	208
1957	445	215
1958	521	210
1959	610	231
1960	681	244

As you can see, the industrial output of the socialist countries in 1960 was 6.8 times greater than in 1937, while the capitalist countries had increased theirs less than 2.5 times. The socialist countries' share in world industrial production was 27 per cent in 1955 and in 1960 it had increased to roughly 36 per cent.

The ratio of industrial to agricultural production has changed in all socialist countries. The share of industrial production is growing rapidly, the average for the whole socialist community now being about 75 per cent. The economic development of the world socialist system has an industrial trend.

The completion of the organisation of producer co-operatives in agriculture in the majority of the People's Democracies was the great revolutionary event of the period. The socialist sector's share in the total area of farmlands of the socialist countries is now more than ninety per cent. This has resulted in a change in the class structure of society, a stronger alliance between the working class and the peasantry and the abolition of the economic basis for the exploitation of man by man. The moral and political unity of the people, first established in our country, is growing stronger in all socialist countries. Our people feel deep satisfaction over the successes in socialist construction achieved by the great Chinese people and by other fraternal peoples, and wish them further success. (*Prolonged applause.*)

Thanks to economic progress, the living standards of the people in the socialist countries have improved. It is all the more gratifying to note this because the revolutionary reorganisation of society in the fraternal countries during the early years was inevitably accompanied by considerable losses and difficulties and large sums had to be spent to overcome the economic backwardness inherited from capitalism. Now that an important stage in social reorganisation has been completed, more favourable conditions have been created for a further growth of economy and culture and for a higher standard of living for the people.

The appearance of a large group of sovereign socialist states in the world posed the problem of organising their mutual relations and co-operation on a basis that was new in principle. By their joint efforts, the fraternal parties have found and are improving new forms of inter-state relations—economic, political and cultural co-operation based on the principles of equality, mutual benefit and comradely mutual aid. The growing fraternal rapprochement between the socialist countries, together with their political and economic consolidation, constitute one of the decisive factors of the strength and durability of the world socialist system. We joined forces voluntarily in order to march forward to a common goal together. The union was not imposed on us by anyone. We need it as much as we need air.

In the first stage of the development of the world socialist system, relations between the countries were effected mostly by way of bilateral foreign trade and scientific and technical exchanges, the dominant forms being aid and credits granted by some countries to others.

In recent years the experience of the fraternal parties has brought into being a new form—direct co-operation in production. Take, for instance, the co-ordination of the basic indexes of development in certain branches of the economy for the 1956-60 period, agreed upon by the member countries of the Council for Mutual Economic Aid. This was an important step forward. Since 1959 state plans for economic development have been co-ordinated. It has become the practice to arrange periodical consultations and exchanges of opinion between the leaders of parties and governments on important economic and political problems. The collective organs of the socialist states —the Warsaw Treaty Organisation and the Council for Mutual Economic Aid—have grown stronger.

We have every ground for speaking of a durable socialist community of free peoples existing in the world today.

The profound qualitative changes that have taken place in the socialist countries and in relations between them are evidence of the growing maturity of the world socialist system which has now entered a new stage of development. The chief thing now is, by consistently developing the economy of each socialist country and all of them collectively, to achieve preponderance of the socialist world's absolute volume of production over that of the capitalist world. This will be a great historic victory for socialism. The achievements of our country, which is the first to have entered the path of full-scale communist construction, facilitate and accelerate the advance of the other countries of the world socialist system towards communism.

The constant improvement of forms and methods of economic management, the maximum rational employment of internal resources and possibilities, and the observance of scientifically substantiated proportions in the development of the various branches of the economy of each individual country now assume particular significance. As never before, there is now a growing necessity to make the most reasonable and effective use of the advantages arising out of the development of the world socialist system—the socialist international division of labour, specialisation and co-operation in production, the coordination of economic plans and the possibilites of the world socialist market.

In the period under review the trade turnover between the socialist countries has been growing with exceptional rapidity, its rate of growth greatly exceeding that of the capitalist countries. In the 1950-60 period the trade turnover between the member states of the socialist community was more than trebled. The trade turnover between the capitalist countries for the same period was only doubled. In the new stage of the development of the world socialist system, too, mutually beneficial trade between the fraternal countries will occupy an important place. Subsequently, it will probably be effected in accordance with the same principles as trade within each socialist country, that is, with compensation for the expenditure of socially necessary labour. The more fully this principle operates, the more effective will be the economic stimuli in each country and the more rapid will be the development of inter-state co-operation and of the socialist international division of labour based on the principle of sovereignty of each state and taking due account of national interests.

The combination of the effort to develop the economy of each socialist country on the one hand, and the common effort to strengthen and expand economic co-operation and mutual assistance on the other, is the main road to further progress in the world socialist economy.

Comrades, Lenin's statement to the effect that socialism exercises its influence on world development mainly by its economic achievements is today more valid than ever. The all-round, growing effect which the building of socialism and communism is having on the peoples of the non-socialist countries is a revolutionising factor that accelerates the progress of all mankind.

Socialism is firmly maintaining priority in rates of economic development and is ahead of the capitalist countries in the development of a number of highly important branches of world science and technology. The imperialist countries have lost their former monopoly in supplying the world non-socialist market with means of production, and also in granting credits, loans and technical services. The peoples of Asia and Africa who have liberated themselves from the foreign colonial yoke are looking more and more frequently to the socialist countries, and borrowing from them experience in the organisation of certain spheres of economic and social life. In the world socialist system they seek protection and support in their struggle against colonialist encroachments on their liberty and independence.

As the might of the socialist states grows, the material and moral factors for peace become stronger. The cardinal problems of the day, the problems of war and peace, for instance, can no longer be approached only from the standpoint of the laws of capitalism and their operation. Today it is not imperialism with its wolfish habits but socialism with its ideals of peace and progress that is becoming the decisive factor in world development.

The socialist countries have broken the road for new norms of international life by demonstrating to the whole world an example of really equal, fraternal relations between peoples. Under the influence of the ideas of socialism, the working people's struggle for emancipation and the general democratic movement of the peoples are merging into a common world-wide torrent that is washing away the pillars supporting imperialism.

As socialism wins new victories, the unity of the peoples, both within each socialist country and in the world socialist system as a whole, grows stronger.

In the same way as a mighty tree with deep roots does not fear any storm, so the new, socialist world does not fear any adversities or upheavals. The counter-revolutionary insurrection in Hungary, organised by internal reaction with the support of the imperialist forces, and the intrigues of enemies in Poland and the German Democratic Republic showed that in the period of socialist construction the class struggle may, from time to time, grow stronger and take on sharp forms. In the future, too, the remnants of internal reaction may, with imperialist backing, attempt to sever one country or another from the socialist system and to restore the old bourgeois regime. The reactionary forces speculate on the difficulties that are inevitable in an undertaking as new as the revolutionary transformation of society, and continue planting their agents in the socialist countries.

The ruling circles of certain imperialist powers have elevated subversive activities against the socialist countries to the level of national policy. The United States of America expends, with frank cynicism, hundreds of millions of dollars on espionage and sabotage against the socialist countries, and organises so-called "guerilla units" made up of criminal elements, of cut-throats, who are prepared to undertake the vilest of crimes for money. For several years in succession provocative "captive nations weeks" have been held in the United States. The paid agents of the monopolies call "captive" all those peoples who have liberated themselves from imperialist bondage and have taken the path of free development. Truly, imperialist demagogy and hypocrisy know no bounds! Monopolists who howl about "captive nations" are like the crook who has his hands in somebody's pocket and shouts "Stop thief!" (*Animation. Applause.*)

The intrigues of the imperialists must always be kept in mind. Our gigantic successes in building the new way of life must not lead to complacency and relaxation of vigilance. The greater the achievements of socialism and the higher the living standards in each socialist country, the more solidly the people will muster around the Communist and Workers' parties. That is one aspect of the matter, and a very encouraging one. There is, however, something else that must be borne in mind. As the unity of the peoples of all socialist countries grows the hopes the imperialists have of restoring the capitalist regime, of the socialist countries degenerating, are gradually fading away. World reaction, therefore, is more and more turning to the idea of striking a blow at the socialist countries from outside in order to regain capitalist world dominion through war or, at least, to check the development of the socialist countries.

The most rabid imperialists, who act in accordance with the principle "after us the deluge", openly voice their desire to set out on a new war venture. To intimidate the peoples the ideologists of imperialism are trying to instil into them a kind of philosophy of hopelessness and despair. "Better death under capitalism than life under communism," they cry out hysterically. They, you see, do not like free peoples to prosper. They are afraid that the peoples of their countries will also take the path of social ism. Blinded by class hatred, our enemies are prepared to plunge all mankind into the holocaust of war. The possibilities the imperialists have of implementing their aggressive plans are, however, becoming fewer. They behave like a feeble and covetous old man whose strength is exhausted, whose physical capacity is low, but whose desires persist.

The imperialists, of course, may set out on dangerous adventures, but they have no chance of success. They are prepared to try other ways as well. To weaken the socialist community the imperialists try to set the peoples of the fraternal countries at loggerheads or to sow discord among them, to revive the remnants of national strife and artificially stir up nationalist sentiment.

A great historical responsibility rests with the Marxist-

Leninist parties, with the peoples of the socialist countries —to strengthen tirelessly the international brotherhood of the socialist countries and friendship between nations.

As long as the imperialist aggressors exist we must be on the alert, we must keep our powder dry and improve the defences of the socialist countries, their armed forces and their state security organs. If the imperialists, contrary to all common sense, venture to attack the socialist countries and hurl mankind into the abyss of a world war of annihilation, that mad act will be their last, it will be the end of the capitalist system. (*Applause.*)

Our Party has a clear understanding of its tasks and its responsibility and will do everything in its power to ensure that the world socialist system continues to grow stronger, gather fresh strength and develop further. We are confident that socialism will win in the competition with capitalism. (*Prolonged applause.*) We are confident that the victory will be won in peaceful competition and not through war. We have always stood for, and shall continue to stand for, the peaceful coexistence of states with different social systems; we shall do everything to strengthen peace throughout the world. (*Prolonged applause.*)

2. Aggravation of the Contradictions in the Capitalist Countries. Growth of the Revolutionary Struggle and Upsurge of the National-Liberation Movement

Comrades, the Twentieth Congress of the Party analysed the situation in the capitalist countries and drew the conclusion that they were moving steadily towards new economic and social upheavals. This conclusion has been borne out. In the years that have elapsed there has been further aggravation of contradictions both within the capitalist countries and between them, colonial empires have been disintegrating and the struggle of the working class and the national-liberation movement of the peoples have assumed huge proportions.

The general trend—the further decay of capitalism—has continued to operate inexorably. Although there has been some growth in production, the economy of the capitalist countries has become still more unstable and reminds one of a man sick with fever, so often do its short-lived recoveries give way to depressions and crises. The U.S.A., the chief capitalist country, has experienced two critical recessions in five years, and there have been four such recessions in the post-war period as a whole. The crisis of 1957-58 involved countries whose share in capitalist industrial output amounts to almost two-thirds of the whole. With the incomes of the monopolies increasing to a fabulous degree, real wages of the working people have increased very slightly and far more slowly than the productivity of labour. The social gains achieved by the working class in the past are gradually being reduced to nought. In general, the condition of the working people, especially in the underdeveloped countries, is growing worse.

During the past five or six years mankind has made great progress in science and technology, particularly in the fields of atomic energy, electronics, jet propulsion and rocketry. As Lenin pointed out, however, the evils of capitalist production hamper the rational use of those achievements. As far back as 1913 he wrote: "Whichever way you turn, at every step you come up against problems that mankind is fully capable of solving *immediately*. Capitalism is in the way. It has amassed enormous wealth and has turned people into the *slaves* of that wealth. It has solved the most complicated technical problems, but the application of technical improvements is hampered by the poverty and ignorance of the people, by the stupid miserliness of a handful of millionaires.

"Under capitalism, the words civilisation, freedom and wealth call to mind a rich glutton who is rotting alive but will not let that which is young live on."* How apt those words of Lenin's sound today!

---

* V. I. Lenin, *Collected Works*, 4th Russ. ed., Vol. 19, p. 349.

The application of new scientific and technical achievements, far from eliminating the insuperable contradictions of capitalism, only serves to aggravate them. Capitalist automation has only just begun, but millions of workers have already been thrown out of production. The imperialists hoped to find a way out of these difficulties by militarising the economy, but their hopes did not materialise.

Militarisation, of course, has brought prosperity to the branches of industry producing weapons. In five years direct war expenditure alone in the U.S.A. exceeded 220,000 million dollars; all the NATO countries together have spent over 500,000 million dollars on the arms race during the past ten years. Militarisation, however, gave rise to new disproportions, had a serious effect on other branches of the economy and deprived more millions of working people of their employment. During the past five years the number of totally unemployed in the U.S.A. has rarely been less than three million. In Italy, Japan and a number of other countries, mass unemployment has acquired a permanent character. The greater the amount of money spent on war production, the more unstable becomes capitalist economy and the more acute its contradictions. A glaring contradiction in present-day capitalism is the increasing employment of human labour for the production of means of destruction. A social system that creates such contradictions is discrediting and outliving itself.

No wonder the American millionaire Harriman proposed abolishing the word "capitalism". "Plagiarising from Khrushchev," he said, "we should 'bury' the word 'capitalism'." He had to admit that "people outside America think of the word 'capitalism'" as a synonym "for imperialism, for exploitation of the poor by the rich, for colonialism. It is a dishonoured word, and one that breeds terror". (*Animation.*) Indeed, there is no getting away from the truth! Not even the most thorough cleansing could remove the blood and filth from that sullied word. There is an apt proverb which says, "You can't wash a black sheep white".

(*Laughter. Applause.*) We can only welcome the efforts of Mr. Harriman who has taken up the spade to dig a grave for the word "capitalism". But the peoples of the capitalist countries will draw a more correct conclusion and will bury not the word "capitalism", but the capitalist system with all its evils, a system that is rotten through and through. (*Stormy applause.*)

In recent years there have been some significant changes in the alignment of forces in the capitalist world.

First, the United States of America has lost its absolute supremacy in world capitalist production and commerce. Its share in capitalist world industrial output dropped from 56.6 per cent in 1948 to 47 per cent in 1960, its exports from 23.4 per cent to 18.1 per cent and its gold reserves from 74.5 per cent to 43.9 per cent. The result is that the United States today occupies approximately the same position among the capitalist countries as it did before the Second World War.

Secondly, there has been a noticeable weakening of the position of Britain and France; these states, like Belgium and Holland, are losing their colonies for ever. They have been unable to recover their pre-war position in world industry.

Thirdly, the vanquished countries, especially West Germany and Japan, have made a big leap forward. The share in capitalist world industrial output of West Germany, Japan and Italy combined is now about 17 per cent, that is, greater than it was in 1937, on the eve of the Second World War.

West Germany has drawn level with Britain in industrial output, and as far as exports are concerned takes second place after the U.S.A. In post-war years U.S. monopolies have invested huge sums of money in the economy of West Germany and Japan. For a number of years these two countries were actually relieved of the burden of their own war expenditure because the U.S.A. provided them with armaments at the expense of the American taxpayers. West Germany and Japan have made huge investments in the key branches of the economy to renew their constant capital and reorganise production on modern lines. As a result they are already serious rivals to Britain, France and even the United States in the world market.

The contradictions that existed between the imperialist powers before the war have reappeared and new ones have emerged. The struggle between British and West German imperialism for supremacy in Western Europe is growing fiercer. French imperialism, in its struggle against British imperialism, is seeking support in yesterday's enemy, the West German monopolies. But this unnatural alliance, like a marriage of convenience, is more and more frequently operating against France herself. There are profound contradictions dividing the U.S.A. and Britain and other imperialist states. They are manifested in NATO and other aggressive blocs.

It is becoming more and more obvious that the imperialist powers and their leaders fear a slackening of international tension because in a tense situation it is easier for them to form military blocs and keep the peoples in fear of an alleged threat from the socialist countries. The imperialists are seeking to involve all countries in the arms race, to tie up the economies of other countries with their own and direct them towards militarisation. This line of action is most clearly demonstrated by U.S. policy towards West Germany and Japan. The U.S. imperialists are deliberately drawing West Germany into the arms race. In the event of the outbreak of war it will be to their advantage to pay for the new adventure mainly in the blood of the German people. At the same time they hope that this policy will impair the economy of West Germany and weaken her as a rival in the world market. Much the same policy is being pursued in respect of Japan.

In their talks the leaders of the Western Powers do not conceal that their policy is one of arming West Germany. Their argument is something like this—if West Germany does not rearm and does not spend money on armaments, she may become a still more powerful and dangerous rival. In short, there are some very acute contradictions in the imperialist camp.

In their fear of the future the imperialists are trying to unite their forces and to strengthen their military, political, commercial, customs and other alliances. The reactionaries count on aggression against the socialist countries as a way out. In the pre-war period they placed great hopes on Hitler Germany. Today the role of the chief aggressive force belongs to the United States of America which has become the centre of world reaction. The U.S. imperialists are acting in alliance with the West German militarists and revenge-seekers and are threatening the peace and security of the peoples. In our times, however, it has become dangerous for the imperialists to seek a way out of their contradictions in war.

The position of imperialism in Asia, Africa and Latin America, where the colonialists until recently oppressed hundreds of millions of people, is getting shakier. The revolutionary struggle of the peoples of those continents is rapidly gaining momentum. In the course of the past six years twenty-eight states have won political independence. The sixties of our century will go down in history as years of the complete disintegration of the colonial system of imperialism. (*Applause.*)

It must not be forgotten, however, that although the colonial system has collapsed, its remnants have not been eliminated. Many millions of people in Asia and Africa are still suffering under colonial slavery and are struggling for their liberation. For seven years the blood of Algerian patriots has been flowing in the fight for freedom. The French monopolies do not want to end the war in Algeria although that "dirty war" against a peaceful people is costing thousands of lives and is a heavy burden on the French and Algerian peoples. Portugal, a small state with an area no more than two-thirds of our Vologda Region, holds in bondage colonies with an area nearly twenty-five times its own size. The Dutch colonialists stubbornly refuse to return to the Indonesian people their ancient land of West Irian. The U.S.A. is maintaining its grip on the Chinese island of Taiwan and the Japanese island of Okinawa. Against the will of the Cuban people the U.S.A. retains its hold on the military base of Guantanamo which is on Cuban soil.

The forces of imperialism are opposing any effort on the part of the peoples to achieve liberty and independence, democracy and progress. On the pretext of various commitments, the imperialists strive to smother the national-liberation movement, and by entering into deals with internal reactionary forces intervene brazenly in the home affairs of young states. That was the method they used in Iran, Pakistan and the Congo and are now using in Laos and Kuwait.

Throughout this period the Soviet Union, in fulfilment of its internationalist duty, has been helping the peoples who struggled against imperialism and colonialism. There are those who do not approve of this position. But we cannot help that. Such are our convictions. Our people won freedom in a long and stubborn fight against oppression by the landlords and the capitalists and against the intervention of international imperialism. We remember well enough what that struggle cost us, we remember the sacrifices that had to be made for the sake of victory. From the bottom of our hearts we wish success to those who are struggling for their liberty and happiness against imperialism. We believe that it is the inalienable right of peoples to put an end to foreign oppression and we shall support their just fight. Colonialism is doomed and a stake will be driven into its grave. Such is the will of the peoples, such is the course of history. (*Stormy applause.*)

The countries that have liberated themselves from the colonial yoke have achieved certain successes in national and cultural regeneration. But economic progress in most of the newly-free countries of Asia and Africa is still slow.

The masses of the people are still living in miserable conditions, while the wealth of their countries flows in streams of gold into the coffers of foreign banks and corporations. The U.S. monopolies are making two or three dollars profit on every dollar they spend in the underdeveloped countries. The U.S. monopolists have recently announced that they wish to "grant" 500 million dollars to aid the Latin American countries. What is 500 million dollars among twenty countries over a period of five years? It is nothing more than miserly alms thrown by the rich man to those whom he has been robbing for many years and still continues to rob. The peoples who have been plundered have the right to demand from the colonialists, not aid, but the return of property stolen from them.

Today the colonialists, sensing that their rule is coming to an end, are putting on a good face in a losing game. They assert that they are leaving the colonies of their own accord. Who will believe them? Anyone can see that they are taking this step because they know that anyway they will be driven out in disgrace. The more prudent of the colonialists are getting out, so to say, five minutes before they are given "a kick in the pants", to put it in popular language. (*Animation. Applause.*)

The colonial powers impose unequal treaties on the newly-free countries, locate military bases on their territories and try to involve them in military blocs, one of the new forms of enslavement. Almost a half of the states that have emerged as a result of the disintegration of the colonial system are shackled by unequal, onerous treaties. In the centre of this refurbished but no less disgraceful colonialism stands the United States of America. Its closest allies and at the same time its rivals are British colonialism and West German imperialism, the latter unceremoniously pushing the British and French monopolies out of Africa and the Middle East.

The countries that have gained their freedom from colonial oppression have entered a new phase of development. The struggle for political independence united all the national forces that suffered under the colonialists and shared common interests. Now that the time has come to tear up the roots of imperialism and introduce agrarian and other urgent social reforms, the differences in class interests are coming more and more into the open. Broad sections of the working people and also that considerable section of the national bourgeoisie interested in the accomplishment of the basic tasks of the anti-imperialist, anti-feudal revolution, want to go farther in strengthening independence and effecting social and economic reforms. Within the ruling circles of those countries, however, there are forces that are afraid to go farther in their collaboration with the democratic, progressive strata of the nation. They would like to appropriate the fruits of the people's struggle and hamper the further development of the national revolution. These forces compromise with imperialism outside the country and feudalism within, and resort to dictatorial methods.

The example of Pakistan shows what this policy leads to. Two-thirds of the country's budget appropriations are made for war purposes, the national industry is not developing and foreign capital rules as if it were in its own bailiwick. The sad fate of Pakistan, whose people we wish nothing but good, should set the public thinking in some other countries where influential forces are wrecking national unity and are persecuting progressive leaders, especially the Communists, who have shown themselves to be the stoutest defenders of national independence.

To adopt the path of anti-communism means splitting the forces of the nation and weakening them in face of the imperialists, of the colonialists.

And contrariwise—the sounder the unity of the democratic national forces and the more radically urgent social and economic reforms are carried out, the stronger is the young state. Why did the Cuban people, for instance, rally so solidly around their government? Because the Cuban peasants obtained land and extensive material support from the government. Because the Cuban workers are working for themselves and not for the American monopolies now that industry has been nationalised. Because the small and medium producers in Cuba have been given protection against the arbitrary rule of the monopolies. The Cuban people as a whole acquired broad democratic rights and liberties, the road was opened up to a better way of life, to happiness and prosperity! In the hour of danger, when the American imperialists organised the invasion of Cuba, the entire people stood solid in defence of the gains of their revolution. Under the leadership of that courageous patriot and revolutionary, Fidel Castro, the Cubans speedily routed the American mercenaries and hurled them into the Bahía de Cochinos, which, being translated, means "the Bay of Swine". The proper place for them! (*Laughter. Stormy applause.*)

Imperialist agents are more and more frequently advising the peoples of the newly-free countries not to be in a hurry with their reforms. They would have the peoples of the underdeveloped countries believe that they cannot avoid the lengthy path travelled by the capitalist countries of Europe and America before they reached the present level of economic development. They conceal, however, that that path was a bloody and painful one for the peoples. They prefer to say nothing about the roads and prisons in England, France and Germany from the seventeenth to the nineteenth centuries being filled with vagabonds and homeless people, about the workers in those countries being forced to work from 14 to 18 hours a day even in the middle of the nineteenth century, or about the last plots of land being taken away from the English peasantry to make way for sheep pastures, so that, as was said at the time, "the sheep ate people".

The capitalist path of development would be still longer and more arduous for the peoples of the colonies at whose expense the Western Powers achieved their own affluence. Why should this long and painful road be imposed on peoples today, in the middle of the twentieth century? Communists believe that the age-old backwardness of peoples can be overcome through socialism.

We do not, however, impose our ideas on anybody; we are firmly convinced that sooner or later all peoples will realise that there is no other road for them to happiness and well-being. (*Applause.*)

Comrades, the increasing contradictions of imperialism confront the working class of the capitalist countries with the grave alternative of either throwing itself upon the mercy of the monopolies and continuing in a miserable plight, or fighting for its rights and its future. The workers prefer to fight, and are fighting with great tenacity.

Bourgeois prophets have announced the advent of an era of "class peace". They have claimed that the time of class struggles is a thing of the past and that Marxist theory in general is obsolete. Events have shown the utter absurdity of such prophecies. Strikes by the working people are growing in number and scale and in 1960 alone involved over 53 million people. The mass actions of the French and Italian working people, the Belgian workers' strike, the prolonged strike of American steel workers, in which more than 500,000 people took part, and the strike of British engineering workers will for ever go down in the history of the working-class movement. The Japanese proletariat, for its part, has demonstrated its militant strength on more than one occasion.

New contingents of the working class have stepped into the world arena in recent years. There are upwards of 100 million industrial, office and professional workers in Asia, Latin America and Africa, or about 40 per cent of the wage labour employed in the non-socialist world. The young working class is asserting itself more and more as a revolutionary force.

The struggle which the working people of the capitalist countries are waging for their economic and social rights is becoming ever more acute. For today they are faced, as a rule, not by individual employers but by powerful monopolies which, moreover, have the entire power of the state to support them. More and more often, the working people's actions assume a political character. Over 40 million people, or roughly 73 per cent of the total number of strikers, took part in political strikes in 1960. Powerful actions by the working class and the masses of the people last year brought about the fall of the governments in Japan, Italy and Belgium. The working people of France, who rallied in support of the working class, foiled an attempt by the militarists, by the ultra-reactionaries, to impose a fascist regime on that country.

The social situation that has taken shape in the major capitalist countries during the last five years has also been marked by a growing peasant movement. In France, Italy, West Germany and elsewhere, monopoly domination is ruining the peasantry, and it is participating ever more actively in the struggle against the monopolies.

The experience of recent years has provided more evidence that the working people owe all their gains to joint action. Nevertheless, the split within the working class persists because of the subversive activity of Right-wing Social-Democratic leaders, who are making frantic efforts to divert their parties, and the working class, from the struggle against capitalism. Right-wing Socialist leaders and many trade union bosses have long since betrayed the interests of the working class and faithfully serve monopoly capital. But among the Social-Democratic rank and file, among the functionaries and even within the leadership there are many honest people who sincerely want to take part in the common struggle for working-class interests. They have lately been putting up increasing resistance to the policy of the Right-wing leaders.

That is the reason Communists, while continuing to lay bare the ideological bankruptcy and disruptive actions of the Right-wing Social-Democratic officials, want to cooperate with all the sound elements among the Socialists, to take joint action with them in the struggle for peace, democracy and socialism. This is not a temporary tactical slogan but the general policy of the Communist movement, a policy prompted by the fundamental interests of the working class.

Progress in the working-class movement is inseparably bound up with the activity of the Communist parties. The Communist movement has entered on the highroad of creative activity. In our day the political influence of Communists makes itself felt in any country with a more or less advanced working-class movement. In recent years the close-knit family of Communists has increased by another twelve parties and the total number of Communists, by seven million. (*Applause.*)

The Communist parties are growing all over the world despite the fact that the reactionaries are conducting vicious anti-communist campaigns. Communists are blacklisted, deprived of jobs, declared "foreign agents" or imprisoned. In thirty-six capitalist countries, the Communist parties are compelled to operate deep underground. But the peoples are learning by experience that the Communists are the most loyal and reliable defenders of their interests. Communist ideas cannot be stopped by any barriers; they cannot be shot or put behind stout prison bars. They are winning the minds and hearts of people and are becoming an invincible force.

Of course, the Communist parties in some major capitalist countries are as yet small. But that by no means detracts from their historical role. Whatever the situation, the Communists, who are strong because they realise that theirs is a just cause, stand in the van of the working class. For example, it is well known that the number of Communists in the U.S.A. is small. But that big capitalist power, for all its enormous military and police machinery, is afraid of the Party of Communists, and obstructs its activities in every possible way. That indicates that the small contingent of the U.S. Communists is working as befits Marxists-Leninists. Truly, a little body often harbours a great soul! (*Applause.*)

The Communists of the socialist countries never forget the difficulties and hardships falling to the lot of their brothers in the capitalist countries, who are fighting for the victory of the working class, for the cause of all working people. Today, on behalf of the delegates to this Congress, of all Soviet Communists, we send the most heartfelt fraternal greetings to our fellow-Communists in the capitalist countries, who bear aloft the victorious banner of Marxism-Leninism, to all those in the dungeons of reaction who have not bowed their heads to the enemy, to those who are fighting courageously for the interests of their peoples. (*Stormy, prolonged applause.*)

The decisions of the Twentieth Congress, backed by the fraternal parties, added to the great creative power of the Communist movement and helped restore the Leninist spirit and style to the activities of the fraternal parties and the relations between them. The meetings of Communist and Workers' parties held in recent years were important milestones marking the progress of the world Communist movement. International Communist meetings are one of the forms evolved by the fraternal parties to ensure their militant co-operation.

It is indisputable to Marxists-Leninists that the fundamental interests of the international Communist movement require consistent and unswerving unity of action, and the Communist and Workers' parties are loyal to it. Only the leaders of the League of Communists of Yugoslavia, who are plainly affected by national narrow-mindedness, have turned from the straight Marxist-Leninist road on to a winding path which has landed them in the bog of revisionism. The Yugoslav leaders responded to the 1957 Declaration of the fraternal parties, which resounded throughout the world as a charter of Communist unity and solidarity, with a revisionist, anti-Leninist programme, which all the Marxist-Leninist parties subjected to a severe and just criticism.

Revisionist ideas pervade both the theory and practice of the leadership of the League of Communists of Yugoslavia. The line they have adopted—that of development in isolation from the world socialist community—is harmful and perilous. It plays into the hands of imperialist reaction, foments nationalist tendencies and may in the end lead to the loss of socialist gains in the country, which has broken away from the friendly and united family of builders of a new world.

Our Party has criticised, and will continue to criticise, the Yugoslav leaders' revisionist concepts. As internationalists, we cannot but feel concern about the destinies of the fraternal peoples of Yugoslavia, who fought selflessly against fascism and, on the achievement of victory, chose the path of socialist construction.

The historic November 1960 Meeting convincingly reaffirmed the will and resolve of the Communist parties to uphold the purity of Marxism-Leninism, strengthen the unity of their ranks, and continue their determined struggle on two fronts—against revisionism, which constitutes the main danger, and against dogmatism and sectarianism. The important propositions on the necessity for each party to observe decisions adopted collectively and not to permit any action likely to undermine Communist unity are of tremendous significance in bringing about greater solidity of the working-class parties.

The achievements of socialist construction in the Soviet Union and the People's Democracies are proof of the great power and vitality of Marxism-Leninism. They show mankind what can be achieved when the workers and peasants have taken their destiny into their own hands and are equipped with the most progressive revolutionary theory.

Socialism results from the creative activity of the broadest masses marching under the banner of Marxism-Leninism. Communists are opposed to the forcible, artificial implantation of any particular socio-political system in other countries. We are convinced that in the end the socialist system will triumph everywhere; but this in no way implies that we will seek to achieve its triumph by interfering in the internal affairs of other countries.

Attempts are made to blame us Communists for any action by the masses against their oppressors. Whenever the working people of a capitalist or colonial country rise to fight, the imperialists claim that it is the "handiwork of the Communists", or "the hand of Moscow". To be sure, we are glad to have the imperialists attributing to Communists all the good actions of the peoples. By so doing the imperialists unwittingly help the masses gain a better understanding of Communist ideas. These ideas are spreading throughout the world. But, of course, this is not happening because the Soviet Union and the other socialist countries impose them on the peoples. You cannot bring in ideas on bayonets, as people used to say in the past, or in rockets, as it would now be more proper to say.

Certainly, warring classes have always sought the support of kindred forces from outside. For a long time the bourgeois class had an advantage in this respect. The world bourgeoisie, acting in concert, stamped out revolutionary centres everywhere and by every means, including armed intervention. It goes without saying that even at that time the international proletariat was not indifferent to the struggle of its class brothers; but more often than not, it could express its solidarity with them only through moral support. The situation has changed since then. The people of a country who rise in struggle will not find themselves engaged in single combat with world imperialism. They will enjoy the support of powerful international forces possessing everything necessary for effective moral and material support. (*Applause.*)

The imperialists, who are alarmed by the scale of the revolutionary struggle, continue their attempts to interfere in the internal affairs of peoples and states. That is the reason they have reserved, in military pacts and agreements, the "right" to armed intervention in the event of so-called internal unrest, the "right", that is, to suppress revolutions and popular actions against reactionary regimes. The imperialists claim at every turn that the Communists export revolution. The imperialist gentlemen need this slander in order to camouflage, in some way or another, their claims to the right to export counter-revolution.

It is a strange logic these gentlemen have. They are apparently still under the spell of the times when they were able to strangle the liberation movement of peoples. But those times have gone, never to return. The Communists are against the export of revolution, and this is well known in the West. But we do not recognise anybody's right to export counter-revolution, to perform the functions of an international gendarme. This, too, should be well known.

Imperialist attempts to interfere in the affairs of insurgent peoples would constitute acts of aggression endangering world peace. We must state outright that in the event of imperialist export of counter-revolution the Communists will call on the peoples of all countries to rally, to mobilise their forces and, supported by the might of the world socialist system, repel firmly the enemies of freedom and peace. In other words, as ye sow, so shall ye reap. (*Prolonged applause.*)

3. Peaceful Coexistence Is the General Line in Soviet Foreign Policy. The Peoples Are the Decisive Force in the Struggle for Peace

Comrades, important changes have come about in the alignment of world forces during the period under review. The world socialist system has become a reliable shield against imperialist military ventures not only for the peoples of the countries that are friendly to it, but for the whole of mankind. And the fact that the socialist community of nations has a preponderance of strength is most fortunate for all mankind. The peace forces, furthermore, have grown all over the world.

A few years ago there were two opposing camps in world affairs—the socialist and imperialist camps. Today an active role in international affairs is also being played by those countries of Asia, Africa and Latin America that have freed, or are freeing, themselves from foreign oppression. Those countries are often called neutralist though they may be considered neutral only in the sense that they do not belong to any of the existing military-political alliances. Most of them, however, are by no means neutral when the cardinal problem of our day, that of war and peace, is at issue. As a rule, those countries advocate peace and oppose war. The countries which have won their liberty from colonialism are becoming a serious factor for peace, for the struggle against colonialism and imperialism, and the basic issues of world politics can no longer be settled without due regard for their interests.

In the capitalist countries, too, the masses are taking more and more vigorous action against war. The working class and all working people are fighting against the arms race and the disastrous policy of the warmongers.

Thus the aggressive policy of the imperialist powers is now being opposed by greater forces. *The struggle which the countries of socialism and all the forces of peace are carrying on against preparations for fresh aggression and war is the main content of world politics today.*

In these past years, the forces of war and aggression have jeopardised world peace more than once. In 1956 the imperialists organised, simultaneously with the counter-revolutionary rising in Hungary, an attack on Egypt. In the second half of 1957 the imperialists prepared an invasion of Syria that threatened a big military conflagration. In the summer of 1958, in view of the revolution in Iraq, they launched an intervention in the Lebanon and Jordan and at the same time created a 'tense situation in the area of Taiwan, an island which belongs to the People's Republic of China. In April-May 1960 the U.S. imperialists sent their military aircraft into Soviet air space, and torpedoed the Paris summit meeting. Last spring they organised an armed invasion of Cuba by mercenary bands and tried to bring Laos under their sway, to involve her in the aggressive SEATO military bloc. But all those imperialist sorties failed.

It would be a gross error, however, to imagine that the failure of aggressive schemes has brought the imperialists to their senses. The facts show just the opposite. The imperialists continue their attempts to aggravate the international situation and to lead the world to the brink of war. In recent months they have deliberately created a dangerous situation in the centre of Europe by threatening to take up arms in reply to our proposal to do away with the remnants of the Second World War, conclude a German peace treaty and normalise the situation in West Berlin.

In view of the aggravation of the international situation, we were compelled to take proper steps to safeguard our country against the encroachments of aggressors and save mankind from the threat of a new world war. The Soviet Government was compelled to suspend the reduction of the armed forces planned for 1961, increase defence expenditure, postpone the transfer of servicemen to the reserve and resume tests of new and more powerful weapons. We were compelled to adopt these measures; they were unanimously supported by our people and correctly understood by the peoples of other countries, who know that the Soviet Union will never be the first to adopt a policy leading to war. The Soviet people are only too familiar with the ways of aggressors. We have not forgotten the years of the Great Patriotic War, we remember Hitler Germany's treacherous, wanton attack on the Soviet Union. In the presence of the war menace created by the imperialists, there is no room for complacency and carelessness. (*Applause.*)

Some people in the West assert that the measures taken by the Soviet Government to strengthen the country's defences mean renunciation of the policy of peaceful coexistence. That, of course, is nonsense. The policy of peaceful coexistence follows from the very nature of our system.

I should like to recall the following fact. When our country was beating back the furious attacks of the Whites and foreign interventionists, the Soviet Government was discussing the question of the Soviet coat of arms. The first sketch contained a sword. Lenin raised a sharp objection. "Why the sword?" he said. "We need no conquest. The policy of conquest is utterly alien to us; we are not attacking, we are repulsing domestic and foreign enemies; ours is a defensive war and the sword is not our emblem." As everyone knows, the hammer and sickle, symbols of peaceful, constructive labour, have become the emblem of our country. (*Stormy applause.*)

The principles of peaceful coexistence, laid down by Lenin and developed in our Party documents, have always been the central feature of Soviet foreign policy. The Soviet Government's foreign policy is convincing evidence of the fidelity of the Party and the Soviet people as a whole to the peaceful course charted by Lenin. (*Applause.*)

But it is hard to combat the war menace by unilateral action, in the same way as it is hard to put out a fire if one person pours water upon it while another pours oil. The Western Powers, who should be no less interested in avoiding thermonuclear disaster than we are, must, for their part, show readiness to seek ways of settling disputed issues on a mutually acceptable basis.

Certain pacifist-minded people in the West are simple-minded enough to believe that if the Soviet Union made more concessions to the Western Powers, there would be no aggravation of international tension. They forget that the policy of the imperialist powers, including their foreign policy, is determined by the class interests of monopoly capital, in which aggression and war are inherent. When, under the pressure of the masses, the partisans of a more or less moderate policy gain the upper hand, there occurs an international détente and the clouds of war are dispelled to some extent. But the international situation deteriorates when the pressure of the masses slackens and the scales tip in favour of those groupings of the bourgeoisie that capitalise on the arms race and see war as an additional source of profit.

Hence, the peaceful coexistence of countries with different social systems can be maintained and safeguarded only through the unrelenting struggle of all peoples against the aggressive aspirations of the imperialists. The greater the might of the socialist camp and the more vigorously the struggle for peace is waged within the capitalist countries, the more difficult it is for the imperialists to carry out their plans of aggression.

Peace and peaceful coexistence are not quite the same thing. Peaceful coexistence does not merely imply absence of war; it is not a temporary, unstable armistice between two wars but the coexistence of two opposed social systems, based on mutual renunciation of war as a means of settling disputes between states.

Historical experience shows that an aggressor cannot be placated by concessions. Concessions to the imperialists on matters of vital importance do not constitute a policy of peaceful coexistence but mean surrender to the forces of aggression. That we will never accede to. (*Applause.*) It is high time the imperialists understood that it is no longer they who are the arbiters of mankind's fate and that socialism will exist, develop and gain strength whether they like it or not. (*Stormy applause.*) But for the time being the imperialist gentry do not seem to have understood this. Adventurous actions may well be expected of them, actions that would spell disaster for hundreds of millions of people. That is why we must curb the aggressors and not aid and abet them. (*Prolonged applause.*)

Peace supporters in many countries, who have associated in various unions and movements, have made an important contribution to the struggle against the forces of aggression and war. Everyone will remember how, in the early fifties, hundreds of millions of people called for a ban on atomic weapons and how indignantly the peoples of Europe protested against the establishment of the notorious European Defence Community and West Germany's participation in it. The pressure which the people exerted on parliaments and governments produced a powerful effect.

The work being done by peace supporters is particularly important now that the danger of a new war has increased. In the present situation, men of goodwill can no longer confine themselves to mere utterances in favour of peace. It should be evident that, despite the numerous actions of the general public in defence of peace, the forces of aggression and war are becoming ever more brazen. Indeed, a few years ago no Western politician would have made bold, without risking his career, to hint about rearming the Bundeswehr. But now the militarisation of West Germany is going full blast, and the Bundeswehr has become a major armed force in Western Europe. Strauss, West Germany's war minister, cynically boasts that the Federal Republic of Germany is not merely a member of NATO but has the upper hand there. Moreover, something unheard-of has happened: the governments of Britain and France, that is, of countries which in the past suffered from German militarism, have granted the Bundeswehr proving grounds and barracks on their territories and have placed their armed forces under the command of former Hitler generals. As a result, Bundeswehr soldiers are trampling British soil, which in two world wars they were unable to reach by armed force.

We share the bitterness and indignation of French and British patriots, who see West German revenge-seekers marching across their homeland.

It is said that even a gale of words won't make a wind-mill turn. Still less will talk of peace stop the aggressors' war machine. It is necessary to act resolutely and vigor-ously to stay the criminal hand of the warmongers in good time, before it is too late. Obviously, the struggle for peace, like any struggle, requires sustained effort and per-severance. When fighting, one not only delivers but also receives blows. But is that something to be afraid of at a time when the fate of mankind is at stake? *It must be realised that it depends above all on the peoples them-selves, on their resolve and vigorous action, whether there is to be peace on earth or whether mankind is to be hurled into the catastrophe of a new world war.* It is necessary to heighten the vigilance of the peoples with regard to the intrigues of imperialist warmongers. Vigorous anti-war action by the peoples must not be put off till the war starts; such action must be launched immediately and not when nuclear and thermonuclear bombs begin to fall.

The strength of the peace movement lies in its mass scope, its organisation and resolute actions. All the peo-ples and all sections of society, with the exception of a handful of monopolists, want peace. And the peoples must insist that a peace policy be pursued and must use all forms of struggle to achieve that end. The peoples can and must render harmless those who are obsessed with the insane ideas of militarism and war. It is the peoples who are the decisive force in the struggle for peace. (*Stormy applause.*)

4. Seek the Settlement of International Problems by Peaceful Means. Expose the Intrigues and Manoeuvres of the Warmongers. Improve Relations Between Countries

Comrades, the situation calls for the settling of funda-mental international problems without delay, and in keep-ing with the principles of peaceful coexistence. Following the Twentieth Congress the Soviet Union advanced an extensive and realistic programme of action that would ensure the maintenance and consolidation of universal peace. The purpose of that programme is, in a nutshell, to deliver mankind from the dangerous and burdensome arms race, to do away with the remnants of the Second World War and to remove all obstacles to a healthier international climate.

The struggle for general and complete disarmament is a major feature of the foreign policy of our Party. The Soviet Union has persevered in this struggle for many years. We have always resolutely opposed the arms race, for in the past, competition in this field not only imposed a heavy burden on the peoples but inevitably led to world wars. We are opposed to the arms race still more firmly now that a tremendous technical revolution has taken place in the art of war and the use of modern weapons would inevitably lead to hundreds of millions of people losing their lives.

The stockpiling of these weapons, which is taking place in an atmosphere of cold war and war hysteria, is fraught with disastrous consequences. It only needs an addlebrained officer on duty at a "button" somewhere in the West to lose his nerve for events to occur that will bring down great misfortune on the peoples of the whole world.

It should be plain that the idea of our programme for general and complete disarmament is not the unilateral disarmament of socialism in the face of imperialism or the other way round, but a universal renunciation of arms as a means of settling controversial international problems. As they do not dare to say they are against disarmament, the ruling circles of the capitalist countries, primarily of the United States, Britain and France, have invented the tale that the Soviet Union is against control over disarmament. We exposed the manoeuvre of the capitalist powers and openly declared that we were prepared in advance to accept any proposals for the most rigid international control they might make, provided they accepted our proposals for general and complete disarmament.

To mislead people, the imperialists are hypocritically raising a racket over the fact that we were compelled to carry out experimental blasts of nuclear weapons. But the racket did not prevent the peoples from seeing that we had taken this step only because the Western Powers, after bringing the solution of the disarmament problem and negotiations on nuclear weapons tests to a dead end, had set the flywheel of their war machine turning at top speed in order to achieve superiority in strength over the socialist countries. We forestalled them and thus retained the superior position of the socialist camp, which is defending peace. (*Stormy applause.*)

We were forced to take these measures. It was known that the United States had for a long time been preparing to resume tests, and as for France, she had carried them out repeatedly. In the present conditions, the necessity for the peoples' struggle to get rid of the arms race is all the more obvious. The disarmament problem affects the vital interests of every nation and of mankind as a whole. When it has been solved there will be no more need for nuclear weapons and hence for their manufacture and testing.

The elimination of the remnants of the Second World War is of tremendous importance for the maintenance and strengthening of peace. It is intolerable that sixteen years after the defeat of the Hitler invaders a peaceful settlement with Germany has still not been effected. The Western Powers, headed by the U.S.A., are alone to blame for this unpardonable delay. In flagrant disregard of the interests of the peoples, they set out to revive German militarism as soon as the war was over.

The absence of a peace treaty has already played into the hands of the Bonn revenge-seekers. With help from the U.S. imperialists, they have re-established their armed forces with an eye to further aggression. It is the West German militarists' cherished dream to profit by the unstable situation in Europe to set their former enemies—the powers of the anti-Hitler coalition—upon each other. They dream of absorbing the German Democratic Republic, enslaving other neighbouring countries and taking revenge for the defeat they sustained in the Second World War.

We have always held that a peace treaty would confirm the German frontiers defined in the Potsdam agreement, tie the hands of revenge-seekers and discourage them from adventures. The socialist countries have waited long enough for a treaty to be signed, in the hope that common sense would gain the upper hand in Washington, London and Paris. We are still ready to negotiate with the Western Powers a mutually acceptable and agreed solution.

Recently, while attending the U.N. General Assembly, Comrade Gromyko, the Soviet Foreign Minister, had conversations with the Secretary of State and the President of the United States. He also had talks with the Foreign Secretary and the Prime Minister of Britain. We gained the impression from those conversations that the Western Powers are showing some understanding of the situation and are inclined to seek a solution to the German problem and the West Berlin issue on a mutually acceptable basis.

But there is something strange about the Western countries, above all the U.S.A. In those countries one thing is said in the course of talks between statesmen and another reported by the press, although it is plain that the press is kept informed on the tenor of the talks. The Western press presents the issue of a German peace treaty in an unreasonable, unrealistic vein. It makes the accusation, for example, that someone wants, in settling the German problem, to take the orchard and give an apple in exchange. Perhaps those who say so like this figure of speech. But in this particular instance the figure does not do justice to the real state of affairs.

Everyone knows that the Soviet Government proposes signing a German peace treaty. Peace treaties are concluded to clear the way, as much as possible, to normal relations between countries, to avert the threat of a new war and ease international tension.

We proceed from the actual situation which has arisen since Hitler Germany was defeated, and from the existence of the two German states and the post-war frontiers. Any war, however trying and cruel, must end in the signing of a peace treaty. (*Applause.*) One has to render account and to pay for aggression, for starting wars. That being so, where does the orchard or the apple come in? (*Animation. Applause.*)

Some Western politicians offer us would-be good advice by declaring that the signing of a peace treaty would endanger the Soviet Union and the other socialist countries. What are we to make of that? Since when have wars been considered to endanger one side only? The times when the imperialist powers dominated have gone for ever. The Soviet Union today is a mighty socialist power. The great socialist community, which possesses developed industry and agriculture and advanced science and technology, is making good progress. (*Stormy applause.*)

I trust the imperialists will realise that since we have a developed industry and agriculture, the armaments of our Soviet Army are bound to be up to the latest standards. (*Applause.*)

We consider that at present the forces of socialism, and all the forces championing peace, are superior to the forces of imperialist aggression. But even granting that the U.S. President was right in saying a short time ago that our forces were equal, it would be obviously unwise to threaten war. One who admits that there is equality should draw the proper conclusions. It is dangerous in our time to pursue a position of strength policy. (*Applause.*)

A German peace treaty must and will be signed, with the Western Powers or without them. (*Applause.*)

The treaty will also serve to normalise the situation in West Berlin by making it a free demilitarised city. The Western countries and all the other countries of the world must enjoy the right of access to West Berlin in keeping with international law, that is, must reach an appropriate agreement with the Government of the German Democratic Republic, since all communications between West Berlin and the outside world pass through her territory. (*Applause.*)

Certain spokesmen of the Western Powers say that our proposals for the conclusion of a German peace treaty this year constitute an ultimatum. But they are wrong, for it was as far back as 1958 that the Soviet Union proposed concluding a peace treaty and settling the issue of West Berlin on that basis by transforming it into a free city. A long time has passed since then. We did not rush the settlement of the issue, hoping to reach mutual understanding with the Western Powers. It is fair to ask, therefore, why this talk about an ultimatum? In proposing the conclusion of a German peace treaty, the Soviet Union presented no ultimatum, but was prompted by the need to have this pressing issue settled at last.

The Soviet Government insists, now as before, on the earliest possible solution of the German problem; it is against that problem being shelved indefinitely. If the Western Powers show readiness to settle the German problem, the issue of a time limit for the signing of a German peace treaty will no longer be so important; in that case, we shall not insist that a peace treaty absolutely must be signed before December 31, 1961. The important thing is to settle the matter—to eliminate the remnants of the Second World War by signing a German peace treaty. That is the fundamental issue, the crux of the matter. (*Applause.*)

The solution of these problems will pave the way to further steps in the sphere of peaceful co-operation, both multilateral and bilateral, between states. What else has to be done for the further strengthening of peace, in addition to the conclusion of a German peace treaty?

The problem of effecting *considerable improvement in*

the United Nations machinery has long been awaiting solution. That machinery has grown rusty in the cold war years and has been operating fitfully. The time has come to clean it, to remove the crust that has formed on it, to put fresh power into it, with due regard to the changes that have occurred in the international situation in recent years. It is high time to restore the legitimate rights of the People's Republic of China in the U.N. (*Stormy, prolonged applause.*) The time has come for a decision on the question of the German people's representation in the United Nations. (*Prolonged applause.*) As matters stand now, the most reasonable solution would be to conclude a peace treaty with both German states, whose existence is a reality, and to admit them into the U.N. It is time to grant genuinely equal rights in all U.N. agencies to the three groups of states that have come into being in the world—socialist, neutralist and imperialist. It is time to call a halt to attempts to use the U.N. in the interests of the military alignment of the Western Powers. (*Applause.*)

The problem of the full abolition of colonial tyranny in all its forms and manifestations must be solved in accordance with the vital interests of the peoples. At the same time real and not verbal aid must be rendered to the peoples, and the consequences of colonialism must be remedied. They must be helped to reach, as speedily as possible, the level of the economically and culturally developed countries. We see the way to achieve that goal first of all in making the colonial powers restore to their victims at least part of their loot. The Soviet Union and other socialist countries are already rendering the peoples disinterested, friendly support and assistance in the economic and cultural fields. We shall continue to help them.

The solution of pressing regional political problems could play a fairly important part in achieving a healthier international atmosphere. We attach great importance to the problem of establishing atom-free zones, first of all in Europe and the Far East. A non-aggression pact between the countries in the Warsaw Treaty Organisation and those in the North Atlantic military bloc could go a long way towards promoting security. An agreement could also be reached on the establishment of a zone dividing the armed forces of military alignments, and a start could be made to reduce the armed forces stationed on foreign soil. And if the countries in military blocs were to come to the reasonable conclusion that all military alliances must be disbanded and armed forces withdrawn to within their national boundaries, it would be the best, the most radical, solution of the problem.

In short, given mutual desire, many useful steps could be taken that would help the nations reduce the war danger and then remove it altogether.

We see a way to a better international situation in *more extensive business relations with all countries.*

Our relations with the socialist countries have been, and will continue to be, relations of lasting fraternal friendship and co-operation. (*Applause.*) We shall expand and improve mutually beneficial economic and cultural ties with them on the basis of agreed long-term plans. Such co-operation will enable us all to proceed even faster along the road of socialism and communism. (*Stormy applause.*)

Our people derive deep satisfaction from our expanding co-operation with the great Asian powers of India and Indonesia. We rejoice in their successes and realise their difficulties, and we readily expand business co-operation which helps them promote their economy and culture. Successfully developing on similar lines are our relations with Burma, Cambodia, Ceylon, the United Arab Republic, Iraq, Guinea, Ghana, Mali, Morocco, Tunisia, Somali and other Asian and African countries that have freed themselves from foreign tyranny. We will develop business relations with the Syrian Arab Republic.

After long and painful trials a government which declared itself to be successor to the Patrice Lumumba Government was set up in the Congo. The Soviet Government is prepared to help the Congolese people solve the difficult problems facing them in the struggle to overcome the consequences of colonial oppression.

Our relations with Latin American countries have likewise made progress in the period under review, despite the barriers artificially raised by internal reaction and the U.S. imperialists. The heroic people of Cuba, who have broken down those barriers, are establishing co-operation on an equal footing with other countries. And even though the U.S. imperialists stop at nothing—not even at overthrowing lawful governments—to prevent Latin American countries from pursuing an independent policy, events will nevertheless take their own course.

We shall continue assisting newly-independent nations to get on to their feet, grow strong and take a fitting place in international affairs. Those nations are making a valuable contribution to the great cause of peace and progress. In this the Soviet Union and the other socialist countries will always be their true and reliable friends. (*Prolonged applause.*)

We attach great importance to relations with the major capitalist countries, first and foremost the United States. U.S. foreign policy in recent years has invariably concentrated on aggravating the international situation. This is deplored by all peace-loving peoples. As for the Soviet Union, it has always held that the only way to prevent a world war of extermination is to normalise relations between states irrespective of their social systems. That being so, there is a need for joint efforts to achieve this. No one expects the ruling circles of the United States to fall in love with socialism, nor must they expect us to fall in love with capitalism. The important thing is for them to renounce the idea of settling disputes through war and to base international relations on the principle of peaceful economic competition. If realistic thinking gains the upper hand in U.S. policy, a serious obstacle to a normal world situation will be removed. Such thinking will benefit not only the peoples of our two countries but those of other countries and world peace. (*Applause.*)

We propose to expand and strengthen normal, business-like economic and cultural relations with Britain, France, Italy, West Germany and other West European countries. Noticeable progress has been achieved in this respect in recent years, and it is up to the other side to improve the situation.

The Soviet Union pays special attention to the promotion of relations with its neighbours. Differences in social and political systems are no hindrance to the development of friendly, mutually advantageous relations between the U.S.S.R. and such countries as Afghanistan or Finland. Our relations with Austria and Sweden are progressing fairly well. We have sought, and will continue to seek, better relations with Norway and Denmark. Relations with our Turkish neighbour have been improving lately. We should like them to go on improving.

The Soviet Union would also like to live in peace and friendship with such of its neighbours as Iran, Pakistan and Japan. Unfortunately, the ruling circles of those countries have so far been unable, or unwilling, to disentangle themselves from the military blocs imposed on them by the Western Powers, nor have they been using the opportunities for business co-operation with our country. Their governments' present policies imperil their peoples. Outstanding in this respect is the Shah of Iran, who has gone to the point of agreeing to turn almost half the country into a zone of death in the interests of the aggressive CENTO bloc.

The Soviet Union has exerted considerable effort to improve its relations with Japan. But the government of that country, which is bound to the United States by an unequal military treaty, still refuses to eliminate the remnants of the Second World War. The absence of a Soviet-Japanese peace treaty seriously handicaps wider co-operation between our two countries. The Japanese people are becoming increasingly aware of the great loss Japan is incurring as a result. We hope that sooner or later common sense will win and that our relations with Japan will make proper progress to the benefit of both countries.

The role of *economic ties* as an important element of peaceful coexistence is growing. In the period under survey, Soviet foreign trade has almost doubled in volume. We have stable commercial relations with more than eighty countries. But a great deal more could be achieved in this field if the Western Powers stopped their obstructionist practices and frequent arbitrary actions, which damage business co-operation with the socialist countries. Incidentally, these outmoded practices do more harm to them than to us. Whoever resorts to discrimination, trade barriers and even blockades inevitably exposes himself as a proponent of war preparations and an enemy of peaceful coexistence.

Our country's *cultural relations* have expanded considerably in recent years and we now maintain such relations with more than a hundred countries. Over 700,000 Soviet people go abroad every year, and as many foreigners visit our country. We are willing to continue these mutually beneficial international contacts on a large scale. They can and must play a role in promoting co-operation and understanding among people.

Contacts with the leaders of other countries have become an important factor in Soviet foreign policy. It will be recalled that, despite pressure of business, Lenin, who guided the foreign policy of the Soviet state, received and had talks with American, British, French, Finnish, Afghan, and other foreign leaders. It was his intention to attend the 1922 Genoa Conference. The Central Committee of the Party has regarded it as its duty to follow this Lenin tradition. In pursuing an active foreign policy, members of the Presidium of the C.C. C.P.S.U. have often visited countries of the socialist community. They have paid sixty-five visits to twenty-seven non-socialist countries. I have had to travel far and wide myself. It cannot be helped—such is my duty, such is the need. (*Prolonged applause.*)

We have received many distinguished foreign guests, including the heads of state or government of European, Asian, African and Latin American countries. Party and government leaders of the socialist countries have been frequent and welcome visitors to our country. We are prepared to continue meetings with heads of state or government, individually or collectively.

Comrades, events have shown that the foreign policy of our Party, elaborated by the Twentieth Congress, is correct. We have achieved major victories by pursuing that policy. While our strength has increased very appreciably, we shall persevere in our Leninist policy in an effort to bring about the triumph of the idea of peaceful coexistence. *There is now a prospect of achieving peaceful coexistence for the entire period necessary for the solution of the social and political problems now dividing the world.* Developments indicate that it may actually be feasible to banish world war from the life of society even before the complete triumph of socialism on earth, with capitalism surviving in part of the world. (*Applause.*)

Lenin taught us to be firm, unyielding and uncompromising whenever a fundamental question, a question of principle, is involved. In the most trying conditions, at a time when the only socialist state had to resist the attacks of the whole capitalist world, when the enemy was storming us at the front, in the rear and from the flanks, Lenin spoke with the imperialists in firm, resolute terms, while following a flexible course and always retaining the initiative.

What are the tasks which the present international situation sets before Soviet foreign policy? We must continue:

adhering steadily to the principle of the peaceful coexistence of states with different social systems as a general line of the Soviet Union's foreign policy (*applause*);

strengthening the unity of the socialist countries through

fraternal co-operation and mutual assistance, and contributing to the might of the world socialist system (*applause*);

promoting contacts and co-operating with all who
champion world peace. Together with all those who want
peace we must oppose all those who want war (*applause*);

strengthening proletarian solidarity with the working
class and all working people of the world, and rendering the
fullest moral and material support to the peoples fighting
to free themselves from imperialist and colonial oppression or to consolidate their independence (*applause*);

vigorously extending business ties, economic co-operation and trade with all countries that are willing to maintain
such relations with the Soviet Union (*applause*);

pursuing an active and flexible foreign policy. We must
seek the settlement of pressing world problems through
negotiations, expose the intrigues and manoeuvres of the
warmongers, and establish business co-operation with all
countries on a reciprocal basis. (*Applause*.)

Experience has proved that the principle of the peaceful
coexistence of countries with different social systems, a
principle advanced by the great Lenin, is the way to preserve peace and avert a world war of extermination. We
have been doing, and will do, all in our power for peaceful
coexistence and peaceful economic competition to triumph
throughout the world. (*Stormy, prolonged applause*.)

II

THE SOVIET UNION ENTERS THE PERIOD OF FULL-SCALE COMMUNIST CONSTRUCTION

Comrades, the chief feature determining the activities
of our Party since the Twentieth Congress has been the
effort to carry out the basic tasks of the period of full-scale
communist construction—the creation of the material and
technical basis of communism, the further consolidation of

the economic might of the Soviet Union, the communist education of the working people, and the satisfaction of the growing material and spiritual requirements of the people to an ever greater degree.

The Central Committee is glad to be able to report to this Congress that all branches of the economy are developing at accelerated rates. The living standards of the people are steadily rising. Soviet science and culture have reached new heights of development. The Seven-Year Plan is being implemented successfully. Our country has made a great advance towards the fulfilment of the basic economic task—to overtake and outstrip the more highly-developed capitalist countries in production per head of population. And, it must be said, the population of the Soviet Union has grown considerably. At the time of the Twentieth Congress it was less than 200 million whereas it had grown to almost 220 million by the time of the Twenty-Second Congress. A satisfactory increase, comrades. (*Applause.*)

We have adopted a rapid pace in the development of our economy and are marching with confidence along the path indicated by Lenin, taking one height after another. We are drawing nearer and nearer to our great goal, and can now see distinctly the bright peak on which the Soviet people will in the near future plant the banner of communism. (*Stormy applause.*)

1. The Struggle to Build Up the Country's Economic Might. The Seven-Year Plan, an Important Stage in the Creation of the Material and Technical Basis of Communism

In creating the material and technical basis of communism, heavy industry has a decisive role to play as the foundation of the entire economy. Permit me to quote some figures on the growth of industrial output since the Twentieth Congress. The figures I quote will include the preliminary returns for 1961. Although 1961 has not yet come to an end we may already say that planned targets will be exceeded for many important items.

The increase in industrial output for the six years will be almost 80 per cent. Here are the figures for some leading items:

							Produced in 1955	Expected output for 1961	1961 output as % % of 1955
Pig iron	(000,000 tons)	.	.	.	.	.	33.3	51.1	153
Steel	"	"	.	.	.	.	45.3	71.0	157
Rolled goods	"	"	.	.	.	.	35.3	55.0	156
Coal	"	"	.	.	.	.	391	513	131
Oil	"	"	.	.	.	.	70.8	166	234
Gas (000,000,000 cu. m.)							10.4	59.5	575
Electricity (000,000,000 kwh)							170	327	192
Chemical industry output (000,000,000 rubles)							3.7	7.6	205
Output of machine-building and metal-working industries (000,000,000 rubles)							17	38	224
Cement (000,000 tons)							22.5	51	226

Worthy of special mention are the achievements of the leading branches of heavy industry. In six years the amount of steel smelted has increased by 26 million tons, which is more than Britain's annual output. The extraction of oil has increased by 95 million tons, which is the equivalent of five new Baku oilfields. The output of electric power has increased by 157,000 million kwh, which is the same as fifty additional stations the size of the Lenin Power Station on the Dnieper. (*Applause*.)

With modern heavy industry as the basis, all branches of the economy are making rapid progress; light industry and the food industry are developing well. The Party is paying particular attention to greater output of foodstuffs, clothing, footwear—of everything man needs—to raise the living standard of the people.

Here are some figures showing how the output of consumer goods has increased:

	Produced in 1955	Expected output for 1961	1961 output as % % of 1955
Meat, industrially processed (000,000 tons)	2.5	4.5	178
Butter, factory-made (000 tons) . . .	463	794	171
Whole-milk products (000,000 tons)	2.6	9.0	345
Vegetable oils (000 tons)	1,168	1,730	148
Granulated beet sugar (000,000 tons)	3.2	6.5	200
Fish (catch—000,000 tons)	2.7	3.7	136
Clothing and underwear (000,000,000 rubles)	6.0	9.2	152
Leather footwear (000,000 pairs) . . .	271	443	163
Textiles (000,000 sq. m.)	5,543	6,661	120
Woollen textiles (000,000 sq. m.)	321	452	141
Radio and TV receivers (000)	4,044	6,345	157
Domestic refrigerators (000)	151	731	480
Furniture (000,000 rubles)	491	1,280	261

You can see from this that the output of consumer goods is growing at a higher rate than in the recent past. We can now increase the output of these goods year by year. In only three years of the Seven-Year Plan over 1,000 million metres of textiles and about 70 million pairs of boots and shoes have been produced above plan. The requirements of Soviet people, however, must be met more fully. The Government is additionally allocating for the remaining period of the Seven-Year Plan about 2,500 million rubles to develop the textile and footwear industries and increase supplies of raw materials. *By the end of the seven-year period our industry will be producing over 9,000 million square metres of textiles a year; the annual output of footwear will be nearly three pairs per head of population.*

The Soviet Union's output of these items will greatly exceed that of Britain, France and West Germany combined.

It will, of course, be necessary to extend the area planted to cotton and increase its per-hectare yield. That is a problem that will undoubtedly be solved. After the Nurek Power Station is completed 1.2 million hectares of irrigated land in Tajikistan and Uzbekistan will be put under cultivation and planted to the most valuable, long-staple varieties of cotton. The output of cotton will be substantially increased with the cultivation of the Hungry Steppe in Uzbekistan. However, the implementation of the programme for the building of factories manufacturing artificial and synthetic fibres will ensure the most reliable supply of raw materials for our textile industry.

Our plans are designed for peaceful construction. The Party is working to promote the economic might of the country, and never forgets the need to strengthen its defences. We have established industries producing high-precision instruments, the means for automation, special metals, atomic and electronic equipment, and rockets, we have jet aircraft and a modern ship-building industry. These branches have made a name for themselves, and not only on earth, but in outer space as well. They are reliable in their service to the cause of peace, to defence. We now have at our disposal intercontinental ballistic missiles, anti-aircraft rocket equipment, and rockets for the land, naval and air forces.

The press has announced tests of our new rockets, which have a range of more than 12,000 kilometres. We have stationed our ships where the rockets fall. They record when, and how accurately, they reach the target area. Reports indicate that our rockets are unusually precise.

I must say that there are also American vessels in the area, which observe the flight of the Soviet rockets. The Americans publish appropriate data about the flights of our rockets and we compare their data with ours. We trust the comrades aboard our ships implicitly. But we get something of a double check—ours and the opponent's. (*Applause.*)

Our opponents—we would have liked it better if they were not opponents, but we have to take the nature of imperialism into account—confirm that the Soviet rockets hit the target squarely. That is good! We were sure they would. (*Applause.*)

Since I have digressed from the prepared text, I might as well say that the testing of our new nuclear weapons is going on very successfully. We shall complete it very soon—probably by the end of October. We shall evidently round out the tests by exploding a hydrogen bomb equivalent to 50 million tons of TNT. (*Applause.*) We have said that we have a bomb as powerful as 100 million tons of TNT. And we have it, too. But we are not going to explode it, because, even if exploded in the remotest of places, we are likely to break our own windows. (*Stormy applause.*) We will therefore not do it yet. But by exploding the 50-million bomb, we shall test the triggering device of the 100-million one.

However, God grant, as people said in the old days, that we never have to explode those bombs over any territory. That is our fondest dream! (*Stormy applause.*)

In this hall I see comrades who have developed our wonderful rockets, rocket engines and precision instruments. I also see those who are engaged in improving nuclear weapons. We are proud of them and give them due credit. We rejoice in their achievements, for they serve to increase the defensive power of our country and to promote world peace. (*Stormy applause.*)

The Soviet submarine fleet is being built up with success. Our opponents are building a submarine fleet equipped with ballistic missiles. We are equipping our fleet with both ballistic and target-seeking missiles. It is the situation that compels us to do so. Our opponents, organised in the military blocs, are making preparations to fire at our country and the other socialist countries from submarines. We are ready to retaliate by firing at both ground and sea targets. The Soviet Union is a continental power. Those who will want to start a war against us will have to overcome water barriers. That is why we are building up a powerful submarine fleet equipped also with target-seeking missiles so that we can sink in the ocean, hundreds of kilometres distant, vessels on their way to the borders of the socialist countries.

The atom-powered Soviet submarine fleet, equipped with ballistic and target-seeking missiles, stands vigilant guard over our socialist gains. It will retaliate crushingly against an aggressor, and against his aircraft-carriers, which, in case of war, will make a nice target for our submarine-launched missiles. (*Stormy applause.*)

Permit me to report to the Congress that the re-equipment of the Soviet Army with nuclear and rocket weapons has been completed. Our armed forces are now equipped with weapons powerful enough to enable us to crush any aggressor. While providing our armed forces with rockets and building an atomic submarine fleet, we have not neglected our air force but have continued to develop and perfect it.

Permit me, on behalf of the Congress, to express heartfelt thanks to the scientists, engineers and workers who have produced for the Soviet Army the most up-to-date weapons. (*Stormy applause.*) They have done all mankind a great service! No longer can the imperialists with impunity use threats of war to intimidate the peaceful countries; atomic and hydrogen weapons in the hands of the Soviet people, the builders of communism, do reliable service to the cause of peace. (*Prolonged applause.*)

The Soviet people do not need war; their minds are turned to developing the economy of peace, to the implementation of the great plans for communist construction, to the creation of an abundance of material and spiritual values for all working people.

Important *qualitative changes* have taken place in industry, building and transport since the Twentieth Congress; a huge amount of work has been done to re-equip technically all branches of material production. Thousands of new types of machines, machine-tools, apparatus, measuring instruments and equipment for automation have been designed. The pattern of the country's fuel supply has been radically improved. Oil and gas accounted for 23.5 per cent of the fuel output in 1955 and today the percentage has increased to 42. An economy of over 3,000 million rubles has been effected in the six years by the use of cheaper fuels.

The electric power industry has been provided with a new technical basis. Steam and hydropower turbines of 200,000-225,000 kw capacity are being built. Turbines up to 500,000 kw capacity are being designed. Some of the world's biggest power grids have been established and 500,000-volt transmission lines have been built. Power consumption per industrial worker has increased by about 40 per cent.

The chemical industry is employing natural and oil-well gas as raw material on an ever-growing scale. This has enabled us to effect a considerable reduction in costs and economise a large quantity of unprocessed foodstuffs. Thanks to the fact that raw materials other than foodstuffs are used for the production of alcohol, this year alone over 130 million poods of grain will have been economised. The output of plastics and artificial fibres has been more than doubled in six years.

A great deal is being done to effect the technical reconstruction of all types of transport, the carrying capacity of which has increased by 72 per cent. More than ten thousand kilometres of railway have been electrified. Half of all our trains now use electric and diesel traction; this has provided an economy of about 2,500 million rubles in the period under review. Vessels sailing under the Soviet flag call at ports of more than sixty countries in all continents. The tonnage of the merchant fleet has increased by about 50 per cent. The civil air fleet, equipped with giant air-liners, carries about 100,000 passengers a day. The centralised shipment of goods by road, effected by special motor-transport agencies, has increased six times over.

The industry manufacturing prefabricated concrete elements, which now produces almost 40 million cubic metres as compared to 5.3 million in 1955, has been built up almost from scratch. In recent years radical changes have come about in building techniques. Large-panel building is making rapid progress. The day is not far off when building will be completely transferred to industrial methods and re-equipped with modern facilities. Such are the more prominent features of progress in industry, transport and building in the period under survey.

In the period between 1956 and 1961 state investments in the economy amounted to 156,000 million rubles. That sum is larger than the total investments in the entire Soviet period up to the Twentieth Congress of the Party. About six thousand large-scale state enterprises have gone into production, among them such giants on the Volga as the Hydro-Electric Power Station named after Lenin and another after the Twenty-Second Party Congress, the Karaganda and Kuibyshev steel works, huge ore-dressing plants in the Ukraine, Kazakhstan and in the Kursk ironfield, and numerous engineering, chemical, sugar and textile factories. Over 30,000 kilometres of gas and oil pipeline has been laid. The builders of the Bratsk Power Station, which will be one of the world's largest, have a fine achievement to record—they have erected the first 225,000 kw unit ahead of schedule.

The builders of the hydro-electric power station at Kremenchug have made a fine gift to the Congress—they have completed the construction of the third power station in the Dnieper chain much earlier than scheduled. The commissioning of this power station will increase the stable, guaranteed capacity of the Dnieper Power Station by twenty per cent and greatly improve navigation on the Dnieper. A number of new towns have sprung up lately— Stavropol on the Volga, Volzhsky, Temir-Tau, Rudny, Bratsk and many others.

The years under review have seen a rapid growth of *labour productivity.* In 1961 the 1955 level will be exceeded by 43 per cent in industry, 60 per cent in building and 56 per cent on the railways. Almost 70 per cent of the growth in industrial output has been obtained thanks to greater labour productivity. Production costs have been reduced by about 11 per cent and railway transport costs by 22 per cent. Industry and transport last year yielded profits that were double those of 1955.

All Union republics have recorded important achievements in the development of their economy and culture. Industrial output and investments have increased by fifty to over a hundred per cent as compared with 1955 in all republics.

The Party's policy to develop the productive forces of *the eastern areas of the country* has been consistently implemented. Big power stations are being built to utilise the rich energy resources of Siberian rivers, and cheap coal. Huge iron ore deposits in Kazakhstan and Siberia have been placed in the service of the people. The output of metals and coal is rapidly increasing. The exploitation of gigantic deposits of natural gas in Uzbekistan will provide a dependable fuel supply for the Central Asian republics and cheap gas will be piped in large quantities to Kazakhstan and the Urals. The chemical industry is developing at a high rate.

The reorganisation of management in industry and building has greatly accelerated economic progress. It has affected every aspect of the country's economy, has elevated the role played by the Union republics in economic development, has stimulated the initiative of local Party, governmental and economic bodies and of broad sections of the working people, and has helped put big economic reserves to use.

Comrades, *the Seven-Year Plan for the Development of the Economy of the U.S.S.R.*, adopted by the Twenty-First Congress, has been an important stage in the creation of the material and technical basis of communism.

It will be remembered that the control figures for the seven years envisaged an increase in overall industrial output by about eighty per cent. The absolute growth we planned for the seven years was equal to that achieved during the previous two decades. All the peoples of the U.S.S.R. and millions of working people abroad acclaimed the plan. As for bourgeois politicians, they assessed the Seven-Year Plan as a new Soviet challenge to the capitalist world. And it *was* a challenge—a challenge to engage in a peaceful economic competition.

Among bourgeois politicians there were also those who repeated the old inventions that date back to the first five-year plans. They declared beforehand that it was another piece of propaganda, that the Communists drew up plans without due consideration of their possibilities, and that the Seven-Year Plan would be revised. The plan has now been operating for almost three years.

And what has happened? It must be admitted that we actually had to review some of the Seven-Year Plan targets—seven years is a long time and not everything can be foreseen. We made corrections to a number of important points in the plan and have, so to say, "considered the criticism" of the enemies of communism. To be more exact, the changes were suggested by developments and were made possible by the devoted labour of the Soviet people. The Seven-Year Plan called for an 8.3 per cent average annual growth in industrial output in the first three years. The actual growth in these three years will amount to ten per cent a year. The industries of the Soviet Union will produce goods worth about 19,000 million rubles more than planned for these three years. (*Applause.*)

In this period the country will obtain additionally about two million tons of pig iron, more than nine million tons of steel, about eight million tons of rolled goods, ten million tons of oil and many other items.

This is what the corrected targets for the last year of the plan now look like:

it was planned to smelt 65-70 million tons of pig iron but we now expect to smelt 72-73 million;

instead of 86-91 million tons of steel we shall probably obtain 95-97 million tons or more.

Some people suggested that we increase steel output to 100 million tons a year. But we had to damp their ardour and tell them that all branches of the economy had to be developed proportionately and that, along with steel production, we must think of housing construction, children's institutions, the production of footwear and clothing, and so on.

We must abide strictly by the directives adopted on this score by the Twenty-First Party Congress. (*Applause.*)

The output of rolled goods will be 73-74.5 million tons and not 65-70 as planned;

we shall extract not 230-240 million tons of oil, but more than 240 million;

the output of electric power will not be 500,000-520,000 million kwh but will be more than 520,000 million kwh;

the output of the machine-building and metal-working industries will reach 56,000-57,000 million rubles in value instead of the planned 49,000 million rubles.

These figures may, of course, have to be changed as time goes on; we may have to increase the appropriations for the development of one or another industry, or for cultural and welfare services, by drawing on the accumulations received as a result of overfulfilment of the plan. Evidently, we will be receiving substantial additional accumulations. The Central Committee of the Party and the Government will earmark them for those branches of the national economy where they are most needed and can best be used.

We shall produce more cement, tractors and farm machinery, paper, footwear, butter, sugar, furniture, radio and television receivers, refrigerators, washing machines and many other items for the country's economy and for the general public than envisaged by the control figures.

That is how we "miscalculated" when drawing up the Seven-Year Plan! We are not ashamed to admit such "miscalculations". (*Applause.*) I imagine the Soviet people will accept the amendments without regret. And let those who prophesied the failure of our plans think of a way out of the bog into which they have floundered, that is not our headache. (*Laughter. Applause.*)

You will recall, comrades, that even at the time of the earliest five-year plans our rate of industrial growth exceeded that of the U.S.A. but that we lagged behind noticeably in absolute growth, to say nothing of the considerable difference that existed in the level of production. *In recent years our country has continued to keep far ahead of the U.S.A. as far as the rate of growth is concerned, and has begun to outstrip that country in the absolute growth in the production of many important items.* The matter is now one of rapidly closing the gap between production levels, of the Soviet Union gaining first place in the world for the output of a number of foodstuffs and manufactured goods.

I will cite some facts. The average annual rate of industrial growth in the Soviet Union in the 1956-61 period amounted to 10.2 per cent, that of the U.S.A. to 2.3 per cent; the average annual output of manufactured goods per head of population increased by 8.2 per cent in the Soviet Union and by 0.6 per cent in the U.S.A.; the average annual increase in investments in the past six years has been 12 per cent in the U.S.S.R. and in the U.S.A. there has been no increase, but, on the contrary, a slight decrease.

And how do matters stand with the absolute growth of production and the closing of the gap in the level of production? In the last six years the output of steel in our country has increased by 26 million tons while that of the U.S.A. has decreased by 15 million tons; oil extraction in the U.S.S.R. has increased by 95 million tons and in the U.S.A. by approximately 20 million tons.

Industrial output in the U.S.S.R. today amounts to more than 60 per cent of American output. Here are the relevant figures for the more important items for 1961 (a preliminary estimate):

	U.S.S.R.	U.S.A.	U.S.S.R. as %% of U.S.A.
Pig iron (000,000 tons)	51.1	62.0	82
Steel (000,000 tons)	71.0	91.0	78
Coal, oil, gas and other fuels (reduced to a single conventional fuel—000,000 tons)	724	1,430	51
Electric power (on the bus bars—000,000,000 kwh)	306	872	35
Electric power used in industry (000,000,000 kwh)	213	425	50
Cement (000,000 tons)	51	54	94
Cotton textiles (unbleached—000,000,000 sq. m.)	5.3	8.5	62
Woollen textiles (000,000 linear metres)	353	270	131
Leather footwear (000,000 pairs) . . .	443	610	73
Granulated sugar (000,000 tons) . . .	6.5	3.7	175

I would remind you that a mere ten or eleven years ago Soviet industrial output was less than 30 per cent that of the U.S.A. At the present time the U.S.S.R. has already outstripped the United States in the extraction of iron ore and coal, the production of coke, prefabricated concrete elements, heavy diesel and electric locomotives, sawn timber, woollen textiles, sugar, butter, fish and a number of other items. (*Applause.*)

Our country now accounts for almost a fifth of the world's industrial output, or more than Britain, France, Italy, Canada, Japan, Belgium and the Netherlands combined. Yet these are all highly-developed countries with a total population of 280,000,000 people. The fact that our country with a population of 220,000,000 has surpassed them in total volume of industrial production shows how swiftly and surely socialist economy is progressing. (*Applause.*)

The implementation of the Seven-Year Plan will bring our country up to such a level that little more time will be required to outstrip the United States economically. *By fulfilling this basic economic task the Soviet Union will achieve an historic victory in the peaceful competition with the United States of America. (Prolonged applause.)*

2. Make Fuller Use of the Untapped Potentialities of Soviet Economy, Eliminate Waste and Mismanagement. Effect an All-Round Increase in Labour Productivity

Comrades, as you see, things are going well with us. We have every possibility not only of fulfilling, but of overfulfilling the Seven-Year Plan, and thus laying a sound foundation for the still greater tasks set out in the draft Programme of the Party. For those possibilities to become realities we shall have to work a lot, make better and wiser use of our potentialities and persist in our improvement of the planning and management of the economy.

The chief thing on which attention must be concentrated is *an all-round increase in the productivity of labour.* Experience shows that the Seven-Year Plan target for the growth of labour productivity can be surpassed. This is a big task and an important one. Real heroism will be needed to carry it out. Heroism in our day, however, is not merely enthusiasm, doggedness and industriousness. It is also ability, knowledge, a high level of culture, advanced technology and innovation.

Our forefathers composed the well-known song about the cudgel (*Dubinushka*) that men sang at work. It is true that words cannot be removed from a song, but even before the Revolution our people had substituted in it the word *mashinushka** for *dubinushka*, the cudgel. Even at that time they realised the great power of machinery. Today the Soviet Union is a technically advanced country. In the struggle for high, genuinely communist labour productivity we must place firm reliance on powerful machinery.

While giving our technical achievements their due, we cannot but see that there are still many unsolved problems. One still comes across instances of new technology being introduced into production too slowly. Take the Likhachov Automobile Works in Moscow, for example. It is still turning out 4-ton lorries of the type first produced fourteen years ago, only slight changes having been made in the design. How do the executives of the works and the leading people on the Moscow City Economic Council justify their infatuation with obsolete machines? Why has the design of a new lorry been under way for six long years? After all, the works has been given considerable help in organising the production of an improved vehicle.

The introduction of the new sometimes involves certain production outlays, extra worries and even disappointments. How much easier it is to go on doing quietly today what you did yesterday, and tomorrow what you are doing today. Unfortunately we still have executives who want to spend the rest of their days in peace. But we cannot

---

* The Russian diminutive of the word *mashina*, i.e., machine.
—*Tr.*

have Soviet executives working that way. Routine and stagnation are alien to the very nature of socialist production which is dynamic, revolutionary and always forward-looking. We must *employ more speedily and to the full everything that science and technology create in our country, we must take more boldly the best of what foreign experience offers, we must more extensively develop specialisation and co-operation and accelerate the rate of the overall mechanisation and automation of production.* We cannot tolerate conservatism in technology when we are building a communist economy. You can't clear high jumps on an old nag, as the saying goes.

At every factory, mine and building site we must thoroughly and painstakingly examine its technical equipment: we must replace whatever is obsolete, and wherever there are no production lines we must organise them. We must build new enterprises and technically re-equip those now in operation and we must produce the most up-to-date machine-tools, organise production lines, introduce automation and perfect technological processes.

Electrification plays the leading role in technical progress. It is the basis on which are developed automation, radio engineering, electronics and cybernetics, all the modern equipment that determines the technical level of production. New power installations must be put into operation more rapidly and the electrification of all branches of the economy must proceed at a faster pace.

The overall electrification of the country, the building of gigantic hydro-electric power stations, will make it possible to begin simultaneously the fulfilment of other complex economic tasks. We must complete the chains of power stations on the Volga and the Dnieper to provide new deep waterways and irrigate millions of hectares of land.

On the Volga, the Kama and the Dnieper, ten hydro-electric power stations are in operation at full capacity and four are under construction. To complete the reconstruction of the Volga-Kama basin, we have yet to build four hydrotechnical units and erect the installations for the transfer of water from the northern rivers, the Pechora and the Vychegda, through the Kama and the Volga to the Caspian Sea. A sixth station—the Kanev hydro-electric station—will have to be built on the Dnieper, and the River Pripet reconstructed to link the Baltic Sea with the Black Sea through the River Niemen and a system of canals. (*Applause.*)

Such are the magnificent plans being elaborated by the Party of Lenin. We can start realising them in the present seven-year period.

The question of questions, comrades, is *capital construction.*

The Seven-Year Plan envisaged state investments to the amount of 194,000-197,000 million rubles. Some of our opponents hissed at the time that we would not be able to realise such huge investments. What has actually happened? The average annual growth of investments was planned at 8.6 per cent, and the actual average has been 11 per cent per annum for the first three years. This over-fulfilment of the plan for investments means that in the course of three years out of the seven we are investing an additional sum of more than 3,500 million rubles in the economy.

There is no doubt that we are now building better and more quickly. There are, however, still very many short-comings in building. At the present time there are over a hundred thousand construction sites in the country, a half of them are for industry. With this huge number of projects in hand simultaneously, funds and materials are scattered and many enterprises go into production two or three years later than technical possibilities permit. Funds expended are frozen over a long period, they lie idle and the state does not get its money back.

Why is that so? It is because the desire for great things militates against a reasonable and realistic approach. It frequently happens that plausible excuses of solicitude for state interests are used to cover out and out parochialism; to put it crudely, it is grabbing on a regional, territorial and at times even a republican scale. Republican Councils of Ministers, economic councils, ministries, and local Party bodies try to get funds to start the greatest possible number of projects without considering whether the necessary building materials, manpower, and equipment can be supplied, and the planning bodies do not prevent these acts that contravene the interests of the state. This leads to stoppages, low labour productivity, prolongation of schedules, extra expenses and higher building costs.

If we overcome this defect—and overcoming it depends entirely on the ability to give guidance, on our will—we shall create conditions for a further speed-up in building. It seems that we shall have to stop starting new industrial building projects for a time, for a year, say, and devote all the funds that will accumulate in that period to the earliest possible completion of building projects already begun. Exceptions can only be sanctioned for particularly important projects and then only by decision of the Union Government. The Central Committee and the Soviet Government have recently adopted a decision laying down the sequence for capital construction.

Matters must be so arranged, planning must be so organised, that proportionality in the development of the economy is strictly observed and all potentialities are used to the full. An important role in this respect should be played by the recently organised enlarged economic areas and the boards set up in those areas to co-ordinate and plan the work of economic councils.

Of tremendous importance is the correct, economically justified selection of the way in which the different branches of economy are to develop. Projects for the building of new enterprises and the reconstruction of those already in operation should employ the best technological methods that can be implemented at the lowest cost.

Considerable economic interest, for example, attaches to the question of how the steel industry is to develop. Experience has shown that the production of steel in converters with the use of oxygen is far more profitable than in open-hearth furnaces; the economy effected in initial investments amounts to about six million rubles on a million tons of steel and more than a million is economised during exploitation. Despite the obvious advantages of the use of converters, far from sufficient attention is being paid to it.

You will remember that at the Twentieth Congress sharp criticism was levelled at those conservatives who regarded themselves as specialists in railway transport. Their ideologist was Kaganovich, who called himself the "iron commissar". For a long time they clung to their steam locomotives and barred the way to electric and diesel traction. Then we broke down their resistance, and the technical re-equipment of the railways went ahead at top speed. In some other branches of economy, too, conservatives cling to the old like the devil to a sinner's soul.

Socialist economic management demands an ability to analyse profoundly and with knowledge the economic aspect of the work of enterprises, building projects and whole branches of industry. We cannot leave at the helm of economic construction executives who are either not accustomed or who are unable to count the money of the state, and who regard their mission to be the fulfilment of plans at all costs. Take, for instance, the leaders of Perm Economic Council. It would seem that all is well with them, they report punctually on the fulfilment of targets for total output. But look how they run their economy. Last year every third enterprise in Perm Economic Area failed to fulfil its plan for profit, with the result that 27 million rubles were lost to the accumulation funds. The Economic Council paid out over eight million rubles in various fines, lost seven million rubles in spoilage and ended the year with a deficit of 26 million rubles in circulating funds.

Do you think that Comrade Soldatov, chairman of the Economic Council, was seriously criticised? Not at all. He was promoted to a leading post in the All-Russia Economic Council. (*Animation.*)

A ruthless war must be declared on the waste of raw and other materials and electric power. How many times has it been said, for instance, that a tremendous amount of metal is expended irrationally. Over four million tons of metal goes annually into shavings and, furthermore, no little effort, working time, electric power and tools are expended on them.

And are we at all thrifty in the way we deal with natural and oil-well gas? During the past three years about 30,000 million cubic metres of gas have been dissipated in the atmosphere or burnt to destroy it in the oilfields. To give you a clearer idea of what such mismanagement costs the state, it is enough to say that the natural gas lost would satisfy the annual needs of big industrial centres like Moscow, Leningrad, Kiev, Minsk and Magnitogorsk combined, while the oil-well gas lost would be sufficient to produce about a million tons of synthetic rubber.

Financial control must be made stricter in all spheres of production. Economy in big and little things, the proper utilisation of natural resources and material values must be elevated to the level of state policy.

Planning practice must be radically improved. It must be said that planning bodies not infrequently make mistakes and miscalculations in estimating the volume of production. Output plans do not always dovetail with plans for the supply of materials and machines and with co-ordinated deliveries, and building plans are not always adapted to financial allocations, supplies of materials and deliveries of equipment. In any economy there must always be certain reserves, the planning must not be from hand to mouth, so to say.

We are now in a position to build up the necessary circulating funds at enterprises. It was difficult to do this in the past when dozens of ministries had a hand in every economic area and each of them tried to isolate itself within its own boundary posts. Those boundary posts have now been removed. The economic area has become a single economic entity under the guidance of the economic council and it is this body that must provide its enterprises and building sites with sufficient materials both for production and for repairs.

Party and economic bodies must be made to account more strictly for their fulfilment of the decisions and directives of the Party and the Government, and Party and state discipline must be enhanced throughout the apparatus. No high-handed methods or lack of discipline can be tolerated in a planned economy. A number of economic councils, for instance the Dnepropetrovsk, Bryansk and Uzbek councils, expended more than their quota of certain materials and equipment on the needs of "their own" economic areas; plans for deliveries to other economic areas suffered in consequence. This is the work of those who follow the principle "How can you refuse a favour to a friend!" Unprincipled executives who are prepared to "do a favour" to the local authorities at state expense, who are guilty of malicious breaches of Party and state discipline, must be severely punished.

Our task is to increase considerably the output of goods by improving the organisation of production, by the extensive employment of the methods of advanced workers in all branches of industry and in building.

The best methods must be more vigorously introduced and the lagging and so-called average enterprises must be brought up to the level of the best.

The wonderful successes of our industry, building and transport have been achieved by the devoted labour of the heroic Soviet working class, engineers, technicians, designers and scientists. Relying in the future, too, on their experience, knowledge and political and labour activity we shall attain those great aims of communist construction that the Twenty-Second Congress will define. (*Prolonged applause.*)

3. A Highly-Developed Agriculture Is a Necessary Condition for the Construction of Communism. The Development of Virgin Lands Is a Great Achievement of the Soviet People

Comrades, in the period under review the Party has devoted special attention to the development of agriculture. And this is understandable, for, as a result of the war, and also of errors and shortcomings in the management of collective and state farms, our agriculture found itself in a difficult position.

The Party was faced with a vital and most pressing task, namely, speedily to eliminate the lag in agriculture and meet the food requirements of the people and the raw material requirements of industry. The September 1953 and subsequent plenary meetings of the Central Committee disclosed the causes of the errors and shortcomings in the management of agriculture and devised a comprehensive programme to promote its progress. The Twentieth Congress unanimously approved the measures taken, and instructed the Central Committee to work with unflagging energy for a rapid increase in the output of grain, industrial crops, meat, milk and other products.

In these past years important measures have been carried out in agriculture. They have already benefited communist construction and will benefit it still more in the future. With the active co-operation of the people, the Party set about the effective solution of many cardinal problems in agricultural development.

The material and technical basis of the collective and state farms has been strengthened. From 1956 to 1960 investments in agriculture amounted to 27,200 million rubles compared with 13,900 million in the previous five years, or were almost doubled. Our farms were supplied with 747,000 tractors as against the 427,000 delivered in the previous five years; large quantities of other machinery were also provided.

The machine and tractor stations have been reorganised, which has made it possible to put the land and machinery in the same hands and to create conditions for the better use of the productive forces in agriculture.

Immense tracts of virgin and disused land have been developed. As a result there have been decisive increases in grain production and opportunities have been provided for a more rapid development of livestock farming.

The role of the state farms in communist construction has been increased. In seven years over 3,000 new state farms have been set up, and their total number is now almost 8,000. Many of the state farms are highly productive model farms which set an example of the socialist organisation of farm production. The cultivated area of the state farms has grown from 15 to 80 million hectares, and their share in sales to the state is: grain 43 per cent, meat 28, milk 32 and wool 31 per cent.

A new system of planning has been introduced. It is based on the principle of combining state guidance with the encouragement of the creative initiative of the people. This has increased the activity of the working people in the countryside and made collective farms and local government bodies more immediately responsible for the better use of land and technical equipment.

The Leninist principle of giving material incentives to the collective farmers, state-farm workers and specialists to increase agricultural production *has been restored.* The state has replaced obligatory deliveries by purchases; it has substantially raised purchase prices and has reduced the prices of capital goods for the rural areas.

The collective and state farms have been reinforced by leading cadres and specialists. At the call of the Party, hundreds of thousands of Communists and non-Party people have gone to work in the countryside.

These, then, are the more important measures carried out by our Party. They had a truly revolutionising effect on the development of agriculture and the entire socialist economy. Total agricultural output has gone up 43 per cent in the past five years as against the preceding five years. The output of grain, meat, milk and other farm produce has increased very considerably. Thanks to greater collective production, the money incomes of the collective farms and their non-distributable assets have doubled. The living standard of the farmers has improved as a result of the progress made in collective farming.

Now let us look at the condition of the major branches of agriculture.

The Central Committee has been directing the efforts of the working people in the countryside towards a *greater output of grain* as the basis of agricultural progress. The Party has criticised the indiscriminate use of grass-arable rotation. Steps have been taken to effect a considerable expansion of areas under more productive and valuable crops—wheat and maize—and seed cultivation has been improved to an appreciable degree.

The development of virgin and disused lands is prominent among the measures implemented by the Party. The Central Committee is happy to report to the Congress that this task has been successfully accomplished. In the boundless steppes of Kazakhstan, Siberia, the Volga region, the Urals and other eastern areas, 41,800,000 hectares of new land have been cultivated and put at the service of the people. (*Applause.*) The new lands now account for over 40 per cent of the grain purchased by the state. *Their development is a great feat which our heroic people have performed in building communism. It is an achievement that will live through the ages.* (*Prolonged applause.*)

The newly-developed lands have radically changed the grain balance of many areas of our country. It is with pride and elation that we speak of this historic fact—the increase in the country's grain output achieved through the development of new lands. Before the new lands were developed, the regions concerned produced an annual average of 1,386 million poods of grain; between 1956 and 1960, their output averaged 3,363 million poods a year. (*Applause.*)

Grain sales, too, have greatly increased. Here are some data to illustrate this.

Grain Sales to the State

(yearly averages, 000,000 poods)

	1949-1953	1956-1960
R.S.F.S.R.	1,196	1,734
Altai Territory	49	245
Orenburg Region	43	115
Omsk Region	36	89
Novosibirsk Region	26	80
Krasnoyarsk Territory	44	73
Kazakh S.S.R.	111	705
Tselinny Territory	63	508
Tselinograd Region	13	152
Kustanai Region	17	138
Kokchetav Region	12	93
Pavlodar Region	5	74
North Kazakhstan Region	16	51

That shows you the capacity of the new lands. There you have some of the fruits of the Party's policy. It is gratifying to note that the peoples of all the fraternal republics of the Soviet Union took part in the development of the new lands, particularly our fine youth, our Leninist Komsomol. In response to the call of the Party, hundreds of thousands of patriots went to unsettled steppes. There they accomplished feats of labour heroism and brought fame to their great country. (*Prolonged applause.*)

The value of the new lands goes beyond the additional thousands of millions of poods of grain our country obtains there. Their development is radically transforming vast areas in the East. Large state farms, modern settlements, research institutions and educational establishments have sprung up in the steppes, where you can also see new railways and roads, and high-voltage transmission lines. The Party and the people developed a vast industrial area in the East. And now, thanks to the development of new lands, we also have a vast area in the East supplying grain and livestock products. All the riches of the Soviet East will thus serve the great cause of communist construction. We have here an example of truly communist renovation of the earth. (*Applause.*)

While promoting grain farming, the Party is also working to increase the output of sugar beet, cotton, flax, sunflower seeds, potatoes, vegetables, fruit (including citrus fruits), grapes, and tea. We have noteworthy achievements in these fields as well. The growth of agricultural production can be seen from the following table:

| | Average Annual Output | | 1956-1960 |
	1951-1955	1956-1960	in %% of 1951-1955
Grain (000,000 poods)	5,442	7,742	142
Sugar beet (at refineries)			
(000,000 tons)	24.0	45.6	190
Cotton (000 tons)	3,888	4,365	112
Sunflower seeds (000 tons)	2,456	3,672	150
Flax (000 tons)	234	438	187
Potatoes (000,000 tons)	69.5	88.3	127
Vegetables (000,000 tons)	11.2	15.1	134
Fruit (000 tons)	2,100	2,905	138
Grapes (000 tons)	1,021	1,592	156
Tea (000 tons)	105.8	134.0	127

Agricultural output has thus grown considerably in five years. The result is that state purchases of grain and the other farm products have increased to a large extent.

While formerly the state purchased about 2,000 million poods of grain, in recent years it has been purchasing 3,000 million poods or more.

The problem of developing livestock farming holds a special place among the more urgent problems of agricultural development. It will be remembered that until very recently this vital branch was in a state of extreme neglect and there occurred serious difficulties in supplying the population with food. Tremendous effort was required to do away with that protracted lag. It was first of all indispensable that the problem of increasing feed production be solved. The planting of maize was a most important condition, along with the development of new lands, for a better feed supply. Maize growing for ensilage at the milk-wax stage extended the area of cultivation and made it possible to push that valuable crop almost into all areas of the country. In 1953 the area under maize was 3,485,000 hectares, whereas today it is almost 26 million hectares. The collective and state farms have been producing more fodder grain and have sharply increased the amount of silage. Much has been done in the way of building premises for livestock and poultry and for dairy farms, and mechanising labour-consuming operations.

We now have every reason to assert that *radical changes have come about in livestock breeding on collective and state farms.* Take the livestock population. For a long time it remained at one and the same level and only in the last few years has the situation changed noticeably. This is how the livestock population has increased on farms of all categories:

	1955	1960	1960 in % % of 1955
	(000,000 head)		
Cattle	58.8	75.8	129
Cows	27.7	34.8	126
Pigs	34.0	58.7	173
Sheep	103.3	133 0	129

It is important to note that the livestock population has been growing chiefly on the collective and state farms.

In the last five years the number of cattle on the farms has gone up by 68 per cent and that of pigs, by 150 per cent.

The growing purchases of meat, milk and other products vividly illustrate the work carried out in the field of livestock farming.

| | Purchased | | 1956-1960 |
| | (annual average, 000 tons) | | in % % of |
	1951-1955	1956-1960	1951-1955
Meat (live weight)	3,523	6,111	173
Milk	10,987	22,231	202
Eggs (000,000)	2,582	4,841	187
Wool	190.6	310.6	163

You will see that the purchases of livestock products have substantially increased. It is important to stress that the collective and state farms have now become the decisive factor in supplying the country with livestock products. Their share in meat sales last year was 87 per cent and in those of milk, 93 per cent. This is a big victory for the policy of our Party, a victory for the socialist economic system. (*Applause*.)

Comrades, our progress in agriculture is appreciable and indisputable. But the question arises: Why are we still short of certain products, particularly meat, and why, despite our important overall achievements, we still have considerable difficulty in supplying the population with livestock products?

This is due, first of all, to the fact that the rate of growth of agricultural production is still lower than that of industrial production and still does not meet the growing requirements of the population.

Let us look into the changes that have occurred in our country in late years. Our population has increased considerably. As I have said, compared with 1955, it has increased by more than 20 million. The incomes of the working people have been growing year after year. Thanks to higher wages, the abolition of taxes, the discontinuance of the floating of state loans, and increased pensions, the incomes of the population in 1960 were greater than in 1955 by 24,000 million rubles. Needless to say, the workers and office employees do not hoard their money but spend it on food and other goods. It is natural, therefore, that meat, milk and butter consumption should greatly increase. State and co-operative sales of livestock products to the population have increased in the following proportions:

	1953	1960
	(000 tons)	
Meat and meat products	1,757	4,158
Milk and whole-milk products	1,980	8,214
Butter	330	613

We all rejoice in this increased consumption of the more valuable food products. The Party is working to ensure that the Soviet people eat better and that the general standard of living improves. Consumption will continue growing, and this implies that we must always keep agricultural problems in the foreground and ensure that agricultural production is always ahead of demand. Yet many Party and government organisations in 1959-60 slackened attention to agriculture, with the result that the rate of output, especially as regards meat and milk, fell far short of Seven-Year Plan targets.

This fact caused understandable concern to the Party. The January 1961 Plenary Meeting of the Central Committee sharply criticised shortcomings in agricultural management and condemned all manifestations of complacency and overconfidence. The Central Committee meeting, as well as zonal conferences, went deeply into the question of ways and means of promoting agriculture and outlined definite measures for increased production.

The Soviet people gave their full support to the measures planned by the Party; they felt confident that these measures were realistic and have been vigorously putting the decisions of the January Meeting of the Central Committee into practice. It is true that but little time has passed since the Party decided on those measures and they have, therefore, not yet had their full impact on the situation in agriculture. But what has been done so far, the results achieved this year, warrant the conclusion that it will not be long before agricultural production shows a steep rise.

What have we accomplished in 1961? The total grain harvest is greater than last year. State purchases of grain are also greater. By October 15, purchases mounted to 3,086,000,000 poods, or 354,000,000 poods more than on the same date last year. Total state purchases for the year will be roughly 3,300,000,000 poods, or 450,000,000 poods more than last year. And this is a big victory for the Party and the people, a victory all the more valuable because it has been gained in a year that has not been particularly good as far as weather conditions are concerned. *(Applause.)*

What enabled us to produce and purchase more grain than before? The decisive fact was that the collective and state farms, in carrying out the decisions of the Central Committee Plenary Meeting, revised their cropping plans and replaced less productive by more productive crops, mainly by maize and legumes, although it must be pointed out that not all collective and state farms carried out these important measures.

The Ukraine is a good example of the way agriculture has benefited from the measures adopted by the Party. You will recall that at the January Plenary Meeting of the Central Committee the leaders of the Communist Party of the Ukraine, the Council of Ministers of that republic, regional Party committees and executive committees of regional Soviets were sharply criticised for shortcomings in agricultural management, especially for low grain output. Last year the Ukraine sold the state a mere 359,000,000 poods of grain.

You remember it, of course, comrades from the Ukraine; I'm sure you haven't forgotten.

Voice: The Ukrainians aren't the only ones to remember.

Khrushchov: That's good!

The Party organisations of the Ukraine drew proper conclusions from the criticism levelled at them. They organised and led the working people of the countryside in carrying out big new tasks. The republic's collective and state farms made better use of the land and of their potentialities, and launched an emulation movement to fulfil commitments and plans. Millions of people were taught progressive methods of maize-growing. This year the area planted to maize for grain was greatly expanded and there was a considerable improvement in the yield per hectare. The area planted to peas has been increased by 342,000 hectares and the average yield was 1.74 tons per hectare. These facts have played a decisive role in increasing grain production and sales to the state.

The following data indicate changes in grain sales in some regions of the Ukraine:

Grain Sold to the State

Region	1961 (by October 15)	Annual average 1956-1960
	(000,000 poods)	
Poltava	73	22
Dnepropetrovsk	70	44
Kharkov	60	25
Kirovograd	60	31
Zaporozhye	54	41
Vinnitsa	41	27
Lugansk	40	10
Cherkassy	37	20

Altogether the collective and state farms of the Ukraine will this year sell the state something like 850,000,000 poods of grain (*applause*) of which 744,000,000 poods had already been sold by October 15. (*Applause.*) It is important to note that although they have sold so much grain, the collective and state farms have made ample provision for seed and have unprecedented quantities of grain in stock for use as fodder. The collective farms supply their members with ample quantities of grain as payment for work-day units and pay bonuses for high yields in full.

That is splendid, comrades. I have spent many years in the Ukraine and know the hard-working Ukrainian people quite well. I worked with them before the war, and after the war too, when they were rehabilitating their economy. But I must confess that in those years our imagination never soared to the heights the Ukraine has attained today in grain production. We often say that being determines consciousness, and in jest sometimes observe that "beating", for its part, stimulates consciousness. (*Applause.*) The criticism levelled at the Ukrainian comrades has been severe but fair. It made the right impression and was duly appreciated. It roused people, and they showed how much they could do. We give praise to them, and expect them to lift agricultural production to a still higher level. (*Applause.*)

The Communist Party of the Ukraine and the Ukrainian people as a whole have achieved an outstanding victory. Great credit accrues to the working people of the Ukraine, who can report such remarkable achievements to this Congress. (*Prolonged applause.*)

The working people of many regions in the Russian Federation have this year achieved gratifying successes in the struggle for grain. By October 15, the collective and state farms of the republic had sold the state 1,828,000,000 poods of grain, or 91,000,000 poods more than by the same date last year. The state will apparently purchase 2,000,000,000 poods of grain in the Russian Federation; in this republic, as in the Ukraine, maize played an important part in meeting food and fodder requirements.

A big maize harvest has been gathered over large areas. Take Krasnodar Territory. On account of the spring drought, this year's corn crop in the Kuban area is only 1.9 tons per hectare or two-fifths of a ton less than last year, when 2.3 tons were gathered from each hectare. The amount of grain produced and the amount sold to the state, however, have been considerably increased. By October 15 the collective and state farms of the territory had sold the state 116,000,000 poods of grain, or 35,000,000 poods more than by the same date last year. How has this been done? The collective and state farms of the territory have obtained high maize yields over an area of 400,000 hectares. They were thus able to sell the state 33,000,000 poods of maize by October 15, 1961, whereas only 16,000,000 poods of maize had been sold by the same date last year.

Collective farmers and state-farm workers have this year obtained significant results in increasing grain output in the Central Black-Earth regions and some regions of the Volga area, the Urals and Siberia, thereby showing that the Russian Federation possesses tremendous resources for a bigger output of farm produce. Here are comparative figures on the amount of grain sold to the state by some regions.

Grain Sold to the State

	(000,000 poods)	
Region	1961 (by October 15)	Annual average 1956-1960
Stalingrad	125	75
Voronezh	66	38

This is the Voronezh Region which, as you may recall, demonstrated the "new method" of harvesting maize with a rail. After they were criticised, the Voronezh comrades tried another method of land cultivation. As you see, their results are not bad. (*Animation.*)

	1961 (by October 15)	Annual average 1956-1960
Tambov	42	28
Penza	42	27
Belgorod	37	19
Kursk	36	23
Lipetsk	28	17

These successes have been achieved by the devoted labour of the collective farmers, state-farm workers and agricultural specialists, and through the extensive organisational and political work of Party organisations which have developed a widespread emulation movement for the fulfilment of commitments.

This year the Ukrainians have shown what they can do, and it is up to the comrades of the Russian Federation to see what's what and to draw the right conclusions. The Russian Federation has great potentialities. It must realise its strength and tackle the matter in all earnest. (*Animation.*)

Many Western politicians say:

"We do not question the achievements of your industry, but we cannot imagine how you will put things straight in agriculture."

Speaking to them, I said:

"Just wait, we'll still show you where you get off in agricultural output as well." (*Stormy, prolonged applause.*)

We have inexhaustible potentialities. But they have to be fully appreciated and properly used. It seems that after this Congress we shall have to repeat the round of agricultural conferences held in the republics, territories and regions. We must stir a few people in a few places into action, so to speak, to clear their pores as people do in steambaths to normalise the supply of oxygen they get. (*Animation.*)

I should like to express confidence in the ability of the working people of the Russian Federation to make still fuller use of their potentialities and achieve fresh successes in developing all branches of agriculture. (*Applause.*)

The January Plenary Meeting of the Central Committee pointed out that in a number of areas there were intolerable lags in the production of cereals and legumes. This year there is a noticeable increase in the production and sales of these crops. Last year 21 million poods of legumes were sold to the state but this year the figure is 41 million poods. More buckwheat and millet has been purchased.

The production of cotton, sugar beet, sunflower seeds and other crops has also increased. This year, in the face of difficulties occasioned by a shortage of water for irrigation, the collective farmers and state-farm workers of the Uzbek, Tajik, Turkmen and Kirghiz republics and the South Kazakhstan Region of the Kazakh Republic showed great perseverance and tenacity. They raised a good cotton crop and are successfully meeting their commitments. By October 15, state cotton purchases amounted to a total of 3,000,000 tons of cotton, or 663,000 tons more than last year; Uzbekistan, the biggest cotton-grower, has sold 1,982,000 tons to the state, or 453,000 tons more than last year.

The collective and state farms of Georgia have, as last year, produced an excellent tea harvest. They have sold the state 154,000 tons of tea, fulfilling the plan by 107 per cent.

These, then, are the preliminary results of this year's farming. As for stock breeding, we have made some progress in this field as well. The cattle population of the collective and state farms has grown by 4,000,000 head within the year, the increase in the number of cows being 1,700,000; the number of pigs is up by 5,000,000 head and that of sheep, by 3,000,000 head. The output and state purchases of livestock products have increased.

The rate of growth of meat and milk output, however, is still far below the necessary level. Much hard work will have to be done and, most important of all, all potentialities will have to be utilised to effect a considerable increase in the production of these items as early as 1962.

4. Press Forward Agricultural Progress. Meet the Population's Demand for Farm Products More Fully

Comrades, our potentialities are immense. Within the next few years we shall be able *to increase grain purchases to 4,200 million poods, meat to 13 million tons and milk to 50 million tons annually* as envisaged by the decisions of the January Meeting of the Central Committee. In what way can production be substantially increased and purchases of farm produce brought up to such a level?

For a greater *grain output*, the important thing is to continue improving the crop pattern and to raise productivity. The less productive crops must be firmly ruled out to make room for those with a high yield, and a correct rotation must be established. This is indeed a basic task in agriculture, and one that is most pressing, comrades. We still have many areas where farming is irrational. The Kirov, Kostroma and Yaroslavl regions are particularly indicative in this respect.

Kirov Region, for example, last year planted 477,000 hectares to oats and 515,000 hectares to annual and perennial grasses. These crops were planted on a million hectares, or 44 per cent of the total crop area. Another 514,000 hectares were under clean fallow. When we consider that annual grasses yielded 0.7 to 0.8 ton of hay, and oats 0.5 to 0.7 ton of grain per hectare, we realise that more than half the arable area was virtually unused. The area under maize and peas was 155,000 hectares, or only seven per cent of the region's sown land. In the light of these facts, how could there have been sufficient grain or feed and how can anyone have developed livestock farming with such a crop pattern? More than a few speeches were delivered in Kirov Region on farming efficiency but the speakers all forgot the main thing.

What do we mean by efficient land cultivation? First of all the maximum yield per hectare of land and per unit of labour expended. But this can only be achieved if the most productive crops are planted and crop rotation is properly organised, and if the collective and state farms make extensive use of scientific achievements and the experience of innovators. It is this purpose—the greatest possible output, the best utilisation of the land, and higher fertility—that the cropping system should serve.

Unfortunately, many of our scientists, agronomists and farmers are still under the spell of grass-arable rotation, whose indiscriminate application has caused a great deal of harm to agriculture. The sooner we get rid of indiscriminate practices in agriculture, the more creative imagination we display in solving urgent problems and the more fully we take account of the experience of the foremost collective and state farms and research institutions, the sooner we shall increase the output of grain and other farm products.

In revising the crop pattern, special attention should be paid to *greater output of maize grain and legumes*. In the more favourable maize-growing areas—the Ukraine, the southern regions of the Russian Federation, in Moldavia, Georgia, Azerbaijan, the southern areas of Kazakhstan and in the Central Asian republics—we can harvest five tons of maize per hectare on large areas. We must select appropriate varieties and hybrids and must raise maize for its grain in the Central Black-Earth regions, the Volga region and elsewhere and push maize northwards.

It is essential to realise, comrades, that without maize the collective and state farms cannot achieve the required level of grain production. Maize has shown its potentialities in every area of the Soviet Union. If there are some parts of the country in which maize is not properly cultivated and the collective and state farms obtain low harvests, the blame should be put on the management and not on the climate. Where maize refuses to grow there is an "ingredient" which hampers its growth. That "ingredient" is to be found in the leadership, first of all on the collective and state farms, and then also at district, regional, territorial and even republican level. We must replace officials who have grown as dry as dust and are causing a valuable crop like maize to wither like themselves and are preventing it from proving its worth to the full. (*Applause.*)

The experience of many thousands of collective and state farms this year has shown beyond all doubt that one of the main sources of increased grain production is, along with maize, a sharp increase in the share of peas and beans among the spring crops. On an expanse stretching from the Carpathian foothills to the virgin steppes of Siberia and Kazakhstan, peas yield harvests of two, three or more tons per hectare. *The introduction of maize, peas and feed beans on a large scale is not just a task like any other but a highly important trend in the development of cropping.*

The further development and better use of new lands is a major source of increased grain production. Within the next few years we must develop not less than another 8,000,000 hectares, which will raise the total of new land in use to 50 million hectares. The proper utilisation of these land areas is a task of national importance. I must say that there are serious defects in the use of new lands. In Kazakhstan, for example, the one-crop system is practically dominant; the state and collective farms have for many years been sowing nothing but spring wheat, that is, grain upon grain. The result is that the fields have become weedy and the growth of productivity has been checked. The Central Committee of the Communist Party of Kazakhstan and the Council of Ministers of that republic hardly gave thought to the future of the newly-developed lands and took an incorrect stand on the solution of problems of crop farming on them.

The errors that have been committed must be rectified. The fullest use must be made of the new lands; it is essential to expand the fallow row-crop area, introduce maize, peas, feed beans and sugar beet and keep clean fallow wherever necessary. On the new lands, the machinery used must be suited to the row-crop system. Row crops there may be introduced only if their cultivation is highly mechanised.

It is important to introduce the strictest agronomic regulations, to make the relevant set of agrotechnical measures as obligatory as technological operations are at a factory, and raise the role of the agronomist on the collective and state farms to the same high level as that of the engineer in industry.

The development of new lands is an accomplishment of our Party, comrades, something our people may well be proud of. We must make farming on the new lands a symbol of the efficiency of socialist agriculture.

Increased grain output will also enable us to solve the problem of expanded livestock farming all the more speedily. We deliberately treat the production of grain, meat and milk as a single problem. It would be wrong to separate the solution of the grain problem from that of livestock farming. The two problems should be dealt with and solved jointly. What do I mean by the solution of the grain problem? I mean the attainment of a grain production level sufficient to meet the demand for both food and feed. And what do I mean by the solution of the livestock problem? I mean primarily greater output of meat, milk and butter. As we say in Russian, a dry spoon will scratch the tongue. If anyone is to eat his bread with relish, he must be able to "flavour" it with butter, bacon, meat and other livestock products, which cannot be supplied in adequate quantities unless grain production is adequate. The solution of the livestock problem also means an increased supply of manure and, therefore, higher crop yields.

To meet the people's demand for meat and milk in full

and to overtake and outstrip the United States in per capita output of livestock products, the collective and state farms must draw on the progress made so far and use the experience they have gained.

There are American newsmen present here. They like to ridicule this slogan of ours. But I want you to know, gentlemen, that if we say so, our people will do it without fail. (*Applause.*) When the Party advances a slogan, the people support it and put it into practice. Our people will do it without fail! (*Applause.*)

Our immediate task is to produce in our country an average of not less than 7.5 tons of meat per hundred hectares of arable and 1.6 tons per hundred hectares of other farmland. We now have all we require to achieve such a level on every collective or state farm. These, of course, are average indexes for the country as a whole. Many areas of the Russian Federation, the Ukrainian, Byelorussian, Lithuanian, Latvian, Estonian and Moldavian republics can and must produce much more meat and milk per hundred hectares of arable and other farmland.

I have already mentioned, comrades, the role which the newly-developed lands have played in increasing grain output. But we have thus fulfilled only our first task, and passed the initial stage of development on the new lands. We must go further, for agriculture on the new lands must not be restricted to one branch, such as grain production. Our task now is to persevere in the development of livestock farming, using grain farming as a basis. That will be the second stage in new land development.

Large-scale, well-organised livestock farming in the newly-developed areas will be a valuable means of increasing the production of meat, milk and butter, and will enable us to meet the requirements of the people more fully. *The new lands have supplied our people with thousands of millions of poods of grain; they must also provide, in addition to grain, millions of tons of meat, milk and other livestock products.*

Maize, legumes and sugar beet are dependable factors in the development of livestock farming. If we learn to raise large quantities of these crops everywhere, we shall be able to produce any pre-set amount of meat, milk, etc.

One of our important tasks is to meet in full the demand of the urban population and industrial centres for fresh milk and dairy products, high-quality potatoes and the widest assortment of vegetables. Not so long ago a great deal was said in our country about setting up vegetable and milk-producing areas around cities, but actual progress in this field has been slow.

The Central Committee of the Party and the Government have now found a more rational way for the speedy solution of the problem of meeting the demand for these products. The Party is carrying out an extensive programme for the establishment of specialised state farms around our cities and industrial centres. We must work still better and more purposefully to ensure that the demand for milk, potatoes and vegetables is fully met through production on the specialised state and collective farms surrounding our cities and industrial centres.

State interests require a rapid increase in cotton production. During the remaining years of the Seven-Year Plan we must increase cotton harvests by nearly 50 per cent.

It is important to expand the area under cotton and extend as quickly as possible the irrigated lands of Central Asia. At the same time the cardinal task is to increase yields by better use of the irrigated lands and mechanised cultivation.

The cotton-growing regions of the Uzbek, Tajik, Turkmen, Kirghiz, Kazakh, Azerbaijan and Armenian republics are now faced with a double task: to achieve high productivity of cotton as their basic crop and to have a developed livestock farming. While producing more cotton for industry, the cotton belt must also provide an adequate supply of feed and must satisfy the demand for meat, milk and other products. To achieve this aim, they must carefully study crop rotation in order to increase feed production simultaneously with an increase in cotton output. Adequate quantities of feed can be provided above all by sowing maize in the irrigated areas and raising the productivity of alfalfa and sugar beet.

In the next few years every collective farm and every state farm must increase cotton yields to not less than 2.5 tons per hectare. When that has been done, we shall have, in the areas now in use, an additional quantity of cotton in excess of one million tons. Two and a half tons is a yield attained by average collective farms; many of the advanced farms gather four or more tons of cotton per hectare.

With regard to the production of *sugar beet, sunflower seeds, flax, hemp, potatoes, vegetables, fruit, grapes, tea, etc.*, an effort must be made to increase yields and to use machinery on a larger scale. This is the way to reduce labour expenditure and put out cheaper produce.

Comrades, our objectives in agriculture are dictated by the fundamental interests of communist construction. We all realise that progress in agriculture is a major condition for the continuous improvement of the standard of living of the people.

The Party is outlining the prospects for agricultural progress in the coming twenty years. It envisages a very substantial increase in the output of grain, meat, milk and other farm produce. The accomplishment of this task will call for higher labour productivity in all branches of agriculture, labour heroism, a high standard of organisation, the provision of collective and state farms with modern machinery, and better utilisation of machines. It is important for the workers and collective farmers, for Communists and non-Party people, for all Soviet men and women, to realise that the groundwork for the effective implementation of this great plan is being laid today through the fulfilment of the Seven-Year Plan. By fulfilling the Seven-Year Plan, we shall lay a solid foundation on which we can achieve further progress in agriculture.

The further development of agricultural production is a matter for the entire Party and all Soviet people. It is a height on the road to communism which we must scale by using the whole might of the Soviet system. (*Prolonged applause.*)

5. Improvement in the People's Living Standards. The Flowering of Science, Education, Literature and Art

Comrades, the main purpose of the Party's activity is to raise the living standard of the Soviet people, to promote their material and spiritual requirements and meet them ever more fully. The socialist system in our country has reached a period of maturity when its potentialities are revealing themselves more fully than ever. The superiority of socialism in rates of economic development is more and more favourably affecting not only material production but consumption as well.

Under socialism the greater the national income, the higher the living standard. In the Soviet Union three-quarters of the national income goes to satisfy the personal requirements of the people. In 1960 the national income of the U.S.S.R. had increased by more than 50 per cent as compared with 1955, and in the last ten years the national income per head of population has increased by 120 per cent. *The national income per capita is increasing much more rapidly in the Soviet Union than in the most highly-developed capitalist countries.*

On the basis of the growth of the national income the real incomes of factory, office and professional workers per employed person have increased by 27 per cent in the past five years, and those of collective farmers by 33 per cent. Under the Seven-Year Plan the real incomes of factory, office and professional workers and collective farmers will increase by as much as 40 per cent.

We have set ourselves the task of achieving a higher standard of living than that of the more advanced capitalist countries. In propounding this task we have in mind only those spheres in which our country must overtake and surpass the capitalist countries. In many respects the Soviet Union has already achieved indisputable advantages over the most highly-developed capitalist countries. Free education, free medical services, the absence of unemployment, not to mention many other benefits enjoyed under socialism, have long since become normal for Soviet people, something they take for granted. These, comrades, constitute *the greatest of gains, and our people are justly proud of them. In this sphere we have long since left the capitalist countries behind.* Much effort will be required of the working class in the capitalist countries, they will have to wage a stubborn struggle to achieve such gains as these. (*Applause.*)

Consumption is steadily growing in the Soviet Union. In 1960 the volume of retail trade through state and co-operative shops increased by more than 50 per cent over that of 1955; in the first three years of the Seven-Year Plan the rate of growth of trade was higher than envisaged by the control figures. Soviet people are consuming more and more meat, milk, dairy products and sugar; sales of clothes, footwear, furniture, household and other goods are increasing. The popular demand for these goods, however, is still not being fully met. The lack of certain goods in the shops is a serious criticism of our work. In order to satisfy the growing requirements of the population the Party and the Government have decided to increase the output of consumer goods.

The time has come when we must raise more sharply the question of greatly improving the quality of all goods. The variety of goods in our shops is often not wide enough, although warehouses are often chockfull of "unmarketable goods". What kind of goods are these? Poor-quality goods that nobody will purchase. The demand for footwear, for instance, is not being fully met, although footwear to the value of more than 1,500 million rubles has accumulated in warehouses. Or take the quality of clothes. Everybody agrees that Soviet fabrics wear well, but there is criticism of the styles and finish of suits and coats. All too often poor-quality articles are made out of good material, and then big sums are spent on removing the defects. Here I might cite an old saying:

"Akulya, why are you sewing the thing askew?"

"It doesn't matter, Mother, I mean to rip it apart anyway." (*Laughter. Applause.*)

How much longer will certain of our executives work after the fashion of an Akulya?

The work of the light industry enterprises has to be improved; all consumer goods must be not only of high quality, but also attractive.

In its efforts to better the life of the people, the Party devotes much attention to questions that are basic in ensuring rising living standards. The general normalisation of wages and salaries is drawing to a close, and the minimum is being raised. In the past five years about 4,000 million rubles have been spent on raising wages and salaries. At the same time excesses in the payment for some categories of labour have been done away with.

At the present time nearly forty million factory and office workers are receiving wages according to the new rates of payment. Within the next few years the new rates will be introduced throughout the national economy. It is planned to raise the salaries of such a numerous contingent of the intelligentsia as teachers and doctors. During the remaining period of the Seven-Year Plan minimum wages will be raised to 50-60 rubles. Also the wages and salaries of average paid factory, office and professional workers will be increased.

The working people are receiving a new, very tangible addition to their wages as a result of the measures abolishing taxes. Beginning with October 1, 1960, when the first stage in the abolition of taxes began, this addition totals 360 million rubles a year. The second stage of the abolition of taxes, which began on October 1 of this year, will give the working people an extra 400 million rubles annually. By the end of 1965 the population will be tax free. *The abolition of taxes will be a signal social gain for the Soviet people. (Prolonged applause.)*

In 1960 all factory, office and professional workers went over to a seven- or six-hour working day. The working week was thus reduced by six and a half hours with no reduction but even increases in wages. Within the next few years it is intended to introduce a 40-hour working week for all factory and office and professional workers now working a seven-hour day.

Wage increases and a shorter working day and working week must go hand in hand with greater productivity of labour. The higher the productivity of labour the greater are society's opportunities to improve the living standard of the people. *All for society, society for all—such is our hard and fast principle.(Applause.)*

Important measures have been taken in recent times to improve the pension system. The average amount of old-age pensions has been more than doubled; disability pensions and pensions in the case of loss of the breadwinner have been increased. State expenditure on pensions increased from 3,000 million rubles in 1955 to 7,600 million rubles in 1961. In 1963 the minimum amounts of pensions will again be raised. As the collective-farm economy develops pensions for collective farmers will be introduced on an ever wider scale.

Housing construction in the Soviet Union has acquired a truly unprecedented scale. The building crane has indeed become the symbol of our times. The 1956-60 state housing programme has been fulfilled. More houses were built in the past five years than in the preceding fifteen years. In other words, comrades, nearly 50 million people, or almost one-quarter of the entire population, have moved into new houses. (*Prolonged applause.*) *In volume and in rates of housing construction the Soviet Union ranks first in the world. In recent years our country has been building twice as many flats per thousand inhabitants as the United States and France, and more than twice as many as Britain and Italy. (Applause.)*

But we still have a housing shortage, the housing problem remains acute. The growth of the urban population in the U.S.S.R. during the past few years is considerably in excess of estimates. By the end of the Seven-Year Plan the urban population will have increased by approximately 15 million more than was expected, which means that more dwellings will be needed. The Central Committee and the Soviet Government are taking measures to accelerate house building. In the remaining four years of the Seven-Year Plan about 400 million sq. metres of housing will be built—60 per cent more than under the fourth and fifth five-year plans taken together. Over four million houses will be built in rural localities.

Housing in the countryside calls for special attention. During the past few years more comfortable dwellings, well-appointed schools, clubs, hospitals and shops are being built in the villages. However, rural housing development is often conducted without proper attention to the prospects of economic advance and improvements in living conditions. Although big funds are allocated for building, houses in the rural localities are all too often scattered, they lack proper modern conveniences. Newly-created communities in the rural areas, especially those of the state farms in the newly-opened lands, should be built as urban-type settlements.

We are doing a lot of building. But we must give thought to another aspect of the matter: sometimes as a result of haste new buildings are put into exploitation with many defects. The working people, naturally, are highly annoyed at this, and rightly so! Those responsible for such defects in newly-built houses should be rapped over the knuckles. There must be stricter order in the allocation of flats, the general public must participate in the work, and priority must be given to those acutely in need.

In the Soviet Union the state has taken upon itself protection of the health of the people. How it is coping with this lofty task can be seen from the fact that the death rate in the U.S.S.R. is the lowest in the world, and the expectation of life is steadily increasing. (*Applause.*) We must continue to improve health services and promote physical training and sports, must build more sanatoria, hospitals, outpatients' clinics and other medical institutions, especially in the rural areas and the eastern regions of the country.

Communal services are not a minor, unimportant matter. The mood of people and the productivity of their labour to a large extent depend on living conditions and good services. The way to solve this problem is through the establishment of modern, well-equipped shops, canteens, dining-rooms, service establishments and food factories.

Our Party's policy is imbued with the lofty idea of communism: *everything for the sake of man, for the benefit of man. (Prolonged applause.)*

Should we continue to solve the problem of raising living standards only by direct wage increases and price reductions? Wages and salaries will, of course, for a long time to come continue to be the basic form of material incentive for the worker, one that will depend on his labour contribution to social production. But the Soviet citizen is, at the same time, receiving an ever bigger share of material and cultural benefits through public funds.

Today the people's needs are to a great extent being covered by public funds. In 1940 payments and benefits made to the population from public funds totalled 4,200 million rubles, whereas in 1960 the figure was 24,500 million rubles. Under the Seven-Year Plan public consumption funds will increase, allowing for changes that may be introduced, to as much as 40,000 million rubles in 1965. At present over twenty million pensioners are maintained by these funds; nearly four million students in higher, secondary and vocational and technical educational establishments receive state scholarships and hostel accommodation; over 600,000 children in boarding-schools are maintained for the most part by the state. Over seven million factory workers, collective farmers, office employees and their children spend their annual vacations in sanatoria, holiday homes and Young Pioneer camps at the expense of social insurance and collective-farm funds. About seven million mothers receive benefits from the state. That is how we use our public funds! (*Applause.*)

Comrades, we have every right to be proud of the fact that Soviet society has become the most highly educated society in the world, and that Soviet science holds leading positions in the more important fields of knowledge.

When the first Soviet artificial earth satellite orbited our planet a special committee was set up in the United States to look into the country's educational system. After comparing the two systems the committee arrived at the conclusion that the Soviet system of education is superior. It was at that time, however, that our Party decided to reorganise the school system with a view to giving the pupil a more thorough grounding in the fundamentals of science and linking the school more closely with life.

The experience of this reorganisation has confirmed the timeliness and need for the Party's measures. On the whole, the school's ties with real life and production have grown stronger, and the labour training of the pupils has improved. Secondary-school graduates are working successfully in the economy. The number of schools for young workers and farmers is growing from year to year. Hundreds of thousands of young people are studying in their spare time.

Much has been accomplished in this sphere. But there are facts of a bureaucratic attitude to the reorganisation of the schools. Not all educational workers have understood their tasks in the field of polytechnical education.

New types of educational establishment—boarding-schools and extended day-care schools—have been set up in our country and have received public approval. About 1,500,000 pupils are attending these educational establishments. In 1965 two and a half million children will be studying in boarding-schools alone.

Universal compulsory eight-year schooling has been introduced in the Soviet Union, and the necessary conditions exist for all those who wish to receive a full secondary education to do so. The next task in the field of education is to introduce universal compulsory secondary education.

The education of the individual in a communist spirit places new and higher demands on schools. Schools must keep pace with the rapid development of modern science and production. The training of teaching personnel must be extended so that there are enough teachers for all schools; teachers must be shown every consideration and respect. Factories and collective farms must help the schools reorganise, and help pupils acquire sound knowledge and the skills that are needed. More schools must be built to do away with shifts. This is a formidable task when it is remembered that in 1965 nearly 43 million children will be going to school.

The development of higher and specialised secondary education and vocational training is proceeding hand in hand with the reorganisation of the school. Here, too, the purpose is to bring education and vocational training closer to life, to production. More than half of the day-time students enrolled in the country's higher educational establishments this year have practical production experience. About half a million specialists with a higher education have been graduated by our evening and correspondence institutes during the past five years.

The Soviet Union trains three times the number of engineers the United States does; in all, there are more than twenty million brain workers in our country. When these figures were made public they caused confusion among the enemies of socialism who had frequently described our society as backward and as having a low cultural level. They are now obliged to make a painful reappraisal and sometimes even have to fall back on stupid inventions. In order to fool people they have spread the tale that the greater the number of educated people in the Soviet Union the greater the chances that they will turn away from communism. (*Animation.*)

What can we say to these ideologists of capitalism? Let them demand from their governments bigger appropriations for public education. According to their way of reasoning, the more educated a society is, the more firmly it clings to capitalism. Nobody any longer believes yarns of this kind, however, and least of all those who invent them. (*Applause.*) *Communism gives knowledge to all; it draws strength and confidence for its progressive movement from this knowledge of the masses, from their high cultural level. (Prolonged applause.)*

The flourishing of Soviet science is vivid evidence of this. We have more than 350,000 scientific workers. There are about four thousand research institutions in the country, and what is particularly noteworthy is the steep rise in the past five to six years in the number of research institutions in the Union republics. A major role in the development of research in the eastern part of the country is being played by the Siberian branch of the Academy of Sciences.

Soviet scientists are performing their duty to their country with credit. Widely known are the achievements of our scientists in physics, mathematics and cybernetics, in the creation of high-speed computing machines, the elaboration of the chemical theory of chain reactions and the chemistry of polymers, in biology, in the discovery and prospecting of huge mineral deposits, in the development of automation and remote control, radio engineering and electronics, in metallurgy, mechanical engineering, and other fields. Soviet scholars also have a number of achievements in the social sciences to their credit.

Soviet scientists are engaged in extensive research on one of the cardinal problems of our day, that of controlling thermonuclear reactions. Their investigations and co-operation with scientists of other countries have won wide recognition. Continued promotion of thermonuclear research in our country will accelerate the solution of the problem of the peaceful uses of nuclear energy for the good of man. The successes scored by Soviet science in the exploration of outer space have ushered in a magnificent era in the advance of scientific knowledge. The Soviet Union launched the world's first artificial earth satellite. Soviet space rockets were the first to overcome the force of the earth's gravitation and orbit in interplanetary space. We were the first to place our pennant on the moon and to photograph its hidden side. The Soviet citizens Yuri Gagarin and Herman Titov, delegates to this Congress, were the first to venture forth from their cradle, the earth, and perform triumphant flights into space. (*Stormy, prolonged applause.*)

We have every reason to be proud of the great achievements of Soviet science. Allow me, comrades, from this high rostrum to express our heartfelt gratitude to all Soviet scientists, and to wish them new, big victories for the glory of their Soviet land and the triumph of communism! (*Prolonged applause.*)

The Soviet Union's successes in space exploration have compelled the capitalist world to take a different view of the achievements of socialist society, of the advance of science and industry in the U.S.S.R. The U.S. statesman Chester Bowles, for instance, stated that until the first Soviet sputnik "almost no one had questioned America's industrial, military and scientific superiority. Then suddenly there was Sputnik, ringing the earth, and millions began to ask whether communism was not the winning side after all". (*Animation. Applause.*)

It is, Mr. Bowles. Even that twin soul of yours, Wernher von Braun, the German rocket specialist now working in the U.S., has had to admit that the Russians have created, on the basis of their philosophy, a system which assures them these successes, and that, unfortunately, the system he is living under does not make it possible to achieve the successes scored by Russia. He could not have put it better, comrades. (*Applause.*)

Today, when our country is putting into effect magnificent plans for communist construction, new and more majestic tasks confront Soviet science. Scientific investigations must be carried out more purposefully, young forces must be given broader access to science. Our task is to win leading positions in all the more important fields of science and technology. (*Prolonged applause.*)

Comrades, the lofty message borne by Soviet literature and art has won them immense prestige throughout the world. The art of the Soviet writer, composer and artist, of the cinema and theatre worker, has won high recognition. In the past few years new works of literature and art have been produced which give a faithful and vivid picture of socialist reality.

The achievements of our art and its traditions are of tremendous significance; they mark an important stage in the aesthetic development of mankind. The experience of our country has proved that socialism alone offers the broadest scope for free creative endeavour in art, for the active participation of the masses in the creation of cultural values. Soviet art is enriching the spiritual treasurehouse of mankind, is blazing the trail to the triumph of communist culture.

Lenin said that the road to a common culture in a communist society lies through the thriving of the national culture of every people that has liberated itself from capitalist oppression. Through intercourse within the community of socialist nations new features common to Soviet culture as a whole emerge, develop and bring benefit to all. Our task is to give thoughtful support and encouragement to the international unity of the socialist cultures. The people expect and are confident that our writers and art workers will produce works in which they will fittingly portray the present heroic era of the revolutionary transformation of society. The Party maintains that the purpose of art is to educate people above all by depicting positive examples from life, to educate them in the spirit of communism. The power of Soviet literature and art, of the method of socialist realism, lies in their faithful depiction of what is most important and decisive in life. Serious attention should be paid to the aesthetic education of Soviet people, to the moulding of their artistic tastes. Lack of taste should be resolutely combated, no matter what form it takes, whether it is a fad for formalism or a vulgar concept of "beauty" in art, in life, and in the home.

The most beautiful thing in life is the labour of man, and what more noble task can there be than to portray faithfully the new man, the man of labour, the richness of his spiritual interests, his fight against all that is obsolescent. We must give Soviet people interesting works which reveal the romance of communist labour, which spur their initiative and perseverance in achieving their aims.

Our Party is confident that Soviet literature and art will continue to be a reliable weapon of the Soviet people, a good and intelligent counsellor in their life. (*Applause.*)

6. Development of Socialist Social Relations into Communist Relations. Promotion of Soviet Democracy. Socialism and Freedom of the Individual

Comrades, in carrying out the decisions of the Twentieth Congress the Party has paid considerable attention to the development and perfection of socialist production relations and other social relations. Our Party believes this to be the principal path of transition to communist social relations—the most perfect type of relations between free, harmoniously developed and socially conscious people, relations based on friendship and fellowship. We might here recall that the first international workers' organisation founded under Marx's leadership was called the International Workingmen's Association. The word "associate" expresses identity of views, equality, fraternity, respect, and co-operation.

The socialist principle is—"From each according to his ability, to each according to his work". In order to advance to the communist principle "From each according to his ability, to each according to his need" time and certain definite conditions are required. The lofty and inspiring principles of communism have a tremendous appeal. We all want them to become a part of our life as soon as possible.

Why then are we not introducing these principles right away? Why does the Party need two decades to build, in the main, a communist society? Are we not taking too much time in implementing communist principles? No, comrades. We would, of course, like to introduce these principles as soon as possible, but the mere subjective desire is not enough. We must proceed from objective conditions, must take the laws of social development into account.

The transition to communist principles is possible, but not before the necessary material and technical basis has been created, not before people have reached a high degree of social consciousness, not before the principles of socialism have developed in full and their progressive potentialities had their full effect. There is no other path to communist social relations than through the development and perfection of socialist relations.

During the past few years the Party has carried out important socio-economic measures in all spheres of Soviet life. *These measures have revolutionary significance not only because they have helped consolidate the material and technical basis, but also because they have played an important part in developing social relations and bringing the two forms of socialist property closer together.*

The new features in the character of labour and in the relations between workers in production are becoming increasingly evident. The important thing here is that ever larger sections of the working people are developing the habit of working conscientiously, to the best of their abilities. For many of them work is no longer simply a means of earning a livelihood, but a social calling, a moral duty. We have the example of Valentina Gaganova, who has been elected to the Presidium of this Congress. Of her own free will she left an advanced work team to work with a team that was lagging behind. She was not prompted by selfish motives but by a high sense of duty and devotion to our common cause. Gaganova's example has been followed by many others.

The Party always encourages the desire of Soviet people to learn to work and live in a communist way. We attach great importance to the movement of communist work teams and communist shock workers. As time goes on, practice will undoubtedly suggest other, even more perfected forms of socialist emulation.

Social relations are progressing also in the sphere of the distribution of material and cultural values. In what way?

Primarily, it is to be seen in the continued development of the socialist principle of distribution according to labour, which is an essential requisite for the transition to the communist principle of distribution according to needs. The Party consistently implements the principle of material incentive in work and emphatically rejects wage levelling. Our premise is that until we have an abundance of material values and until work has become a vital necessity for the individual, there are no grounds for discarding the socialist principle of distribution, for relaxing public and state supervision over the amount of labour and the amount of consumption.

The experience of socialist construction in our country has borne out the correctness of Lenin's principle of material incentive. Lenin's genius was in his ability profoundly to analyse and to interpret social phenomena, to find the right solutions for every specific period in socialist construction.

Recall how Lenin, with the foresight and boldness so characteristic of him, called for a fundamental change in policy immediately after the Civil War, how he shifted the lever from War Communism to the New Economic Policy.

The transition to NEP was not easy, it caused a number of difficulties within the Party itself. Some Communists dropped out of the Party because they did not understand the essence of NEP. Lenin was well aware of the difficulties involved but this did not deter him from introducing NEP, and the Party as a whole supported Lenin's policy in the fight for the victory of socialism. If Lenin's policy had not triumphed at the time, we should not have been able to build socialism. It was necessary to strengthen the alliance of the working class and the peasantry, to get the workers of town and country materially interested in developing the economy, in building socialism. The egalitarian principle was replaced by the principle of payment according to the quality and quantity of work done.

Lenin taught us to be realistic in politics. We could draw a picture of the most rosy prospects, plan the highest rates of economic development, but unless the working people themselves realise the need for the reconstruction of society, unless they are materially interested, no plans will be of any avail. To ignore the principle of material incentive means to be guided by purely subjective considerations, means skipping a definite stage of development, means damaging socialist and communist construction.

We should always learn from Lenin how to work with people, taking them as they are. We cannot afford to be subjectivists in politics, to act according to the rule "I do as I please". We must closely observe the life of the people, study it, heed the voice of the people. In the combination of the material with the moral stimulus, the Party sees the true road to the life of plenty and distribution according to needs which it will reach without fail, the road to the triumph of communist labour.

The idea that abundance implies the unrestricted growth of personal property is an idea that is alien to us, to communism. The working man's personal ownership of a large number of things, as a form of personal consumption, is not at variance with the principles of communist construction as long as it keeps within reasonable bounds and does not become an end in itself. But under certain circumstances, excessive personal property may become, and frequently does become, an obstacle to social progress, a breeding ground for private-property instincts; it may lead to petty-bourgeois degeneration. The individual then falls a prey to things and becomes a slave to them.

Communists reject the ethics of bourgeois society where the concept "mine" is the supreme principle, where the prosperity of some is possible only at the expense of the ruin of others, where the corrupting psychology of egoism, greed and a lust for money is cultivated. To the world of private property the Communists oppose public property, and to bourgeois individualism, the principle of fellowship and collectivism.

The progress of all aspects of socialist production relations is leading logically to the gradual obliteration of the distinctions between town and country, between the classes and social groups of Soviet society, and to the implementation, on an ever wider scale, of communist principles in relations between workers, peasants and intellectuals. The two friendly classes of our society—the working class and the collective-farm peasantry—are drawing closer together and their unbreakable alliance is growing still stronger. The Soviet peasantry is drawing level with the working class in skills and working conditions, and in cultural and technical standards. The peasants enjoy the same political rights as the workers, the basic interests of the two classes are identical. In all essentials the distinctions between the working class and the peasantry have been eliminated; the final elimination of class distinctions will now proceed more rapidly.

The basic distinctions between mental and physical labour are being eradicated on the basis of technical progress and the rising cultural and technical standards of the working people. Today the labour of the industrial worker and the collective farmer, armed with advanced technology and knowledge, combines elements of both physical and mental work. Forty per cent of the country's industrial workers and over 23 per cent of its collective farmers now have a secondary or higher education. Nowadays it is often difficult to distinguish the front-rank worker from the engineer, the front-rank collective farmer from the agronomist.

Thus, *class relations in our country have now entered a new stage.* Proletarian democracy is becoming socialist democracy of the whole people. We note with great satisfaction that we are nearing the goal set by Lenin: to enlist all citizens without exception in the work of governing the state. Tens of millions of Soviet people take part in the administration of the country through the Soviets and their committees, through the elective bodies of the co-operatives, the trade unions, the Komsomol and other mass organisations, and through the performance of public duties.

Every Soviet citizen should take an active part in the management of public affairs—that is our slogan, our task. (Applause.)

While laying the prime accent on the task of steadily perfecting government bodies and reorganising the Soviets of Working People's Deputies into bodies of self-government by the people, our Party will continue handing over an ever larger number of government functions to mass organisations. It is important here, however, to take into account the level of development of the respective mass organisations and the extent of their independent activity. Our purpose is not just a change of signboards, but a fundamental reorganisation.

The transfer of many important government functions to mass organisations, with persuasion and education gradually becoming the principal method of regulating the life of Soviet society, does not imply relaxed supervision over strict observance of Soviet law, labour discipline or moral behaviour. *We must educate people to have a respect for Soviet law. The power of the law and the power of public influence must be made full use of.*

Our Party has been working, and will continue to work, on the development of social relations in all spheres of life. Not only economy and politics, but also the everyday life, culture, psychology and the social consciousness of people offer a wide field for shaping the new relations— relations of friendship, fellowship, mutual assistance and collectivism. Real freedom and the all-round development of the individual, the harmonious combination of personal interests and the interests of the whole of society are possible only in a socialist society, on the basis of the new relations between people.

Our ideological enemies keep reiterating that communism inevitably brings the individual into conflict with society and suppresses his personality. True, the enemies of socialism admit our successes in the sphere of material production, but hasten to assert that they have been achieved by infringing on the liberties and rights of the individual. The imperialists measure things according to their own standards; to them personal freedom means anarchistically opposing personal interests to public interests, the individual to the collective. Their moral code is: "Eat lest you be eaten".

The criterion of real freedom and happiness is a social

system which frees man from the tyranny of exploitation, gives him broad democratic liberties and the opportunity to live in fitting conditions, a system that inspires him with confidence in the morrow, unfetters his individual abilities and talents and makes him feel that his labour is for the good of society. Socialism is such a social system. *Of all the values created by the socialist system, the greatest is the new man—the active builder of communism.* The Soviet people are demonstrating what the really free man of the new society is capable of. (*Applause.*)

The ideologists of imperialism call the world of capitalism the "free world". But what has capitalism to offer in place of the real freedom, economic progress, prosperity, culture and the development of the individual achieved in the Soviet Union? Freedom for the rich to exploit and rob the poor, "freedom" from work for millions of people, mounting taxation, a reckless arms drive, racial discrimination, the dictatorship of the money bag, the banning of democratic organisations? Theirs is anything but a free world. Just the reverse. It is a world of slavery and exploitation.

The ideologists of imperialism call the capitalist countries an "open society", and the Soviet Union a "closed society". We quite agree that our socialist state is indeed closed to exploitation and robbery by monopoly capital, to unemployment, to the corrupting ideology of decadence. The imperialist gentry would, of course, like to see the doors of our socialist society open to espionage. But our doors are tightly closed to subversive activities against socialism. (*Applause.*)

Our society is open to all people from abroad who come to us with an open heart. It is open to fair trade, to the exchange of scientific, technical and cultural achievements, to truthful information. If we are to speak of an "iron curtain", then surely this "curtain" exists in the capitalist world which from time to time shuts its doors, in sheer fright, to Soviet cooks or to chessplayers though it calls itself the "free world". There was a case of a state which calls itself the most "open" being afraid to admit Soviet dancers. Perhaps they were afraid that the foundations of the capitalist world would give way under the feet of the Russian dancers. (*Animation.*)

We have long since proposed to the capitalist world that it compete with us, not in the arms drive but in improving the life of the working people. We are positive that capitalism would be the loser in such a competition; we are positive that ultimately all peoples will make the right choice, and will prefer the genuinely free world of communism to the so-called "free world" of capitalism. (*Applause.*)

* * *

Comrades, when the Party mapped out its far-reaching measures to develop the country's economy the bourgeois politicians and economists asserted that the Communists were sacrificing the vital interests of people to heavy industry, that production in the Soviet Union exists only for the sake of production. What a malicious slander of socialism! *Not production for the sake of production, but production for the sake of man is the sacred principle which the Party and the Soviet state adhere to in all activities.* Everybody, even the most incorrigible sceptics, can once more see for themselves that our Party always honestly carries out its obligations to the people. (*Applause.*)

In the sphere of home policy our Party sets before the Communists, before the Soviet people the following tasks for the immediate future:

1. All the people's efforts must be directed to fulfilling and overfulfilling the Seven-Year Plan, an important stage in the creation of the material and technical basis of communism. We must continue to raise the level of production and keep the country's defence potential up to the mark. As the Soviet economy advances to new heights,

we must not forget that only continuous progress will assure us absolute superiority and bring closer the day of our great victory in the peaceful economic competition with capitalism.

2. We must accelerate technical progress in all branches of socialist industry without exception, especially in electric power development, chemistry, mechanical engineering, metallurgy and the fuel industry. We must more widely promote specialisation of enterprises, work for the comprehensive mechanisation and automation of industrial operations, accelerate the application of the achievements of advanced science and technology and the production experience of innovators. Continuous growth in labour productivity, reduction of production costs, improvement in the quality of products, must be the law for all Soviet enterprises.

3. Industry and agriculture must achieve a level which will make it possible to satisfy the needs of the population in manufactured goods and foodstuffs more fully. Money accumulating as a result of the overfulfilment of industrial plans is to be directed mainly to agriculture, the light and food industries and other branches producing consumer goods.

4. Development of agriculture is the concern of the whole Party, of the whole people. Party and government bodies must daily concern themselves with agricultural production, drawing extensively on the experience of the leading collective and state farms. It is necessary to ensure fulfilment and overfulfilment of the Seven-Year Plan targets in the production and purchases of grain, cotton, sugar beet, oilseeds, tea and other crops, meat, milk, wool, eggs, and other farm products.

5. There must be further advance along the highroad of cultural and social development, and continued promotion of Soviet science, public education, literature and art. The living standards of the people must be raised and the measures to normalise wages and salaries must be completed

and the planned reduction of the working day and working week effected. Housing development must proceed at a rapid rate; the pension system, trade, public catering, medical and other public services must be improved.

Our country is in the full tide of its creative endeavour. All the peoples of the multi-national Soviet Union regard the building of communism as their common cause; they are working in unison and are making their invaluable contribution to our common victory. Realisation of the magnitude of the tasks we are tackling makes Soviet people redouble their efforts, makes them more demanding of themselves, more intolerant of shortcomings, stagnation and inertness. We must fully utilise the vast motive forces inherent in the socialist system. (*Prolonged applause.*)

III

THE LENINIST PARTY IS THE ORGANISER OF THE STRUGGLE FOR THE VICTORY OF COMMUNISM

Comrades, we owe our great achievements in both foreign and home policy to the firm and consistent implementation of the Party's Leninist general line, which found forceful expression in the historic decisions of the Twentieth Congress. The Central Committee considers it necessary to report that the policy adopted by the Twentieth Congress has triumphed. Dictated by reality and imbued with a Leninist revolutionary spirit, that policy has become the cause of all Soviet people. The Party has strengthened its bonds with the people and, backed by their tremendous energy, has enhanced the greatness of the Soviet Union. (*Stormy applause.*)

The Extraordinary Twenty-First Congress was a landmark on the road of our progress; it had great historic importance, for it adopted the Seven-Year Economic Development Plan and proclaimed the Soviet Union's entry into the period of full-scale communist construction.

The Twenty-Second Congress of the C.P.S.U. is destined to play an epoch-making role, for it will consider and adopt the new Programme of the Party, a programme for the construction of a communist society, a programme that will become the victorious banner and ideological weapon of the Party and the people in the struggle to achieve the triumph of communism. (*Stormy applause.*)

The Leninist Party of Communists—the flesh and blood of the working class and all working people, their heart and their brain, the exponent of their vital interests and revolutionary will—has travelled a long and difficult road, a road of glory. No other party in the world has been able to accomplish so much in transforming society. (*Prolonged applause.*) You will remember Lenin's prophetic words: "...Give us an organisation of revolutionaries, and we will overturn Russia." Sixty years have passed since he said that and the world can now see that the Bolsheviks have indeed "overturned" their country; the country that was tsarist Russia, an economically backward capitalist country, has become a mighty and prosperous socialist power. (*Stormy applause.*) And today we extend our heartfelt greetings to the old Bolshevik guard who for decades waged, as members of the Leninist Party, a courageous revolutionary struggle for the happiness of the people, for socialism. We salute the splendid representatives of that old guard who have been elected delegates to this Congress. (*Prolonged applause.*)

Our Party is rightfully proud of the fact that it has fulfilled its first and second programmes. By achieving the complete and final victory of socialism in the Land of Soviets, our Leninist Party has honourably acquitted itself not only of its national task, but also of its internationalist duty to the proletarians of all countries, to the world Communist movement. (*Prolonged applause.*)

In the new Programme of the C.P.S.U., whose draft was applauded by the Party and all Soviet people in the course of the discussion preceding this Congress, the construction of a communist society is given as our chief and immediate task. Besides the draft of the new Programme, this Congress will discuss the draft of the new Party Rules, on which Comrade F. R. Kozlov will report to you. We have always been guided by Lenin's statement that the Programme and the Rules of our Party are one indivisible whole. The organisational principles laid down in the Rules must guarantee the fulfilment of the Programme; they must strengthen the unity and cohesion of the Party, the militant vanguard of the Soviet people in the struggle for communism. (*Applause.*)

1. Elimination of the Consequences of the Cult of the Individual. Promotion of the Leninist Standards of Party Life and Principles of Leadership. Enhancement of the Militancy of the Party

Comrades, the restoration and promotion of the Leninist standards of Party life and principles of leadership have been a most important aspect of our Party's work in the period under review. The Twentieth Congress, by condemning the cult of the individual as a practice alien to the spirit of Marxism-Leninism, provided vast scope for the creative energy of the Party and the people. It helped the Party to extend and strengthen its bonds with the people and heighten its militancy.

On the eve of the Twentieth Congress the issue facing us was: either the Party would openly, in Leninist fashion, condemn the errors and distortions committed at the time of the cult of Stalin's person and reject the methods of Party and government leadership that had become an obstacle to progress, or the forces which clung to the old and resisted all that was new and creative would gain the upper hand in the Party. The issue was as crucial as that.

Was it really necessary to criticise, so scathingly and so frankly, the major errors and grave consequences bound up with the cult of the individual?

Yes, it was. The careful analysis and profound study of a number of records, undertaken after the exposure of that inveterate enemy and adventurer, Beria, fully revealed to the Central Committee the flagrant violations of socialist legality, abuses of power, arbitrary acts and repressive measures that had been perpetrated against many honest people, including prominent Party and government officials. The Central Committee, which was well aware of its responsibility to the Party and the people, could not possibly take the line of concealing or hushing up past errors and distortions. Following Lenin's behests, the Central Committee decided to tell the truth about the abuses of power perpetrated at the time of the cult of the individual. It was a moral requirement, the duty, of the Party and its leadership. It was a correct decision and it had tremendous significance for the destiny of the Party and for communist construction. (*Prolonged applause.*)

Lenin called on the Party never to conceal its errors but to criticise them openly and rectify them. "The attitude of a political party towards its own mistakes," he wrote, "is one of the most important and surest ways of judging how earnest the party is and how it *in practice* fulfils its obligations towards its *class* and the toiling *masses.* Frankly admitting a mistake, ascertaining the reasons for it, analysing the conditions which led to it, and thoroughly discussing the means of correcting it—that is the earmark of a serious party; that is the way it should perform its duties, that is the way it should educate and train, first the class, and then the *masses.*" *
(*Applause.*)

_____

* V. I. Lenin, *"Left-Wing"* Communism, an Infantile Disorder, F.L.P.H., Moscow, p. 49.

What would have become of the Party and the country had the cult of the individual not been condemned, had its harmful consequences not been removed and the Leninist standards of Party and government activity restored? The result would have been a cleavage between Party and people, grave violations of Soviet democracy and revolutionary legality, slower economic progress, a lower rate of communist construction and hence a deterioration of the people's standard of living. In the sphere of international relations, the result would have been a weakening of Soviet positions in world affairs and a worsening of relations with other countries, which would have had dire consequences. That is why criticism of the cult of the individual and the elimination of its consequences were of the utmost political and practical importance. (*Applause*.)

Marxism-Leninism has always severely condemned all manifestations of the cult of the individual, which it regards as alien to the spirit of the proletarian revolutionary movement, of communism. Marx, Engels and Lenin saw the people as the real maker of history; they stressed the leading and organising role of the working-class party. Marxism-Leninism does not deny the important role of leaders of the working class, but it emphatically opposes all glorification, to say nothing of the deification, of any particular person. Glorification of any one person inevitably pushes the people and the Party into the background and thus reduces their role and significance.

The Soviet people, led by the Party, have by their labour and heroic struggle made great progress in socialist construction. They triumphed in the Great Patriotic War against fascism. But you will remember that, at the time of the cult of the individual, all the achievements and victories of the Party and the people were attributed to one man. Stalin, of course, must be credited with great services to the Party and the Communist movement, and we give him his due. But it was wrong to associate all the victories of the Party and the people with one individual.

It was a gross misrepresentation of the real state of affairs. (*Applause.*)

The Twentieth Congress restored justice; it put an end to distortions and emphasised the great role of the people, and the role of the Party as the vanguard of the working class and the people as a whole, as the leading and guiding force in the struggle for communism. The Congress instructed the Central Committee consistently to implement measures that would completely abolish the cult of the individual, remove its consequences in all spheres of Party, government and ideological activity, and ensure strict enforcement of the standards of Party life and the principle of collective leadership elaborated by Lenin. (*Prolonged applause.*)

In its principled and firm criticism of the cult of the individual, our Party took guidance from Lenin's directives and from his testament. It is well known that while Lenin thought highly of Stalin, he was also aware of his shortcomings and, indeed, his defects. Being concerned for the destiny of the Party and the Soviet state, Lenin in December 1922, that is, shortly after Stalin was elected Secretary General of the Central Committee, wrote in a message to the forthcoming Party congress:

"Comrade Stalin, having become Secretary General, has concentrated boundless authority in his hands, and I am not sure whether he will always be capable of using that authority with sufficient prudence.... Stalin is too harsh, and this defect of his, while quite tolerable in our midst and in dealings among us Communists, is intolerable in a Secretary General. That is why I suggest the comrades think over a way of shifting Stalin from that post and appointing someone who differs from Comrade Stalin only in one respect, namely, in that he has the advantage of being more tolerant, more loyal, more polite and more considerate to comrades, less self-willed, etc."

As you see, Lenin knew very well that Stalin's negative qualities were likely to do much harm to the Party and the state. Unfortunately, Lenin's warning and advice were not acted upon in good time, with the result that the Party and the country had to pass through many difficulties stemming from the cult of the individual. At its Twentieth Congress, the Party subjected this cult to a devastating criticism. Carrying the Congress decisions into effect, it put an end to distortions and errors, and drew up measures precluding the recurrence of such practices. It was a courageous decision attesting the political maturity of our Party and its Central Committee. (*Stormy, prolonged applause.*)

The Party realised, of course, that the errors, distortions, and abuses of power revealed might arouse a certain bitterness and even discontent within the Party and among the people, that they would cause some damage and setbacks and give rise to temporary difficulties for the C.P.S.U. and the fraternal Marxist-Leninist parties. But the Party boldly faced the difficulties; honestly and frankly, it told the people the whole truth, being deeply convinced that the people would appreciate its line. Nor was the Party mistaken. Our advance to communism has gathered speed. Our carriage is now more erect, our breathing freer, and our vision clearer. Life within the country is making rapid progress. Our industry, farming, science and culture have scored big new successes. As we know, millions of Soviet men and women are playing an increasing part in the administration of government and public affairs.

The Soviet Communists may well declare proudly that they have upheld the honour and dignity of the Leninist Party, whose prestige has grown immeasurably, and that the world Communist movement has reached a higher stage. Today our Party is united more solidly than ever. (*Stormy, prolonged applause.*)

The Leninist policy formulated by the Twentieth Congress had at first to be implemented in the face of fierce resistance from anti-Party elements, from zealous adherents of the methods and practices prevailing at the time of the cult of the individual, from revisionists and dogmatists. The Leninist line of the Party was opposed by a factional anti-Party group consisting of Molotov, Kaganovich, Malenkov, Voroshilov, Bulganin, Pervukhin, Saburov, and of Shepilov, who later joined them.

At the beginning it was Molotov, Kaganovich, Malenkov and Voroshilov who bitterly resisted the Party line aimed at condemning the cult of the individual, fostering inner-Party democracy, condemning and rectifying all abuses of power and exposing those directly responsible for the repressive measures. That stand of theirs was no accident, for they are personally responsible for many instances of the wholesale repression of Party, government, economic, military and Komsomol personnel and for other practices of a similar nature, which occurred at the time of the cult of the individual. At first the group constituted a negligible minority on the Central Committee Presidium.

But when the Party set out to restore the Leninist standards of Party and government activity and to fulfil such pressing tasks as the development of new lands, the reorganisation of management in industry and building, the extension of the rights of the Union republics, the improvement of the living standards of the people and the restoration of revolutionary legality, the factional group stepped up its anti-Party subversion and began to recruit supporters within the Presidium of the Central Committee. The group was joined by Bulganin, Pervukhin and Saburov, and later by Shepilov. Realising that they had succeeded in marshalling a numerical majority on the Central Committee Presidium, the members of the anti-Party group launched an open attack, seeking to change the policy in the Party and the country, a policy laid down by the Twentieth Congress.

After reaching agreement at their clandestine gatherings the factionalists demanded an extraordinary meeting

129

of the Presidium. They expected to carry out their anti-Party schemes and seize leadership in the Party and the country. They wanted to confront the members of the Central Committee and the Party as a whole with an accomplished fact.

But the anti-Party group had miscalculated. On hearing of the group's factional activity within the Presidium, those Central Committee members who were then in Moscow demanded that a plenary meeting of the Central Committee be convened immediately.

The Plenary Meeting of the Central Committee held in June 1957 resolutely exposed the anti-Party group and routed it ideologically. It demonstrated the political maturity and solid unity of the Central Committee, based on the Leninist line of the Twentieth Congress. (*Stormy applause.*) Ideologically defeated in the course of the Plenary Meeting of the Central Committee and faced with unanimous condemnation by the Meeting, the members of the anti-Party group admitted that there had been collusion among them and that their anti-Party activity was harmful. Comrade Voroshilov admitted his errors in a speech at the Meeting, saying that he had been "misled by the factionalists", that he fully realised his errors and emphatically condemned them, just as he condemned the entire subversive activity of the anti-Party group.

As you know, the Plenary Meeting of the Central Committee passed its decision on the anti-Party group unanimously; the members of that group, too, voted for it, with the exception of Molotov, who abstained. Afterwards, when the results of the Plenary Meeting were being discussed by the primary Party organisation, Molotov stated that he, too, considered the decision of the Plenary Meeting correct and accepted it.

The struggle against the anti-Party group was a sharp political struggle over principles, a struggle between the new and the old. The point at issue was whether our Party should continue the Leninist policy outlined by the

Twentieth Congress or whether the methods typical of the period of the cult of the individual, methods condemned by the entire Party, would be revived.

The struggle was complicated by the fact that the line of the Party, and the course adopted by the Twentieth Congress, was opposed by a group of political figures some of whom had for a long time held prominent positions in the Party and the government. There have been many cases in history of particular leaders proving their worth at a certain period in their lives and playing a notable role but later stopping short in their tracks, as it were, and gradually fading out.

The reasons for this phenomenon may vary: some people become exhausted; others lose touch with reality, become conceited and do not work properly; still others turn out to be unprincipled, spineless people who have adapted themselves to circumstances and who lack staunchness in the struggle for their party's cause. Meanwhile, in the course of the struggle, new political leaders emerge; they oppose all that hampers the development of the new, and overcome the resistance of the old. It is something akin to the phenomenon astronomers call light from extinct stars. Certain stars, which are very far removed from earth, seem to shine on even though they have been extinct for a long time. The trouble with some people who find themselves in the position of stars on the social horizon is that they imagine they continue to radiate light even though they have long since become nothing but smouldering embers. And that is exactly what happened to certain political leaders who began a factionalist, anti-Party struggle. (*Stormy applause.*)

The decisions of the June Plenary Meeting of the Central Committee won the unanimous approval of the entire Party and all Soviet people. Somewhat later, in October 1957, the Plenary Meeting of the C.C. C.P.S.U. firmly repelled attempts by the former Defence Minister, Zhukov, to take an adventurous course, to dissociate the Armed

Forces from the Party and oppose the Soviet Army to the Party leadership. Casting aside the bankrupt factionalists and scheming careerists, the Party closed its ranks; it strengthened its bonds with the people and rallied all forces for the implementation of its general line. *(Prolonged applause.)*

The course adopted by the Twentieth Congress was applauded by the world Communist movement, by the fraternal Marxist-Leninist parties. This found expression in decisions passed by congresses of the fraternal parties, as well as in other records of those parties, and in the documents of the meetings of representatives of the Communist and Workers' parties in 1957 and 1960.

To cite an example, the Statement of the Moscow Meeting of 1960 said: "The historic decisions of the Twentieth Congress of the C.P.S.U. ... have initiated a new stage in the world Communist movement, and have promoted its development on the basis of Marxism-Leninism."

I must say, however, that our Party's policy aimed at eliminating the harmful consequences of the cult of the individual did not, as it became obvious afterwards, meet with due understanding on the part of the leaders of the Albanian Party of Labour. Indeed, they began to oppose that policy.

Everyone knows that until recently there were good, friendly relations between the Soviet Union and the People's Republic of Albania, and between the Communist Party of the Soviet Union and the Albanian Party of Labour. The peoples of our country were giving Albania all-round disinterested help to enable her to develop her economy and carry on socialist construction. It has always been our sincere desire, and it still is, that Albania should be a prosperous socialist republic, and her people happy and enjoying all the benefits of a new life.

For many years the Albanian leaders signified their complete agreement with the Central Committee of our Party and the Soviet Government on all matters pertaining to the international Communist movement. They repeatedly voiced support for the course adopted by the Twentieth Congress. Enver Hoxha, First Secretary of the C.C. of the Albanian Party of Labour, noted that in his speeches at the Twentieth and Twenty-First congresses of our Party. The Third Congress of the Albanian Party of Labour, held shortly after the Twentieth Congress, fully endorsed the criticism levelled at the cult of the individual, as well as the steps taken to eliminate the harmful consequences of that cult.

We Soviet people believed the Albanian leaders, believed that there was mutual understanding and unity of views between our Party and the Albanian Party of Labour.

The facts show, however, that the Albanian leaders have lately reversed their policy for no apparent reason, despite their previous assurances and contrary to the decisions of the congress of their own Party, and have set out to seriously worsen their relations with our Party, with our country. They have begun to depart from the common agreed line of the Communist movement of the whole world on major issues of the day, something which became particularly noticeable in the middle of last year.

The Albanian leaders no longer conceal their disapproval of the course adopted by our Party with a view to completely eliminating the harmful consequences of the cult of Stalin's person, severely condemning abuses of power and re-establishing the Leninist standards of Party and government activity.

It would appear that in their hearts the Albanian leaders disagreed with the conclusions of the 1957 and 1960 meetings of the fraternal parties, which, as we all know, approved of the decisions of the Twentieth Congress and our Party's policy directed towards eliminating the harmful consequences of the cult of the individual. This stand of the Albanian leaders is due to the fact that they are, to our deep regret, themselves using the same methods as were current in our country at the time of the cult of the individual.

It is with concern for the destinies of the heroic Albanian people that we are watching events in Albania. We are pained to see that rank-and-file Communists in Albania, and the Albanian people as a whole, who have a vital interest in friendship and co-operation with all the socialist countries, have to pay for the erroneous policy of the Albanian leaders. We are deeply concerned about the situation and have never stopped our earnest search for ways and means of overcoming the divergences that have arisen.

The policy elaborated by the Twentieth Congress of our Party is a Leninist policy, and we cannot make a concession on this fundamental point either to the Albanian leaders or to anyone else. To depart from the course adopted by the Twentieth Congress would amount to ignoring the wise advice given by Lenin, who discerned the danger of a cult of Stalin's person when it was still in embryo. It would amount to disregarding the costly lessons of history and forgetting the price which our Party had to pay because it had not acted in good time on the warning given by its great leader.

The Albanian leaders, who oppose the course adopted by the Twentieth Congress, are now trying to pull our Party back to practices which they like but which will never recur in our country. Our Party will press forward with determination the policy of its Twentieth Congress, a policy which has withstood the test of time. No one can divert us from the Leninist road. (Stormy, prolonged applause.)

If the Albanian leaders hold dear the interests of their own people and of socialist construction in Albania, and if they really want friendship with the C.P.S.U. and the other fraternal parties, they must renounce their erroneous views and revert to the path of unity and close co-operation within the fraternal family which is the socialist community, to the path of unity with the world Communist movement as a whole.

As regards our Party, it will continue, in keeping with its internationalist duty, to do all in its power that Albania may march shoulder to shoulder with all the socialist countries.

From the rostrum of this Congress we declare that the purity of Marxism-Leninism and an uncompromising attitude to all distortions of its great principles are law for our Party. *(Prolonged applause.)* Communists place the cause of the revolution, the cause of the people, above all else, and its leaders are worthy of the name only when they express the vital interests of the working people and follow the right path. Such leaders are steeled in the course of the struggle; they gain prestige by serving the people and the communist cause; they serve the people and must be subject to control by the people. *(Stormy applause.)*

Comrades, in our Party every major issue of home and foreign policy is discussed collectively, and the decisions taken are an expression of the collective experience of the Party. This is genuine implementation of Leninist principles. It has become the rule for the whole Party membership and the entire people to discuss all the questions submitted for the consideration of plenary meetings of the Central Committee and sessions of the Supreme Soviet of the U.S.S.R. The measures taken to restore revolutionary legality, promote Party and Soviet democracy, extend the rights and increase the role of local Party and government bodies, and encourage the creative initiative of the working people have yielded good fruit.

The Central Committee has taken special care to ensure the regular convening of all elective bodies, beginning with Party congresses and Central Committee plenary meetings. We know how very regularly Party congresses were held in Lenin's lifetime. In the difficult first seven years of Soviet power they were convened every year, and they discussed the main tasks of the Party and the young Soviet state. In the period of the cult of the individual that system was grossly violated; following the Eighteenth Congress no congresses were convened for almost fourteen years, though the country had gone through the Great Patriotic War and a period of great and strenuous effort to rehabilitate the national economy. Plenary meetings of the Central Committee of the Party were very few and far between. Such a situation was conducive to abuses of power and gave certain leaders an opportunity to put themselves beyond the control of the Party and the people.

Such things do not and cannot exist in the Party today. In the nine years since the Nineteenth Congress, the Twentieth, the Extraordinary Twenty-First and the present Twenty-Second Congress of the Party have been convened. Plenary meetings of the Central Committee, called at regular intervals, examine the more important problems of the life of the Party and the country. They sharply criticise the activities of some Party organisations and their leaders, including the activities of individual members of the Central Committee and of the Presidium of the C.C. C.P.S.U. Officials who have not justified the confidence placed in them by the Party have been relieved of their posts.

The period of the cult of the individual, now a thing of the past, saw the widespread employment of harmful methods of Party, government and economic leadership, such as high-handed administrative methods, the hushing-up of shortcomings, indecision in work, and fear of anything new. In the situation, many sycophants, hosanna-singers and falsifiers emerged. The Party resolutely combats, and will continue to combat, all violators of Party and state discipline, people who deceive the Party and the state. It boldly develops principled criticism and self-criticism, which it uses as its keenest and most effective weapon.

The promotion of inner-Party democracy, the extension of the rights and the enhancement of the role of local Party bodies, and adherence to the principles of collective leadership have increased the Party's militancy and strengthened its ties with the masses. The Party's inseparable links with the people find vivid expression in the growth of its membership, in the continuous influx of fresh forces.

In the period under review the membership of our Party has increased by almost 2,500,000. The Party had a membership of 7,215,505 at the time of the Twentieth Congress; its membership had grown to 9,716,005 shortly before this Congress (October 1, 1961). Factory workers account for 40.7 per cent of those admitted into the Party; 22.7 per cent are collective farmers, 35.6 per cent are office and professional workers and one per cent are students. What are these office and professional workers that have been admitted into the Party? Almost two-thirds of them are engineers, technicians, agronomists, livestock-breeding experts and other specialists.

I must say that the very concept of office and professional workers has undergone a change. In the early years of Soviet power the intelligentsia consisted mainly of people who before the Revolution had been connected with the propertied classes. Certain restrictive measures were therefore taken in respect of office and professional workers. Things are entirely different now; today the overwhelming majority of professional and office workers are former industrial workers or collective farmers, or their children. That is why the attitude to professional and office workers has changed too. As science, technology, automation and mechanisation of production advance, the category known as professional and office workers will grow, and play an ever more important role in production. The time will come when we shall have no need to divide Party members into industrial workers, collective farmers, and professional and office workers, since class distinctions will have completely disappeared, and all will be workers of communist society. (*Applause.*)

It is gratifying to report, comrades, that the number of well-educated people in the ranks of our Party is increasing. Today one out of every three Communists has a higher or secondary education. Particularly noteworthy is the fact that *over 70 per cent of all Party members and candidate members are today engaged in the sphere of material production.* The majority of Communists are employed in the decisive sectors, that is, in industry or agriculture.

The C.P.S.U. comprises representatives of the more than a hundred nations and nationalities inhabiting the Soviet Union. Our Party came into being, and has been developing, as an internationalist organisation of the working class that embodies the great unity and fraternal friendship of the equal socialist nations making up the close-knit family of builders of communism. (*Applause.*)

The supreme mission of every member of the Leninist Party lies in selfless service to communism. A Communist must do his job with ardour; he must devote heart and soul to the cause of the people. There is no room in the Party for a member who fails to live up to his lofty duties. In the last six years over 200,000 people have been expelled from the Party for various reasons. By getting rid of those chance people, the Party has become stronger and more solid. (*Applause.*)

It must be admitted that there are still people who regard Party membership as a way to a career. How are we to safeguard the Party against such time-servers? In the early years of the Revolution, and also during the Patriotic War, Communists were tested in the struggle. This reminds me of an incident which took place during the Civil War. When our unit had entered a village freed by the Red Army the local schoolmaster asked me:

"What job will you assign me if I join the Bolshevik Party?"

"We'll give you the most honourable job. We'll give you

a rifle and we'll send you to fight against the bourgeoisie, for Soviet power," I replied.

"Oh no, that sort of job doesn't suit me," said the man. (*Animation.*)

That made things as clear as daylight. You know that there were many intellectuals in our Party, including teachers, who nobly defended the gains of the Great October Revolution, who fought for the cause of the Party.

Now that the struggle for communism is in full swing we must demand that all those who join the Party should be everywhere in the forefront of communist construction. The Party Rules make it incumbent on Communists to set an example of a communist attitude to labour, of the utmost devotion to our ideology, of an uncompromising attitude to all shortcomings, to money-grubbing and parasitism, to be considerate and sympathetic to others, and loyal to the Party and the people. A Communist must be a model in the struggle to establish the lofty principles of communist morality. (*Applause.*)

That is why all Party organisations must strictly adhere to the principle of individual selection and must fully appraise the personal qualities of applicants for membership. We must continue to admit into the C.P.S.U. the foremost workers, collective farmers and intellectuals, that is to say, the finest members of Soviet society.

Our Party, with its membership of almost 10 million, will continue fulfilling Lenin's behest as a sacred duty—will continue to raise the prestige of the name of Communist. (*Stormy applause.*)

2. The Party's Organisational Work and the Training of Cadres. The Active Participation of the Masses in Public Work Is the Key to New Successes

Comrades, of recent years the Party has turned its attention to questions of the practical guidance of the national economy. The Central Committee has focussed the attention of Party organisations and leading cadres on the careful study and extensive introduction of progressive methods in industry and agriculture; it has used specific examples of good work as models of how our great communist construction should be conducted.

How should the work of a Party official be appraised? What yardstick should be applied for one official to be considered a skilful and energetic organiser, and another reproached and criticised? It is common knowledge that the quantity and quality of the work done by a steel smelter, a farmer or a builder can be fairly easily measured. The work done by Party functionaries should be appraised according to the concrete results in the functioning of the factory or construction project, the collective or state farm, the research institution, the district, region or republic they are responsible for.

The success of organisational work and the level of leadership depend in great measure on the links between the leaders and the masses, on the ability to organise and direct human effort towards the solution of the principal tasks. However, the links with the masses may differ: they may be strong and permanent, or superficial and temporary. To be able to maintain close links with the masses a Party official must possess a number of qualities. Among them are a knowledge of the field he is working in and a progressive approach to the various aspects of economic and cultural construction. A leader must enrich his knowledge all the time by keeping abreast of life, and by studying the progressive experience amassed by innovators in industry and agriculture and the achievements of science and technology. Such knowledge can be accumulated by a Party official only if he adheres consistently to the Marxist method in analysing the phenomena of life, only if he is keen in discerning what is new and helps uphold it and put it into effect.

This should not be taken to mean that a Party leader has to be a specialist in all fields. Of course, he should know a lot, be well educated and well informed, but the important thing is his all-round knowledge in the field entrusted to him; he should profoundly understand people and enjoy working with them. *The strength of Party leadership lies in its collective spirit, which helps to fuse, as it were, the talents, knowledge and experience of many people into a single talent capable of accomplishing great things.*

The decisions of the Twentieth Congress spoke of the necessity of enhancing the role played by Party primary organisations and district committees in organisational and political work. It is here, in these primary organisations and district Party bodies, that the most various and burning problems of economic and cultural activity are tackled. The primary organisations are the backbone of the Party, and it is they that carry on day-by-day work among the masses. There are 41,830 primary organisations at industrial enterprises, 10,427 at building sites, 18,938 in the transport services, 44,387 on collective farms, and 9,206 on state farms. The success of our cause depends in great measure on the level of the organisational and political work in these lower units of the Party.

To raise the level of the work being done by the primary organisations, the Central Committee has kept all Communists regularly informed on the more important measures of home and foreign policy, and on questions of ideological work and the international Communist movement. On many occasions the Central Committee has addressed to primary Party organisations and to district Party committees letters specifying the urgent tasks of communist construction.

We can all say that to us Communists nothing can be more interesting or more important than Party work, whose central feature is live contacts with the people. To devote our all to such work, without classifying it as more important or less important, to show consideration for others, no matter on what business they come to us, to be broad-minded and approach matters from the standpoint of

Party principles, and always keep pace with developments—such is our duty and our responsibility to the Party and to the people. It is only such enthusiastic, creative work that can fire people's hearts, and inspire them to do great things in the field of labour and in the struggle. (*Applause.*)

We must always remember that the strength of the Party stems from the activity, the political consciousness and militant unity of its members. Party work is essentially a sphere of public activity, and participation in it is the duty of every Communist. We are marching towards communism, under which people will run the affairs of society without any special government machinery.

In our country socialist government is gradually developing into self-government by the people. As the vanguard of a people engaged in building a communist society, our Party must also be in the van in organising its own internal activities and set an example in evolving the best forms of communist self-government by the people. In practice this could mean that the paid apparatus of Party bodies, for instance, would be reduced more and more, while the ranks of unpaid Party functionaries would swell. Party bodies should have more commissions, departments, secretaries of district and city committees and other functionaries working on a voluntary basis. Stronger bonds with the masses, the direct contacts with people that were characteristic of Lenin, the urge to live and work among people and share their joys and sorrows, and communist ardency in the struggle for what is new and progressive, are all features that should be typical of a Party leader. (*Applause.*)

Comrades, the Party has reared a great number of mature and ideologically tested leading cadres for all fields of work. These people see their supreme duty in selfless service to the people. In the past many local Party officials awaited directives and instructions from above on all and every occasion and frequently had no opportunity to display their own initiative. But now that the powers and responsibilities of local Party bodies have been extended, they must show greater independence and a creative approach to matters. We now have cadres capable of this, and it is they who set the tone in all work.

However, there are still officials who display neither energy nor initiative in their work, and who have grown accustomed to their factory, district, region or republic trailing along in the rear. We still do not always present sufficiently high demands to such people, and they keep their jobs for a long time. If an industrial enterprise fails to fulfil its monthly or quarterly plans, its director will obviously not keep his job for long. Non-fulfilment of an industrial enterprise's plan is justly considered intolerable and impermissible.

Then why is it that this same principle is not always applied to executives in the agricultural sphere? We have not only collective farms but entire districts and regions which have "won" the "right" not to fulfil plans, the "right", if I may say so, to consume, not produce. They become consumers because their agricultural techniques are extremely poor and they are satisfied with harvests of five to seven centners of oats per hectare. I have already spoken about the situation in Kirov Region, where for over eight years Comrade Pchelyakov was secretary of the Regional Committee. When he was finally relieved of his post for serious failures in his work and for falsification, he was surprised and demanded an explanation—for what reason and on what grounds, he wanted to know, had he been relieved of his post? But how can such a person stand at the head of a Party organisation?

Then there are executives of another type—those who like living at state expense. Year after year some directors of industrial enterprises, collective farm chairmen, state farm managers and heads of various departments keep asking for production plans to be reduced, and payrolls and investments increased. Such officials cannot be regarded as genuine leaders since they do not organise people to work better, do not inspire them by example, but instil in them a spirit of dependence on others. If such leaders, who consider themselves Communists, gave serious thought to what the consequences would be if all enterprises, and all state and collective farms were to start asking for lower plans of output and larger budget appropriations, they would realise that with such an approach we cannot make progress. It should be clear to everyone that we can create an abundance of everything and satisfy the steadily increasing requirements of the people only when each enterprise, and each Soviet man and woman makes proper contribution to the common cause of communist construction. *(Applause.)*

A lot of damage is done to our cause by swelled-headed officials. More often than not one meets among these people those who do not bother to improve their professional qualifications, their theoretical and political knowledge, and therefore often slide into political turpitude, become hucksters and windbags.

In general, comrades, work with cadres, and the ability to select and educate them properly, is a delicate matter calling for no little skill. Sometimes a man is promoted to a certain job and fails to cope with it. The causes may vary, and they should not always serve to cast blame on the person in question. However, it becomes clear that the promotion was a mistake and as a result the work suffers. It is obvious that the mistake must be rectified. But in the case of some comrades it is not easy to return them to the old job, where they were doing good work. It is, in fact, almost impossible. Why? The reason is, you see, that they have won the right to be called functionaries at regional, republican or even Union level, and will take mortal offence if offered work they can cope with. In this case, riding the high horse, displaying conceit and arrogance, means displaying qualities unworthy of a Party member. *(Voices: "Hear, hear!" Applause.)*

Working with personnel calls for strict observance of the Leninist principle of a proper combination of old and experienced leaders, who have been tested in the struggle for the Party line, and young, energetic organisers with a sound knowledge of their field. It is very important that continuity be observed in our work, for it helps to preserve and develop the best traditions of the Party, and encourages an influx of young forces, with their innate sense of the new, with their ability to take the initiative and to get things done quickly. It is quite impermissible for a leading Party post to be held by one who falsifies reports or is a hide-bound bureaucrat. The Party will always condemn, with the full force of Party and Soviet law, all falsifying of reports and other acts of deception. *(Applause.)*

Our Party and the Soviet people are rich in talents. The promotion and training of people for various branches of Party and government work, for employment in the economy or in cultural spheres is the prime duty of Party organisations. The school of life, of practical activities, provides the finest training and the best political instruction. The struggle for the implementation of the Party line and the fulfilment of the tasks of communist construction evolves and develops those qualities that are required in a Party or government worker of the Leninist type. We must solicitously train such cadres.

Comrades, at the present time primary significance attaches to the problem of *Party, government and public control* from top to bottom and from bottom to top. Control is an effective means of improving leadership in communist construction. The work of any organisation, of any leading Party body, should be appraised first and foremost by the way it puts into practice the Programme and the Rules of the C.P.S.U., and the directives given by the Party.

In the early years of Soviet rule, Lenin attached tremendous importance to all aspects of supervision and to the verification of fulfilment of Party decisions. How much greater must be our care of such things now that our national economy has expanded so immensely! Just as a skilled mechanic senses the pulse and operation of a

145

huge machine in his charge so that the slightest sound will tell him whether the machine is out of tune, just as he seems to discern the slightest speck of dust which may lead to a stoppage, so we must daily and hourly keep a finger on the throbbing pulse of the huge Soviet land, eliminate manifestations of red tape, and notice in time and remove all that delays progress.

Party organisations must take the lead in exercising stricter supervision and verification of the execution of decisions. There must be more system in the way local Party bodies render account to higher Party bodies and to the rank and file on their fulfilment of Party decisions. We must remember and unswervingly carry out the Leninist demand—supervise the work of people, and verify what has actually been done.

Much work has to be done to improve state control. Until recently there were big shortcomings in the work of the Soviet Control Commissions. In the first place, they were very poorly linked up with practice, with the masses, without whose co-operation the state control bodies cannot properly perform their functions.

The system of Party, state and public control is a powerful means of improving leadership in communist construction on genuinely democratic principles, it is a splendid school of communist education for the masses. That is why the advice given by Lenin in his article "How We Should Reorganise the Workers' and Peasants' Inspection" should be more widely applied, with due attention to present-day conditions.

Supervision by the general public, with strict verification of the way decisions have been carried out, is a method by which the principle of criticism and self-criticism can be given effect. The new features that are appearing in our life, the shoots of communism, call for the greatest care, and we must clear the communist field of weeds and wild grasses, must promote the creative activity of the great army of builders of a communist society.

The great successes achieved by our people under the leadership of the Party are clear to everybody. They are gratifying to all Soviet people and give them confidence that the further progress of the country will be ever successful and more rapid.

Lenin taught the Party never to permit conceit and complacency, to see the shortcomings in the work as well as the successes, and to concentrate efforts on the solution of unsolved problems. We still have many such problems. There are still quite a number of shortcomings to be overcome in the work of Party and government bodies.

We must bend all our efforts towards effecting a more rapid growth of the economy and towards improving the living standards of the people. We must work for a further increase in farm produce, for the fulfilment of housing plans, for higher labour productivity in all branches of the economy and for considerable improvement in the quality of goods produced, especially consumer goods.

The more we support and use in production everything that is new and progressive, and the more ruthlessly we expose and eliminate shortcomings, the more speedily we shall accomplish the tasks confronting us. Communist construction is the great cause of millions, the cause of the entire people.

In all its activities, the Party has working side by side with it such *mass organisations of working people* as the Soviets, the trade unions, the Komsomol and the co-operatives.

Born in the fire of revolution as organs of the people's struggle for power, the *Soviets* have now become an all-embracing organisation of the people and the embodiment of their unity; they have become a school of public activity for the millions, the like of which mankind has never before seen.

The activities of the Soviets are the best confirmation of the highly democratic character of our society. The very fact that the total number of deputies to the Soviets is now about two million speaks volumes. Besides these deputies, there are over two million people working on a voluntary basis on the standing committees of the Soviets. No other social system could provide such confirmation of its genuinely democratic and popular character. The Soviets must strengthen their ties with the masses and devote close attention to problems of state administration and economic and cultural development.

Great changes have taken place in our country in the 25 years that have passed since the adoption of the present Constitution of the U.S.S.R. The Soviet Union has entered upon a new stage of development, and socialist democracy has reached a higher plane. The new Constitution of the U.S.S.R., the elaboration of which we are beginning, must reflect the new features that have appeared in the life of Soviet society in the period of the full-scale construction of communism.

The role and importance of the *trade unions* are growing. Following the Twentieth Congress, the rights and functions of the trade unions in handling all problems affecting the working people's vital interests were considerably expanded. With their membership of over 60 million, the Soviet trade unions are a school of education, administration and management, a school of communism for the working people. At the present stage, the struggle for the implementation of the programme of communist construction must hold priority in trade union activities. Concern for the working man is the prime duty and responsibility of the trade unions. Our trade unions, applying the traditional principles of trade union work and enriching that work with new, communist forms and methods, must draw the working people into the management of production and of all the affairs of society.

As Soviet society advances towards communism, the functions of the trade unions will expand, and new problems, formerly the concern of state bodies, will enter their sphere of activity. Our Party will encourage the growth of trade union activities in economic management, and in particular in transforming the standing production conferences into ever more effective agencies helping to improve the work of enterprises.

Special stress must be laid on the trade unions' tasks in promoting communist consciousness among the working people, organising emulation for communist labour and in helping the masses learn to administer state and public affairs.

The trade unions must today improve forms and methods of work. Developments in our country call imperatively for the greatest possible application of the principle of voluntary work in the trade unions, so that their paid staff may be reduced. The more extensively this principle is applied, the more actively will the working people participate in the affairs of society.

We all highly appreciate the activities of our splendid *Leninist Young Communist League* [Komsomol], the Party's militant helper. The lives of many of us are linked with it. Many Communists have passed through the school of the Komsomol. The Komsomol is our future and our reserve. At all stages of socialist construction the Komsomol, the Soviet youth, have displayed a clear understanding of the tasks set by the Party. By their work they have shown that they are worthy heirs to the great revolutionary traditions, and are carrying on the glorious cause of their parents.

It would be hard to enumerate the splendid exploits of the Komsomol, of the Soviet youth. Our people are proud of their youth, and rightly so.

More and more young Leninists are growing up in the Young Pioneer organisation, and the Party has entrusted to the Komsomol the task of educating these young Leninists with solicitude and love, and of teaching them to face up to all difficulties life may present to them.

We must not forget that the old world continues to try to encumber our path with old ideas and habits. We must not lose sight of the fact that some young people are sullied by the dirt of the past; they yield to philistinism and the corrupting influence of bourgeois ideology.

The principal task of the Leninist Young Communist League is to educate young people on the heroic traditions of revolutionary struggle, on examples of devoted labour set by workers, collective farmers and intellectuals, and on the great ideas of Marxism-Leninism.

Splendid prospects, great and fascinating goals are opening up before the youth. The Programme of the C.P.S.U. opens the door into the future wide before them. To build communism—what a great and wonderful aim! However, building communism means first and foremost developing the economy, increasing the production of material and spiritual values, and fostering in everyone features of a member of communist society. The youth are called upon to help develop our natural wealth, and build factories, state farms, and cities. It is not near Moscow or Leningrad that the bowels of the earth hold wealth, but in the taiga, in the mountains and deserts. To make this wealth serve the people, it must be extracted from the earth.

The young people of Moscow and Leningrad, Kiev and Gorky, all young people living in the older seats of population, must set out boldly to provide our people with new wealth. Wherever there is man and his labour there will be everything. As Nekrasov once said: "Man, with his will and his labour, is a miracle-worker indeed!" Such was the case in Nekrasov's time, when men used pick and shovel, saw and axe to do their work. Today the Soviet youth heading for the construction sites in the country are equipped with sound knowledge and the most up-to-date machinery. They have done much good work in our country, and will do much more, inspired by the great plans of communist construction.

The Party has confidence in the Komsomol, in the Soviet youth, and calls to our young people: Forward, take your places on the construction sites of communism. *(Stormy applause.)*

3. The Ideological Activities of the Party; Strengthening Bonds with the People in Their Day-to-Day Life. Communist Construction and the Development of Revolutionary Theory

Comrades, the Twentieth Congress opened up wide vistas for the creative development of Marxism-Leninism. We are glad to note that in the years since that Congress the Party has restored and developed Lenin's principles in ideological work, and has successfully tackled urgent theoretical problems of communist construction. After eliminating the harmful consequences of the cult of the individual, the Party re-oriented ideological work in conformity with the requirements of the day, and embarked on a policy of strengthening the unity of theory and practice. It based its policy on a scientific, Marxist-Leninist foundation and devoted all theoretical, ideological and educational work to the fulfilment of concrete tasks of communist construction.

Of great significance in advancing ideological and theoretical work was the publication of a second edition of the works of Marx and Engels, the fifth edition of the complete works of Lenin, collections of Party decisions, a thoroughly documented biography of Lenin, a number of manuals and books on theory, the history of the C.P.S.U., philosophy, political economy, and the history of the Civil War and the Great Patriotic War. By a decision of the Central Committee, work has begun on a many-volume history of the C.P.S.U. which is to sum up the experience gained by the Party and the Soviet people in the struggle for the victory of communism.

The Party proceeds from Lenin's thesis on the growing role of the masses as the conscious makers of history. The Party consults the people on all the most momentous and most urgent issues of the day. The ideological work of the Party organisations enhances the communist consciousness and the labour and political activities of the masses, and serves as a most important, permanently operating factor in the building of communism.

A significant part in deepening and expanding the Party's ideological influence on the masses is played by political training, lectures, educational work among the masses in the fields of politics and culture and by the press, radio, television, cinema, literature and art. It is indicative that in the past five years the circulation of newspapers has increased by twenty million copies, and the annual circulation of magazines and other periodicals by 417 million copies. More books are published in the Soviet Union than in any other country. That, comrades, is an outstanding success recorded by the Party in the development of socialist culture and the dissemination of communist ideology. *(Applause.)* The Party and the Soviet people think highly of those who conduct propaganda and agitation, workers in the fields of science, education and culture, that huge army of ideological workers, active fighters for the triumph of the ideas of Marxism-Leninism. *(Applause.)*

In the forefront of ideological work today is the task of thoroughly explaining to the working people the new Programme of the C.P.S.U. which equips the Party and the entire people with a great plan of struggle for the triumph of communism. Our new Programme will serve as the basis on which to educate the masses in the spirit of communism. The Party programme, said Lenin, is a most powerful weapon in our propaganda and agitation. "Every section of our Programme," he said, "is something that every worker should know, should learn and understand."*

Ideological work is not an end in itself, but is an important means of fulfilling the basic tasks of communist construction. For this reason, a high level of efficiency is an essential requirement for educational work in the field of ideology under the conditions now obtaining.

---

* V. I. Lenin, *Collected Works*, 4th Russ. ed., Vol. 29, p. 168.

The building of communism requires a great labour effort on the part of the people, on the part of literally every Soviet man and woman. Without labour there cannot be a prosperous society, there can be no well-being and happiness for man. The good things of life do not drop like manna from heaven. Every working man and woman must realise this and do his or her bit in the nation-wide cause of communist construction.

You know how industrious bees are; every bee brings its drop of nectar into the common hive. We may well imagine Soviet society as a big communist hive. In our society everyone must increase the national wealth by his labour, and in due time we shall be able to meet all requirements. But just as there are drones in a beehive that the bees themselves and the bee-keeper try to drive out, so there are still some people in our Soviet society who want to live at the expense of society without giving anything in return. There are still people among us who are inclined to regard communism as a society of idleness and indolence. It is unfortunate that a one-sided and simplified picture of the future society is frequently drawn in oral and even in printed propaganda, and there are people who think that under communism a man will neither sow nor reap but only eat cake. (Animation.) Such a conception of communism is typical of people that are poor in spirit, of philistines and parasites.

Communism and labour go hand in hand. The great principle, "He who does not work neither shall he eat", will continue to operate under communism and will, in fact, become a sacred principle for everyone. Man's beauty and his fame stem from his work, from what he does, from that which he has created or that which he has performed. The abilities and talents of people, the genius of man, are revealed in labour, the immortality of man is in his labour. (Applause.)

The training of man for his life's work, the steeling of people through labour, the inculcation of love and respect for labour as a vital necessity, is the central feature of all work in the field of communist education.

The moulding of the new man is a long and complicated process. People cannot be mechanically transported from the realm of capitalism to the realm of communism. A man steeped in capitalist prejudices cannot be taken into communism. He must first be freed from the burden of the past. It will take time and effort to eliminate the survivals of capitalism in the minds of men, to change in millions of people customs and habits that have evolved in the course of centuries—to complete the change that was begun by our revolution. Survivals of the past are a terrible power that weighs on the minds of people. They persist in the lives and in the minds of millions of people long after the economic conditions that engendered them have disappeared.

At the present stage of communist construction a still more vigorous struggle must be waged against such survivals of capitalism as indolence, parasitism, drunkenness and rowdyism, swindling and money-grubbing, against recurrences of dominant-nation chauvinism and local nationalism, against bureaucratic methods, a wrong attitude towards women, etc. These are weeds that should have no place in our field. *(Applause.)*

Communist education implies the emancipation of the mind from religious prejudices and superstitions which still prevent some Soviet people from displaying their creative ability to the full. A more effective and better organised system of scientific atheist propaganda is needed, one that will embrace all sections and groups of the population, and will prevent the dissemination of religious views, especially among children and adolescents.

Nor must it be forgotten that the survivals of capitalism in the minds of people have to be overcome and a new man educated under conditions of a fierce ideological struggle between the world of socialism and the world of capitalism. The ideologists of imperialism are doing everything they can to maintain and revive bourgeois morals and prejudices in the minds of Soviet people in order to hamper our progress towards communism.

The education of the new man requires great effort and a wise approach. We are dealing with human beings. Everything in man is rationally interconnected. But it is not the sort of interconnection that exists between the parts of a machine. It is something far more complex. One day, when the Dnieper Power Station was being built, Maxim Gorky saw how the rapids were being cleared. Workers placed explosives under the rocks, there was a dull explosion, the water raged for a time, the rocks subsided and the broad Dnieper flowed smoothly on its way. And Gorky said: "If one such explosion could remove from society all the rocks, all that belongs to the past, all that is ignorant and barbaric, how wonderful that would be!" In the reconstruction of society, however, everything is more intricate and difficult. Human society cannot be cleansed of that which prevents a happy and joyous life without a great deal of sweat and much vexation of spirit.

The shaping of a new type of citizen, a man of great ideals and high moral principles, is one of the greatest achievements of our Party. Our opponents are scared by the political and cultural growth of Soviet people and by their loyalty to communism. It stands to reason that this has not arisen automatically, but has been achieved as a result of the Party's many years of educational work. We are now in a position to propose and put into effect those most noble principles of relations between people that many generations of working people have dreamed of. Those principles are given concrete form in the Communist Moral Code.

The interests of communist construction demand that questions of communist education should be in the centre of the attention and activities of every Party organisation and the general public.

The time has come to put an end to any underestimation

of ideological work and to its divorce from organisational work. Any contraposing of ideological and organisational work is incorrect and harmful. The ideological worker, if he really strives to make his work bear fruit, must be a political organiser of the masses. On the other hand, we must always remember that the principal methods of organisational work imply convincing people and educating them in a proper spirit. A higher level of ideological work is an essential condition for the success of our practical activity.

Comrades, our Party's strength lies in its having been able to merge the theory and practice of scientific communism into a single whole in the work of effecting revolutionary transformations. The historic successes achieved by the Soviet people are most convincing evidence of the Party's correct application and creative development of Marxist-Leninist theory. In recent years the scope and significance of the Party's theoretical work have greatly increased.

The great doctrine of Marx, Engels and Lenin always has been and remains our guide to action. The Party will continue to hold high the all-conquering banner of Marxism-Leninism and to preserve its purity, will resolutely sweep from its path all revisionists and other renegades who, under the guise of "renewing" communist theory, attempt to distort it and deprive it of revolutionary principles.

The creators of scientific communism foresaw that ever new problems would arise out of real life and that Communists would have to develop revolutionary theory persistently and in close connection with the socialist transformation of society. This sounds particularly forceful and urgent in our own times, in the period of the rapid, revolutionary recasting of social relations, of radical developments in the history of mankind. Now that those men of genius, the founders of scientific communism, are no longer with us, and day-to-day practice confronts us with a growing number of new questions, the answer to them must be provided by the disciples and followers of Marx and Lenin.

It is a specific feature of the epoch of the full-scale construction of communist society that it confronts us with more and more theoretical questions, the answers to which are to be sought, not only in books, but first and foremost in the living, everyday practice of communist construction. We would be betraying the spirit of our theory if, under these new conditions, we were unable to apply and develop Marxism-Leninism in a creative spirit, if we did not enrich it with new theoretical propositions and conclusions, if we had not courage enough to bring up to date those formulas and propositions that had ceased to conform to new historical experience.

Reality is much richer than any formula. Theoretical propositions must be brought up to date and changed relevantly to changes in the life of society. Our Party has provided excellent examples of such a thoroughly Marxist-Leninist attitude to revolutionary theory.

In the life of our Party the period under review is one in which constructive solutions have been found to many important questions in the building of communism and to many urgent problems of the world emancipation movement. Among them are some major theoretical conclusions—on the dictatorship of the proletariat under present-day conditions; on the laws governing socialism's development into communism; on the ways of creating the material and technical basis of communism; on the formation of communist social relations and the education of the new man; on the variety of forms for the transition from capitalism to socialism; on the more or less simultaneous entry of the socialist countries into communism; on the possibility of preventing a world war in our times; on the nature of the present epoch, and so on.

The great theoretical work of the C.P.S.U. is most fully embodied in its new Programme, which is the philosophical, economic and political basis of the building of communism in our country. The Party's elaboration of this Programme is not only evidence of historic achievements in economic and cultural development, but demonstrates its great and varied theoretical work. The development of revolutionary theory has become a matter for the entire Party. *(Applause.)*

Our practical successes in the building of communism are at the same time successes in the development of theory. It is precisely from this point of view that we must judge the huge social and economic measures carried out by the Party in recent years. Among them are the reorganisation of management in industry and building, the reorganisation of the machine and tractor stations and the further strengthening of the collective-farm system, improvements in economic planning, the adjustment of school programmes to meet the needs of life, further progress in developing the educational system, and a number of others. The measures effected by the Party constitute a truly revolutionary step forward in the development of Soviet society and are, at the same time, a major contribution to Marxist-Leninist theory. They were important decisions dictated by the requirements of the objective laws of communist construction. The Party proceeded from the need to change certain methods of leadership in the economic and cultural fields which, after having played a positive part in the past, had ceased to meet the requirements of life under the new conditions, and might have hampered our development. In implementing important measures the Party takes into consideration both the need to solve current economic and political problems and the perspective of the Soviet Union's advance to communism.

Creative Marxism-Leninism does not tolerate stagnation of thought, or the worship of formulas that do not accord with the real state of affairs, with the objective situation. Nothing contradicts the essence and creative spirit of revolutionary theory so much as attempts to hang on to propositions whose unsoundness has been proved by the realities of life. An example is the thesis, current for a long time in our economic literature, and, indeed, not only in economic publications, that under socialism the purchasing power of the population should always keep ahead of production, and that this is even one of socialism's specific advantages over capitalism and one of the motive forces of our development. This obviously erroneous assertion, one that contradicts the Marxist-Leninist theory of the relation between production and consumption, arose out of the uncritical, dogmatic acceptance of Stalin's erroneous thesis that in the U.S.S.R. "the increase of mass consumption (purchasing power) continuously outstrips the growth of production...".

It did not worry the champions of this point of view that they were actually justifying the shortage of articles of primary necessity and the perpetuation of the ration-card system and its psychology.

Socialist economy is planned economy. We can and must give every consideration to the population's demand for goods when planning the volume and type to be produced. Lenin said that socialism means "the planned organisation of the process of social production to ensure the well-being and all-round development of all members of society...". On more than one occasion he stressed the need to ensure a rate of production development sufficient to create an abundance of goods for the people. We must be guided by these propositions of Lenin's. Our Party is devoting its efforts to the full satisfaction of the material and spiritual requirements of the people. (*Applause.*)

The creative development of Marxism-Leninism is the very foundation of all Party activity, the decisive factor of our successes in communist construction. Guided by the Leninist principle of the unity of theory and practice, our Party will continue to regard the defence and creative development of the principles of Marxism-Leninism as its most important duty to the peoples of our country and the working people of the entire world.

Comrades, our Congress will discuss the great tasks of building a communist society, the achievement of that great goal which was scientifically substantiated by the great thinkers and revolutionaries Marx, Engels and Lenin. The decisions of the Twenty-Second Congress and the new Party Programme will determine the entire political, organisational and ideological work of the Party.

What are our principal tasks in the field of Party work?

1. First and foremost the Party will direct the efforts of the Soviet people to the creation of the material and technical basis of communism, to the perfection of the new social relations and the education of all Soviet people in the communist spirit. The Party, its organisations, all Communists must ensure correct leadership in communist construction, set an example, be in the vanguard, bring a high degree of organisation and planning into all work for communist construction and develop the creative initiative and activity of the masses.

2. The Party must concentrate its attention on the fulfilment of the Seven-Year Plan, on a steady rise in labour productivity and on improving the working people's living standards. Party organisations must head the struggle for technical progress in all branches of the economy, for the wide application of the methods used by innovators and by those who have taken the lead in socialist emulation, and for the all-round development of the movement for communist labour.

3. In conformity with the demands of its new Programme and Rules, the Party will unswervingly observe Leninist standards in Party life and the principle of collective leadership, will make Party bodies and their members more strictly accountable to the Party and the people, will foster activity and initiative on the part of all Communists and their participation in the elaboration and implementation of Party policy, and will develop criticism and self-criticism. The Party will continue to strengthen the unity of its ranks, preserve the purity of Marxism-Leninism,

and conduct an implacable struggle against all manifestations of factionalism and group activity, both of which are incompatible with the Marxist-Leninist Party spirit.

4. The Party will in every way help extend and improve the activities of the Soviets of Working People's Deputies, the trade unions, the Komsomol and other mass organisations, will help enhance their role in communist construction and communist education, will help develop the creative initiative of the masses and strengthen the friendship of all nations of the Soviet Union. The growing scale and complexity of the tasks of communist construction make it imperative to strengthen Party, state and public control over, and systematic verification of, fulfilment of decisions. Improvements in the system of control must be effected on a broad public basis to transform it into genuine control by the people.

5. Ideological work, that powerful factor in the struggle for the victory of communism, must be raised to a higher level. The Party will continue working on the new theoretical problems arising out of practice, will educate all Soviet people in a spirit of loyalty to Marxism-Leninism, intolerance of all manifestations of bourgeois ideology, in a spirit of greater political vigilance in face of the intrigues of the enemies of communism.

6. The Party regards communist construction in the U.S.S.R. as the fulfilment of its internationalist duty to the working people of all countries. It will continue to work untiringly to strengthen the world socialist system and the unity of the entire international Communist and working-class movement. Our Party will develop fraternal contacts with all Communist and Workers' parties and, together with them, will conduct a determined struggle for the purity of Marxism-Leninism, against the various manifestations of opportunism, against present-day revisionism as the gravest danger, against dogmatism and sectarianism.

Loyalty to the great theory of Marxism-Leninism and

ties with the people were in the past, are in the present, and will be in the future the foundation of all our victories, a guarantee of the triumph of communism! *(Stormy applause.)*

* * *

Comrades, this Congress is to examine and discuss magnificent plans for the building of a communist society. These are plans for peaceful creative work, for a gigantic economic and cultural growth, for higher living standards. All the countries of the mighty socialist community are making great headway. Great and clear-cut prospects are ahead of us.

The peoples building socialism and communism do not need war. They adhere to and thanslate into practice the principle of peaceful coexistence inherited from the great Lenin.

In the name of the Communist Party and the Soviet people, we solemnly proclaim from the rostrum of the Twenty-Second Congress:

The Soviet Union will continue to pursue unswervingly the Leninist peaceful foreign policy, and will try to establish mutual trust and co-operation with all states irrespective of their social system. The Soviet Union will continue to strive for the easing of international tension and for general and complete disarmament under strict international control. *(Applause.)*

We have appealed and again appeal to the governments and peoples of the countries that fought together with the Soviet Union against nazi Germany, to put an end to the remnants of the Second World War and remove everything that hinders the strengthening of peace and friendship between nations, everything that holds the threat of a new war. The Soviet Union's proposals to conclude a peace treaty with Germany and, on that basis, to settle the question of West Berlin, involve no detriment to the interests of other states. The proposals show nothing but solicitude for the strengthening of peace between peoples. We should like to believe that in the end reason will triumph. *(Applause.)*

Under the conditions obtaining today, when there are terribly destructive weapons in the hands of the great powers, it is criminally dangerous to play with fire by fomenting war. We call on the governments of all countries to strive towards mutual understanding and co-operation, towards the peaceful solution of urgent international issues. It is the sacred duty of the peoples to conduct a persistent and energetic struggle, using all available means, for the preservation and consolidation of peace on earth. *(Applause.)*

* * *

Comrades, the Twenty-Second Congress of the Party is taking place on the eve of the anniversary of the Great October Socialist Revolution. The fact that at this Congress our Party is adopting a new Programme is evidence of the historic victories of socialism and communism, is a triumph for the cause of the Great October Revolution, a further victory for Marxism-Leninism. *(Prolonged applause.)*

Only forty-four years ago, in the revolutionary days of 1917, our country was faced with the crucial question of choosing a path, of deciding how Russia was to be saved from an imminent national catastrophe. At that time one of the Menshevik leaders said that there was no party in Russia that could assume responsibility for the destinies of the country. It was precisely at that time, in the grim days of 1917, that the leader of the proletarian revolution, Lenin, proclaimed boldly and proudly to the whole world:

"There IS *such a Party!" (Stormy, prolonged applause.)*

Speaking at the First All-Russian Congress of Soviets, Lenin announced, on behalf of the Central Committee, that the Bolshevik Party was prepared to take power, to assume responsibility for the destinies of our country. He unfolded a breath-taking programme for the victory of the revolution, for the transformation of Russia on socialist lines. Everybody now sees how very right Lenin was when he spoke these momentous words. Our Party took upon itself a tremendous burden, assumed responsibility for the destinies of the country, for the future of its people. The broad shoulders of the Party of Communists proved mighty enough to carry this burden. In the van of the working class and all working people, the Party has, in a brief historical period, fully lived up to its undertaking to transform the country, to make it mighty and prosperous. (*Stormy applause.*)

Everybody now sees and admits this. Yet at the time Lenin announced the readiness of the Party of Communists to assume government of the country, the Russian bourgeois press launched a savage campaign against the Communists, ridiculed and made mock of them. Here is what the monarchist newspaper *New Times* wrote:

"Let us suppose for a moment that the Communists are victorious. Who will rule us then? The cooks, perhaps, or the firemen, the stablemen and furnace-hands. Or perhaps nurse-maids will hurry to a meeting of the State Council between washing babies' napkins. Who? Who are these statesmen? Stablemen, nurse-maids, cooks—according to the Communists these are the people whose vocation it is to rule the country. Will that come to pass? No! Is it even possible? History will give the Communists a potent answer to that imbecile question."

And sure enough, history has answered that question with great force. The magnificent victories of the Soviet people in building socialism and communism, in all spheres of economic activity, in the development of science and culture have dispersed like smoke the legend that the working masses are incapable of creative effort, of governing the state. These victories have shown convincingly that the working people—factory workers, peasants, miners, furnace-hands and cooks—who have taken power into their own hands can govern the state better and more wisely, and develop economy, science, and culture more successfully than, for example, the members of the Russian State Council, the princes, counts, capitalists and landlords who ended their days ingloriously on the émigré scrap-heap. *(Applause.)*

The example of the Soviet Union is an inspiration to all progressive mankind. Never has the great vitality of the theory of Marxism-Leninism been as obvious as it is today, when socialism has gained a complete and final victory in the Soviet Union, when socialism is achieving new successes in all the countries of the world socialist community, when the world Communist and working-class movement and the national-liberation struggle of the peoples are rapidly growing and expanding. The revolution released the enormous energy of the peoples and this energy is transforming the world on socialist and communist lines. Tremendous changes are taking place and will continue to take place in the world under the influence of the achievements of communism. The triumph of communism is inevitable! *(Stormy applause.)*

Ninety years ago Marx, saluting the heroic deeds of the Paris Communards, called them heroes storming the heavens. That was a high assessment of the deeds of the fighters of the Paris Commune, a passionate call for revolutionary struggle. We are proud to be able to say today that the peoples of the Soviet Union, who have built socialism and are now successfully erecting the edifice of communist society, are really storming the heavens both figuratively and literally. *(Prolonged applause.)*

The great army of Communists, of Marxists-Leninists, is the vanguard of the peoples in the struggle for peace and social progress, for the bright future, communism. Ever more millions of people will rally about the great banner of communism. The cause of progress, the cause of communism, shall triumph! *(Stormy applause.)*

Long live the great, heroic Soviet people, the builder of communism! *(Stormy applause.)*

Long live the unbreakable unity and fraternal friendship of the peoples of the world socialist community! *(Stormy applause.)*

Long live the heroic Party of Communists of the Soviet Union, created and welded by the great Lenin! *(Stormy applause.)*

Long live the unshakable unity of the international Communist and working-class movement, the fraternal solidarity of proletarians of all countries! *(Stormy applause.)*

Long live world peace! *(Stormy applause.)*

Under the all-conquering banner of Marxism-Leninism, under the leadership of the Communist Party—forward to the triumph of communism! *(Stormy, prolonged applause. All rise. Ovation.)*

N. S. KHRUSHCHOV

ON THE PROGRAMME
OF THE COMMUNIST PARTY
OF THE SOVIET UNION

REPORT TO THE 22nd CONGRESS OF THE C.P.S.U.

October 18, 1961

Comrades, the Twentieth Congress instructed the Central Committee to draft a new Programme of the Communist Party of the Soviet Union. The Central Committee has done so, and submits the draft, after it has been discussed by the Party and the people, to the Congress for consideration.

Our Congress will go down in history as a congress of the builders of communism, the congress that considered and adopted the great programme for the building of the first communist society in the history of mankind.

From the rostrum of our Congress we address our first words of affection and loyalty to Marx, Engels and Lenin, the geniuses of mankind, the great leaders of the working class. (*Prolonged applause.*) Socialism, which Marx and Engels scientifically predicted as inevitable, socialism, the building of which was outlined by Lenin, has been translated into reality in the Soviet Union. Our country is now on its way to new summits—the summits of communism. (*Applause.*)

In their struggle the working class and its Communist Party go through three historic stages of world impact— overthrow of the rule of the exploiters, and establishment of the dictatorship of the proletariat; construction of socialism; the creation of a communist society.

Our Party and people have passed the first two stages. And the fact that the Party was invariably successful in each of these stages is due, to a very great extent, to its having a true compass—its militant revolutionary Party programmes built upon the granite foundations of Marxism-Leninism. The first two Programmes were worked out with the immediate participation and guidance of Vladimir Ilyich Lenin. When working out the third Programme we constantly turned to Lenin for advice, and were guided by his masterly prevision, his brilliant ideas about the building of socialism and communism. This is why we have every reason to call this Programme, too, a Leninist one. (*Prolonged applause.*)

The twentieth century is a century of striking communist triumphs. In the earlier half of the century socialism gained a firm footing on our planet, and communism will do so in the latter half. The way to this is shown by the new Party Programme, rightly described as the Communist Manifesto of the present epoch. (*Applause.*)

The draft Programme embodies the collective thought of the Party. All Soviet people say: This is our Programme, it accords with our hopes and aspirations.

The ideas set forth in the Programme express the cherished aspirations of all mankind. The draft has been heartily approved by the fraternal parties. It has been received with great enthusiasm by the proletariat, by working people the world over. This speaks of the power of communism, of the great significance of our Programme for the future of mankind.

I

THE HISTORIC VICTORIES OF SOCIALISM

1. Lenin's Programme Has Been Translated into Reality

Comrades, in October 1917 the Party won its first great victory on the historic path to communism—the rule of the exploiters was overthrown and the dictatorship of the proletariat was set up. The Party Programme adopted at the Second Congress was fulfilled. The country entered upon the glorious, though unexplored, path of socialist transformation.

A fearless helmsman, our dearly beloved Lenin, stood on the bridge of the Soviet ship. He drew up a brilliant plan of socialist construction. Lenin's Party Programme, adopted at the Eighth Congress, was a daring scientific forecast, a clearcut plan for the building of the new society and an ardent revolutionary appeal to the masses, all in one. The Party proceeded from the fact that we had everything needed to build socialism. It had deep faith in the revolutionary potentialities of the new system and the heroism of the working people.

The difficulties of building the new system were countless. War was raging throughout the vast country. The joint forces of international reaction and domestic counter-revolution bore down upon the Soviet Republic in an attempt to block mankind's road to socialism at its very inception.

The imperialist war and the invasion of interventionists played havoc with Russia's national economy, which had economically lagged 50 to 100 years behind the principal capitalist countries to begin with. In 1919 industrial output in the country was one-fifth that of 1913. Agriculture was at a low ebb.

The difficulties were amplified by the fact that we lacked the experience of organising life along socialist lines, and had to blaze new paths in history. The Soviet people could not obtain any material or technical assistance from without. The country was in a hostile capitalist encirclement and had to carry on in a state of siege.

Truly titanic efforts were demanded of the Party and the people to surmount all these immense difficulties, and pave the way for the building of the new life.

Our enemies described us Communists as people capable not of building or creating, but only of destroying. Indeed, we tore down the exploiter system hateful to the people. But we did so in order to build up communism, a new and most just social system, on soil cleared of the filth and abomination of capitalism. *The Communists have entered*

*history as the greatest creative force, a force transforming
and renewing the world. (Prolonged applause.)*

The facts of history have confirmed that the Communists
are the most consistent patriots, the truest sons of their
country, the most courageous champions of its interests.
It was we, the Bolsheviks, who saved the country from
national disaster, from enslavement by foreign imperialists,
and who made it great in the eyes of all mankind.

The bourgeois parties, politicians and ideologists met the
plan for the building of socialism in Russia with savage hatred and scornful derision. They chanted in unison that the
"Bolshevist experiment" would inevitably fail. Churchill
predicted a complete decline of all forms of life in Russia
and the complete failure of the socialist and communist
theories. Today, we could ask Mr. Churchill: Who was the
one that failed? Our country, which was economically last
among the world's principal countries, has now become the
second industrial power and stands in the van of historical
progress. Great Britain, in the meantime, once the first
power in the world, has irretrievably lost its positions.
There you have visual proof of the great transforming power
of socialist ideas and of the failure of imperialist ideas.
(Applause.)

The leaders of the Second International also tried to
prove that it was impossible to build socialism in Russia.
"Any radical destruction of capitalism is out of the question. . . . Capitalism will revive, it must revive, and probably
very soon." This is what Karl Kautsky predicted for our
country. He stated bluntly that the Bolshevik Party would
not succeed in executing its programme. The Mensheviks
and the Right Socialist-Revolutionaries chimed in with him.
An official document of the Central Committee of the Right
Socialist-Revolutionary Party said that "the attempts to
turn an economically backward country with a demolished
industry and disorganised transport into a socialist basis
will do no more than ravage the national economy and
plunge the country into chaos and anarchy."

The bourgeois and Social-Democratic quasi-prophets strayed far from the truth. If the Right-wing Socialist leaders had been in the least honest, they would have had to admit that the Bolsheviks were right. The Communist Party turned out to be the only party that knew where to lead the people. It surmounted enormous difficulties, swept aside the Trotskyites, the Right-wing opportunists, the nationalist deviators and other defeatists, and translated its plans into reality, showing unparalleled consistency of word and deed. (*Applause.*)

The chief result of the activities of the Party and the people is the complete and final victory of socialism in the U.S.S.R. A great feat of world-wide historic impact has been accomplished. Mankind has been furnished with a science, tested in practice, on the establishment and development of socialism. It is now easier for the other peoples to advance to socialism.

The establishment and consolidation of the socialist state, a state of a new type, and of socialist democracy, a democracy of the highest type, is the principal achievement of the Party and the people in the *political sphere.* The Soviet Union is a country of truly popular rule, freedom and equality.

Our principal historic gains in the *economic sphere* are: the establishment of social ownership and the abolition of private ownership of the means of production which engenders acute conflicts between classes and nations. The bourgeoisie proclaimed that private property, which had existed for thousands of years, was everlasting and sacred. We Communists boldly assaulted that principle. Socialism ushered in an era of social ownership and put an end to anarchy in production, to economic crises and other social upheavals.

In an amazingly short time, a powerful industry was built up, forming the material basis of socialism, the cornerstone of our country's power and prosperity. The Party, equipped with Lenin's co-operative plan, solved the most difficult task next to taking power, that of helping the peasants go over to the socialist path. The voluntary co-operation of the peasantry is an outstanding development in the socio-economic history of mankind.

Take a mental glance at our country, compare it with the past, and you will see how strikingly its face has changed, what a grand path we have travelled in these years.

Russia was regarded as a land of the pick and the barrow, the wooden plough and the spinning wheel. It had one-tenth of the machinery that the United States had, and one-fifth of what Germany had. Today the Soviet Union is a country of advanced technology, of high-powered machine tools and high-precision instruments, of automatic production lines, electronic computers and spaceships. In 1961 the output of our machine-building and metal-working industry was 350 times greater than in 1913, and nearly 1,000 times greater than in 1919.

Russia was regarded as a land of timber, straw and bast, and experienced a real metal famine. Today the Soviet Union is a country of steel and aluminium, of cement and plastics. We produce nearly as much steel as Britain, Federal Germany and France combined.

Russia was regarded as a country of the paraffin lamp and the taper. When the delegates to the Eighth Congress of Soviets were discussing the GOELRO Electrification Plan there was barely enough electric power in Moscow to light the building in which the Congress convened. Today the Soviet Union has the world's mightiest power-producing giants. We generate more than 300,000 million kwh of electricity. In 1961 there will be about 160 times more power generated than in 1913, and 650 times more than in 1919.

Back in the days when the country was starting socialist construction, Lenin, speaking of the immense tasks that faced us, recalled Nekrasov's famous lines, filled with deep pain for his country and undying faith in its powers:

> Poor and plentiful you are,
> Mighty and impotent you are,
> Mother Russia!

It was the unbending resolve of the Bolsheviks, Lenin proclaimed, "to achieve at any price that Russia should cease to be poor and impotent and should become mighty and plentiful in the full meaning of the word".* And we have achieved that! (*Stormy applause.*)

In the *social sphere* the Party has realised the age-long hopes of the masses. All forms of oppression of man by man have been wiped out. The exploiting classes have been abolished. The working class has become the guiding force of society. The peasantry have gone over to socialist farming. Socialist unity of the entire Soviet people has emerged. Women have been given the same rights as men and every opportunity to follow constructive pursuits for the good of society.

In the *ideological sphere* there has been a revolution most far-reaching in content and great in its social significance and consequences. The Communists have raised aloft the torch of knowledge and science. The cultural revolution has wiped out illiteracy, and millions of people have gained access to the achievements of culture and science. A people's intelligentsia has come into being. We have long since moved into first place in the world in the training of engineers. A socialist culture, the prototype of the universal culture of the future, has developed. Marxism-Leninism has become the ideology of Soviet society. The man-hating ideas nurtured by private ownership have receded into the past. Collective principles have triumphed in the life and work of Soviet people.

The Party has solved *the problem of relations between nations*, a most complicated problem that has troubled mankind for centuries and persists to this day in the

---

* V. I. Lenin, *Collected Works*, 4th Russ. ed., Vol. 27, p. 134.

capitalist world. Tsarist Russia was known as a "prison of the peoples". The Soviet Union is known as a fraternal family of the peoples, a country where nations live in friendship, and flourish. The Soviet system has roused to new life and led to prosperity all the previously oppressed and under-privileged peoples who stood at different stages of historical development, from the patriarchal clan to the capitalist system. With the help of the more developed nations, above all the great Russian people, the previously backward peoples have by-passed the capitalist path and risen to the level of the advanced peoples. A new historical community of people of different nationalities possessing common characteristics—the Soviet people—has taken shape in the U.S.S.R. They have a common socialist motherland, the Union of Soviet Socialist Republics, a common economic basis, the socialist economy, a common social class structure, a common world outlook—Marxism-Leninism—a common goal, that of building communism, and many common features in their spiritual make-up, in their psychology. (*Applause.*)

People's living conditions have been altered radically as a result of all these colossal transformations. In tsarist Russia the worker's toil was hard and often lasted 12 to 14 hours. His wage was barely enough to keep body and soul together. Many workers lived in slums. The peasants were in the grip of a veritable land famine. Every third family had no horse to plough with. Taxes and other impositions claimed the greater part of the harvest. Most of the peasants were undernourished. They had meat on big holidays only, and sugar was a luxury they could not afford. Each year thousands of peasants were ruined, and swelled the army of unemployed in the towns.

Socialism has given the peoples a different life. Unemployment, that terrible scourge of the workingman, has long been wiped out. With account of the elimination of unemployment and of reductions in the working day, the Soviet workers' real wages have risen 480 per cent, and the real incomes of Soviet peasants more than 500 per cent. Gas, electricity, television, radio, refrigerators, books and newspapers have all come to the homes of the working people. House rents in our country are the lowest in the world. A law abolishing taxes is being put through. The fact that the average life span has risen to 69 years is striking testimony to our successes. Socialism has thereby more than doubled life expectancy. Communism will yield a further rise in life expectancy and make a reality of the poet's dream—"We'll live to longevity, never reaching senility". (*Applause.*)

Socialism has, for the first time in history, provided man with the basic social rights—the right to labour, leisure, material security in old age, sickness and disability, and the right to education. Socialism has given Soviet people a great sense of faith in their own and their children's future, a sense of security, and has moulded them in the spirit of historical optimism.

The colossal power of socialism was demonstrated in the Great Patriotic War, in which the German fascist hordes, considered unbeatable, were crushed.

The victory of socialism has brought about far-reaching changes in the character of social development. For thousands of years people suffered from the spontaneous operation of objective social laws, whose pawns they were. Under socialism people not only become cognizant of objective laws, but master them. The workers and peasants, whom the exploiters treated as an inarticulate and inert mass, have revealed, in the socialist environment, a truly boundless capacity for creative endeavour, wonders of heroism, unparalleled bravery and titanic strength. In the working people of all countries the example of the Soviet Union has nurtured confidence in their strength.

The basic advantages displayed by the socialist system in our country provided the most conclusive answer to the question of what path mankind is to take. The facts show that all the plans of the bourgeois and Social-Democratic parties have fallen through: these parties have not lived up to their promises. They have not solved any of the basic social problems, nor could they have solved any. History has corroborated that the Communists constitute the only socio-political force that actually solves the social problems troubling mankind and fulfils its programmatic undertakings.

2. The Chief Results of World Development

Comrades, the Party Programme adopted at the Eighth Congress pointed out that the development of imperialism and of its contradictions "has made inevitable the downfall of capitalism and transition to the highest type of social economy". The Programme declared that the era of worldwide proletarian, communist revolution had begun. All subsequent historical development proceeded just as the Marxists-Leninists had foreseen.

Let us compare the political maps of the world in 1919 and in our day.

What do these comparisons reveal? The great revolutionary forces of modern time have radically refashioned the face of the earth. Imperialism has irretrievably lost its hold on the bulk of the peoples. The main avenue along which mankind advances has been established. It is socialism.

The formation of the world socialist system is the principal result of the progressive development of society in our epoch. The triumph of socialist revolutions in China and in a number of other European and Asian countries has been the biggest development in world history since October 1917.

The world socialist system is a young system. But it has already accumulated enough experience to draw conclusions of enormous significance for the charting of the ways of mankind's further development.

	1919 Area		1919 Population		1961 Area		1961 Population	
	million sq. km	% %	millions	% %	million sq. km	% %	millions	% %
I. The world	135.4	100	1,777	100	135.4	100	3,017	100
1) The socialist world	21.7	16.0	138.0	7.8	35.1	25.9	1,072	35.5
2) The rest of the world . . .	113.7	84.0	1,639	92.2	100.3	74.1	1,945	64.5
II. The big imperialist powers (U.S.A., Britain, Germany—F.R.G., France, Japan, Italy) and their colonies	60.3	44.5	855	48.1	18.6	13.7	541.5	17.9
III. All colonies, semi-colonies and dominions	104.5	77.2	1,230	69.2	14.2	10.5	85.4	2.8
IV. Former colonies and semi-colonies that won independence after 1919 (excluding socialist countries) . .	—	—	—	—	72.2	53.4	1,228	40.7

That the socialist system inevitably replaces the capitalist has now been confirmed by the experience not of just one country, but of a large group of countries. The decisive advantages of socialism have been proved. The new system has ensured high rates of development of the productive forces, steadily rising living standards for the working people, freedom from exploitation, and broad social and political rights for the individual.

The glorious Marxist-Leninist parties of the fraternal countries have contributed substantially to the collective experience of socialist revolution and socialist construction. Besides the vast experience of the U.S.S.R., the international working-class movement is now equipped with the experience of people's democracy, a new form of the dictatorship of the proletariat; the experience of peaceful transition from the democratic phase of revolution to the socialist phase; the experience of utilising parliament and the multi-party system in the interests of socialist construction; the experience of building socialist society in industrially developed countries; the experience of economically underdeveloped countries by-passing the capitalist stage of development in their transition to socialism; and the experience of socialist change in the countryside without nationalising land, in view of the long-time tradition of deep attachment which the peasantry has for private landownership.

Socialism has developed a new type of economic and political relations between states and peoples. Socialist internationalism, all-round comradely co-operation and fraternal mutual assistance, and complete equality of all sovereign countries—those are the main features of the relations obtaining in the socialist community. The age-old antagonism between nations has been wiped out in the socialist community and the principles of fraternity and friendship among the peoples prevail. (*Prolonged applause.*)

The socialist system is turning more and more into a dominant factor of world development in the interests of peace and social progress. By the force of its example the socialist community is inspiring the working class and all the working people in other countries to intensify their struggle against capitalist oppression, for their essential rights and interests, for social and national liberation, and lasting peace. The facts of life are leading the masses up to the realisation that socialism is the true spring-tide of the world and that capitalism is its yesteryear. (*Applause.*)

The collapse of the colonial system is second in historical significance among the results of world development. The emergence and consolidation of socialism ushered in the era of liberation for the oppressed peoples. It was only when socialism became a powerful force that a historic development such as the liberation from colonial oppression of more than 1,500 million people, could occur. The national-liberation revolutions inflicted a staggering blow to the Bastille of colonialism. Forty-two sovereign states have sprung up on the ruins of colonial empires.

Imperialism turned entire continents into prisons for the peoples. It put chains of slavery on hundreds of millions of people and fenced them off for centuries from civilisation. It warped the economies of the Asian, African and Latin American countries, making them one-sided, with an emphasis on agriculture and raw materials. Judge for yourselves, comrades. In terms of the capitalist economy countries inhabited by more than two-thirds of the population of the non-socialist world produce as little as about one-tenth of the output of the manufacturing industry, approximately 3 per cent of the machinery and equipment, and 5 per cent of the metals. In the underdeveloped countries of Asia and Africa the annual income per head of the population is 20 to 25 times lower than in the United States of America.

After the many years of "care" which the capitalist "civilisers" dispensed to the colonies, millions of people in Asia, Africa and Latin America are literally starving to death. The average life span in those regions is about half of what it is in their former metropolitan countries. In Africa child mortality is extremely high. Over 80 per cent of Africa's adult population and over 40 per cent of Latin America's can neither read nor write. Such is the terrible price paid for the so-called civilisation of the "free world". It is only natural that the peoples are tearing down the disgraceful system of relations created by the colonialists.

The third result of world development is an acute all-round weakening of capitalism and a fresh sharpening of its general crisis. The facts have fully corroborated Lenin's analysis of capitalism and of imperialism, its highest stage, presented in the second Programme of our Party. This is why we have deemed it necessary to reproduce the fundamental theses on this matter in the new Party Programme as well.

The socialist and national-liberation revolutions, the growth of the world socialist system and the disintegration of the colonial system—those are decisive factors deepening the general crisis of capitalism, which has in recent years entered a new, third stage. But they are not the only factors adding to the crisis of capitalism. The crisis of world capitalism is a far-flung and all-embracing process involving all aspects of life in bourgeois society— the economy, domestic and foreign policy, and the ideological superstructure.

To begin with, it should be noted that the *economic instability of capitalism has increased steeply and the uneven development of some countries in relation to others has become far more marked.* The rates of the economic development of the capitalist system are dropping, and in some countries are barely ahead of the growth of population. Economic crises are becoming more frequent, especially in the United States. War production has become a permanent element of the economy. Militarism has swelled to enormous proportions. Fifteen to twenty per cent of the national income is spent on armaments. A substantial portion of the manpower is not being used to produce material values. The chronic underloading of the production apparatus is all the time increasing in scale. During crises underloading of productive capacities in some industries amounts to as much as 50 per cent. In many countries mass unemployment, to say nothing of agrarian over-population, has assumed the proportions of a real national calamity. According to official statistics 8-10 million out of 85 million industrial workers in the developed capitalist countries of North America and Western Europe, and in Japan and Australia are fully unemployed. This means that on the average one person in every nine is unemployed.

The political instability of world capitalism has increased, especially as a result of mounting class antagonisms. This is indicated convincingly by the deepening of the contradictions between the handful of monopolists and all the other sections of the people, and by the vast scale of the working-class struggle, the mounting struggle of the peasants, and the mass actions of the working people in defence of democracy, against fascism and the despotic militarist regimes. It is also strikingly illustrated by the ever-growing role and influence of the Communist parties.

The structure of imperialism is afflicted from top to bottom by an acute and deep-going crisis. This does not mean, of course, that imperialism is in a state of complete stagnation, that its productive forces are bogged down. A more rapid growth of capitalist economy may be observed at different periods in different capitalist countries under the influence of incidental factors. But on the whole, capitalist relations of production are increasingly inhibiting the development of modern productive forces. In our time it is the rates of growth of production in the socialist countries that constitute the criterion of their development. In the past decade the average annual rate of growth of the capitalist economy did not, on the whole, exceed 5 per cent, while it was nearly 14 per cent in the socialist world.

Imperialist ideologists and politicians are vainly trying to prove that capitalism still commands great possibilities and "reserves" of development. The Right-wing Socialists and other defenders of imperialism capitalise on the new phenomena in capitalist economy to infer that capitalism is changing its nature and, of all things, evolutionising towards socialism. All that is nonsense, of course. In effect, these new phenomena could not do more to confirm Lenin's analysis of imperialism. They show that there is no such thing as "transformation" of capitalism, and that the process of its growing enfeeblement, sharpening of contradictions, increasing decay and parasitism is well under way.

What, in substance, are the apologists of imperialism pinning their hopes on? Above all on state-monopoly capitalism. But, as we know, state-monopoly capitalism has been operative for quite some time. And what do the facts show? They reaffirm that state-monopoly capitalism by no means signifies the emergence of a new stage of capitalist development distinct from imperialism, that it does not signify the development of the bourgeois state into a mediator, a supra-class force safeguarding private and public interests and the interests of both labour and capital, to an equal degree. State-monopoly capitalism constitutes a fusion of the strength of the monopolies and that of the state into a single mechanism subordinating all aspects of the nation's life to the interests of the financial oligarchy. The monopolies remain the basis of the economy, and not just within the framework of individual countries, but also on the scale of the capitalist world as a whole. Suffice it to say that nearly one-third of world capitalist production is concentrated in the hands of only 200 major monopolies. Like giant octopuses, they have fastened their tentacles upon entire countries and continents, sucking the lifeblood out of the peoples.

True, the transition to state monopolies and increasing intervention by the state in the process of capitalist reproduction make it possible to exercise a certain influence on the development of the productive forces and facilitate a mobilisation of resources in the interests of the financial oligarchy. The state's intervention in economic relations in the interests of the monopolies has had a certain effect, inducing some growth of production and renewal of basic capital in the post-war period. Conscious of the far-reaching social consequences likely to follow economic crises of the scale of 1929-33, the monopoly bourgeoisie is trying to soften by methods of state control the destructive impact of the economic upheavals inherent in capitalism. However, state-monopoly capitalism does not cancel—nor can it cancel—the objective economic laws of capitalism, eliminate spontaneity and anarchy of production, economic crises and the other evils of the capitalist system.

In the U.S.A. state-monopoly capitalism is highly developed. But what good has it done the country? It is in the United States that underloading of plants is most acute. At a time when vast multitudes starve in the capitalist world, U.S. monopolists hand out premiums for curtailments of sown areas and reductions in the output of agricultural produce. In place of the vaunted "full employment", the U.S.A. has a permanent army of many millions of fully and partially unemployed.

It follows that the hopes pinned on state-monopoly capitalism as a means of salvaging imperialism are essentially groundless.

American imperialism aspires to the role of citadel and saviour of world capitalism. The United States is, undeniably, the richest and mightiest power of the capitalist world. But it is becoming more and more the epicentre of capitalism's economic difficulties. Furthermore, the fact should also be noted that for all of the last decade the share of the U.S.A. in world capitalist production and commerce has been dropping steadily. American capitalism has passed its prime, and is declining.

There is yet another reason why the designs of the United States to "integrate" the whole capitalist world under its aegis proved futile. It is the ineradicable economic strife between the imperialist states. The international state-monopoly organisations springing up under the guise of integration of the capitalist countries, of alleviating the problem of markets are in effect new forms of redividing the world capitalist market and are becoming sources of acute strain and conflict. Objectively, there are two trends that operate and intertwine in the imperialist camp. One is the trend towards joining all its forces against socialism, and the other towards an aggravation of the contradictions between the imperialist powers, and also between the imperialist powers and the other countries of the capitalist world. The United States has not succeeded, and will not succeed, in overcoming the latter trend. The American financial oligarchy does not have the strength or the means to implement its claims to the role of saviour of capitalism, to say nothing of its claims to world domination.

Comrades, the more acutely the exploiting essence of capitalism, its anti-popular ideology and moral degradation come to the fore, the more stridently the advocates of the bourgeoisie try to extol capitalism. But what has capitalism given mankind? It warps the achievements of man's creative genius and turns them against him. It has turned the release of atomic energy into a menace to mankind. Capitalism turns every new technological advance against man. The wealth of a few countries is maintained by the poverty of the peoples of many other countries. Even the pure light of science, as Marx put it, is unable to shine under capitalism but on the dark background of ignorance.

Not only does a mere handful of millionaires and multi-millionaires arbitrarily control the entire wealth of the capitalist world; it makes the destinies of entire nations a coin of exchange. Within the lifetime of a single generation the imperialists have started two world wars. The price paid by mankind for the policy of the imperialists amounts to about 80 million dead or crippled, to say nothing of the incalculable destruction of material values. Some investigators estimate that the cost of the wars and war preparations in the early half of the twentieth century

(1900-53) added up in the whole world to a truly astronom-
ical figure—more than $4,000,000 million.

Let us see what could have been done for man's benefit
with these funds. The entire population of our planet could
have been supplied free bread for half a century. Comfortable dwellings could have been built with these funds for
500 million families, i. e., for two-thirds of the world population. At present imperialism compels mankind to spend
at least $100,000 million annually for military purposes.
If only 20 per cent of that sum were annually spent on
helping the underdeveloped countries in the course of
25 years, it would be possible to build power stations to-
talling 230 million kw and steel works producing 185 million tons of steel a year, irrigate more than 100 million hectares of land, and do many other big things to improve the
life of peoples. All this demonstrates once again how urgent
the struggle for disarmament is to all the peoples.

To summarise the principal results of world development,
we can say: History is developing the way Marx and Lenin
predicted. The forces of socialism, all the forces of world
progress, are on the upgrade. The peoples are more and
more resolutely breaking away from imperialism. The
downfall of imperialism and the triumph of socialism on
a world scale are inevitable. (*Prolonged applause.*)

II

COMMUNISM IS THE GREAT GOAL
OF THE PARTY AND THE PEOPLE

Comrades, the new Programme is a new milestone in the
history of our Party and of Soviet society as a whole. Each
of our Party Programmes corresponds to a definite historical stage in the country's development. Yet all our Programmes are interlinked. Taken as components of a single
whole, they form an integral Marxist-Leninist theory of
socialist revolution, of socialist and communist construc-

tion, a theory confirmed by experience. The Programmes of the Party may be compared to a three-stage rocket. The first stage wrested our country away from the capitalist world, the second propelled it to socialism, and the third is to place it in the orbit of communism. It is a wonderful rocket, comrades! (*Stormy applause.*) It follows the exact course charted by the great Lenin and by our revolutionary theory, and is powered by the greatest of all energies—the energy of the builders of communism. (*Applause.*)

What are the main features of the draft Programme?

The main thing is that *it is a concrete, scientifically substantiated programme for the building of communism.* The draft shows clearly how the bright edifice of communism is to be erected. We see how it should be built, how it looks from within and without, what kind of people will live in it, and what they will do to make it still more comfortable and attractive. We can proudly tell those who want to know what communism is: "Read our Party Programme." (*Prolonged applause.*)

The draft Programme marks *a new stage in the development of the revolutionary theory of Marx, Engels and Lenin.* The Programme furnishes an explicit answer to all the basic questions of the theory and practice of the struggle for communism and to the key questions of present-day world development. The Twentieth and Twenty-First congresses of the C.P.S.U., which introduced much that was new in principle into the solution of the fundamental issues of Party life and the life of Soviet society, and into the analysis of the processes of world development, have been of enormous, truly historic importance in the drafting of the Programme. It would have been much harder for us to work out such a Programme if there had been no Twentieth and Twenty-First congresses of the C.P.S.U.

The spirit and content of the draft reflect *the unity and indivisibility of Marxist-Leninist theory and the practice of communist construction.* The Programme defines concrete tasks in industry, agriculture, development of the state, science and culture and in communist education. Comrades, just think of the heights the Soviet people have scaled, if they can chart the perspective of social development for so considerable a historical period.

The third Party Programme is a programme of the whole Soviet people. When the Party was adopting its first Programme it was followed by small groups of politically conscious workers. When it was adopting its second Programme it was followed by the working class and the bulk of the working peasantry. Now it is followed by the whole Soviet people. Our people accepted the Party Programme as their own cause, as the greatest purpose of their lives. *(Prolonged applause.)*

The new Programme signifies a full realisation in practice of the Party slogan, "Everything for the sake of man, for the benefit of man". It gives predominance to matters concerning the further improvement of the people's material well-being and culture, the flowering of the human personality. And that is as it should be. The Bolsheviks hoisted the flag of revolution in order to make the life of the working people joyous and happy. The third Party Programme ushers in a period when all the difficulties and hardships borne by the Soviet people in the name of their great cause will be rewarded a hundred-fold.

The draft Programme proceeds from the new international conditions: *Communism is being built not in a capitalist encirclement, but under the conditions created by the existence of a world socialist system, the increasing superiority of the socialist forces over those of imperialism, of the forces of peace over those of war.* The imperialist countries naturally strive to impede the economic and social progress of the Soviet land in every way, forcing it to incur defence expenditures. If this were not so, our rates of development would be still higher. However, as the forces of socialism increase and world imperialism grows weaker, more favourable conditions will arise for our economic and cultural development.

Our Programme is imbued with the spirit of socialist internationalism. Lenin's Party has always honourably fulfilled its obligations with respect to its brothers abroad. In October 1917 it brought the dawn of liberation to the world. It erected the beacon of socialism, and all peoples can see it. That beacon illumines their way towards the new social system. Lenin's Party will bear aloft the banner of internationalism in the future as well. The Party now considers it its prime internationalist duty to build communism in a brief space of history. (*Applause.*)

The draft Programme is *a document of true communist humanism; it is imbued with the ideas of peace and fraternity among nations.* We place the continuously expanding might of our country at the service of peace and mankind's progress. When the Soviet Union will have become the first industrial power, when the socialist system will have fully become the decisive factor of world development, and when the peace forces the world over will have grown still greater, the scales will tilt once and for all in favour of the forces of peace and the barometer of the international weather will show: "Clear. The menace of world war is gone never to return." (*Prolonged applause.*)

Comrades, communism is mankind's age-old dream. The working masses trusted that slavery and dependence, tyranny and poverty, the bitter struggle for one's daily bread, and wars between peoples would give place to a society where Peace, Labour, Freedom, Equality and Fraternity reign supreme. (*Applause.*) The spontaneous movement of the masses produced utopian theories of a future golden age.

Spokesmen of utopian socialism produced trenchant criticism of the system of exploitation and its evils. They depicted the society of the future. But they were closer to the truth when they spoke of what would be absent in that society than when they outlined the ways of achieving socialism. For all that, behind the imaginings in these pictures of an ideal social system we still find germs of brilliant ideas. We gratefully recall the names of the great Utopian-Socialists Saint-Simon, Fourier, Owen, Campanella and More, and of our Russian revolutionary democrats—Chernyshevsky, Herzen, Belinsky and Dobrolyubov, who came closer than others to scientific socialism.

But it was Marx, Engels and Lenin who created the theory of scientific communism and indicated realistic ways and means of establishing the new society and the revolutionary forces destined to destroy the old world and build the world of communism.

Marx and Engels defined the most characteristic features of communism. Today, when we are building communist society in practice, we cannot but admire the brilliant foresight of our teachers. Their vision actually reached across an entire century.

Lenin, the great founder of our Party, developed the Marxist teaching of communist society further. He furnished a clear-cut definition of the two phases of communism, charted the plan of building socialism and revealed the objective laws of its development into communist society.

Our conception of the communist system is based entirely on the scientific conclusions of the founders of Marxism-Leninism. But we have an advantage over them in one, very essential respect: we live in the latter half of the twentieth century and have at our disposal vast and invaluable practical experience of socialist and communist construction. And not on some small island of Utopia cast away in the ocean, as Thomas More pictured it, not in a City of the Sun, as depicted by Tommaso Campanella, and not on a strip of land in distant America, as Robert Owen planned. No, the new life is being built on an immense section of the earth.

Not only are we able today to picture communist society more accurately, but also, and this is most important, to define the practical ways of building it, to impart concrete substance to the principles of scientific communism. We see more clearly and distinctly much that was hidden to our forerunners by the veil of time, because the trends of development of socialist society which lead to the victory of communism have by now become quite tangible. It stands to reason that even now, faithful to the example set by our teachers, we do not attempt to define all the details of a developed communist society.

The draft Programme gives the following definition of communism:

"Communism is a classless social system with one single form of public ownership of the means of production and full social equality of all members of society; under it, the all-round development of people will be accompanied by the growth of the productive forces through continuous progress in science and technology; all the springs of collective wealth will flow more abundantly, and the great principle 'From each according to his ability, to each according to his needs', will be implemented. Communism is a highly organised society of free, socially conscious working people in which public self-government will be established, a society in which labour for the good of society will become the prime, vital requirement of everyone, a necessity recognised by one and all, and the ability of each person will be employed to the greatest benefit of the people."

Let me go into some of the aspects in the description of communist society. Communism implies highly-organised production centralised on the scale of society as a whole and managed along the broadest democratic lines. Communist society is not an association of self-contained, autarkic economic organisms. By no means. Communist society, more than any other, will need unified economic planning, organised distribution of labour and regulation of working time. The need of this springs from the demands presented by the development of the productive forces, from the far-reaching inter-relation of the various branches of economy, the interests of continuous technical progress and from the communist principles of distribution and consumption. Development of the communist economy is impossible, unless the entire people participate most actively in the management of production.

For the first time, the draft elaborates upon the concrete ways and means of effecting the great communist slogan, "From each according to his ability, to each according to his needs". It is a proper combination of material labour incentives and increasing distribution through public funds that leads up to the implementation of the principles of communist equality.

Some people picture living conditions under communism wrongly and narrow-mindedly. They grasp at just the second part of the formula, "according to needs", and reason something like this: "Under communism you work if you wish, or drift from the Far East to the west, and from the west to the south if you wish; you'll be provided according to needs all the same." A big spoon is all they are equipping themselves with for communism. (*Laughter. Applause.*)

We have to disappoint them from the very outset. Their notion has nothing in common with communism. Communist society will have the most advanced technology, the most advanced and best organised production, the most advanced machinery. But it will be people that operate the machines. Machines are dead things, unless there is a man to operate them. Thoroughness, good organisation and discipline are therefore a golden rule, an obligatory standard of behaviour for every workingman. He will not be made to perform his duties by the goad of hunger, as under capitalism; he will perform them consciously and of his own free will. Everyone will be conscious of the duty to contribute his labour to the creation of both the material and spiritual blessings. All Soviet people must work so well as to be able to say, when the bright edifice of communism is built: I have done my bit for it as well.

The classics of Marxism-Leninism emphasised that communism is not fenced off by a wall from socialism, that communism and socialism are two phases of one and the same socio-economic formation, distinguished from one another by the degree of economic development and the maturity of social relations.

Socialism does not develop on its own foundation. For all its immense achievements of world historic significance, in many respects—the economic, legal and moral, and in the consciousness of men—it still bears an imprint of the old system, from which it has emerged. Communism is a higher and more perfect stage of social life, and can develop only after socialism is fully consolidated. Under communism all the after-effects of the capitalist system will be completely eliminated.

The fact that communism develops on its own foundation predetermines the distinctive features of its construction. The transition from capitalism to socialism is effected under conditions of class struggle. It involves a radical break-up of social relations, a sweeping social revolution and the establishment of the dictatorship of the proletariat. On the other hand, the transition to communism proceeds in the absence of any exploiting classes, when all members of society—workers, peasants and intellectuals—have a vested interest in the victory of communism, and work for it consciously. It is natural therefore that the building of communism is effected by the most democratic methods, by way of improving and developing social relations, with due account of the departure of the old forms of life and the appearance of new forms, of their interlacement and mutual influence. Society will no longer experience the difficulties induced by class struggle within the country. All this will serve to accelerate the rates of social development in the period of transition to communism.

The historical limits of the draft Programme are 20 years. Why did we set this term? When the draft Programme was being discussed, some comrades wondered whether the time allocated to the task was not too long. No, comrades. To prepare society for the establishment of the principles of communism we have to develop the productive forces enormously and create an abundance of material and spiritual values. And that takes a certain amount of time. The bowl of communism is a bowl of abundance, and it must always be full. Everyone must contribute his bit to it, and everyone must take from it. It would be a fatal error to decree the introduction of communism before all the necessary conditions for it have matured. If we were to proclaim that we introduce communism when the bowl is still far from full, we would be unable to take from it according to needs. In that case we would only discredit the ideas of communism, disrupt the initiative of the working people and retard the advance to communism. We base ourselves on strictly scientific estimates, which indicate that we shall, in the main, have built a communist society within 20 years. (*Prolonged applause.*)

What does it mean to build communism in the main? It means that:

in the *economic* sphere the material and technical basis of communism will be created; the economy of the Soviet Union will surpass that of the most developed capitalist countries and move into first place for production per head of the population, the world's highest living standard will be ensured and all the conditions created to attain an abundance of material and cultural values;

in the sphere of *social* relations the still existing remnants of distinctions between classes will be eliminated; classes will fuse into a classless society of communist working people; the essential distinctions between town and country, and then between physical and mental labour, will, in the main, be eradicated; there will be greater economic and ideological community among nations; the features will develop of the man of communist society, a man harmoniously combining ideological integrity, broad education, moral purity and physical perfection;

in the *political* sphere all citizens will participate in the administration of public affairs, and society will prepare itself for the full implementation of the principles of communist self-government through a most extensive development of socialist democracy.

III

FROM SOCIALIST TO COMMUNIST ECONOMY

1. Creation of the Material and Technical Basis of Communism

Comrades, the draft Programme sets out a majestic perspective for the building of unprecedentedly powerful productive forces in our country, the development of the Soviet Union into the world's leading industrial power. V. I. Lenin said: "We value communism only when it is economically substantiated." The draft Programme furnishes this substantiation.

A material and technical basis for communism will be built up in the U.S.S.R. in the course of two decades. This is the principal economic task, the cornerstone of our Party's general line.

The building of the material and technical basis of communism is the decisive link in the chain of economic, social and cultural tasks, and is prescribed by the internal as well as the external conditions of our country's development. It will enable us to carry out the following most important tasks:

fistly, to build up unprecedentedly powerful productive forces and move into first place in the world for production per head of the population;

secondly, to achieve the world's highest productivity of labour, which, in the final analysis, is the most important, the principal thing for the victory of the new social system, and to equip the Soviet people with the most advanced technology, to turn labour into a source of joy, inspiration and creative endeavour (*applause*);

thirdly, to develop the production of material values for the satisfaction of all the requirements of Soviet people, to ensure the highest standard of living for the whole population, to create all the conditions for the ultimate transition to distribution according to needs;

fourthly, to gradually convert the socialist relations of production into communist relations, to create a classless society, to erase the essential distinctions between town and country, and later on between mental and physical labour.

Last but not least, it is only in building up the material and technical basis of communism that we can win the economic competition with capitalism and always maintain the country's defences at a level adequate to crush any aggressor who dares to draw the sword against the Soviet Union, the socialist world as a whole. (*Prolonged applause.*)

Do we have all we need to build up the material and technical basis of communism in two decades? Yes, comrades, we do. We have a social system of giant creative power, immense production capacities and inexhaustible natural resources. We have a first-class technology and the most advanced science in the world. The Soviet Union has developed splendid qualified personnel equal to the tasks of communist construction. The Soviet people is led by a wise and battle-hardened Party. (*Applause.*)

The creation of the material and technical basis of communism will, naturally, call for tremendous funds. Capital investments in the national economy of the U.S.S.R. over the coming 20 years have been set at approximately 2,000,000 million rubles. Just think of the scale our capital construction has now assumed, comrades! We have to count in trillions!

Will the mobilisation of such immense resources entail hardships and sacrifices, as in the period of industrialisation? We have every reason to say that it will not. And primarily because a mighty industry has been built up in our country.

The role of heavy industry in the improvement of the people's welfare and in the solution of the problem of accumulation now presents itself in a new way. We know that heavy industry has two categories of plants—firstly, those that produce means of production for industries that also produce means of production, and, secondly, plants that produce means of production for the light and food industries, for agriculture, housing construction and for the cultural and public services. At the time when our heavy industry was only being built up we had to concentrate our resources primarily on the development of plants of the first category and restrict investments in the second category of plants. At present we are able to increase our capital investments considerably in the second category of plants as well, which will step up the rates of growth of popular consumption. In 1980 the output of the first category of plants will have increased about six-fold over 1960 and that of the second category —13-fold. Besides, our heavy industry will produce increasing quantities of cultural and household goods to meet the growing demand. In developing heavy industry, we proceed from Lenin's thesis that "means of production... are not manufactured for their own sake, but only because more and more means of production are demanded by the branches of industry manufacturing articles of consumption".

The 20-year national economic development plan (the general perspective) envisages a considerable approximation between the rates of growth in the production of means of production and the production of articles of consumption. In 1929-40, in industry, the average annual rates of accretion in the production of means of production exceeded the rates of accretion in the production of articles of consumption by nearly 70 per cent, whereas in 1961-80 the difference between them will be approximately 20 per cent.

Heavy industry has always played, and will continue to play, the leading role in extended reproduction. The Party will continue to show constant concern for its growth, since it regards heavy industry as the decisive factor for the building of the material and technical basis and for rapid technical progress, as the basis for the consolidation of the socialist state's defence capacity. At the same time, the Party will do its utmost for heavy industry to ensure a steadily growing output of consumer goods.

We are equal to the planned scale of capital investment also because all social production and the national income will rise steeply. The farther we advance, the greater is the "weight" of each per cent of the national income set aside for accumulation, and, consequently, the greater are the funds we can allocate to capital investment. And one more important circumstance. The further development of technology and rising productivity of labour will serve to increase output per each invested ruble.

On the strength of our experience and our realistic estimates of the future, we are able to fix the approximate scale of production and to speak about time limits for the building of the material and technical basis of communism in terms of concrete figures. Here are a few estimates made by our planning bodies.*

The aggregate social product is the most general index for all branches of social production. It is planned to increase it about five-fold in the coming twenty years. The industrial output will rise not less than six-fold, and the aggregate agricultural output approximately 3.5-fold. This is tantamount to saying that another five industrial and more than two agrarian countries like the Soviet Union today, will be created in our bountiful land. (*Prolonged applause.*) *In twenty years Soviet industry will produce nearly twice as much as is now produced in the whole non-socialist world.*

---

* See p. 201.

In the coming 20 years the production of the means of production in our industry will increase approximately seven-fold. Our country's basic production assets will be five times as great as they are today. This means, in effect, that our industries will be totally re-equipped with the latest machinery. The production apparatus of the Soviet Union will be the most powerful, the newest and the most advanced. The accumulation of new production assets is a gradual process. It is therefore necessary to make the best use of all the means of production in operation, of all available machinery, raising its efficiency to the utmost.

The Soviet economy will continue to develop at a rapid pace. In the coming twenty years the average annual increase in industrial output will amount to not less than 9-10 per cent. This means that our rates of economic growth will continue to be much higher than those of the capitalist countries.

The draft Programme of the C.P.S.U. has mapped out *the basic trends in the building of the material and technical basis of communism.*

The building of the material and technical basis of communism implies an advance to a new level of technology and proficiency, of organisation of production, and an increasing development of the processes of concentration, specialisation, co-operation and combination. Science is becoming more and more of a productive force, and production, a technological application of modern science. As Lenin repeatedly stressed, communism can never be built without the latest technology, without new scientific discoveries.

What new implements of labour, to use Marx's words, form the bone and sinew of communist production? They are a system of machines for comprehensive mechanisation and automation. Under the conditions of communist construction automation ushers in a new era in the development of technology. The development and use of chemical products, of new highly-efficient materials, new

Development of Soviet Industry in 1960-80
(in prices of July 1, 1955)

	1960	1970	1980	Number of times greater than in 1960
Aggregate industrial output in wholesale factory prices (000 million rubles) . . .	155	408	970-1,000	6.2-6.4
including:				
Production of means of production—group "A" (000 million rubles) . . .	105	287	720-740	6.8-7
Production of consumer goods—group "B" (000 million rubles) . . .	50	121	250-260	5 5 2
Electric power (000 million kwh) . . .	292.3	900-1,000	2,700-3,000	9.2-10.3
Steel (000,000 tons) . . .	65	145	250	3.8
Oil (000,000 tons) . . .	148	390	690-710	4.7-4.8
Gas (000 million cu. m) . . .	47	310-325	680-720	14.4-15.2
Coal (000,000 tons) . . .	513	686-700	1,180-1,200	2.3-2.34
Output of engineering and metal-working industries (000 million rubles) . . .	34	115	334-375	9.8-11
Mineral fertilisers (in conventional units—000,000 tons) . . .	13.9	77	125-135	9.9.7
Synthetic tars and plastics (000 tons) .	332	5,300	19,000-21,000	57-63
Artificial and synthetic fibre (000 tons) . .	211	1,350	3,100-3,300	14.7-15.6
Cement (000,000 tons) . . .	45.5	122	233-235	5.1-5.2
Textiles (000 million sq. m) . . .	6.6	13.6	20-22	3-3.3
Leather footwear (000,000 pairs) . . .	419	825	900-1,000	2.1-2.4
Cultural and household goods (000 million rubles) . . .	5.9	18	58-60	9.8-10.1

objects of labour and widespread application of chemical methods will play an increasing role in production. There is a pressing need to increase greatly the durability and reliability of metals and other materials, especially those subjected to extra-high pressures, temperatures and speeds. In the long-term view, sources of raw materials will be greatly increased by deeper penetration into the bowels of the earth and the use of the biological and mineral resources of the oceans and seas.

The draft Programme points to the prime importance of *the electrification of the whole country*. Lenin said that "electrification upon the basis of the Soviet system will achieve final victory for the foundations of communism". Lenin's idea of complete electrification is the keynote of the entire programme of communist economic construction.

Lenin presented the first comprehensive plan for the development of the country's economy—the GOELRO Plan, and described it as the Party's second programme. It was envisaged to raise the output of electric power to 8,800 million kwh a year. The plan was implemented ahead of schedule. As far back as 1947 our country had moved into first place in Europe and second place in the world for electric power output.

The overall capacity of our power stations in 1960 amounted to 66,700,000 kw.

We are on our way to developing new sources of energy and new methods of generating it. A solution of the problem of direct conversion of other types of energy into electric power, with a steep rise in efficiency of power-generating plant, will be highly important.

The general perspective envisages the priority development of electric power production. It is envisaged to raise power output to 2,700,000-3,000,000 million kwh in 1980, i.e., to produce nine or ten times more than in 1960.

In 1980 our country will be generating roughly 50 per cent more power than all the other countries of the world combined are generating today. The result will be an eight-

or nine-fold increase in the electric power consumption per industrial worker. (*Applause.*)

By then the Soviet Union is to exceed the United States not only in electric power output but in kilowatt-hours generated per head of population.

This increase will result in a large-scale electrification of transport, agriculture and communal facilities in town and country.

The electrification of the whole country will thus play a key role in advancing all branches of the national economy and stimulating technological progress.

What grand, truly breath-taking plans, comrades! Indeed, the sun of communism is rising over our land! (*Prolonged applause.*)

The Party and the people are determined steadily to carry out their plans for construction, which will guarantee the fulfilment of Lenin's programme for the complete electrification of the country.

Our planning bodies have worked out a tentative scheme for the construction of major thermal and hydropower stations. This scheme is subject to most thorough deliberation with respect to each individual station. Considerable alterations may be effected in it by further technical progress.

In the coming 20 years we are to build 180 mighty hydropower stations, about 200 district thermal stations up to 3,000,000 kilowatts each, and 260 big heat-and-power stations.

In Eastern Siberia, we shall complete the Bratsk and Krasnoyarsk hydropower stations and by 1980 plan to build a few more large-scale ones, such as the Sayan, Ust-Ilim, Boguchany, Yeniseisk and Osinovka stations on the Angara and Yenisei, and a station on the Lower Tunguska. The capacity of each of these is to exceed 4,000,000 kw. (*Applause.*)

In addition, we shall build two groups of highly effective super-powerful thermal stations there, fuelled with coal from the Kansk-Achinsk Basin—the Itat-Bogotol group in the vicinity of Krasnoyarsk, and the Irsha-Borodino group (each of 3,000,000 kw and up) in the area of Kansk-Taishet.

Large hydropower stations of importance both for electrification and irrigation are to be built in Central Asia. These include the Nurek and Rogun stations on the Vakhsh River and the Toktoghul and Toguztorou stations on the Naryn. A number of large power stations will be built in Kazakhstan, including an Irtysh power group.

The building of the Saratov, Lower-Volga and Cheboksary hydropower stations and of two stations on the Kama River will complete the Volga-Kama hydropower cascade. A six-million-kilowatt hydropower station in the lower reaches of the Ob River will give its power to the single power grid of the European part of the country. In addition, construction is envisaged of a number of powerful thermal stations near Saratov, Stalingrad, Gorky and in the Kuibyshev-Ufa-Orenburg area.

Powerful thermal stations will go up in the Central and Central-Black Earth areas of the European part of the U.S.S.R., south and north-east of Moscow, in the Ukraine near Kiev, Kirovograd and Nikolayev, in the Donets Basin, in Latvia and in Byelorussia. The power industry in the Caucasus will be developed through utilisation of hydro-resources and other sources of energy.

Realisation of the plan will solve the important problem of the Greater Volga and Greater Dnieper. This will, naturally, entail considerable investments. But they will be returned in a comparatively short time. Estimates show that the output of cheap electric power by the Volga-Kama and Dnieper hydropower stations will almost double. More than 20 million hectares of arid land east of the Volga and in the South will be guaranteed against weather hazards, and it will be possible to reclaim more than 4 million hectares of marshland in the Polesye area and the Baltic republics.

Much freight from the north-western and other regions of the country, and freight from the Baltic Sea will then be shipped to the Mediterranean via the Black Sea ports, and not via Gibraltar, and from the southern regions along the Dnieper, via the Pripet and the Niemen, to the Baltic Sea. The route to the eastern section of the Mediterranean will be reduced by about one half.

The Party Programme envisages a formidable development of machine-building. That is the only way to effect the plan of *comprehensive mechanisation and automation*. We must arrange for the mass production of many types of highly efficient and economical machines, instruments and appliances, of various automatic and radio-electronic devices. We must develop perfected systems of machines for industry, agriculture and building. In the 20 years we shall build 2,800 new engineering and metal-working plants, chiefly in the eastern regions of the country, and reconstruct 1,900 old ones. This will enable us to raise the aggregate output of the machine-building and metal-working industry 10- to 11-fold, including a more than 60-fold rise in the output of automatic and semi-automatic lines.

The *chemical industry* assumes exceptional importance. In the 20 years its output is to rise about 17-fold, coupled with a broad enlargement of the range of products. Polymer chemistry is to advance substantially. The output of synthetic tars and plastics is to increase about 60-fold. The output of artificial and synthetic fibre, of special importance to the production of consumer goods, will climb about 15-fold. The production of mineral fertilisers is to be raised 9- to 10-fold.

Considerable attention is focussed in the general perspective on such important branches of heavy industry as the *fuel and metallurgical industries*. Production of all types of fuel will increase about 4-fold. In the 20 years, gas extraction is to be raised 14- to 15-fold, and coal extraction from 513 million tons in 1960 to 1,200 million tons in 1980. In 1980 oil extraction is to be 690-710 million tons. I might point out for the sake of comparison that in 1960 the U.S.S.R. extracted 148 million tons of oil, while the United States extracted 348 million tons.

The iron and steel industry is to have an annual output capacity of some 250 million tons of steel. In 1960 the Soviet Union produced 65 million tons of steel, and the United States 90 million. In as little as nine years Soviet steel production will exceed the present U.S. output by about 55 million tons. Economists estimate that we can raise steel production to a still higher level. But for the time being we have adopted the target of about 250 million tons. The rapid development of substitutes for ferrous metals, improvements in the quality of metals, added economy of metals, and achievements in the designing and manufacturing of machines, will possibly enable us to get by with a smaller amount of steel. In that case the plans for the development of metallurgy will be accordingly amended.

Owing to the demands of such rapidly-growing branches as electric power engineering, chemistry, electronics, instrument-making, atomic and space engineering and high-speed transport, non-ferrous metals will claim a bigger share in the overall metal balance. The output of alloying non-ferrous metals, rare metals and semi-conductor materials will have to be increased. The use of aluminium will expand to an especially marked degree.

The building materials industry should be developed at a high rate. Cement output in 1980 will amount to about 235 million tons, marking an increase of more than 400 per cent in 20 years.

In the coming 20 years the output of all the consumer goods industries is to increase approximately 5-fold. By 1980 the output of textiles, for example, is to rise more than 3-fold, bringing the annual figure up to 20-22 thousand million square metres. The annual output of leather boots and shoes is to amount to something like 1,000 million pairs. The output of cultural and household goods, the demand for which is rising rapidly, will increase 10-fold. This calls for a more expeditious and efficient utilisation of capital investments in the light and food industry, and for hundreds of new factories. The concern shown for consumer and household goods, for domestic appliances, for all the things that make the life of Soviet people easier and more attractive, should not be less than, say, the concern shown for metallurgical equipment.

Comrades, we must take good heed of the fact that productivity of labour is decisive in the achievement of a communist level of production. Rising productivity of social labour is the yardstick of our progress and the most important source of improvement of the living standard. Every other approach to the matter is idle speculation.

We are faced with the formidable task of increasing production, of creating abundance. How to do it if the numerical growth of our labour resources has a limit—in 20 years it will amount to about 40 per cent, with a substantial portion of it going to the non-productive sphere, chiefly education and public health—and considering reductions of the working day. There is only one answer to this question: the productivity of labour has to be raised accordingly. Our planning bodies estimate that over nine-tenths of the increase in the national income in 1961-80 is to be derived from the rise in labour productivity. In the next ten years the labour productivity in Soviet industry will rise approximately two-fold, and in 20 years 4- to 4.2-fold. In view of reductions in the working day, the growth of output per working hour will be still higher.

In the coming 20 years the distribution of the productive forces is to be further improved. This will enable us to economise social labour to the maximum, to achieve high rates of growth of production and to bring new colossal natural wealth into the service of society.

In the sphere of *distribution of the productive forces* it is proposed:

to build up powerful fuel and power-producing centres in Siberia, using surface deposits of cheap coal and the vast hydropower resources of the Angara and Yenisei;

to turn Central Asia into a key power-producing area, based on its immense resources of gas and hydropower;

to build up new powerful metallurgical centres, so that by 1980 the country should have five all-Union metallurgical bases—in the Urals, the Ukraine, in some regions of Siberia and the Far East, in Kazakhstan and in the central regions of the European part of the U.S.S.R.;

to establish large centres of the chemical industry in areas rich in cheap natural and oil-well gases, and of the oil-refining industry, primarily in the Urals, in the Volga area, the Ukraine, the Northern Caucasus, Siberia and Central Asia;

to build in regions east of the Urals powerful machine-building industries to meet the bulk of the needs of these areas in machines and equipment;

to carry out large-scale works, transferring large masses of water from the northern regions of the European part of the U.S.S.R. to the Volga basin; to supply water to Central Kazakhstan, Tselinny Territory, the Donets Basin and the Urals; to build water-regulating reservoirs in Central Asia, on the Volga, the Dnieper, the Bug and the Dniester; and to develop on an extensive scale irrigated and meliorated agriculture.

Such are the general prospects for the development of our industry. They are truly grand prospects. But we know perfectly well that the plan of today will become reality tomorrow. The determination of our Party and the people, a people of giant strength, is an earnest thereof! (*Stormy, prolonged applause.*)

2. The Development of Agriculture and Social Relations in the Countryside

Comrades, the draft Programme of our Party furnishes a thorough analysis of the social, economic and political changes that have taken place in the countryside as a result of the victory of the collective-farm system and the consolidation of the socialist system of agriculture. The establishment in the U.S.S.R. of a socialist system of agriculture is a historic victory for our Party, for the Soviet people as a whole.

When the working class accomplished the Revolution under the leadership of Lenin's Party, our enemies took solace in the hope that the Bolsheviks would not succeed in solving the peasant problem, that the peasant would never agree to give up his strip of land and that it would be impossible to turn the peasant-proprietor into a peasant-collectivist.

But the hopes of our enemies foundered. Lenin worked out his brilliant co-operative plan. Guided by it, the Party rallied millions upon millions of peasants to a new life. Not only did the deep socialist furrow erase the boundaries between the individual land-holdings; it also refashioned the private-owner mentality of the peasant. Today we are witnessing the triumph of Lenin's ideas in the reorganisation of agriculture, and in the millions of peasants joining communist construction. *Our Party can take legitimate pride in the fact that it has brought up a new type of peasant, one who marches in step with the heroic working class, and is an active builder of the new life. (Prolonged applause.)*

Along with industry and its striking force, heavy industry, Soviet agriculture constitutes a powerful socialist economy that knows no crises or upheavals.

We have fulfilled the first part of Lenin's co-operative plan by having guided the peasantry along the kolkhoz path, developed a far-flung network of state farms, and consolidated the collective and state farms. We shall now have to take a new decisive step forward, ensure an advancement of all the collective and state farms, and raise their production to a level worthy of communism.

At the present stage of communist construction, the C.P.S.U. considers the following to be *the chief tasks in the sphere of agriculture*:

to achieve an abundance of high-quality products for the people and of raw materials for industry;

to ensure a gradual transition of the Soviet countryside to communist social relations and to eliminate, in the main, the distinctions between town and country on the basis of a powerful expansion of the productive forces in agriculture.

Let me go into the basic problems of agricultural development, posed by life and the practice of communist construction, and constituting most important theses in the draft Party Programme.

The Communist Party has proclaimed a grand and noble goal—the full satisfaction of the growing material and cultural requirements of man. It will take an unprecedentedly high level of material production to attain that goal. That is why the draft Party Programme presents to the people an imposing plan of agricultural development. As we discuss the Programme we speak in specific terms both about our creative effort of today and about the future of socialist economy. That was how Lenin taught us to approach the tasks of communist construction. In the spring of 1920, Lenin wrote in a letter to Party organisations concerning preparations for the Ninth Party Congress, "We must go forward, we must look ahead, we must bring to the Congress the *practical experience* of economic development, weighed and carefully *summed up* jointly, by the common effort of all the Party members."*

Such practical experience of economic development has been put into our economic plans, into the agricultural targets. The draft Programme envisages that in twenty years the aggregate agricultural output will rise about 3.5-fold, the aggregate output of grain more than 2-fold, of meat nearly 4-fold and of milk nearly 3-fold.

What products, and how much of them must we produce to satisfy the requirements of the people in full, given the prospective development of Soviet society? On the instruc-

---

* V. I. Lenin, *Collected Works*, 4th Russ. ed., Vol. 30, p. 379.

tions of the Central Committee of the Party, the State Economic Council has submitted estimates of the volume of production our country must attain in the coming 20 years. Let me cite these estimates.

Production of Agricultural Produce in 1960-80

	1960	1970	1980
Grain (000 million poods)	8.2	14	18-19
Meat (000,000 tons, dead weight) . .	8.7	25	30-32
Milk (000,000 tons)	61.7	135	170-180
Eggs (000 million)	27.4	68	110-116
Wool (000 tons)	357	800	1,045-1,155
Raw cotton (000,000 tons)	4.3	8	10-11
Sugar beet (at refineries, 000,000 tons) .	57.7	86	98-108
Oil-bearing seeds (000,000 tons) . . .	4.3	8	9-10
Potatoes (000,000 tons) . . . ·	84.4	140	156
Vegetables and melons (000,000 tons)	19.2	47	55
Fruit and berries (000,000 tons) . . .	4.9	28	51

As you see, the Party has big plans. Such a vast output of agricultural produce may appear too ambitious to some people. The figures are indeed staggering. To be sure, for many decades, right up to 1954, the aggregate grain harvest in our country was about 5,000 million poods. It is only in the last few years that we began to harvest 8,000-8,500 million poods of grain by virtue of the virgin land development and the introduction of maize. For a long time, the state procured about 2,000 million poods of grain, and it is only in the last few years that the procurements were raised to 3,000-3,500 million poods. By 1980 grain production is to be raised to 18,000-19,000 million, and state purchases to 7,000 million poods.

In making our great plans, we firmly believe that they will be successfully fulfilled. Our confidence stems from realistic estimates, the incalculable potentialities contained in the socialist system of economy, and from the devoted labour of the Soviet people and its good organisation.

Let us look into the prospective growth of grain production in the major republics—the Russian Federation, and the Ukrainian and Kazakh republics. As for the Byelorussians, we are going to have a talk with them in Byelorussia. We shall say a few things in each other's ear—there are lots of things to be said. (*Laughter. Applause.*)

What contribution is to be made by the working people of the *Russian Federation* to the tasks set in the draft Party Programme? In 1960 the collective and state farms of the R.S.F.S.R. produced 4,800 million poods of grain, and sold the state 1,800 million poods. By 1980 they are to raise production to 12,000 million poods, and grain sales to the state to 4,000-5,000 million poods.

The bourgeois press will perhaps comment on this, saying that in speaking of plans for agricultural production Khrushchov let his imagination run away with him. Let those gentlemen comment if they wish, but let them not forget that this has been said at a Party Congress, on instructions from the Central Committee. This Congress will address a call to Party and people, and the people can move mountains. (*Stormy, prolonged applause.*)

It follows that *the Russian Federation is to increase the production and procurements of grain 150 per cent.* It stands to reason that the task is impracticable with the present crop structure, with millions of hectares sown to oats and other unproductive crops and with vast areas in the humid zone idle under so-called clean fallow.

I would say in jest that if certain officials persist in taking up land with oats, we will feed them on oatmeal. (*Laughter, applause.*) And it won't be the oatmeal that goes into making porridge for children but the coarser stuff, the kind of which Red Army men used to say during the Civil War: "Dash it, you can never tell whether it's food or fodder rations you're getting." (*Laughter. Prolonged applause.*)

But if we act upon the experience of the foremost farms and research institutions and revise the crop structure, if we replace the less productive crops more boldly and resolutely and make the most of the available opportunities of raising the yielding capacity, the projected grain output will definitely be achieved, and earlier than 1980.

Through the use of what reserves do we expect to carry out the task? A certain amount of grain will be obtained by cultivating lands that lie idle at present. But it is by substituting more productive for less productive crops and by increasing the yield of all crops that we will achieve most of the increase in grain output.

The Bureau of the Central Committee of the Party for the Russian Federation and the Council of Ministers of the Russian Federation have, jointly with scientists and specialists, worked out a new crop structure, which offers great prospects of raising grain production. What is new about this structure? The areas under unprofitable and unproductive crops are to be sharply reduced, those under oats by 6,000,000 hectares, and under fodder grass by 9,000,000 hectares. The clean fallow in the humid zone is to be abolished on an area of 9,000,000 hectares.

All in all, 24,000,000 hectares are to be released for more valuable crops. This land will be used for increasing the areas under maize for dry grain, peas, fodder beans and other valuable crops.

The collective and state farms plan to expand *areas under maize* for dry grain from 2.4 million to 7 million hectares. In terms of a harvest of 40 centners of maize per hectare, this will yield *1,700 million poods of grain.*

The area under *leguminous crops* in the republic will expand from 2.6 million to 19 million hectares, including 16.5 million hectares under peas and fodder beans. In terms of a harvest of about 20 centners per hectare, this will yield *2,300 million poods of grain.*

The *area under wheat* and other cereals will amount to 68 million hectares. In terms of a harvest of 20 centners per hectare, the total yield of these crops will exceed *8,000 million poods.*

The introduction of maize (for grain), peas and beans, and the increase in the yield of all crops will thus enable the collective and state farms of the R.S.F.S.R. to produce more than 12,000 million poods of grain a year and to sell the state 4,000-5,000 million poods. To present the feasibility of growing so much marketable grain more visually, I want to draw your attention to the following figures. In 1961 the Russian Federation, according to plan, is to sell the state 2,100-2,200 million poods of grain. If we sow leguminous crops in place of the 9 million hectares of unproductive fodder grass and on the 9 million hectares of the above-mentioned clean fallow, and harvest 20 centners per hectare, this alone will yield 2,200 million poods of grain. In effect, this will be marketable grain, since the collective and state farms get practically nothing from the above-mentioned areas at the present time. It follows that another 2,200 million poods will be added to the present grain sales figure stipulated in the plan, and the state purchases will add up to more than 4,000 million poods of grain. Thus, selling the state 4,000-5,000 million poods of grain is, after all, not too high a hurdle for the collective and state farms of the Russian Federation to take. Let us applaud them, comrades. (*Applause.*)

We are confident that when a decision has been taken, the working people of the Russian Federation will rally their forces and fulfil the task. (*Stormy applause.*)

The yielding capacity of wheat and other grain crops, and of leguminous crops is estimated for the R.S.F.S.R. at 20 centners per hectare. An average yield of 20 centners per hectare in 20 years, comrades. Surely we can cope with a more difficult assignment than that, surely that is not the limit. Far from it!

It will not be long before the Soviet Union takes in the world grain market a place that will show the imperialist gentlemen how our agriculture can grow. (*Stormy applause.*)

An estimate like that for a term of 20 years is even moderate. Many collective and state farms in our country are now already harvesting 25 to 30, and even 40, centners of wheat and other cereals per hectare. They get this yield at the present level of organisation of production, of agricultural science and technology. But science will advance from year to year, providing practice with great new opportunities. Better grades and hybrids of agricultural plants will appear, and the output of organic and mineral fertilisers, herbicides and other chemicals will rise steeply. The collective and state farms will get improved agricultural machinery. All this will make it possible not only to attain, but also to surpass, the projected level of grain production and state purchases.

Let us take the estimates submitted by the Central Committee of the Ukrainian Communist Party and Council of Ministers. Prior to the extensive introduction of maize, the *Ukraine*'s grain potential amounted to something like 1,300-1,500 million poods, and its procurements to 400-500 million poods.

Now that such highly productive crops as maize, peas and fodder beans are being extensively cultivated, *the working people of the Ukraine are quite sure that they will raise grain production to 3,800 million and state purchases to 1,500 million poods.*

How will the crop pattern change on the Ukrainian collective and state farms? An area of 6.5 million hectares will be sown to winter wheat, over five million hectares, or 28 per cent of the grain acreage, to maize, and about four million hectares, or 21 per cent of the grain acreage, to leguminous crops. Maize and leguminous crops, being the most productive, will comprise nearly half the grain acreage in the Ukraine, and their share in the aggregate grain output will be 60 per cent.

It is planned to obtain the following yields (in centners per hectare):

```
Grain crops . . . . . . . . . . . . . 35
                  including:
Winter wheat . . . . . . . . . . . . 30
Maize  . . . . . . . . . . . . . . . 50
Peas . . . . . . . . . . . . . . . . 30
Fodder beans . . . . . . . . . . . . 32
```

This year's practice shows that these figures are realistic, for many collective and state farms grew 70 to 80 centners of maize and 30 to 40 centners of wheat and peas per hectare.

The Party assigns *Kazakhstan* a big role in raising the grain output. The republic has its distinctive features. Save for its southern regions, maize is grown there chiefly for silage. The increase in grain output will therefore have to be effected through higher yields, extensive cultivation of leguminous crops and a further development of new land. In the future, when scientists will have produced strains of maize with a shorter period of vegetation, maize will probably be grown for grain in the virgin-land development area as well.

I must say that as I was preparing this report I received a letter from an Azerbaijan plant-breeder. He wrote that he had succeeded in evolving a maize variety whose period of vegetation lasts about 60 days. If that is so, it will offer immense opportunities of expanding the area under maize and pushing maize to the north, to grow it there for grain.

Mr. Rusk told me in Vienna that there is such a variety of maize in America. But his statement has not been borne out, though he promised to prove it to be true. Americans who are familiar with maize, such as Mr. Garst, say there is no such maize in the United States. But if there is none in that country, it would be a good idea to develop such a variety in the Soviet Union. (*Prolonged applause.*)

But we should realise that this is a very difficult problem. We are not making progress in agriculture conditional on the solution of this problem. Even if we have no such maize, we shall, with the varieties we do have, fulfil and, indeed, exceed our plans. (*Applause.*)

What crop structure is taking shape in the virgin-land development area of Kazakhstan? All in all, including land to be newly developed, about 32 million hectares in the republic are to be sown to wheat, other grain crops, leguminous crops and maize for silage. Of this acreage 50-55 per cent are to be sown to wheat and other grain crops, 30-35 per cent to peas and fodder beans, and 10 per cent to fodder maize and sugar beet. Those are tentative estimates for just the chief crops. The economy will, naturally, need a wider range of crops; we'll need potatoes, vegetables and oil-bearing plants. But, all the same, chief emphasis in the virgin-land development area will be on wheat, peas, fodder beans, maize for grain and silage, and on sugar beet for fodder.

Given this crop pattern, the grain balance will shape out as follows:

An area of 17.6 million hectares will go to wheat and other grain crops. Given a yield of 20 centners per hectare, this will amount to 2,150 million poods of grain. Of this amount the state farms and kolkhozes will be able to sell about 1,500 million poods to the state.

Peas and fodder beans will occupy an area of 11 million hectares. With an expected yield of 20 centners per hectare, the aggregate output will amount to *1,350 million poods*. Of this amount about 600 million poods can be sold to the state.

It is possible, therefore, to raise the aggregate grain harvest in Kazakhstan to 3,500 million poods, and to sell more than 2,000 million poods to the state.

Kazakhstan, like the other republics, has tremendous potentialities for raising per-hectare yields. When the Party set the task of developing the virgin lands, the expected yield was estimated at eight centners per hectare. As experience accumulated and farming techniques improved, the yields rose considerably at many farms. At present some state farms and kolkhozes in the newly-developed areas get 20 and more centners of grain, chiefly of wheat, per hectare on large areas.

The Mamlyutsky State Farm, of North-Kazakhstan Region, annually harvests 20-22 centners of grain per hectare. High yields are obtained on the Kustanaisky, Petropavlovsky, Kiyalinsky, Chandaksky and other state farms.

Farms that sow large areas to row and leguminous crops, which are a good predecessor to spring wheat, obtain especially good results. The Fyodorovsky State Farm, of Kustanai Region, this year obtained the following yield of spring wheat sown after maize: 26 centners per hectare on field No. 3, and 22 centners per hectare on field No. 7.

We have similar examples not only in Kazakhstan. Many of you know the Altai Agricultural Research Institute. It has been getting a high and stable grain yield for some years by extensively cultivating maize, leguminous and other row crops. In 1961 the Institute harvested 20 centners of grain per hectare on an area of 6,359 hectares, including 20.4 centners of wheat per hectare on an area of 5,140 hectares. And the new Barnaulka-32 wheat yielded 44 centners per hectare. The Strana Sovietov Collective Farm, of Altai Territory, has averaged 20.5 centners of grain per hectare for the last five years. The team headed by Alexander Bekker, who is a delegate to our Congress, harvested an average of 23 centners of grain per hectare.

The experience gained by collective and state farms suggests ways of developing agriculture on new lands. We cannot any longer restrict crop farming to spring wheat. Along with wheat, we must cultivate more maize, peas, fodder beans and fodder sugar beet, which are important for more efficient agriculture, bigger crop yields, for the rapid progress of livestock farming and the development of the state farms set up on the new land into highly productive farms.

Why does the Party attach so much importance to maize and leguminous crops in the solution of the grain and livestock problem? Many years of experience show that these crops have no equal in yielding capacity and other merits. It has already been noted in the Central Committee Report how much maize has done to raise grain production in the

Ukraine, Krasnodar Territory and other parts of the country.

It will probably be right to put leguminous crops on a par with maize in importance. Peas and beans are ancient crops, known to peasants for centuries. There is scarcely a peasant in the Russian Federation, the Ukraine, Byelorussia, or the Baltic Republics who did not grow good pea harvests. Unfortunately, the people who had for long headed the Ministry of Agriculture of the U.S.S.R., brought leguminous crops to ruin.

But there were enthusiasts who cultivated leguminous crops with loving care and showed all the collective and state farms the proper way to obtain bigger grain harvests.

Vasily Mikhailovich Kavun, chairman of the Stalin Collective Farm, of Vinnitsa Region, is a delegate to the Twenty-Second Party Congress. He has enlightened many people with regard to leguminous crops. His kolkhoz has been producing good pea harvests year after year. In 1960 he got 27 centners per hectare on an area of 520 hectares, and 31 centners per hectare on an area of 708 hectares in 1961. The collective farm devotes considerable attention to maize. Its maize yield per hectare on an area of 900 hectares was 60 centners. Peas constitute 21 per cent and maize 30 per cent of the grain acreage, which adds up to more than half of the total grain acreage. As a result, the average grain yield at the kolkhoz was 38 centners per hectare. (*Applause.*)

All in all, Vinnitsa Region produced 20.7 centners of peas per hectare on a total area of 180,000 hectares this year, and Cherkassy Region 21.5 centners of peas per hectare on an area of 89,000 hectares. (*Applause.*)

Good pea harvests are not confined to the Ukraine alone. The Petrovsky State Farm, of Lipetsk Region, headed by Comrade Volovchenko, a delegate to the Twenty-Second Party Congress, produced 36 centners of peas per hectare on an area of 110 hectares. Depending on the sowing method and the seeding rate, the yield amounted to (in centners per hectare):

wide-row with 45-cm inter-row spacing and 110 kilograms of
seed per hectare 22
ordinary row with 15-cm inter-row spacing and 270 kilograms
of seed per hectare 33
narrow-row with 7.5-cm inter-row spacing and 270 kilograms
of seed per hectare 42.2

This merits close attention. (*Applause.*) Before the war, the deceased Academician P. I. Lisitsyn told me that the Shatilov Station, where he worked, used the narrow-row method of sowing and obtained the highest yields. What we need is to give the foremost methods a thorough test and to appraise them on their merits, in order to fling the doors open to them in production.

There are many collective and state farms in the central regions of the Russian Federation, in Byelorussia, Latvia, Lithuania, Estonia, regions of Siberia and Kazakhstan, that obtain big harvests of peas on large areas.

We will probably not have the necessary amount of bean seeds for the next year or two, but more peas. Fodder beans could be replaced by peas, which are also a highly valuable grain crop.

Extensive cultivation of leguminous crops offers agriculture new big possibilities. Leguminous crops do three things simultaneously:

firstly, they yield good harvests and are an important factor for greater grain production, both for food and the needs of animal husbandry. They have a comparatively brief period of vegetation and resist the spring frosts— an extremely valuable property for Siberia and Kazakhstan. The early ripening of leguminous crops takes the strain off the harvesting; the fields can be cleared more quickly and prepared for the next crop.

Peas may be sown early. This is very important for the southern Ukraine, the Volga area and some other regions exposed to hot winds. Peas will ripen earlier there and thus escape the hot winds. Early sowing and their short vegetation period make peas a good first crop for the Krasnodar and Stavropol territories, and in the Kabardinian-Balkar, North-Ossetian and Checheno-Ingush republics in growing two crops a year. It may be recalled that maize is sown at a soil temperature of 10-12 degrees. Peas may be sown much earlier—approximately two or three weeks earlier. They have a vegetation period of 70 to 80 days. If sown late in March or early April, they will ripen by mid-June. After harvesting the peas, which are a good predecessor, maize may be sown on the same fields in the last ten days of June. Four months are left for the latter crop. That is ample time for grain maize to ripen. Thus, peas offer good opportunities of obtaining two harvests a year in the southern regions of the country;

secondly, leguminous crops have a large protein content and will help to radically solve the problem of supplying animal husbandry with protein feeds;

thirdly, leguminous crops raise land fertility. They are a kind of factory of nitrogen, which they extract from the atmosphere. Other farm crops do not take nitrogen from the air but use up soil nitrogen to grow. Let me quote a few figures supplied by specialists.

Given a yield of 20 centners per hectare, peas extract 105 kg of nitrogen from the atmosphere, leaving 47 kg of nitrogen in the soil after harvesting. In the case of a 30-centner yield they extract 160 kg of nitrogen from the atmosphere and leave 70 kg in the soil.

Given a yield of 20 centners, fodder beans extract 142 kg of nitrogen from the atmosphere and leave 63 kg per hectare in the soil. With a 30-centner yield, they absorb 213 kg of nitrogen from the atmosphere and leave 95 kg in the soil.

In the future, approximately 30 million hectares, and perhaps more, will be sown to leguminous crops in our country. As a result, immense quantities of nitrogen, a highly valuable and, in effect, cost-free fertiliser, will accumulate in the soil. To produce this fertiliser the chemical industry would have had to build many big factories and invest hundreds of millions of rubles.

Some planning officials will probably think:

"How nice! The crops will procure their own fertiliser from the atmosphere, and we can therefore build fewer chemical plants."

No, comrades, one of today's most urgent tasks is to develop the chemical industry, raise the output of mineral fertilisers, including nitrogen fertilisers, as well as herbicides and other chemicals to control weeds and pests. It is no exaggeration to say that we must put the production of fertilisers on an equal footing with mechanisation of agriculture, for both are decisive factors in promoting a greater output of agricultural produce. (*Applause.*)

The Party plans to raise the output of mineral fertilisers to 125-135 million tons against the 14 million tons produced last year. We must see to it that the supply of fertilisers for agriculture is raised to the utmost in the current seven-year period.

An extensive programme for the production of mineral fertilisers, a sharp increase of the acreage of leguminous crops, of the density of the cattle population and accumulation of manure will tend to greatly improve yields.

In each zone there are collective and state farms that have shown in each specific case the best methods to rapidly increase yields. I cannot name these farms for every zone, so let me cite but one example.

Many of you know the collective farm in the village of Kalinovka, of Kursk Region, of which I have spoken on a number of occasions. The chairman of that farm, V. V. Grachov, is a delegate to the Twenty-Second Party Congress. The kolkhoz has 6,000 hectares of arable. In 1961 it obtained the following harvest (in centners per hectare):

Winter wheat	32.6
Rye	24.3
Barley	21.6

Millet 20
Peas, with 320 kg of seed per hectare 28
Fodder beans, wide-row sowing 25.6
Sugar beet 350
Maize on cob, for silage 700
Clover (one hay crop) 39

How was it possible to obtain such yields on heavy loam soil? It was possible by virtue of the large number of cattle and, hence, of manure. Only a few years ago Kalinovka (and the collective farms that amalgamated with it) had 91 cows. Today it has 1,050. The grain harvest at the time was 8-10 centners, while today it is 25-30 centners per hectare.

Why has its cattle population grown? Because the collective farmers began cultivating maize, ploughed up the clean fallow, and sowed it to valuable crops. This meant more fodder, more cattle, more manure, and better crops.

There are similar farms in other parts of the country too. They have paved the way for good harvests, and the task now is to raise all collective and state farms to their level. But raising them does not mean speechifying; it means actually pulling up lagging farms to the level of the advanced ones, or "pulling out" of the saddle those who are in charge of collective and state farms but do not know their job and hamper progress. (*Prolonged applause.*)

Greater production of grain will promote a rapid development of animal husbandry. Given an ample supply of grain, silage and other feeds, we can increase the livestock population in a short time and ensure the output of meat, milk and other products required to fully satisfy the requirements of the people.

In working out the agricultural development plan, our Party attaches special importance to irrigation. Irrigation is an integral part of Lenin's electrification plan. Lenin regarded the building of power stations and the development of irrigation as an indivisible whole. Already in the early years of Soviet power, Lenin dreamt of irrigating the fields of Transcaucasia and Central Asia, and of bringing water to the arid Volga steppes.

Now that we have a powerful industry the time has come to draw up and implement an extensive irrigation plan in order to create a stable groundwork to guarantee agricultural production in all circumstances.

On the instructions of the Central Committee of the Party, the State Economic Council is drawing up a long-term plan of irrigation development. There are today nine million hectares of irrigated land in the country. The task is to raise that figure to about 28 million hectares.

It is proposed:

to develop a new large cotton-growing region in the basin of the Syr-Darya River, where, according to preliminary estimates, 800-850 thousand hectares of the Hungry Steppe in Uzbekistan, Kazakhstan and the Tajik Republic can be irrigated;

to build a hydropower station on the Nurek to irrigate up to 1,200,000 hectares of land in the Uzbek and Tajik Republics for cotton, rice and other crops;

to irrigate and develop 600 thousand hectares of land in Turkmenia by means of the Kara-Kum Canal, in order to advance cotton growing;

to develop new rice-growing regions in the lower reaches of the Amu-Darya and Syr-Darya rivers, with irrigated land amounting to about 900 thousand hectares;

to make comprehensive use of the land and water resources of the Volga-Akhtuba flood-plain and the Volga delta in order to develop irrigated farming, to produce vegetables, rice and maize, and to improve conditions for fish and waterfowl breeding;

to irrigate land in the Volga area with the energy of the Lenin Hydropower Station and Twenty-Second Congress Hydropower Station on the Volga;

to use the water resources of the Don, Kuban and other rivers in the south of the European part of the Russian Federation in order to irrigate over one million hectares of land and expand rice, grapes, vegetables and industrial crops;

to irrigate an area of 4.5 million hectares in the Crimea and other regions in the south of the Ukrainian Republic and in Moldavia with the waters of the Dnieper, Bug, Dniester and Danube, in order to expand production of rice, maize, sugar beet, grapes, fruit and vegetables, and to develop animal husbandry;

to carry out major irrigation schemes in Transcaucasia.

Once the irrigation programme is completed, our country will be able to produce additional millions of tons of cotton, maize, rice and sugar beet, and more animal products.

Our Party will achieve the deliverance of man from the vagaries of the elements, and give man mastery over nature. (*Prolonged applause.*)

Comrades, when I analysed the trends of development to be followed by our industry, I said that raising the productivity of labour was the paramount problem of communist construction. This applies equally to agriculture.

In the draft of its Programme the Communist Party envisages a rise of not less than 150 per cent in the labour productivity of agriculture for the first ten years, and a 5- to 6-fold increase for the twenty years. That is a difficult task. But the ways of solving it have been found. We now have in all branches of agriculture models of labour worthy of communist society.

Take the productivity of labour attained by the foremost farmers in the principal branches of agriculture.

Grain growing. The average outlay per centner of grain for the country's state farms is 2.1 hours at 4 rubles 10 kopeks.

The Gigant State Farm, of Rostov Region, in the meantime, takes 38 minutes, or about one-third, at a cost of 1 ruble 53 kopeks to produce 1 centner of grain.

Sugar-beet production. The country's average outlay per centner of sugar beet grown on state farms is 3.2 hours at a cost of 1 ruble 80 kopeks, while the team of V. A. Svetlichny, of Krasnodar Territory, where cultivation of sugar beet is mechanised, expends 17 minutes, or one-eleventh, at a cost of 30 kopeks, or one-sixth of the country's average outlay.

Cotton growing. An average of 52 hours at a cost of 25 rubles 30 kopeks is expended by the state farms of Uzbekistan to produce a centner of cotton, while Comrade Kuchiev's comprehensively mechanised team of the Malek State Farm, of Tashkent Region, takes 10 hours at a cost of 7 rubles 30 kopeks.

Livestock products. The average yield of milk for state farms with manual labour is 30-40 tons a year per milkmaid tending 10-12 cows. Zinaida Zabotina, milkmaid at the Shuisky State Farm, of Ivanovo Region, has different results. She works on a mechanised farm equipped with herringbone-type installations. In 1960 Comrade Zabotina tended 150 cows and milked 307 tons. In 1961 she was joined by her husband, Dmitry Zabotin, who is a mechanic. The two of them tend 300 cows and have undertaken a yield of 650 tons of milk, of which they have already turned in 510 tons. They spend 4.8 man/hours per centner of milk, whereas 14 hours are expended on an average by the state farms in the country.

What are the conclusions to be drawn from these examples? Today already the foremost state and collective farms exceed the productivity of labour registered at most of the state and collective farms 5-6 and more times over. It should be noted that it did not take them decades to make this advance in labour productivity, but no more than the last few years. It is our task so to organise production as to have the entire mass of collective and state farms attain that productivity of labour in the near future.

This is a difficult task. It will call for considerable effort on the part of the Party and the people, and a substantial material outlay by the state. But that is not all. We must stop letting things drift, for that is still holding up the development of agriculture in many respects. There is still not enough active intervention and competent in-fluence on agricultural production on the part of some Party organisations. The past is still making itself felt in this respect—when the collective farms used not the manpower required, but all the manpower they happened to have.

The situation is different now. Agriculture is becoming more and more mechanised, and the demands imposed on it are rising. The old approach and outmoded notions about agriculture have got to go. The main thing is to ensure the maximum output with the minimum outlay of labour.

It is one of the most important tasks, therefore, to work for the further mechanisation and electrification of agri-culture in every sector, and for a better utilisation of ma-chinery. And that depends, almost entirely, on the experi-ence and organising ability of our cadres, on the people into whose care the machinery has been entrusted. Labour productivity on collective and state farms must not be raised by over-exerting muscular power, but by supplying agriculture with more of the latest machines. All collective and state farms should, in the shortest possible time, be supplied sets of machines in keeping with the advanced technology of agricultural production. Special emphasis should be laid on developing machines for more progressive methods of grain harvesting, fully mechanising the culti-vation of maize, cotton, flax, sugar beet and potatoes, and for mechanising jobs in animal husbandry.

We must introduce more efficient machines, especially tractors, combines and transport facilities. We can, and must, for example, organise production of new powerful high-speed 200-220 h. p. tractors, complete with imple-ments, for the country's steppe lands. The C.C. C.P.S.U. and the Council of Ministers of the U.S.S.R. have already passed appropriate decisions. They will be 3 to 4 times more efficient than the DT-54 tractors now in use, and will yield tremendous economic advantages. Let me cite the estimates submitted by specialists to show the advantages of powerful tractors in ploughing one million hectares of arable:

	DT-54	200-220h. p. tractor
Average daily performance	7.6 hectares	21.2 hectares
Tractors required for autumn plough- ing (20 days, 2 shifts daily) . .	6,600	2,400
Tractor operators required	13,200	4,800

These estimates are for one million hectares. But there are about 80 million hectares of ploughland in the country where we could use powerful tractors. The economic advantages of such tractors would therefore increase many times over.

We must take serious measures to develop further the production of tractors and farm machinery. We must increase the capacity of the tractor works and other plants producing agricultural machines and equip them with up-to-date plant. The designing offices should be staffed with experienced personnel able to develop new machines.

Comrades, the draft Party Programme regards the development of the productive forces in the countryside and the formation of communist social relations as being indivisibly connected. This is only natural, because communist social relations evolve in the process of labour, in the process of developing production, in the country-wide struggle for communist construction.

What will be typical of our countryside in its advance towards communism? In technical equipment and organisation of production socialist agriculture will approach the level of industry. This means that there will be far-reaching qualitative changes in the nature of labour. In step with the rising cultural and technical level of collective farmers and state-farm workers and the equipment of all branches of agriculture with modern machinery, farm labour will develop into a variety of industrial labour.

In communist construction in the countryside, we must draw on the wealth of experience accumulated by our country in developing socialist agriculture. What does this experience show? Two types of socialist enterprises have emerged in Soviet agriculture—the state farms and the collective farms.

The state farms were founded on Lenin's initiative as state-operated socialist agricultural enterprises. Their purpose was to show the advantages of large-scale socialist farming over small-scale individual peasant farming, to serve as models for the peasants around them.

Our Party has successfully accomplished Lenin's plan of state-farm development. The state farms have become a big force. They have become highly productive enterprises widely employing modern machinery and the latest achievements of science. They have attained a higher productivity of labour, and are consequently producing cheaper agricultural products. In 1960 labour outlays per centner of grain (excluding maize) amounted to 2.1 hours at state farms and to 7.2 hours at collective farms. The respective outlays per centner of milk were 14.2 and 20.8 hours. The state farms expended 66 man/hours and the collective farms 118 man/hours per centner of gain in the weight of cattle, and 57 man/hours and 133 man/hours respectively per centner of gain in the weight of pigs.

As already noted in the Central Committee Report, the share of state farms in the output of agricultural products has increased very greatly in the last few years. The advantages of state farms came to the fore with new force in the virgin-land project, and in solving the problem of supplying big cities and industrial centres with milk, potatoes and vegetables.

It stands to reason that not all state farms are today models of good agricultural organisation. Much work has still to be done for every state farm to use the reserves and possibilities of large-scale mechanised farming better and more fully.

The other form of large-scale socialist agriculture are the kolkhozes. They are a form worked out by Lenin to effect the transition of millions of small-scale individual peasant farms to socialism. The kolkhozes have been a school of communism for the Soviet peasantry. They did much to overcome centuries-old private-owner habits and engaged the peasants in collective labour and in large-scale collective farming. The collective farms have gone a long way in their development. The present-day collective farms are a far cry from the original agricultural artels, where primitive equipment was used and the standard of labour organisation was low, and where the principle of distribution according to the number of mouths prevailed. The collective farm of today is a large-scale mechanised farm. In recent years, as a result of the measures taken by the Party, the collective farms have grown much stronger. Their collective assets have expanded, their output of agricultural produce has grown, and the living standard of collective farmers has risen.

Some comrades ask which trend—the collective-farm or state-farm trend—agriculture will follow in its further development? The Party considers that communist construction in the countryside will proceed through the development and improvement of the two forms of socialist production. One socialist form of farming should not be contraposed to the other. The collective, as well as the state farms, are large-scale socialist enterprises allowing for an effective use of the achievements of technology and science, and for a rapid expansion of social production. Given equal material resources, good organisation of production and competent management, both forms can produce good results.

If the productivity of labour in many collective farms is at present lower, and costs of production higher than at state farms, this is not due to the kolkhoz form having, as it were, exhausted itself and ceased to correspond to the development of the present productive forces. The reason for it lies elsewhere—above all in the organisation of production, in the management, and in the level of technical equipment. Wherever experienced personnel, good organisers and specialists are available, wherever the proper accent is laid on mechanising production and the principle of material incentives is properly applied, the state farms and the collective farms flourish alike. It is important to stress in this connection that the objective conditions for a rapid advancement of the kolkhoz economy are available literally everywhere.

The main thing is to help the collective farms to improve their organisation of production, to make the most of modern machinery and scientific progress, and thereby to attain a higher productivity of labour. It is important to reinforce the weaker collective farms with competent personnel—chairmen, brigade leaders and farm specialists. The task is to bring all collective farms up to the level of the foremost state farms.

The state shows enormous concern for strengthening and developing the collective farms. In turn, each collective farm should make it a sacred duty to fulfil the state plans strictly, to expand its production and other collective assets, and to ensure that collective farmers' incomes rise in step with the rising productivity of their labour.

The role of the state farms, those foremost socialist agricultural enterprises in the countryside, in the further development of agriculture and in providing an abundant supply of farm produce, will continue to increase. We must make the state farms into first-class factories of grain, cotton, meat, milk, wool, vegetables, fruit and tea. It is also important that the state farms become models not only of a better organisation of production, but also of living conditions, culture and communist education.

As production on the collective and state farms develops and social relations there advance, agriculture will ascend to a higher level that will make it possible to go over to communist forms of production and distribution. The principle of material incentives will play an important part in attaining this goal. We must continue to combine moral and material stimuli, to encourage those who produce more products for society, and to promote good discipline and communist consciousness by propagating the best models of labour.

Comrades, our Party has drafted a grand plan of agricultural development. All of us remember the difficult circumstances in which we built up socialist agriculture. Taking guidance from Lenin's behests, the Communist Party skilfully surmounted the difficulties and led the peasantry along the socialist path. Now we have emerged on the high road of communist construction. Wonderful prospects have opened before us. This does not mean, of course, that our advance will be all plain sailing, effortless and easy.

To build up an ample supply of agricultural produce, we shall have to climb quite a few steep gradients, and cope with many complicated problems. Enriched by its great historic experience, the Party will lead the peasantry boldly and confidently to communism. (*Prolonged applause.*)

3. Improvement of the People's Well-Being and Achievement of the Highest Living Standard

Comrades, the C.P.S.U. is advancing a great task—to achieve in the coming twenty years a living standard higher than that of any capitalist country and to create the necessary conditions for achieving an abundance of material and cultural values.

Within the first ten years already all sections of the Soviet people will be enjoying sufficiency, and will be well provided for. Communism will thereby demonstrate its decisive advantages over capitalism in a matter which directly concerns everybody without exception. *For the first time in history insufficiency will be fully and finally eliminated.* This will be an imposing achievement of the new society. No capitalist country can set itself this task.

There are two basic conditions that will enable the Soviet people to attain the highest living standard. Firstly, a growth of labour productivity, of all social production and of the national income that exceeds the possibilities of capitalism. Secondly, application of the growing productive forces and social wealth in the interests of the entire people. The Communist Programme of abundance, therefore, rests upon a solid foundation, whereas the numerous bourgeois publicity projects for "public welfare" are no more than new attempts to deceive the masses.

The Party considers that, while continuing to develop heavy industry and other branches of the national economy, we can and must, in the immediate future, achieve accelerated rates of growth in the living standard. The real income per head of the population will double in the next ten years, and increase more than 250 per cent in twenty years. This rise in the real incomes of the population will derive from the growth of the *national income* of the U.S.S.R. By 1980 the latter will amount to an annual 720-750 thousand million rubles, i.e., to approximately five times that of 1960.

What are the basic trends to be followed in the improvement of the people's living standard?

Within the next few years *all sections of the population will get good, high-quality food.* The following rise is envisaged in food consumption per head of the population in the 10 years: meat and meat products—2.5-fold, milk and milk products—2-fold, butter—1.5-fold, vegetable oil—2-fold, eggs—2.2-fold, fish and fish products—1.5-fold, sugar—1.5-fold, vegetables and melons—2.3-fold and fruit and berries—nearly 5-fold, while bread and potato consumption is to drop somewhat. This means that the share in the diet of the most nourishing and high-grade food products will rise. Public catering will be developed to the utmost. In the next 10 years it will expand more than 3-fold, and approximately 13-fold in 20 years. It will gradually take precedence over home cooking. Prices at catering establishments will be steadily reduced.

In the coming 10 years *all Soviet people will be able to acquire consumer goods in adequate quantities, and in the subsequent ten years the consumer demand will be met in full.* The plan envisages that in 20 years consumption per head of the population will increase approximately 3.5-fold for clothing and footwear, and 5.5-fold for cultural and household goods. The output of furniture is to be raised 6- to 8-fold. Up-to-date electric domestic machines and appliances will effect the electrification of the home.

State-operated and co-operative retail trade in town and country will increase (in comparable prices) 2.5-fold in 10 years and 5-fold in 20. The popular demand for public laundries and repair shops for clothing, footwear and domestic appliances will be met. We must develop all types of public services, so that all who wish could substitute them for household work.

The Communist Party and the Soviet state attach special importance to a complete solution of the housing problem. No social system has been able to solve that problem. Today, housing construction in our country has assumed an unprecedented scale. In the last five years alone, nearly 50 million people were given new housing accommodation. *In the course of the next 10 years we must put an end to the housing shortage. At the close of the second decade every family will have a separate comfortable flat.* This will involve an increase of the country's housing facilities by about 200 per cent in 20 years. Average annual housing construction will climb roughly from about 135 million sq. m in 1961-65 to 400 million sq. m in 1976-80, surely a truly colossal programme!

While preserving the big cities as industrial and cultural centres and, concurrently, checking their excessive growth, we should develop and build well-appointed small and medium towns. Our communities should conform increasingly to the conception of "green towns" or "garden towns". They will combine all the best features of a modern city— comfortable dwellings, thoroughfares, communal and public services, children's, cultural and sports institutions—with all the best features of a rural community—abundant greenery, ponds, and healthful air.

The draft Programme envisages further *reductions of the working day*, which will make for a rapid improvement of the people's cultural and technical level, and for adequate leisure. We have already effected a reduction to a 7-hour and, in a number of branches, to a 6-hour working day. Within the first ten years a 6-hour working day, or a 35-hour working week, will be established for the bulk of the working people, and still shorter working time (30 hours a week) for the rest. *The country building communism will have the world's shortest working day.* Rising labour productivity will enable us to effect further reductions of working hours.

At the same time, the length of paid vacations will be increased for industrial and office workers to three weeks, and subsequently to a month. Gradually, the system of paid vacations will also be extended to collective farmers.

Comrades, we shall proceed from the socialist principle of distribution according to labour to communist distribution according to needs. Besides an abundance of material and cultural values, this will depend on a no less important condition—the transformation of labour into a vital necessity for one and all. Until this condition is met, attempts to "introduce" communist distribution irrespective of a citizen's labour contribution would be outright levelling that would disrupt production. The Party is resolutely opposed to any such "line".

The Party considers that in the coming twenty years payment according to labour will remain the chief source of satisfaction of material and cultural requirements. The principle of payment according to labour is a powerful incentive for greater production. It stimulates the growth of the working people's cultural and technical level and contributes thereby to a gradual elimination of the essential distinctions between physical and mental labour. It is an important source of growth of the real incomes of the population and, as social wealth increases, makes it possible gradually to reduce the disparity between the higher and lower wage brackets. While developing and strengthening moral labour stimuli in every way, we must apply the principle of distribution according to labour consistently and to the fullest extent as an important lever in the building of communist society.

A task of historic significance will be fulfilled in the U.S.S.R. within the next ten years: *the bracket of low-paid industrial and office workers will disappear*. The process of narrowing the gaps between the wage brackets has nothing whatsoever in common with wage-levelling, because it is indivisibly connected with the replacement of unskilled labour by skilled labour. The wages of skilled workers must keep pace with the rising productivity of labour. On collective farms, where labour productivity will rise more rapidly, the average incomes in the coming twenty years will climb at a faster rate than those of industrial workers. Pay increases are envisaged for such sections of the Soviet intelligentsia as engineers, technicians, agronomists, medical personnel, teachers and cultural workers.

Yet another avenue of raising the living standard—*extension of the public consumption funds*—will also assume ever-increasing importance. Distribution among members of society through these funds proceeds regardless of the quantity and quality of their labour, that is, free of charge. It is envisaged in the draft Programme that these funds will rise more rapidly than wages, inasmuch as they lead directly to communist distribution. An increase is planned of the annual public consumption funds by over 900 per cent, from 24,500 million rubles in 1960 to 255-265 thousand million rubles in 1980. At the close of the twenty years they will comprise about half of the total income of the population.

It is important that the growth of public funds be properly combined with the principles of material incentives and distribution according to labour. The draft Programme sets out the following main trends in the development of public consumption funds for the coming twenty years: gradual transition to maintenance at public expense of children and all the incapacitated, free education and medical treatment of the population, rent-free housing and free communal and transport facilities. Maintenance at public expense of children and the incapacitated is a lofty and humane undertaking consistent with the lofty ideals of the new system. And we are proud, comrades, that we shall soon be equal to it. (*Prolonged applause.*)

The time is not distant when we shall be able to provide free hot meals at all schools and supply school children with free textbooks and school uniforms. This is to be followed by the abolition of maintenance fees at nurseries and kindergartens, and at day-care schools. At present the greater part of children's maintenance expenses is paid by the working people, whereas at the close of the coming twenty years about 75 to 80 per cent of the cost of the maintenance and education of children will be covered by society. State allocations for the maintenance of children and adolescents will increase more than 10-fold in 1961-80.

The fact that society is increasingly undertaking the maintenance and education of children, as well as the maintenance of public services, has an immense social impact, since it will serve to eliminate the last remnants of women's inequality in daily life. These measures also tend to do away with the inequality that falls to the lot of large families.

Full maintenance of all persons non-able-bodied at public expense will be provided at the same time. The pensions will gradually rise. The network of boarding-houses for old people and invalids will be extended to a point where it will meet the demand. In the second decade we shall be able gradually to adopt a single system of pensions for all the non-able-bodied.

All these measures will create conditions for a further

improvement of the health of Soviet people and a rise in life expectancy. An extension of the network of public health institutions will play a big part in this. The urban and rural population's requirements of all forms of qualified medical services will be met in full. Special emphasis will be laid on measures to prevent diseases. It is planned to increase considerably the number of hospitals, sanatoria, holiday homes and boarding-houses. In addition to free medical treatment, instituted in our country a long time ago, there will be free accommodation of patients at sanatoria and free dispensation of medicines.

Rent-free modern housing and free basic communal services for every family will be a wonderful achievement of communist construction. In the second decade we shall also launch another major social development—free public catering (meals) at enterprises and offices, and for collective farmers at work.

The Soviet people already enjoy such social advantages as are out of the reach of the working people in the capitalist countries. They know nothing of exploitation, unemployment, crises, or racial and other pay discriminations. They are confident of the future. (*Applause.*) However, at present the Soviet Union is still behind the United States in average per capita consumption and the general level of real incomes per head of the population. Two things should be borne in mind in this respect: the level at which we began, and the price that, unlike the United States, we have had to pay for the war. In 1980 the real per capita incomes in the U.S.S.R. will exceed the present level of incomes of the working people in the U.S.A. by about 75 per cent. But we should also bear in mind that hidden behind the average per capita figures in the case of the United States are millions of fully and partially unemployed, semi-skilled and unskilled workers getting low wages, living in slums and lacking the bare necessities. In our country every family will be adequately provided for, and will ultimately enjoy material and cultural advantages in plenty. (*Applause.*)

The draft Programme points out that the projected plans of improving the living standard can be fulfilled successfully in conditions of peace. Moreover, an easing of international tension and an attendant reduction of military expenditures would enable us to raise the people's standard of living still higher. Our struggle for peace is an integral part of the struggle for communism, for the flowering of the Soviet land and the improvement of the people's well-being.

Comrades, the imposing programme for improving the living standard of the Soviet people is imbued with immense social content. It reveals in a striking way the noble features of our popular system and evokes the admiration of broad sections of people the world over. Western bourgeois propaganda admits that the targets set in the draft Programme are feasible, and considers this the "main challenge" to the Western Powers.

Well, we think it is high-minded to issue a challenge for the creation of better living conditions for the people. Why should not the capitalists, who have amassed vast capital by plundering the peoples, accept a challenge like that? Why should not they convert the industries working for war to civilian production, and raise workers' wages? We think the working people in the capitalist countries would also welcome abolition of house rents, which in some countries consume nearly one-third of their earnings. Would not the American people welcome it if medical services, on which they spent nearly $20,000 million in 1960 alone, were made free?

But, as we know, capitalism's motto is to suck man dry. And when a person is no longer fit for work capitalist society abandons him to his lot: if you have no money, starve; if you have no home, sleep under a bridge. That is what the "free world" is like, that is what bourgeois "freedom" is like. Socialism has put an end to these man-hating canons. The motto of communism is, "Everything for the sake of man, for the benefit of man". And under communism, which is being built by the people and for the people's happiness, the word Man will sound prouder than it has ever sounded before! (*Prolonged applause.*)

4. Planning and Management Must Meet the Demands of Communist Construction

Comrades, to implement successfully the enormous tasks set in the draft Programme, we must see to it that planning and management live up to the demands of full-scale communist construction. This is stipulated, firstly, by the tremendously growing scale of production and building, and by the development and extension of economic ties; secondly, by swift scientific and technical progress; thirdly, by the immense social, cultural and technical advances in the sphere of labour; and, fourthly, by the extension of the democratic foundations of economic management and the mounting activity of the masses.

Communist construction calls for proper and effective use of all production resources and a rational economy of labour. Lenin's wise words, "Socialism means accounting", are acquiring still greater significance in the period of communist construction.

Here is what the figures tell us. Within the term of the general perspective, the savings derived from reductions in the cost of industrial production alone are to yield 1,400-1,500 thousand million rubles, or nearly three-quarters of the aggregate capital investment in the national economy. At present each per cent of the funds saved in production and building becomes a tremendous source of additional production rises and improvements in the living standard. Yet even what would seem an insignificant slip in planning or an incidental misuse of funds entails a loss of many millions.

The 2,000,000 million rubles to be spent on capital construction in twenty years is six times as much as the sum invested in all the years of Soviet power. Dealing on so big a scale we cannot make literally a single step without heeding the popular rule: "Measure thy cloth thrice and cut but once". In so doing, we cannot proceed without the most precise of calculations of *what, how* and *where* to build to the greatest advantage at the least cost. The slightest slow-up in the commissioning of so great a number of new projects would reduce enormous sums to dead stock. On the other hand, what considerable resources would be released if the schedule were reduced, and how many more dwellings, children's institutions, schools, hospitals and holiday homes could be built on these resources in excess of the plan!

Life itself calls for scientific grounding and economic foresight of a new, far higher order in the fields of planning and management. The drafting of plans and endorsement of economic measures should be preceded by a thorough-going scientific analysis of the problems of economic and technical development. Economic and technical research should further the proper solution of economic problems. In other words, it should help us work out the most advantageous proportions in the national economy, make the most effective use of natural resources, production capacities and new machinery, effect the best distribution of the national income and capital investments, find additional ways and means of accelerating rates of economic development, etc.

What are the demands exacted of planning in our time? It is essential, firstly, that we should have progressive planning standards for the use of all types of instruments of labour, raw and other materials, for technological methods and time limits for various jobs; it should be law for every manager to introduce those standards and to abide by them strictly. Secondly, every plan should be accurately balanced with respect to its various elements and provided with the necessary reserves.

Economic organisation and planning should lay a still

stronger accent on modern technology, to give it what people call "the green light". After all, the material and technical basis of communism is already being laid in technical projects, in plants that are being commissioned today and which will also be operating in 15 or 20 years. It is up to the designers to reflect the latest scientific and technical discoveries and improvements in their new projects to the fullest extent and in good time. It is essential to make more effective the system of introducing new technology on a centralised basis, from above, and to promote a country-wide mass movement for technical progress, from below.

Enterprises which have done well in putting to use new machinery and turning out new products should be encouraged materially and morally, and should have precedence over those that are conservative and cling to the old. We should achieve well-adjusted co-operation throughout the country, co-ordinated in time, among specialised enterprises manufacturing various elements of every type of new machinery. Establishment of close and business-like collaboration among scientists, designers, technologists and workers at all stages, from designing and surveying, and the manufacture of experimental samples, to mass production, acquires special importance. Finally, it is essential that a technical project should be considered and approved only after its economic efficiency has been thoroughly proved.

It is safe to say that our progress towards communism and the Soviet people's standard of living will depend to a very great extent on how well we succeed in accelerating construction, reducing its cost and improving its quality, in making effective and wise use of investments and production facilities, and in getting the maximum of output per unit of production capacity at the lowest cost. It is essential for this purpose that we reorganise planning and accounting, state and public control, socialist emulation, and all the ways of evaluating and encouraging the work of every employee, team, factory-shop, enterprise and economic administrative council, in such a way as to obtain the greatest productive effect of each machine tool, machine, and the equipment, in order that capital investments are returned as quickly as possible. As I have said in the Central Committee Report, we must uproot the erroneous practice of scattering and "spreading out" resources among a multitude of projects.

It would do no harm if we were also to learn from the foremost capitalist models how to speed up construction, and start up and run new enterprises. In his day, Lenin said that we should learn how to trade. Much water has run under the bridge since then. We have accumulated tremendous experience in building and management, and possess an incomparable advantage over capitalism. But even now we should not scorn useful foreign experience, and should discerningly borrow from the West all that is technically and organisationally useful, including methods of accelerating the turnover of funds and getting greater returns from capital investments.

In the course of communist construction *continuous improvement of the quality of output* is a prime economic and political task. The slogan, "Soviet-made means the best", advanced in the pre-Congress period, should be a guiding principle for every enterprise.

The draft Programme is imbued with the idea that highly productive and scientifically organised labour equipped with the finest machinery is the cornerstone of communism. For this reason, *a rational use of manpower* is the most important aspect of planning and management.

The introduction of new machinery will release millions of people, including people engaged in ancillary and auxiliary jobs. It will also release many people engaged in farming. The managerial, administrative and office apparatus will shrink considerably. Millions of women will be relieved of household work. They will reinforce the ranks of the working people engaged in the national economy. In view of the most extensive development of public health, education and culture, the number of people engaged in these and other non-productive spheres will grow to the greatest extent—nearly 3-fold in 20 years.

In terms of the country as a whole this will require a well-organised system of mass training and extension courses, and planned re-distribution of manpower strictly on the basis of free choice and the principle of material incentive. Suitable living and cultural conditions should be created to encourage people to move to jobs in new regions.

The growing scale of construction and the mounting rates of technical progress call for continuity in planning. It is now absolutely impossible to draw up one-year plans for production, machinery, capital investments and labour, without thoroughly considering all the aspects of long-term development. Each annual plan should be an organic part of the long-term plan for a number of subsequent years. At the same time, it is necessary in the case of long-term plans to, so to speak, make them "down-to-earth" and amend them with due account of the actual fulfilment of annual plans.

In the period of communist construction the role and importance of centralised planning, which co-ordinates all spheres and branches of our economy, are enhanced. The priority of the interests of the state, effective control over the maintenance of state discipline in economic activities everywhere and by all without exception, and resolute elimination of all manifestations of parochialism and a narrow departmental approach, are essential premises for the advance towards communism.

The Leninist line—*to develop in every way the democratic foundations of economic management in combination with centralised administration by the state*—is clearly expressed in the draft Programme. Centralised administration by the state must draw upon the creative initiative of the masses and give this initiative ever greater scope. This calls for a further gradual extension of managerial powers and of the responsibility of local bodies, and of enterprises. The role and the rights of trade unions and other mass organisations, particularly the primary ones, should be extended to the utmost; the personnel should participate more broadly and actively in the management of enterprises.

Our policy, our line for the entire period of communist construction, is to effect a proper combination of material and moral stimuli. So long as society is in the socialist stage, it cannot dispense with distribution according to labour, with commodity-money relations and with such categories as price, profit, finance and credit. In our country these economic tools have a socialist content and serve the building of communism. When communism will have been built, they will be outdated and replaced by the superior economic categories of direct assessment and distribution of social labour.

In the course of communist construction it is our task to make still greater use of, and to improve, the financial and credit levers, financial control, prices, and profits. We must elevate the importance of profit and profitability. In order that enterprises fulfil their plans better, they should be given more opportunities to handle their profits and use them more extensively to encourage the good work of their personnel, and to extend production. (*Applause.*) It is highly important to work out and introduce forms of collective incentives, in order to make each workingman materially interested not only in the results of his own labour, but in those of collective labour as a whole.

Comrades, the plan for the development of the productive forces of our country for the coming twenty years is truly imposing. It is not merely breath-taking figures showing the increase in the output of coal, steel, oil, grain, meat and milk. It is a magnificent plan for the creation of a society where man will be a genuine master of nature and of social relations, and where a high living standard will be attained for the whole people. (*Prolonged applause.*)

It is worth living, working and fighting for such grand goals. There is no loftier task, no task more purposeful and interesting for our Party, trade union and Komsomol organisations than that of organising the struggle for the realisation of the general perspective, for the building of communism. (*Prolonged applause.*)

IV

THE DEVELOPMENT OF COMMUNIST SOCIAL RELATIONS, AND THE MOULDING OF THE NEW MAN

Comrades, in the transition to communism the mighty growth of the productive forces is accompanied by a gradual development of socialist social relations into communist relations. The establishment of a communist economy, the advancement of social relations, and the moulding of the new man are interlinked processes. The economy is the basis for change in social relations and man's consciousness, while the advancement of social relations, and the growth of the communist spirit, culture and activity of people are a necessary condition for economic progress.

1. The Building of a Classless Society in the Soviet Union

The development of the Soviet Union has reached the historical period when the task of building a classless communist society of free and socially conscious working people is being solved directly.

The wealth of experience accumulated by Soviet society confirms the Marxist-Leninist conclusion that the abolition of classes and class distinctions necessitates:

First, *overthrowing the rule of the exploiting classes, the landlords and capitalists, and abolishing their private ownership of the means of production, which constitutes the economic basis of exploitation of man by man.* In our country this task was carried through as a result of the October Revolution, the nationalisation of land and capitalist property, and the restriction and ousting of the capitalist elements.

Secondly, *converting individual small-scale commodity production into large-scale collective production, completing the construction of a single socialist system of economy, and abolishing the last of the exploiting classes, the class of kulaks.* This task was accomplished by collectivising the countryside, organising the handicraft in co-operatives, and abolishing the kulaks as a class.

Thirdly, *removing the class distinctions between workers and peasants, the essential distinctions between town and country, and creating conditions for an organic fusion of physical and mental labour.* How is this third task being accomplished? It stands to reason that our further advance to a classless society is bound up, above all, with a rapid growth of the productive forces. It is precisely a high level of the productive forces and socialist relations of production that actuate the gradual obliteration of the distinctions between the labouring classes.

And that, comrades, is something we know not only from theory. We see it in practice. The character of the peasant's labour, and his general make-up, are changing under the effect of the wide use of machinery and electric power. He is steadily approaching the industrial worker in technical knowledge.

National property, the property of the whole people, is the basis for the life of the entire population, the kolkhoz peasantry included. At the same time, features characteristic of national property arise and take root in co-operative-kolkhoz property. Life itself is steadily bringing the national and co-operative forms of property closer together, and will ultimately lead to the emergence of a single, communist property and a single, communist principle of distribution.

247

In the process of communist construction, as a result of major changes in production techniques and in the nature of labour, yet another very important social problem will be gradually solved—removal of the essential distinctions between physical and mental labour. We already observe these processes in our daily life. Millions of people with a secondary education have come to work at industrial enterprises and the collective and state farms. Tens of thousands of workers and collective farmers are getting a higher education in their free time. The worker's labour is gradually approaching that of the engineer. Take the foreman, for example. He unquestionably belongs to the bracket of engineers and technicians, to the intelligentsia. Yet he is also a worker. Or take the army of innovators, of workers-rationalisers. The contribution they make to technical progress is often of a kind that only a major specialist would be equal to. The same may well be said of the foremost farm workers, who are veritable professors in their field.

The elimination of distinctions between classes, now under way, makes for an ever greater social homogeneity of society. It stands to reason that this is a gradual and long process. The class distinctions will not be removed to the last until a full communist society is built.

Hand in hand with this process, and indivisibly linked with it, there will emerge *communist equality*, that is, complete social equality of people implying identical relations to the means of production, complete equality in distribution, and harmony of individual and society on the basis of an organic blending of personal and public interests. Classless communist society will thus constitute the highest form of organisation of the human community.

2. From the Dictatorship of the Proletariat to a State of the Whole People

The draft Programme of the Party raises, and resolves, a new important question of communist theory and practice —the development of the dictatorship of the working class into a state of the whole people, the character and the tasks of this state, and its future under communism. *The state of the whole people is a new stage in the development of the socialist state, an all-important milestone on the road from socialist statehood to communist public self-government.*

Half a century ago our Party was the only party to put the Marxist-Leninist idea of the dictatorship of the proletariat into its programme. If we managed to survive in the bitter struggle against domestic and world reactionaries, if we managed to translate into reality mankind's age-old dream of socialism, we owe this, to a tremendous degree, to the fact that we possessed a powerful instrument for the transformation of society—a state of the dictatorship of the proletariat. The experience of the Soviet Union and the People's Democracies has fully confirmed the Marxist-Leninist thesis that the victory of socialism is possible only if the dictatorship of the proletariat is established.

The dictatorship of the proletariat is born of the conditions created by the class struggle between the proletariat and the bourgeoisie. In the process of its establishment, socialism has to overcome the resistance, often of a most bitter kind, of the reactionary forces of the old world. Comrades, remember the fierce resistance put up against us by the landlords and capitalists with the most active support of the forces of world reaction. One could also refer to an event of the relatively recent past—the counter-revolutionary insurrection in Hungary in 1956. It furnished added proof that to effect the transition to socialism, the working class must have a power capable of crushing the resistance of the exploiters, consolidating the victory of the revolution, preventing in time all attempts to restore the rule of the bourgeoisie, and ensuring defence against aggressive acts by international reactionaries.

It should be stressed that the proletariat resorts to force solely against the capitalists and landlords, and their abettors, and not against the labouring classes. It is this that accounts for the profoundly democratic nature of proletarian power. The bourgeois state is a dictatorship of the exploiting minority over the overwhelming majority of society, whereas the proletarian state expresses the interests of the vast majority of society. The working class leads the peasantry and the other labouring sections of society, its allies and brothers-in-arms, and helps them to take the socialist path of their own free will. This leadership, being a characteristic feature of proletarian power, sets it poles apart from the bourgeois state, which knows no other relations but those of domination and subjection.

Lenin taught us that the working class needs dictatorship to build a socialist society, to wipe out all exploitation of man by man. "This goal," Lenin explained, "cannot be achieved overnight. It requires a fairly long period of transition from capitalism to socialism, because reorganisation of production is a difficult thing, because it takes time to effect radical changes in all spheres of life, and because the tremendous force of habit for the petty-bourgeois and bourgeois way of economy can only be broken through a long and dogged struggle. That is why Marx speaks of the entire period of proletarian dictatorship as of a period of transition from capitalism to socialism."*
It follows, according to Marx and Lenin, that the dictatorship of the proletariat is a state of the period of transition from capitalism to socialism.

It stands to reason that when socialism had triumphed *completely and finally* in our country and we entered upon the *period of full-scale communist construction*, the conditions which necessitated the dictatorship of the proletariat disappeared, its domestic purposes were fulfilled.

The working class is the only class in history which does not entertain the purpose of perpetuating its domination. When the conditions which gave rise to its dictatorship disappear, when the tasks which society could accomplish

---

* V. I. Lenin, *Collected Works*, 4th Russ. ed., Vol. 29, p. 358.

solely with its help are consummated, the state gradually develops, under the leadership of the working class, into a nation-wide organisation of all the working people of socialist society. With the victory of socialism and the country's entry into the period of full-scale communist construction, the working class of the Soviet Union has on its own initiative, consistent with the tasks of communist construction, transformed the state of proletarian dictatorship into a state of the whole people. That, comrades, is a fact unparalleled in history. Until now the state has always been an instrument of dictatorship by this or that class. In our country, for the first time in history, a state has taken shape which is not a dictatorship of any one class, but an instrument of society as a whole, of the entire people. (*Stormy applause.*)

Communist construction no longer requires the dictatorship of the proletariat. All working people in our society have equal rights. To be sure, the working class continues to play the leading role in society also during the transition to communism. It retains this role because it is the most advanced and most organised class, a class associated with machine industry, one that is the most consistent bearer of communist ideals.

It would be wrong to think that there is a wall between a state of the dictatorship of the proletariat, which represents the interests of the overwhelming majority of society, and the state of the whole people. From the moment of its inception, the dictatorship of the proletariat contains features of universal socialist democracy. As socialism develops, these features become accentuated, and following its complete victory they become determinant. The state develops from an instrument of class domination into an organ expressing the will of the whole people.

The might of our society and state, far from diminishing, increases many times over in the course of its development from the dictatorship of the proletariat into a state of the whole people, because new sources of strength appear alongside the old. Coupled with the continuous growth of its economic potential, the social basis of our state has gained added strength and has expanded, and society has become more united and monolithic than ever before. Therein lies the chief source of strength of the state. Every worker, every peasant, every intellectual can say: We are the state; its policy is our policy, and the task of developing and consolidating it, of defending it against all encroachments, is our common task. (*Prolonged applause.*)

But why, for all that, is the state as such being retained, though the antagonism of classes, the main thing that gave rise to it, has disappeared? It is being retained because the tasks which society can solve only with the aid of the state are not as yet consummated. These tasks and functions of the socialist state are clearly specified in the draft of our Party Programme.

The state will remain long after the victory of the first phase of communism. The process of its withering away will be a very long one; it will cover an entire historical epoch and will not end until society is completely ripe for self-administration. For some time, the features of state administration and public self-government will intermingle. In this process the domestic functions of the state will develop and change, and gradually lose their political character. It is only after a developed communist society is built in the U.S.S.R., and provided socialism wins and consolidates in the international arena, that there will no longer be any need for the state, and it will wither away.

The fact that the dictatorship of the proletariat is no longer necessary does not in any way imply any relaxation of public order and legality. The Party attaches great importance to a further strengthening of legality and of law and order, and to the protection of the rights of citizens. The rights, freedom, honour and dignity of the Soviet citizen will be closely protected by society and by the state. Those who expect that public order in our country will be less rigid, are in for a woeful disappointment. Alongside the state organs, public organisations of working people will play an increasing role in combating anti-social and criminal elements. The fight against misappropriators of public property, against parasites and rowdies will be waged still more effectively, since it will have become the business of all working people and their organisations.

Comrades, you know that in the last few years, especially after the Twentieth Congress of the C.P.S.U., tremendous effort has been put into restoring the Leninist standards of Party and government activity, and into further extending Soviet democracy. We do not consider, of course, that the task of perfecting our political system is already consummated. We must do everything to perfect and develop the state of the whole people, to draw the masses more and more into administration and control of the organs of state.

To begin with, a word about *the role of the representative organs of power*. The terms of reference of the Soviets will expand. They will be, to a still greater extent, "the working corporations" performing the practical function of managing the economic and social processes that Marx and Lenin had in mind when analysing the nature of truly popular power. Many of the matters which are today allotted to the competence of the executive bodies of state power and administration will be handled directly by the Soviets and their committees.

The transition to communism calls for a continuous *improvement in the work of the state and economic apparatus, and for the development in it of democratic principles and principles of social work*. The apparatus of the government, economic and other organs must be made still simpler, still cheaper to run, and still more efficient, and should respond promptly and considerately to citizens' requests. It is essential that we completely eradicate such survivals of the past as officialism, indifference, formalism and red tape, and not only publicly censure, but strictly prosecute, administratively and legally, officials guilty of a bureaucratic treatment of the needs and requests of the working people.

The advancement of socialist democracy is bound up with *a heightening of the role of mass organisations,* such as the trade unions, the Komsomol, the co-operatives and the cultural and educational societies.

Lenin called the trade unions schools of administration, schools of management, schools of communism. This fundamental appraisal by Lenin of the role of the trade unions has special significance during the transition to communism. Through the trade unions industrial, professional and office workers exert a mounting influence on economic affairs, help improve the work of enterprises and control over production. Furthermore, the role of the trade unions is made greater by virtue of the rights of legislative initiative that are being given them, and of some of the functions previously performed by state bodies.

The activities of the *Komsomol,* the militant organisation of Soviet youth, play an important part in the life of our society. The youth, comrades, are our replacements. They are the future of our country. They are an active and creative force which can move mountains in the struggle for our ideals. We must show daily, truly paternal concern for the education of the Komsomol members.

The administration of our state is effected *for* the working people and by the working people. We set ourselves the task of drawing all citizens without exception into the administration of the affairs of society.

How do we plan to solve this task?

First, by creating ever better material and cultural living conditions for every workingman and woman.

Secondly, by perfecting the forms of popular representation and the democratic principles of the Soviet electoral system.

Thirdly, by extending the practice of nation-wide discussions of the more important matters of communist construction and of draft laws of the Soviet state.

Fourthly, by extending in every way the forms of public control over the activities of the organs of state power and administration, and by making this control more effective.

Fifthly, by systematically renewing the composition of the governing organs, by increasingly and consistently implementing with regard to leading officials of the state apparatus and of public organisations the elective and accountability principle, and gradually extending this principle to all leading officials of state and public organisations, and cultural institutions.

Our ideological opponents keep vociferating that capitalism is a free world and try to discredit our socialist democracy in every way. But the truth about socialist democracy, the finest democracy on earth, cannot be concealed. After all, it is an incontestable fact that the socialist world is steadily and consistently developing and extending democracy, while the capitalist world is abridging and curtailing what stunted democracy there is in bourgeois society.

Never before has actual power in the leading imperialist countries been concentrated in the hands of so small a handful of monopolists as today. The Americans themselves described Eisenhower's administration as a Big Business administration. Indeed, more than a score of its members were either millionaires themselves, or were in the employ of the biggest corporations. Of the 19 ministers in the British cabinet 12 are directly associated with the monopolies, and in Adenauer's government 12 of its 18 members are direct representatives of big concerns and stock companies. In the governments of the imperialist countries individuals change, one millionaire or his protegé replacing another, but all of them serve the interests of the monopolies.

Bourgeois ideologists speak of equality in capitalist society. But what is the equality they imply? Take the social structure in the capitalist countries. It is a monstrous pyramid of social inequality. At its apex are a handful of industrial and financial oligarchs. Like the corrupt nobility of the Roman Empire in its decline, they wallow in luxury and over-satiation. In the meantime, the hundreds of millions of people who constitute the base of this pyramid are condemned to privation and lack of rights. In the United States a handful of moneybags, one per cent of the population, controls nearly 60 per cent, and in Britain a group of no more than one per cent controls over 50 per cent, of the national wealth.

Now take the electoral system in the capitalist countries. It is being continuously refashioned and adapted to ensuring to a maximum the interests of the monopolies, and to distorting the true will of the electors. The present electoral system in France is a good example. At the latest elections there, the Communist Party, which polled 3,882,204 votes, won a mere ten seats in the National Assembly. In the meantime, the reactionary U.N.R., which polled 3,603,958 votes, i.e., less than the Communists, won 188 seats. If this is not outright dictatorship of monopoly capital, then what is? If this is not mockery of the will of the people, then what is? The working people comprise the overwhelming majority of electors. But are they represented in the parliaments? Is it not a fact that there is not a single worker, not a single small farmer, in the Congress of the United States, a country with more than 50 million factory and office workers and working farmers?

The monopoly bourgeoisie makes the utmost use of all levers—the press, the radio, television and all other means of indoctrination—to deceive the masses, to blunt their minds and paralyse their will. Whose will, for example, can the press controlled by millionaire Hearst reflect? It reflects just one will—the will of the monopoly tycoons.

The bourgeoisie employs the police and army more and more frequently in its struggle against the people. Think of all the blood of the people shed in the capitalist countries in the last decade! The police baton and police bullets hold an increasingly prominent place in bourgeois democracy's arsenal of "arguments".

Such is their "free world", a society with no true freedom and no democracy, a society based on social and national oppression and inequality, on the exploitation of man by man, on the flouting of human dignity and honour.

The flowering of democracy in the socialist countries, on the one hand, and on the other the increasing curtailment of the already curtailed democracy in the capitalist countries—these are the *two opposite trends in the political development of the contemporary world.* We are doing our utmost, and will continue to do our utmost, to further perfect our social system and our democracy as a model of the socialist way of life for all peoples. *(Prolonged applause.)*

3. The Growing Closeness Between Nations and Consolidation of Friendship Among the Peoples

The draft Programme sets *a course towards a further economic and cultural advancement of the Soviet Republics, and a still greater all-round rapprochement between nations in the process of full-scale communist construction.*

Under socialism, two interlinked progressive tendencies are operating in the national question. First, there is a rapid, all-round development of each nation. The rights of the Union and Autonomous republics are expanding. Secondly, the socialist nations are drawing closer and closer together under the banner of proletarian internationalism; they influence and enrich each other more and more.

Full-scale communist construction is a new stage in the development of national relations in the Soviet Union. Closer co-operation among nations depends, above all, on correct economic policy. The draft Programme envisages a comprehensive development and specialisation of economy in the Union republics. The economy of each will continue to develop as an integral part of a single Soviet economy. The greater the contribution which each republic makes to the common cause of communist construction, the broader and the more comprehensive become the interrelations between the Soviet nations.

The economic development of each Soviet republic is the result of fraternal co-operation and mutual assistance among all the Soviet peoples. Take the development of the virgin land in Kazakhstan. The republic would never have coped with so formidable an undertaking on its own. Russians, Ukrainians, Byelorussians, and people of many other nationalities gave it a helping hand. Or take our factories and building projects. They are friendly, multi-national collectives, where workers are esteemed not for the colour of their skin or for the tongue they speak, but for their attitude towards their work, their contribution to the communist cause. The population in the various republics is becoming more and more mixed in national composition. There is an exchange of qualified personnel between them. All this strengthens international bonds between the peoples of the U.S.S.R.

Improvements in the forms of national state organisation of the peoples of the Soviet Union are another expression of the development of the socialist nations. The Party will continue to meet all the requirements that arise in this sphere. Full use must be made of all the possibilities provided by the Soviet principles of federation and autonomy. Even today the realities prompt the setting up of some inter-republican zonal bodies for a better co-ordination of the efforts of the various republics in implementing the plans of communist construction.

The growing closeness among the nations and nationalities of our country is also promoted by cultural development and ideological work. The exchange of spiritual values among them is on the upgrade. The cultural achievements of one nation are made available to others. This leads to a mutual cultural enrichment of the peoples of the Soviet Union, to a strengthening of their internationalist foundations, to the formation of the future single, universal culture of communist society.

The forms of national culture do not ossify; on the contrary, they develop continuously. Outmoded forms inconsistent with the tasks of communist construction drop away, and new forms emerge. National flavour is quite natural in literature and art. But all too often we have encountered archaisms in this respect. In architecture, for example, obviously outmoded forms are sometimes extracted from the dim past, though they are absolutely inconsistent with present living conditions and people's requirements. And we know that only forms that are in keeping with our epoch have a future.

The Party will continue to ensure the free development of the languages of the peoples of the Soviet Union, ruling out all restrictions, privileges and coercion in the use of the various languages. Every citizen enjoys, and will enjoy, complete freedom in the choice of the language of instruction for his or her children. There are no hindrances whatsoever to the development of national languages in our country. But their development must not lead to any accentuation of national barriers; on the contrary, it should lead to a coming together of nations.

It is to be noted that the non-Russian peoples show a growing inclination to learn the Russian language, which has in effect become the second native language of the peoples of the Soviet Union, a medium of inter-national intercourse, an avenue whereby each nation and each nationality achieves access to the cultural wealth of all the peoples of the U.S.S.R. and to world culture. (*Applause.*) The voluntary study of the Russian language, now under way, is a positive factor in the development of co-operation among the nations. (*Applause.*)

A rapprochement of nations is proceeding in our country, and their social homogeneity is growing. Complete unity of nations will be achieved as the full-scale building of communism proceeds. But even after communism will have been built in the main, it will be premature to proclaim a fusion of nations. Lenin, it may be recalled, pointed out that state and national distinctions will exist long after socialism will have triumphed in all countries.

We come across people, of course, who deplore the gradual obliteration of national distinctions. We reply to them: Communists will not conserve and perpetuate national distinctions. We will support the objective process of the increasingly closer rapprochement of nations and nationalities proceeding under the conditions of communist construction on a voluntary and democratic basis. It is essential that we lay greater stress on the education of the masses in the spirit of proletarian internationalism and Soviet patriotism. Even the slightest vestiges of nationalism should be eradicated with uncompromising, Bolshevik determination.

The friendship of the peoples of the Soviet Union is one of our greatest gains. Let us guard it as the apple of our eye! (*Stormy applause.*)

4. Communist Education and the All-Round Development of the Individual

Comrades, education of people in the communist spirit is an all-important element of communist construction.

The creation of the highest productivity of labour, the development of communist social relations and the firm establishment of the standards of communist behaviour are inconceivable without an advancement in the consciousness and cultural level of all members of society. The higher the consciousness of the members of society and the fuller and broader their creative activity, the better and more rapidly shall we implement the programme of communist construction.

What are the tasks we have in view when we speak of the moulding of the new man? They are:

consolidation of the communist world outlook: deep faith in the communist ideals, a conscious attitude to civic duty, socialist internationalism and patriotism, loyalty to country, readiness to defend it even at the cost of one's life;

education through labour, development of the communist attitude to labour, to social production;

consolidation of the principles of communist morality, voluntary observance of the standards of communist behaviour;

cultural development, knowledge of the fundamentals of science, general and polytechnical education, aesthetic and physical education.

Communism ennobles man. *Communism is the full flowering of humanity and of the individual.*

While instilling new, communist traits of character in all members of our society, the Party attaches special importance to the communist education and training of the youth. The Party and the people have brought up a wonderful generation of devoted builders of socialism and heroic defenders of our country, who have won undying glory. Today we are preparing people for life in communist society. The communist generation have to be moulded from childhood. They have to be cared for and steeled from their youth. We must see to it in all earnest that there are no moral cripples in our country—no victims of incorrect education and bad example. Whenever young fruit-trees have been damaged to any degree, much effort has to be put into tending them back to healthy growth. Furthermore, these efforts are not always successful. It is the same with the people of the new generation.

The new man is moulded not only under the influence of the educational work of the Party, the Soviet state, the trade unions and the Komsomol, but also of the very pattern of life of society—the mode of production, the forms of distribution, the public services, the socio-political activities, the legal norms and the court practices. We must make the most of all economic, social and family, political and legal levers to develop the communist consciousness of people and to eradicate survivals of bourgeois psychology and morals.

The bourgeoisie associates the freedom of the individual with private property. But millions of people in the capitalist countries have no property, and to them bourgeois property is not an earnest of freedom, but a heavy burden. To the petty proprietor property is not a condition for the development of the individual; rather, it is a chain that keeps him fully dependent on monopoly capital. It is only to capitalists that private property furnishes complete freedom to exploit the working people and to amass fabulous profits. The wealth of experience accumulated in our country, and that of the world socialist system as a whole, shows that it is not private but commonly-owned property that delivers man from all types of social dependence and provides broad opportunities for the free development of the individual. Our people have become imbued with the lofty sense of collectivism, comradeship and loyalty to civic duty.

The draft Programme attaches great importance to the further moulding of the progressive scientific world outlook of Soviet people. And that is only natural. After all, man cannot successfully develop spiritually if his head is stuffed with mystical ideas, superstitions and false conceptions.

For the first time in history, the world outlook of millions of people rests on the scientific basis of Marxism-Leninism, which has become the ideological weapon of the people in the struggle for a better life, for the victory of communism. Marxism-Leninism has placed mankind in the correct, accurately computed historical orbit leading to the bright communist future! (*Applause.*)

We are revolutionaries and internationalists, and cannot be indifferent to the propaganda of reactionary views. We cannot reconcile ourselves to the bourgeoisie obscuring and corrupting the minds of people, and fomenting chauvinism. The Party will continue to expose imperialist ideology.

Communist consciousness is fashioned and consolidated in the active struggle for communism, in work for the common weal. Communist ideas must logically lead to communist deeds in the behaviour of every man, the work of every collective, every organisation and institution.

It is creative labour that constitutes the basis of communist education, of the all-round development of the individual. Labour has always been, and always will be, the source of man's existence and development. The motto, "He who does not work, neither shall he eat", exists in different forms in all languages, among all peoples.

The Communists have made it their purpose to deliver people not from labour, but from the exploitation of their labour. Man's labour and his being provided with all the good things of life are blended organically in the communist principle, "From each according to his ability, to each according to his needs."

Communist education has the all-important purpose of instilling in each man the awareness that man cannot live without labour, that he cannot live unless he creates the means of life. All the good that Soviet man does is done for himself and for society as a whole. Doing one's work conscientiously, doing all things well and in time means showing concern for one's comrades, who also work for everybody, oneself included. It is this that embodies the comradely co-operation and mutual assistance of the people of the new society.

The bourgeoisie oppresses and humiliates working people. The Communists extol and glorify free labour as a source of life and of the well-being of all men, and as an earnest of social progress and prosperity. (*Applause.*)

The draft Programme contains the *moral code of the builder of communism*, the ethical standards of the new society, its moral tenets.

For over a hundred years bourgeois ideologists have been accusing the Communists of negating morals, of undermining the moral pillars of society. The bourgeoisie needs this falsehood to cover up its own immorality. What is the basis of the moral tenets of the exploiting classes? It is most clearly illustrated by sayings such as these: "What will not money do?", "Cheat your fellow lest he cheat you", "Money doesn't smell", and "Man is to man a wolf".

We do, indeed, negate these brutal and cynical canons. We contrapose to them the moral principles of collectivism and humanism expressed in the following magnificent words: "One for all, and all for one", and "Man is to man a friend, comrade and brother". (*Prolonged applause.*)

It is our task to make the new moral principles a vital need for all Soviet people. Much still has to be done to wipe out the vestiges of the past. In public life the progressive is not fenced off from the old and backward. The progressive wins in the end, but the survivals of the old retard progress. The force of good example grows, and that is the basis of our education. But, as you know, weeds grow fast if they are not controlled in good time.

We must induce the general public to pay greater attention and take a more exacting attitude to people's behaviour. After all, ill deeds are committed by people who are mostly members of some collective, of an organisation, of a trade union, the Komsomol, a collective farm, or of some cultural and educational society or association, and sometimes even members of our Party. We must use the moral weight and authority of public opinion more actively in combating those who break the rules and standards of socialist behaviour.

We want to make all people harmoniously developed. What other class besides the working class, and what other ruling party besides the Communist Party, has ever set the task of developing the capacities and gifts of *all* working people?

It is in the cultural advancement of the people that the

*Party sees the earnest of victorious communist construc-
tion.* Our country has reached the final stage of the cultural
revolution, whose main purpose is to build up all the
necessary ideological and cultural premises of communism. The most important task at this stage is to raise the
cultural and technical level of all workers and peasants to
the level of the intelligentsia, so as to eliminate, in the
main, the essential distinctions between mental and
physical labour.

In the coming 20 years the bulk of members of society
will, through one medium or another, receive a full secondary, specialised secondary or a higher education. That is a
formidable, but quite feasible task.

*General and polytechnical secondary (11-year) education
for all children of school age is to be brought into effect* in
the course of the coming 10 years. According to the School
Law the children must, after completing eight years of
schooling, work at enterprises or at collective farms, and
study simultaneously to obtain a full secondary education.
This creates the opportunity both for a higher education and
for highly-skilled work at the factory or farm.

It is also essential that in the coming ten years the young
people employed in the national economy who have no
secondary education should get an education equal to at
least eight years of schooling. This is an important and
urgent task. It should be borne in mind that during the war
many boys and girls were unable to receive a secondary
education. Due concern should be shown for these young
citizens of our country.

Soviet schools play an especially important role in the
all-round and harmonious development of man. In educating school children in the spirit of communism, schools
must instil in them the best qualities and habits, prepare
them for conscientious labour according to ability, for
using sensibly the social facilities, for unfailing observance
of the communist moral code and standards of behaviour.
A very big role in the education of the rising generation

devolves on the schoolteachers, who may well be called the spiritual mentors of the youth. The role of the school-teacher should be enhanced in every way, and he should be surrounded with attention and care. (*Applause*).

The Party attaches great importance to the further development of educational establishments—boarding-schools, day-care schools, and pre-school institutions. Public and family education are not opposed to each other. The family's educational influence upon children should blend with their education by society.

People who say that the significance of the family drops during the transition to communism, and that it disappears entirely with time, are absolutely wrong. In fact, the family will grow stronger under communism. Completely disencumbered of material considerations, family relations will become pure and lasting.

While focussing its efforts on instituting universal secondary education, the Party also sets the programmatic goal *of making all forms of higher education still more accessible to everybody*. At present we have an enrolment of 2,600,000 in our higher educational establishments. By 1980 it is envisaged that enrolment at higher educational establishments will rise to eight million, i.e., more than three-fold. The network of higher evening and correspondence schools will expand very greatly.

We still have to eliminate the considerable lag in the cultural and technical level of the rural population behind that of the urban population, so as to remove the essential distinctions between town and country in that sphere as well. It is necessary that all organisations dealing with matters of culture redouble their attention to the raising of the cultural level in the countryside.

In the next few years large-scale measures are to be taken to develop extensively the material basis of culture—paper factories and printing plants, radio and television stations, theatres, film studios and cinemas, clubs and libraries. This will naturally involve large material outlays.

But our society, which is building communism, will not grudge the means to meet the cultural requirements of Soviet people to the fullest.

In our age of rapid scientific and technical progress the development of society and of the individual is inconceivable without a planned and all-round utilisation of the achievements of science. As Lenin once said: "No dark force will withstand the alliance of science, the proletariat and technology."* These prophetic words have become living reality. We have smashed and destroyed the evil force of the exploiters. We have wiped out for good all forms of economic and spiritual oppression. And now we are concentrating more and more of our effort on eliminating man's dependence on the elements, on subjugating them to man's will. Man will thereby take the last hurdle on his road to the realm of true freedom.

Science is called upon to respond to the requirements of the present day, to serve as a militant and effective weapon in solving the pressing problems in the national economy, and in developing the productive forces of society. In the future science will find ways to control thermonuclear reactions so that the limitless sources of nuclear energy will be employed for peaceful purposes; to control the climate and the weather; to conquer disease and ensure longevity for people; to control the vital processes of organisms; to create a countless number of artificial materials with desired properties; and to explore outer space and set up reliable communication routes in the Universe. This will constitute an entire epoch in the history of world science and technology, provide man with inexhaustible resources of energy, and make him the true master of nature.

The importance of the social sciences will increase steadily in the study of mankind's historical path to communism, the investigation of the processes of capitalism's collapse, the elaboration of the scientific foundations of

---

* V. I. Lenin, *Collected Works*, 4th Russ. ed., Vol. 30, p. 376.

planned guidance of social development, economic and cultural construction, in the moulding of the materialist world outlook in people, in the education of the man of communist society and in the struggle against bourgeois ideology. The Party will see to it that all provinces of human knowledge flourish.

It is the honourable and patriotic duty of Soviet scientists to consolidate the already won advance positions of Soviet science in the key spheres of knowledge, and to ensure that Soviet science occupies a leading place in all the basic fields of world science. (Applause.)

Literature and art play a big part in moulding the new man. By upholding communist ideas and genuine humanism, literature and art instil in Soviet man the qualities of a builder of the new world, and serve the aesthetic and moral development of people. The Party calls on all who are engaged in literature and art to use new and bold forms in treating contemporary subjects.

Amateur art, which is spreading widely, offers a great medium for the emergence and development of popular talents and gifts. However, this does not eliminate the need for developing the professional arts. It will be the artistic activities of professional companies and distinguished men of the arts that will, in the future as well, serve as a model for amateur art. In its turn, amateur art will serve as an inexhaustible source for the enrichment and advancement of professional literature and art.

Socialist and communist culture is a new, and the highest, stage in man's cultural development. We have all the necessary conditions to scale successfully the summits of communist culture. (*Prolonged applause.*)

V

COMMUNISM AND MANKIND'S PROGRESS

Comrades, fulfilment of our Party Programme will exert a most profound influence on the course of world history. By the force of its example, communism in the making attracts to the banner of Marxism-Leninism new hundreds of millions of working people all over the world. The building of communism means, first and foremost, a rapid development of the productive forces, a steep rise in the people's cultural and living standards, and creation of conditions for a peaceful and happy life. The entire course of social development has borne out Lenin's prevision that it is through their economic construction that the countries of victorious socialism exert their chief influence on the development of the world revolution. Peaceful economic competition is the main arena of the contest between the socialist and the capitalist systems.

The outcome of this competition will be determined in tremendous degree by the competition between the Soviet Union and the United States of America.

The Party sets the task of converting our country, within the next decade, into the world's leading industrial power, of winning preponderance over the United States both in aggregate industrial output and in industrial output per head of the population. By approximately the same time, the U.S.S.R. will exceed the present U.S. level of agricultural production per head of the population by fifty per cent, and will surpass the U.S. level of national income.

But that is only the first objective. We shall not stop at that. *In the course of the second decade, by 1980, our country will leave the United States far behind in industrial and agricultural output per head of the population.*

The economy of all the countries of the world socialist system, and not only that of the Soviet Union, is developing far more rapidly than the economy of capitalism. Compared with the pre-war level, the countries of the socialist community have increased gross industrial output almost seven times over, while the increase for the countries of capitalism is less than two-and-a-half times. Preliminary estimates indicate that by 1980 the socialist system will account for about two-thirds of the world's industrial output.

Some say that figures are dull. But the figures showing the growth of our system are pleasant to quote and, I think, pleasant to hear. I remember that in our young days we had a song, "Race forward, steam locomotive! The goal is communism". Today it is not on a steam locomotive that we and the entire socialist system are speeding forward, but on a powerful electric locomotive. There can be no doubt that our socialist express will outrace capitalism, and leave it behind. Capitalism has neither the strength nor the hauling power any more. (*Prolonged applause.*)

Communist construction in our country is an integral part of the building of communist society in the socialist community as a whole. The successful development of the world system of socialism opens up prospects for the transition of the socialist countries to communism at more or less the same time, within one and the same historical epoch. The world system of capitalism is governed by the law of uneven economic and political development, this leading to an aggravation of contradictions and an intensification of the rivalry between states. The development of the world socialist system is governed by diametrically opposite laws. It is marked by a steady and planned economic growth of each country, by a more rapid development of the states that were economically backward under capitalism, and by all countries drawing level in their development.

Countries that once lagged behind because of specific features in their historical development have, within the framework of the world socialist system, come very close to the level of the advanced socialist countries in a very brief period thanks to the all-round assistance and support of the latter. However, the degree of development of their productive forces is not yet the same. These are the objective factors that rule out any one definite "hour" of entry of all the socialist countries into the higher phase of the new society. It is only natural that the full-scale building of communist society will begin in those countries as the necessary conditions for it arise. This accords with the interests of the socialist system as a whole, because it will accelerate the common advance of the peoples to communism and create more favourable conditions for greater support and aid for the other socialist countries by those in which communism has been victorious.

It is indisputable to Marxists-Leninists that the basic interests of the socialist states call imperatively for the maximum strengthening of their community. Any course steered towards the construction of socialism in isolation, separately from the world socialist community, runs counter to the objective laws of development of a socialist society. Such a course is harmful, since it may weaken the forces of socialism in the face of the united front of imperialist reaction; it encourages nationalistic tendencies, and in the long run may lead to a loss of the socialist gains.

Whatever guise it may don, nationalism is the most dangerous political and ideological weapon employed by international reaction to undermine the unity of the socialist countries. As the draft Programme states, "The Communists consider it their prime duty to educate working people in a spirit of internationalism, socialist patriotism, and intolerance of all possible manifestations of nationalism and chauvinism. Nationalism is harmful to the common interests of the socialist community and, above all, to the people of the country where it obtains, since isolation from the socialist camp holds up that country's development, deprives it of the advantages deriving from the world socialist system and encourages the imperialist powers to make the most of nationalist tendencies for their own ends."

Soviet people have the most friendly feelings for their brothers in the socialist countries in Europe and Asia. They rejoice at their successes and take pride in their victories. They have helped them in building up a new life, and will continue to do so. In fair weather and foul, the peoples of the socialist countries act according to the principle—all for one and one for all. Whoever lifts his hand against the socialist gains of the peoples of our community will be hurled back by a thousand million builders of socialism and communism. (*Prolonged applause.*)

As regards Yugoslavia, I have said in the Central Committee Report that we have fought, and will continue to fight, against the revisionist views of the leadership of the League of Communists of Yugoslavia; at the same time we have stood, and stand now, for the all-round promotion and strengthening of state relations with Yugoslavia. Concerning the struggle for peace, our views coincide on many points with those of Yugoslavia. The Soviet Union advocates bringing closer together and consolidating all the forces that are fighting against the imperialist warmongers, for peace and friendship among the peoples.

Comrades, the draft Programme of the C.P.S.U. gives expression to the incontrovertible fact that communism has become the most powerful force of our times. Today Communist parties are working in 87 countries of the world, and have a membership of about 40 million. And what vast numbers of people follow the Communists, share their views and convictions, and approve and support their policies. Communism has struck deep roots and is developing mightily. More than one-third of mankind are building a new life under its banner. In many non-socialist countries, too, the working class is dealing sledge-hammer blows at the foundations of capitalism.

The world is going through an epoch of revolution. *Socialist revolutions, anti-imperialist national-liberation revolutions, people's democratic revolutions, broad peasant movements, popular struggles to overthrow fascist and other despotic regimes, and general democratic movements against national oppression—all these merge in a single world-wide revolutionary process undermining and breaking up capitalism.*

The draft Programme delineates the paths of peaceful

and non-peaceful development of revolution. In this question, as in all others, our Party stands solidly on the principles collectively formulated by the world Communist movement in the 1957 Declaration and the 1960 Statement.

In the present epoch more *favourable international conditions* have arisen for the development of the world revolutionary movement, due mainly to the consolidation of the forces and the growth of the influence of the socialist system. The example set by socialism is exerting a powerful influence on people's minds, making them active fighters for the new system. Peoples rising in revolution can rely on support from the socialist countries in the struggle against any attempts by world reaction to export counter-revolution. In building a new society they can get help of every kind from the socialist countries.

The *internal conditions* for the transition of new countries to socialism are also more favourable in the present epoch. Among these conditions are the general weakening of capitalism, and the deepening of its contradictions; the numerical growth and the better organisation and consolidation of the working class, and its greater influence on society; the growing number of allies of the working class, who are objectively interested in the struggle against imperialism and in the abolition of the omnipotence of monopolies; and the founding and consolidation of Communist parties in almost all countries of the world.

But we should not lose sight of the difficulties that confront the revolutionary forces. Since the war the monopolist bourgeoisie has formed a new reactionary "Holy Alliance"—military blocs spearheaded not only against the socialist countries but also against the revolutionary working-class and the national-liberation movements. It has inflated the apparatus of violence and suppression to monstrous proportions. Concurrently, it is resorting to new and refined methods of splitting the working class and corrupting the trade union movement, for which end it makes extensive use of reactionary social-democratic and trade union leaders. It conducts a frantic anti-communist campaign, and has rallied all the enemies of the working people under this black flag. The possibility is not to be ruled out that the monopoly bourgeoisie will fall back on the most extreme and sanguinary means of retaining its domination. In these circumstances Lenin's words ring still truer today than ever before. The working class, he said, must "gain mastery of *all* forms or aspects of social activity without exception", and must be prepared for "a most rapid and sudden replacement of one form by another".*

In the present epoch the tasks of the popular-democratic, the national-liberation and the socialist revolutions are drawing closer and becoming more interwoven. The logic of social development has led to all these revolutions being directed primarily against one principal foe—imperialism, the monopolist bourgeoisie.

It is often asked what course the world liberation movement will follow.

It stands to reason that in the highly-developed capitalist countries the conditions for the transition to socialism have fully matured. After accomplishing their national-liberation, anti-imperialist revolution, the seething underdeveloped states of Asia, Africa and Latin America will be able to effect the transition to socialism. Today practically any country, irrespective of its level of development, can enter on the road leading to socialism.

The world revolutionary process is extending ever wider, involving all the continents. There was a time when, unable to destroy the first socialist state in the world by military means, the imperialists tried through a *cordon sanitaire* to fence it off from the rest of the world. However, the revolutionary activity of the peoples of Europe and Asia has now extended the borders of socialism from the Elbe to the South China seas. The imperialists have done everything possible to confine the ideas of revolution within

---

* V. I. Lenin, *Collected Works*, 4th Russ. ed., Vol. 31, p. 76.

these bounds, but neither mountains nor oceans are obstacles to the ideas of freedom. This has been vividly borne out by the victorious revolution in Cuba. *(Stormy applause.)*

The freedom-loving Cuban people have raised the banner of the people's anti-imperialist revolution, and cleared their land of the foreign plunderers and their henchmen. Workers, peasants, the intelligentsia and the middle strata of the urban population have rallied around the banner of the revolution. This is one of the chief sources of the strength of the Cuban revolution, and a guarantee of its further social progress. This small, faraway, sea-girt island has now become an unquenchable beacon of freedom, which is lighting the way to progress for all the peoples of Latin America. *(Stormy, prolonged applause.)*

Cuba lies far from the Soviet Union, but our peoples are close. Our hearts are with you, heroes of Cuba, who are defending independence and freedom against U.S. imperialism, and who have inscribed socialist aims on your battle standards. *(Stormy applause.)* Our people have rendered, and will continue to render assistance to the fraternal Cuban people in their sacred struggle for their just cause. *(Prolonged applause.)*

As the socialist system grows stronger, as its advantages over capitalism reveal themselves more fully and socialist and democratic forces all over the world increase, more and more countries at various levels of development will enter upon the path of revolution and join the system of socialism, as streams add their waters to a mighty river.

In its revolutionary struggle, the working class will continue to encounter various opportunist trends impeding consolidation of its forces and achievement of its aims. As long as capitalism exists, these trends will appear time and again, under various guises. That is why the draft Programme emphasises the necessity of a struggle both against the ideology of social-democratism and revisionism, and against dogmatism and sectarianism.

The C.P.S.U. will continue to do its utmost to fulfil its

internationalist duty to the working class and the working people of the whole world honourably; it will continue to work for the greater unity and solidity of the ranks of the great army of Communists of all lands. *(Prolonged applause.)*

Comrades, our successes in communist construction will be of exceptional significance to the destinies of the people of Asia, Africa and Latin America, these vast and long-suffering continents, which are rising to full stature as the makers of their own history and searching for paths towards a rapid rise in their economy and culture.

The national-liberation movement has entered the final phase of the abolition of colonial rule. The newly-free peoples are setting themselves the task of consolidating their political independence, of launching an offensive against economic backwardness so as to eliminate it, and of destroying all forms of dependence on imperialism.

But their path is not an easy one. Imperialism is losing the open battles with the national-liberation movement, but is not laying down its arms. Its methods are becoming subtler. The monopolists want to carry out a far-reaching plan for the preservation and consolidation of their positions in the underdeveloped countries, and are concealing the real essence of this plan with pious talk about aid. In this, the U.S. imperialists are second to none.

Of course there can be no question of the imperialist powers giving disinterested aid to the underdeveloped countries. The monopolies cannot give up their super-profits.

Their aims remain what they have always been—to keep the underdeveloped countries in the position of agrarian appendages and sources of raw material, and to go on exploiting their peoples. If, nevertheless, the imperialists proclaim an "aid" policy, it is an insincere measure, and one that has been forced upon them. It never occurred to the financial oligarchy to extend aid of any kind to the underdeveloped countries while imperialism was in sole control of the world. The situation changed when the Soviet Union and the world socialist system broke the imperialist powers' monopoly of machinery deliveries, of granting loans and credits, and of technical know-how. The imperialists were then forced to change their tactics, and start talking of economic "aid" to the underdeveloped countries.

They expected that in these countries prayers would be sent up and gratitude expressed to those who made dollar hand-outs. Instead, the U.S. imperialists heard curses addressed to them. Why? Because actually the U.S.A. is granting but a tiny fraction of the tremendous sums it extracts from the underdeveloped countries. Indeed, between 1946 and 1959 each dollar invested by the U.S.A. in all the underdeveloped countries brought in $2.5 profit. Soviet economists have calculated that the monopolies of the U.S.A. and other Western countries annually extract $20,000 million from the underdeveloped countries. If that is aid, then what is robbery? And robbers are never thanked, they are only cursed. (*Applause.*)

The monopolists are trying to retain the underdeveloped countries within the imperialist orbit, to keep them in an unequal position in the capitalist world system of economy. This is a vain attempt. The peoples of the underdeveloped countries do not wish to remain tied to imperialism. They see the example set by socialism. It is not from books alone that the peoples now judge socialism, but first and foremost by its actual achievements. The peoples see that it has taken not centuries, but the lifetime of one generation for Soviet power to do away with the country's age-old backwardness, and for the Soviet Union to become a mighty world power.

The achievement of political independence by the former colonies has had a favourable effect on their economic development. The rate of growth of production has gone up. Before the Second World War these countries had an average annual rate of development of one per cent, but of late years this figure has gone up to 4 per cent. In many of these countries a state sector has been set up, and the national industry has begun to develop.

But these are only the first steps. The heritage of colonialism is still deep-rooted. The principal economic problems still await solution. Meanwhile, the upper crust of the bourgeoisie and the feudal landlords, who have linked up their destinies with foreign capital, are doing all they can to keep the underdeveloped countries in the system of world capitalism. The road on which the imperialists and their henchmen want to drive these countries can in no way solve the problems over which the peoples arose in struggle against the colonialists.

What is the way out? History provides a clear answer to this question: the way out should be sought along the non-capitalist path of development. Those who want to know what fruits are to be gathered on this path should take a glance at the flourishing republics of Soviet Central Asia and at the other parts of our country that, after the October Revolution, bypassed the thorny path of capitalist development. *(Applause.)*

A country cannot simply drift on to the non-capitalist path of development. Only active struggle by the working class and all working people, only the unification of all democratic and patriotic forces in a broad national front, can lead the peoples on to that path.

Marxist theoretical thought, by a deep study of the objective course of development, has discovered a form in which the unification of all the sound forces of a nation can be most successfully achieved. That form is national democracy. Reflecting as it does the interests not of any one particular class but of broad strata of the people, a state of this type is called upon to consummate the anti-imperialist revolution for national liberation.

It is the good fortune of the peoples who have achieved national independence that they are entering upon the road of independent development at a time when the forces of imperialism and their ability to affect the course of events are steadily declining, while the forces and influence of socialism are steadily growing. In the circumstances it will be immeasurably easier for them to solve the problems of economic and social development.

The Soviet Union, like the other socialist countries, has no intention of interfering in the internal affairs of the young, newly-free states, or of imposing socialism upon any of them. There has not been, is not, and will not be any export of socialism. But neither must there be any imposition of colonialism, or any export of counter-revolution.

The C.P.S.U. considers alliance with peoples who have thrown off the yoke of colonialism to be a cornerstone of its international policy. Our Party regards it as its internationalist duty to help peoples who have set out to win and strengthen national independence, to aid all peoples who are fighting for the complete abolition of the colonial system. (Applause.)

Comrades, the fulfilment of our vast plans will be of decisive help in carrying out communism's historic mission— the abolition of war, and the establishment of everlasting peace on earth.

The experience of history has shown that war is as inherent in imperialism as the struggle against imperialism and the policy of the consolidation of peace are inherent in socialism. Human memory cannot forget the events inscribed in the annals of history not in ink but in the blood of millions. From the time the U.S.A. unleashed the first war of the epoch of imperialism in 1898, imperialism has plunged the peoples into a succession of "local wars", and has twice hurled mankind into world holocausts of unparalleled fury. Moreover, the ruins of towns and villages were still smouldering and the wounded hearts of millions who had lost relatives in the Second World War had not yet healed when the U.S. imperialists already "staked their claim" to a third world war.

In the imperialist camp, and first and foremost in the U.S.A., groups are operating who behave like reckless gamblers. They give no thought to the calamity that the new war they are hatching would bring mankind. The use of thermonuclear and rocket weapons would turn all continents into zones of the mass annihilation of people and the destruction of material values. In a thermonuclear world war, the factor of distance will lose its former significance, and the Western Hemisphere will become the scene of a terrible holocaust. In our times war cannot, and must not, serve as a means of settling international disputes.

It may be asked: isn't there a contradiction between the recognition that there is a danger of war, and our striving to expel war from the life of society. No, comrades, there is no contradiction in this.

The Party's confidence that already the present generation has every possibility of preventing a world war is grounded in a profound and comprehensive analysis of the forces operating on the international scene. This analysis leads to an indisputable conclusion—the balance of world political, economic and military forces has changed in favour of the peace camp.

What gives it this preponderance? Primarily, the following factors:

First, the Soviet Union, one of the mightiest powers of today, is directing all its efforts towards the preservation and consolidation of world peace. While the growing might of any big imperialist power was invariably accompanied by a growth of its aggressive aspirations and, consequently, led to a more acute threat of war, the growth of the forces of the first socialist state in the world has created, and is creating, effective guarantees against the danger of war, and increasing the chances of its being prevented. Since the time the Soviet Union won first place in the world in the decisive fields of science and technology and placed this preponderance on the scales of the struggle for peace, the possibility that world security can be ensured has increased many times over.

Secondly, another mighty force now stands, together with the Soviet Union, in the way of the imperialist aggressors—all the countries of the world socialist camp. Under the conditions of imperialism the emergence of any alliance of states is aimed at preparing new wars; the countries of the socialist community, on the contrary, are pooling their efforts exclusively to achieve the triumph of the cause of peace and social progress.

Thirdly, one more new force has appeared on the world scene—a large group of young national states in Asia, Africa and Latin America who are interested in the preservation of peace for the accomplishment of the tasks of national regeneration. The majority of these states uphold a policy of peace. The fact that the vital interests of the peoples of these countries and the interests of the peoples of the socialist states coincide is the objective basis for uniting their efforts in defence of peace. Expressing, as it does, the will and the power of two-thirds of mankind, so mighty a front can make the imperialist aggressors retreat.

Fourthly, the role that the masses of the capitalist countries now play in world politics has grown tremendously too. In the presence of the threat of a thermonuclear war, a coalition without precedent in history is in the process of formation, a coalition of heterogeneous mass movements united by a desire to rid mankind for all time of the catastrophe of war. The international working class, which is becoming more and more aware of its historic responsibility for the fate of mankind, has become the great organising force of this coalition. The banner of peace is in the firm hands of the many-million-strong army of Communists of all lands.

Such are the principal forces that, in our times, are blocking the way to war. They are truly countless today. Tomorrow they will become more powerful still. Fulfilment of the economic plans of the socialist countries will be of decisive importance for the consolidation of these forces. The fulfilment of the plans set forth in our Programme will make still more powerful the material basis on which the defenders of peace can rely.

Mankind can and must prevent war. That task, however, can be achieved only given the most active and resolute action by all peace-loving forces. *To curb the imperialists in good time, to give them no opportunity to use lethal weapons, to prevent war and not allow it to flare up—such is the crucial issue today. (Applause.)*

The great service rendered by Lenin, by our Party, lies in their having brought forward the only foreign policy principle correct for the period of the existence of two social systems, that of the peaceful coexistence of states with different social structures, which is now being implemented. The principle of peaceful coexistence is winning the minds of hundreds of millions of people. Even representatives of bourgeois circles, those that are capable of sober thinking, recognise the telling force and role of this principle.

Genuine stability in the relations between states with different social systems can be achieved only when the arms race will no longer be a sword of Damocles hanging over the peoples, that is to say, in conditions of general and complete disarmament. It is not on a foundation of military might, but on a foundation of general disarmament that a genuinely reliable system of international security can be created. That is why our Party, the Soviet Government and the whole of our people are determined to fight for disarmament, to look for paths to that objective, until this historic task is at last fulfilled.

Imperialism wants to turn the policy of "brinkmanship" into a constantly operating norm in international relations. What we want to turn into a constantly operating norm in international relations is durable peace and the general security of the peoples. The politics of imperialism are an expression of the selfish interests of a handful of monopolists. The politics of socialism embody the interests of all mankind. That is why we are convinced that the cardinal principle of socialism's foreign policy—the principle of peaceful coexistence—will be the banner under which all the peoples will rally, all those who want genuine peace and prosperity for mankind. *(Applause.)*

In adopting its new Programme, our great Party solemnly proclaims to the whole of mankind that it sees as the principal aim of its foreign policy not only the prevention of world war but also its expulsion for all time from the life of society, already within the lifetime of our generation. (Prolonged applause.)

Our policy of peace is a principled, outspoken, socialist policy. We are defending the cause of peace not because we are weak. We were able to rout our enemies and ensure ourselves conditions of peace even when the young socialist republic was besieged on all sides by the imperialist wolves, when it was incomparably weaker than the imperialists in the military and economic sense. During the Second World War the Soviet Union made the decisive contribution to the defeat of the Hitler war machine, and saved humanity from fascist enslavement. Can there be any doubt of the fate that awaits the imperialist maniacs if they dare attack the socialist gains of the peoples in the new situation, now that the Soviet Union has tremendous might at its disposal, now that the powerful socialist community is marching by its side in serried ranks, now that we are backed by hundreds of millions of people all over the world? In these conditions the launching of a war will mean the end of the anti-popular imperialist system. *(Stormy applause.)*

Our unshakable confidence in this does not mean that we are underestimating the forces of imperialism in the slightest. We know that imperialism is still strong. The possibility of a new war being unleashed by the imperialists cannot be written off. The imperialist maniacs may dash headlong into adventures, in an attempt to stay the course of history. In a situation like that we have only one path—we must strengthen our might, create the most powerful weapons, and be prepared at any moment to hurl back any attacks made by the aggressors. *(Applause.)* We have declared more than once, and we declare again, that we are prepared to disband our army, and sink our atomic bombs and our rockets in the ocean, but of course only given general and complete disarmament under strict international control. Until the imperialist powers agree to that, we shall see to it that our Armed Forces possess the most up-to-date means for the defence of our homeland —atomic and thermonuclear weapons and rockets of every range—and that all types of armaments are maintained at the due level. The strengthening of the U.S.S.R.'s defences and of the might of the Soviet Armed Forces—such is the paramount task of the Soviet people. *(Stormy applause.)*

Communists are in duty bound to look history boldly in the face. As long as the war danger exists, as long as there are in this world imperialist jungles inhabited by preying tigers, we must educate all our people, our youth, in a spirit of devoted love for the homeland, readiness to defend it, sparing neither strength nor life itself. Our cause is a great one, and to defend that cause the Soviet people will give their all. If the imperialists challenge us to war, we shall not only take up that challenge without hesitation, but, with all the devoted gallantry and courage inherent in Communists, we shall deal the enemy a devastating blow. *(Stormy, prolonged applause.)*

Comrades, all the content of our new Programme confirms the fact that communism serves peace, the creation of conditions for the exclusion of war from the life of society. It is clear to everybody that one who sets oneself such unprecedented tasks in the economic and cultural spheres, and in improving the people's living standards, cannot seek war. The Programme for the construction of communism is at the same time a historic programme for consolidating peace and international security. *(Prolonged applause.)*

<h1 style="text-align:center">VI</h1>

RESULTS OF THE DISCUSSION
OF THE DRAFT PROGRAMME

Comrades, since the day of its publication, political life in the Soviet Union has centred around the draft Programme. The ideas it contains have, moreover, spread far beyond the bounds of our country and have met with a very warm response in the hearts of millions of people living in all countries and continents.

The discussion of the draft Programme has demonstrated with great force the close and unseverable ties between the Party and the people, and the democratic nature of Soviet society, a society in which the people are the masters of their own fate.

Permit me to deal first with the results of the discussion of the draft Programme in the Party and in the country, and then to comment briefly on the response it has aroused throughout the world.

1. Unanimous Approval of the Draft Programme by the Party and the People. Amendments to the Draft

The discussion of the draft Programme acquired dimensions unprecedented even in the history of our Party and the Soviet state. This was only natural because the aims of the Programme and the tasks elaborated in it concern and enthuse each and every one.

The draft Programme has been thoroughly discussed in all its aspects at meetings of all primary Party organisations, at district, city, regional and territorial Party conferences, and at congresses of the Communist parties of the Union republics. Over nine million Communists, that is, the entire Party, took part in those discussions. More than 500,000 meetings were held at factories, collective farms, offices, army, navy and air force units, and trade union and Komsomol organisations, at which the draft Programme was discussed. About 73,000,000 people attended them. More than 4,600,000 people spoke on the draft Programme at Party meetings, conferences, congresses of the Communist parties of the Union republics and at meetings of working people.

In addition to this, the Central Committee of the Party, local Party bodies, the editorial offices of newspapers and magazines, radio and television have received more than 300,000 letters and articles.

Statistics, however, is unable to gauge the exact number of people who participated. The discussion permeated the entire ideological life of the country and was carried on in the most varied forms—at meetings of factory personnel, at state and collective farms, in offices, institutes and schools, and in friendly talks at work and at home. It may be said without exaggeration that the draft Programme was discussed by the whole people and was accepted by the people as their own programme, as the purpose of their life. *(Stormy applause.)*

The Congress has every reason to affirm that the *draft Programme has been unanimously approved by all Communists and by the entire Soviet people. (Stormy, prolonged applause.)* The ideas contained in the Programme and the plans it outlines have been accepted not only in the minds but in the hearts of all Soviet people. The speeches and letters of Party members and non-Party people are filled with lofty thoughts and feelings. In the letters— many of them could more truly be called poems, so inspired and emotional are they—people welcome the new Party Programme with all their hearts and express their firm determination and eagerness to work for its implementation. The thoughts and feelings of the people are reflected in those letters as the sun is reflected in a drop of water. *(Applause.)*

The discussion of the draft Programme was strictly to the point and was conducted on a highly principled ideological level. This is further evidence of the political maturity of the many-million-strong army of Communists, of all Soviet people. It is gratifying to note the profound knowledge of theory and practice with which the Soviet people tackled the wide range of big, new and complicated problems connected with the building of a communist society. The draft Programme has widened the ideological horizons of the Soviet people. They now see more clearly their great goal and the tasks that have to be done. The Programme has imparted great creative power to the nation-wide socialist emulation movement in honour of the Congress. This shows convincingly that the Party and the people have virtually adopted the Programme and are already working for its implementation. *(Stormy applause.)*

Comrades, the numerous proposals for amendments to the draft Programme are marked by a creative effort to find the best solutions to the problems presented; they show the profound interest that all Soviet people have in the building of communist society to proceed as efficiently as possible.

Permit me to report to the Congress that all proposals have been thoroughly studied by the Central Committee. To begin with, I will speak of those proposals that the Central Committee considers acceptable. I shall mention only the most significant of them.

1. The Central Committee supports the proposals to stress more strongly in the Programme the significance of accelerated technological progress, the fuller and more rational employment of production capacities.

2. The Central Committee considers as correct the proposals to include a special point in the Programme on the need to make capital investments more efficacious, the

impermissibility of scattering investments and the importance of concentrating them in the decisive sectors.

In the course of the discussion attention was rightly called to a lack of co-ordination between the erection of new industrial buildings and the provision of equipment for them. We actually do suffer great losses from this lack of co-ordination. For instance, on January 1, 1961, there were industrial buildings with a total floor area of millions of square metres that had not been completely equipped, on the one hand, and stocks of equipment to the value of hundreds of millions of rubles for which the necessary buildings were not ready, on the other. The Central Committee and the Government already have measures in hand to improve capital construction in our country. It is an urgent task to establish strict order in this important matter.

3. At some Party meetings and conferences it has been proposed that the Programme make provision for the establishment of an iron and steel centre in the heart of the European part of the Soviet Union, using the world's biggest ironfield, the Kursk Magnetic Anomaly, as the basis. This proposal is in accordance with plans. I have already said that by the end of the twenty-year period we plan to complete a third metallurgical centre in Siberia, and to establish two more new iron and steel centres. We are of the opinion that it would be desirable to state in the Programme in which areas they are to be built. Party organisations, planning bodies and all executives in the iron and steel industry would then bear greater responsibility for the implementation of the plans.

4. In view of the numerous proposals received, the Central Committee considers it essential to add to the relevant section of the Programme a special point on the conservation of natural resources and their proper use. Our forests, waters, fish and other natural resources constitute tremendous national wealth. As we march forward towards communism we must treasure what nature provides, we must

use our resources wisely and rationally, we must restore and multiply the wealth of our forests, rivers and seas.

5. Comrade Nektov, Hero of Socialist Labour, and many other people working in agriculture quite rightly propose that the Programme emphasise the need for care and good maintenance of farm machinery. We cannot reconcile ourselves to the fact that the efficiency of tractors and other machines in many collective and state farms is low because of poor maintenance and, what is more important, they go out of commission prematurely. A negligent and, at times, even barbarous attitude to machinery hampers the growth of farm output and is a sheer waste of national property.

The Central Committees of the Communist Parties and the Councils of Ministers of the Union republics must immediately elaborate a system of economic, organisational and technical measures that will ensure the long life and better maintenance of tractors, harvester combines and other machinery.

6. Many proposals have been received from working people, especially from women, to reduce the time required for the fulfilment of such an important task as the further expansion of the network of children's pre-school institutions. The draft Programme envisaged the expansion of the network of nurseries and kindergartens to give an opportunity, in the second decade, to all families so desiring to maintain their children in them. The Central Committee, in due consideration of the wishes expressed during the discussion of the draft Programme, deems it essential to meet these wishes and to do everything possible to satisfy the demand for nurseries and kindergartens within the next few years. *(Applause.)*

There have also been proposals that mothers of large families should, at their own request, be permitted a shorter working day and have their wages adjusted accordingly. The Central Committee considers it necessary to instruct our government and trade union bodies to study and elaborate relevant proposals.

Many people have suggested at Party meetings, meetings of working people, and in letters to the Central Committee, that the resolution of the housing problem should be speeded. Taking note of the numerous suggestions on that score, the Central Committee deemed it necessary to point out in the Programme that by the end of the first decade families that are still living in substandard and over-crowded dwellings, will get new flats. *(Applause.)*

In the course of the discussion proposals were made on literally every aspect of the life of our society, all of them permeated with deep concern for the all-round improvement of our economic and cultural development. Many of the proposals concern specific questions of the development of industry, agriculture, planning and management, and the improvement of the work of our state and economic administration, and making it cheaper to run. Many of the proposals concern the expansion of research work on various problems and, most important of all, the application of the latest scientific achievements in industry and agriculture, in the transport services, in building and in communications. Many of the submitted proposals deal with questions of ideological work , communist morality, education, culture, and with further measures to combat parasitism, money-grubbing and other manifestations of private-property psychology. Valuable proposals have been tendered in the sphere of town-planning, especially housing construction and urban and rural improvement. There have been many proposals on other problems as well. The basic line for the solution of these problems is laid down clearly in the draft Programme. But many of the proposals concern important questions of state, economic and cultural development and of political and ideological educational work. They are deserving of serious consideration. The final text of the draft Programme has been edited with due consideration for these proposals. The Central Committee will study all proposals attentively and will instruct the relevant Party, state or other bodies to take the necessary practical steps.

Party members and non-Party people have offered many critical remarks and many proposals on the work of local Party, governmental, economic and trade union organisations and institutions. Defects have been pointed out in production, in trade and public catering, in the distribution of housing and the maintenance of dwelling houses, etc. Instances of bureaucratic methods and red tape and abuse of official status by individual executives have been exposed. Our Congress should instruct Regional Committees, Territorial Committees, and the Central Committees of the Communist Parties of the Union republics to make a thorough study of these criticisms and proposals, to adopt measures to remedy the defects exposed and report on those measures to relevant plenary meetings and then to current Party conferences and congresses.

There have been some proposals, few, it is true, whose authors have an unrealistic approach to the solution of some problems of communist construction. Some comrades, for instance, propose that the Programme should provide for the overall electrification of the country, including that of the farms, within the next ten or even five years. Proposals have also been made that the Programme provide for other no less "resolute" but economically unrealistic measures. We understand the feelings of such comrades, but we cannot agree with them. It would be wrong to include in the Programme anything that we cannot yet accomplish. By such commitments and promises we would only be discrediting the Programme. (Applause.)

There is yet another type of proposal, submitted by people whose approach to the processes taking place in life is, I would say, scholastic, and not creative. Some comrades, for example, are of the opinion that the dictatorship of the proletariat should be retained until the final victory of communism has been achieved. These comrades do not take into consideration the objective conditions that have grown up in our country, and base themselves exclusively on random quotations, losing sight of the essence of the theory of Marx, Engels and Lenin on the state of the dictatorship of the proletariat as the form of state in the period of transition from capitalism to socialism, the first phase of communism. They do not take into consideration the fact that there are now only labouring classes in our socialist society, classes engaged in socialist production, and socially, politically and ideologically united. After the complete and final victory of socialism in our country there is no basis for the dictatorship of one class. And, indeed, in respect of which class can there possibly be a dictatorship in our country? We have no such classes.

Such comrades, moreover, are of the opinion that since the alliance of the working class and the peasantry has remained, the dictatorship of the proletariat should also remain. But they do not understand that the workers' and peasants' alliance needed the dictatorship of the proletariat to combat the exploiting classes, to transform peasant farming along socialist lines and to re-educate the peasantry, and to build socialism. Now that those tasks have been accomplished the alliance of the working class and the peasantry is successfully developing and growing stronger without the dictatorship of the proletariat under the conditions of a socialist state of the whole people. (Applause.)

Those comrades also refer to the fact that the organisational, economic, cultural and educational functions inherent in the dictatorship of the proletariat also remain in the period of the transition to communism. These functions, however, will remain under communism as well. If we are to be consistent, the dictatorship of the proletariat must, according to the logic of those comrades, also remain under communism. The fallacy of such arguments is obvious to everyone.

The proposition on the development of the state of the dictatorship of the proletariat into a state of the whole people as formulated in the Programme, corresponds fully to reality. This state is a product of reality; it expresses our policy on the political organisation of society, a policy aimed at the all-round development of democracy. *(Applause.)*

Some comrades propose forbidding kolkhoz trading, and some of the more zealous propose doing away with trading altogether and replacing it with direct distribution. Is there any need to prove that these comrades are running a long way ahead? The question of whether or not there is to be trading is not decided by somebody's wish or by decree. In order to effect a transition to direct distribution we must create the necessary material and technical basis and an abundance of material values. So long as that does not exist we must not curtail, but, on the contrary, develop and perfect Soviet trade. *(Applause.)* Nor can kolkhoz trading be prohibited since it plays a noticeable role in supplying the population with foodstuffs. The collective farmers need to sell part of their produce. Furthermore, fixed prices on the kolkhoz market cannot be established administratively, as some comrades suggest. A reduction in prices on the kolkhoz market should be effected primarily by increasing the output of farm produce and not by administrative measures. The latter should be applied firmly only against profiteers. At the same time the work of the co-operatives must be improved, they must help the collective farmers realise their surplus produce.

In view of the importance of the continued expansion of Soviet trade, the Central Committee is of the opinion that it would be to good purpose to include in the Programme a point on trade and its improvement in the period of communist construction.

Our Party, being a Party of scientific communism, advances and accomplishes the tasks of communist construction, as the necessary conditions for it arise and mature. Above I gave details of the Party's plans in the sphere of production and living standards. Some comrades, however, propose going considerably farther than the planned targets and extending, in the near future, the principle of the free satisfaction of the requirements of members of society to a broader range of material and cultural values; this would be tantamount to introducing equal pay for all, irrespective of qualifications or the nature of the work performed. Such proposals are profoundly erroneous. To take such a path would be to remove the material stimulus for higher labour productivity, to hamper the building of communism. *(Applause.)*

As we all know, on the initiative of the Central Committee of the Party, considerable work has been done in recent years to bring order into the wages system. These measures have resulted in considerable reductions of high incomes and of the salaries of some categories of employees. At the same time the minimum rate of wages has been raised. The established procedure of abolishing the income-tax is also helping to narrow the gap between the incomes of various categories of working people. In short, much has been done to reduce the gap between the incomes of the various groups of the population. It is stated clearly in the draft Programme that the Party will continue to pursue this course consistently and unswervingly in order that by the end of the first decade, the very category of low-paid workers ceases to exist in our country and the well-being of the whole people rises. *(Applause.)* Simultaneously with wages, the social funds will increase at an accelerated rate, which will eliminate disproportion in incomes and bring about a more rapid improvement in the living standard of low- and medium-paid workers. All wage-levelling tendencies are contrary to the interests of the development of production and the raising of living standards, contrary to the education of the working people in the spirit of a communist attitude to labour.

We must stringently enforce the principle of "he who does not work, neither shall he eat", the principle of pay according to work performed. At the same time we must close all loopholes that enable anti-social elements to rob society, acquire incomes from sources other than labour and live a parasitic life. We must suppress profiteering and similar offences with a firm hand, making full use of Soviet legislation and of the influence of public opinion.

We favour a steady improvement in the living standard of the entire people, but are opposed, at the same time, to any excessive accumulation of property by individuals, which fosters private property psychology.

In the course of the discussion many amendments of an editorial nature have been proposed. The Central Committee has examined these amendments. Some of them improve the text, and have been inserted in the draft Programme distributed to you.

Such are the principal questions presented in the course of the discussion of the draft Programme.

2. International Comments on the Draft Programme

Comrades, the draft Programme of the C.P.S.U. has acquired the character of a document of trully world-wide importance and has already had considerable influence on the political climate of the world. It has aroused the keen attention of the masses in the countries of the socialist camp, of the general public in the imperialist states and of the peoples that have won their independence or are still groaning under the heel of the colonialists. It has penetrated to the most distant corners of the earth, and has forced its way into the columns of even the most reactionary bourgeois publications.

It is naturally gratifying to us Soviet Communists to know that the fraternal Marxist-Leninist parties, the many-million-strong army of Communists of all countries, have given the draft Programme high praise. As internationalists, we are happy when the Communists of other countries state that they draw inspiration for their own practical activities and struggle from the Programme, that the achievements of our Party multiply their forces, the forces of freedom, peace, and socialism throughout the world. Permit me, on behalf of the delegates to the Twenty-Second Congress, on behalf of the members of our Party, on behalf of the entire Soviet people, to express our heartfelt thanks to all the fraternal parties, to Communists throughout the world for their support of our plans and our aims. (*Prolonged applause.*) We assure you, our brothers in other countries, that our Leninist Party, holding high the banner of proletarian internationalism, will do everything in its power to bring mankind closer to a world of peace, happiness and prosperity, to communist society. (*Stormy applause.*)

All people holding progressive, democratic views note that the Programme provides solutions to the most urgent problems of the day, and will play an outstanding part in social movements and in the progressive changes of modern times. As far as the bourgeoisie and its press are concerned, they have to admit that the Programme and its fulfilment will have an exceptional impact on the situation throughout the world.

An examination of the statements made by prominent bourgeois and Right-wing Socialist personalities in respect of the draft Programme of our Party will enable us to draw a number of conclusions that are of significance in matters of principle.

It must first of all be said that a real battle between the two ideologies, the communist and the bourgeois, has developed around the ideas of the Programme. We may safely say that the communist ideas embodied in the gigantic plans for construction vividly demonstrate their immeasurable superiority over bourgeois ideology, over the ideology of violence and destruction, and score fresh victories over that ideology. (*Applause.*)

The first victory is that bourgeois ideologists now admit that communism, as a new socio-economic organisation of society, is becoming an ever more powerful force in our times. In the nineteenth century the bourgeoisie declared that communist ideals were a utopia and those who championed them were persecuted and baited. In the first three decades of the twentieth century they carried out several "anti-communist" crusades on an international scale, and in a number of countries communism was declared to have been buried for all time. In the fifties they were loud in their assertions that communism was suffering from an "incurable crisis". But a few years passed and imperialist reactionaries were forced to take note of the colossal growth of communism, its vitalising force and its growing significance to world history. *(Applause.)*

Extremely typical of the evolution of bourgeois views are the statements made by such a serious bourgeois weekly as the British *Economist*. At the time our Party adopted its second programme the *Economist* asserted that Bolshevism was on its last legs, but is now compelled to admit that the Programme is "a projection of current trends", and that "the promises in the manifesto do not look fanciful". *(Applause.)*

The Communists have shown that they do not waste words, that they fulfil all their promises. They have compelled even their opponents to respect their plans. *(Applause.)* Communism has entered present-day life tangibly and visibly, it has occupied a leading position in it and there is no power that can check its victorious advance. *(Stormy applause.)*

An analysis of world comments permits of still another important conclusion; the great idea of the Programme, that communism and peace are indivisible, is becoming ever more widespread among the population of the capitalist countries. Even many representatives of the bourgeoisie have to admit that a country that has announced such great plans of construction must want peace. In the U.S.A., the citadel of imperialism, the democratic public contrapose the Programme of our Party, that magnificent charter of peace and humanism, to the plans of the American imperialists for military mobilisation, plans bringing sorrow, sweat and blood. The Australian *Sydney Morning Herald,* an old hand at anti-Soviet slander, had to admit that the Soviet Union, having such a grandiose plan in view, calls for peace. And here is what a bourgeois newspaper in another part of the world, the Lebanese *An Nahar,* has to say: "The advocates of war have been dealt a crushing blow. Once the substance of the Programme is understood by everybody, the flag of peace will be raised everywhere."

What do such admissions tell us? They tell us that the Programme has administered a big new defeat to the aggressive forces, to those who worship the hydrogen bomb.

The great ideas of the Programme are shattering to pieces the myths and anti-communist inventions of the bourgeoisie and its lackeys. Communism's power of attraction is growing and the ideas of communism are acquiring more and more supporters. The new Programme is helping ever-growing numbers of people to realise that communism is superior to capitalism economically, politically and morally, that the future belongs to communism. It is not difficult to see the causes of the alarm that has gripped the bourgeoisie and their advocates; they obviously have nothing to contrapose to the Programme of the C.P.S.U. They have nothing to say about the future, they cannot plan for a single year, to say nothing of twenty years. The Burmese writer, Dau A Ma, expressed it very well when she said, "The United States is the monarch of capitalist society, the 'commander-in-chief' in the struggle against communism. That country, even if it wanted to out of spite, could not draw up any plan that would compete with the Soviet plan. The same is true of Britain. She is unable to compile a single plan similar to that of the Soviet Union."

The imperialist bourgeoisie are particularly worried about the effect of the Programme on the peoples of Asia,

Africa and Latin America. Albert Gore, member of the Senate Foreign Relations Committee, warned in alarm that the appeal of the Programme to the under-privileged nations must not be underrated.

The ideas of the Programme really do have great attraction for all people exploited by capitalism. *The Times of India* wrote: "Since the Communist Manifesto, there has not been a more inspiring communist document. The practicability of the Programme is also not doubted; at least the Afro-Asian nations are impressed by Soviet achievements which create a kind of conviction in them that anything that Russia promises it can achieve." Not a bad testimonial for our Programme and our activities! *(Applause.)*

Imperialist propaganda is continually inventing new methods of lauding capitalism and scaring the peoples of the newly-free countries with the difficulties of a non-capitalist path of development. The more the imperialist bourgeoisie do this, however, the more obvious becomes their fear of advanced ideas that inspire the peoples in the struggle for the final abolition of colonialism, in the struggle for social progress. As far as we are concerned, we do not foist our ideas on anybody. If, however, the peoples of the newly-free countries choose to adopt the ideas of socialism, the ideas of progress, all we can say, on the basis of our own experience, is that they will be doing the right thing. *(Applause.)*

Imperialism's ideological lackeys are trying to comfort their masters with sham arguments to the effect that the ideas of communism are not in any way attractive to the population of the Western countries. But they are, gentlemen! The ideas of communism are alive and are gaining ground wherever there are people who toil and are humiliated by capitalism. Do you want to know what millions of people in the countries of your lauded "civilisation" are thinking? Ask any of the workers living in fear of the morrow, or any of the ruined farmers, ask the unemployed in the breadlines, ask all those who want peace and happiness for their children. You will learn that millions of people in your own countries are drawn to communism. I want to quote a letter to *Pravda* from an unemployed American. "This draft and its meaning", he wrote, "holds to all the world an answer to the daily murder of workers everywhere by capitalist crimes against the people of the world. The Soviet people can't imagine what a great source of strength this Programme is to us who live under capitalist rule." This unemployed appeals to the Soviet people: "I can only close by saying, hurry, complete this task, the whole world looks to you in the Soviet Union to fulfil, complete this program, as fast as can be done, and thus save millions who would otherwise die of exploitation, ground down, give up." That document was written in his heart's blood; it is a genuine expression of the thoughts and feelings of our brothers in the capitalist countries.

The ideas of the Programme, the ideas of communism, are spreading over our planet because hundreds of millions of people who are downtrodden and under-privileged see in them the embodiment of their best feelings and aspirations. The witch-doctors of capitalism cannot fence off the peoples from the idea of progress by means of police cordons and "iron curtains". Communism is the hope of the peoples, the guarantee of their radiant future! *(Stormy applause.)*

The imperialist bourgeoisie still do not, of course, want to admit their ideological defeat. That stands to reason, since it would mean political suicide for them to do so. They are making feverish efforts and using any means to minimise the significance of the draft Programme of the C.P.S.U., to weaken its influence on the masses.

The ruling élite of capitalist society are making vain attempts to contrapose their own platform, some plan for the preservation of capitalism, to our Programme. But how often have we read and heard of plans for the rejuvenation of capitalism. Yet capitalism is inexorably decaying. That, too, stands to reason, for there are no means that can save the doomed system. Such a system does not and cannot possess ideas that inspire the peoples. None other than the *New York Post* has provided damning evidence of the poverty of bourgeois ideology. "For several years," says the paper in connection with the draft Programme, "a number of American leaders have been wrestling with the concept of 'national purpose', and have come up with little more than empty abstractions."

Hence, capitalism has no positive programme of its own and no arguments to offer in criticism of our Programme. In this unenviable plight, the legion of bourgeois apologists searched in an arid desert for anti-communist arrows. But they did not find anything except the poisoned arrows of slander, insinuations and rigged quotations. Hence the utter confusion, impotent malice in the camp of the enemies of communism.

Bourgeois critics have shouted in chorus, as though in response to a command—the Programme is not feasible. The familiar incantations that we know since the first Soviet five-year plans have again appeared in the columns of the reactionary newspapers—"utopia", "mirage", "illusion". Perhaps the opponents of our Programme are in possession of some figures, calculations or facts? Nothing of the sort. Every proposition in our Programme is substantiated. They have nothing but noisy declarations. Every figure of ours is computed and proved. They are as afraid of figures as the devil is of holy water. We have given an exact scientific analysis of the course of historical development. They have nothing but hysterical incantations, a fruitless predicting from tea-leaves. They put so much zeal into them that they do not even realise how they drop into obvious contradictions and cannot make their stories hang together. Moreover, they bang their heads together. One group of the critics shouts, "the Programme cannot be fulfilled", while another group shouts, "This is a challenge!

Save yourselves if you can!" The French newspaper *Figaro* maintains that the new Soviet plans are "castles in the air". The Austrian newspaper *Das kleine Volksblatt* calls on the West "not to regard the gigantic aims the Kremlin sets itself as mere castles in the air, for those aims are a challenge to the West in the real sense of the word". Here it is truly a case of "understand if you can"! As you can see these critics lost their way in a forest of not even the three proverbial pine-trees, but merely of two!

The second hobby-horse the critics of our Programme try to ride is the worn-out tale of the absence of the freedom of the individual under communism. The Austrian Social-Democratic newspaper, *Arbeiter Zeitung*, tried to give a "basis" to this absurd assertion. Here is what the paper says: "We believe that on the day after tomorrow a Soviet citizen actually may get a free ticket to travel, but we do not believe that it is at all likely that he will have the right to go where he wants." *(Laughter.)* If anybody were to ask a Soviet citizen whether he could go wherever he wanted, he would look at his interlocutor as at one who was mentally deranged and had escaped from a lunatic asylum. *(Laughter. Applause.)* Soviet people go wherever they like. In answer to the same question, what would the hundreds of Americans, those "freedom riders" who travelled through the southern states and ended up behind bars, have to say?

No less ridiculous is another line in bourgeois propaganda. They announce, without a second thought, that the conditions the Soviet people want to achieve under communism already exist in the U.S.A. and certain other capitalist countries. It would be difficult to imagine a greater mockery of the facts, mockery of the living conditions of working people in the capitalist countries. Just think of it—the American newspapers admit that the "level of unemployment remains a national scandal", that millions of people are actually starving. And yet attempts are being made to delude those millions, who are experiencing all the "joys" of the American way of life, into believing that their requirements are met according to needs. Year after year American newspapers report that medical services are ruinously expensive in America and now they would have us believe that they, too, have free medical attention. Yesterday the American press was telling the whole world that rent is the ruination of millions of families and today, according to their hack writers, housing in the U.S.A. is almost rent-free. They have all got hopelessly mixed up with their lies, those would-be critics!

The Programme of the C.P.S.U. consistently pursues the line of coexistence and peaceful competition. As we see, the call to peaceful coexistence scares those who do not want peace. Some bourgeois newspapers go so far as to say that peaceful coexistence is a "weapon of world revolution". The *New York Times*, one of the leading newspapers of the capitalist world, said in commenting on the Programme that it is a new declaration of war on the free world, a declaration of a military, political, economic and propaganda war.

That, gentlemen, is hysterics. Your nerves have given way. In what part of the Programme did you find anything in the nature of a declaration of war on the capitalist world? Which article, which proposition of the Programme gives you grounds for such assertions? There are not, and cannot be, any such grounds. If the ink-slingers on the *New York Times* are still harping on the old theme, it only goes to show again that they are afraid of peace, of coexistence, since they realise that capitalism cannot stand up to a peaceful competition with socialism. Imperialist circles pin all their hopes on war and are thereby demonstrating again and again how much their plans are inimical to the vital interests of the peoples.

We are not in the least upset that the obscurantists and reactionaries are maliciously attacking our Programme. We should be upset if they were to praise us. If the forces of obscurantism are arrayed against our Programme, the latter must be hitting the mark. We are following our own road, the road of communism, with confidence, and are quite certain that sooner or later all mankind will take that road. *(Stormy, prolonged applause.)*

VII

THE PARTY IN THE PERIOD
OF FULL-SCALE COMMUNIST CONSTRUCTION

Comrades, the grandeur of the new Programme speaks of the grandeur of our Leninist Party. In giving expression to the lofty ideals of communism our Party is creditably performing its mission as leader of the revolutionary transformation of society. *Our Marxist-Leninist Party which came into being as a party of the working class has become the party of the entire people.* In this is manifested the monolithic unity and might of Soviet society, welded by common interests and outlook. At all times, in fair weather and foul, in days of triumph and in days of stress, *the Party is with the people and the people are with the Party. (Stormy applause.)* The Communist Party is the force that rallies the will, the efforts and energies of our people to accomplishing the tasks that confront us in the new stage of historical development.

Today, when our country possesses vast material potentialities, a highly-developed science and technology, when the initiative of the masses is in full tide, the rates of our progress depend chiefly on the correct implementation of the envisaged political line on a country-wide and local scale, on the proper and effective functioning of all our state and public organisations, on their ability to make proper use of the advantages of the socialist system. Hence the need to enhance the directing and organising role of the Party in the period of the full-scale building of communism. *(Applause.)*

Along what principal lines will the Communist Party

develop during this period? We consider that it will be along the lines of:

further enhancing the role of the Party as the highest form of social and political organisation, its guiding influence in all spheres of communist construction;

strengthening the unity between the Party and the people, extending the variety of forms of Party ties with the non-Party masses, raising ever larger sections of working people to the level of Party members in political consciousness and in activeness;

further promoting inner-Party democracy, enhancing the significance of the name of Party member, rousing all Communists to still greater activity and initiative, strengthening the unity and solidity of Party ranks. *(Applause.)*

It should be stressed that a new, higher standard of the Party's political work and organisational leadership has to be attained to correspond to the period of the full-scale building of communism. Adoption of the new Programme is a great historic act. But it is only the first step. The main thing is to implement the Programme. The imposing tasks set out in the Programme place very high demands on the Party as a whole, and on every Party organisation.

The Rules of the C.P.S.U., which our Congress will adopt on the basis of the new Programme, elaborate the Party's organisational principles in conformity with the conditions and tasks of the period of full-scale communist construction.

The question of how elected Party bodies should be formed is one of fundamental importance. The draft Programme proposes a new procedure, which ensures *regular renewal of the composition of the leading Party bodies.* We believe that it would be advisable to apply this procedure also to elected bodies of state and public organisations.

The transition to this system will be a big step forward in the development of our democracy. It is in accord with the new period in the political organisation of Soviet society, when the state has become a state of the whole people, and the Party, the spokesman of the will and interests of the whole people. A distinctive feature of this period is the tremendous growth of the Party's ranks and of its ideological power, the growth of its cadres, and the unprecedented rise in the political and cultural level of the people. *(Applause.)*

When the Party was coming into being, it comprised a handful of advanced workers and intellectuals, who embraced Marxism because they wanted to know the laws of history and were seeking a revolutionary way out of the contradictions existing in society. Professional revolutionaries thoroughly devoted to the communist cause, they formed the guiding core of the Leninist Party, which organised and politically enlightened the working class and the working masses, led them in the assault on the old exploiter system, and secured the triumph of socialism. From its very inception, the strength of our Party lay in its high ideological integrity, in the cohesion and discipline of its ranks, in its ties with the masses, and in the support it was given by the working class and the labouring peasantry.

In the battles for the victory of the October Revolution, in the fire of the Civil War, on the fronts of socialist construction, in the grim ordeal of the Great Patriotic War, and in the post-war years, the strength of our Party multiplied, its ranks grew, its cadres became steeled. Shoulder to shoulder with the Communists, non-Party people too, who in their bulk are kindred in spirit with the Communists, are today actively building communism.

Whereas in the early years of the Revolution we had only a small number of leading Party workers, today we possess inexhaustible possibilities for promoting new people to leading posts. It is necessary to introduce procedures that will make it impossible for comrades who have been elected to leading posts to bar the way to fresh forces and will, on the contrary, give the latter an opportunity to apply their knowledge and ability in responsible posts in Party, government, trade union and other mass organisations, in the leadership of the Party and the country. We have many capable, educated people. All they lack is experience, and that is where our leading comrades should prove their worth as persons capable of training new cadres.

Every organism consists of separate cells and is continually renewed as some cells die off and others are born. The Party and society as a whole are subject to the same process, to the same law of life. This natural process cannot be checked or violated without causing harm to the development of the organism of the Party and society as a whole.

It is an open secret that there are comrades among us who in their time were duly appreciated and elected to leading offices, and that they have been occupying them for dozens of years. During this time some of them have lost the ability to conduct affairs in a creative spirit, have lost all sense of the new, and have become a hindrance. To keep them on at these posts just because they were elected to them in the past would be wrong. Surely we shouldn't confine ourselves perpetually to the same persons, once elected to leading bodies. That is not our policy. (Applause.) Naturally, if Party comrades are not re-elected to a Party body after the expiration of their term of office, this must not be a reason for discrimination. If a Communist has done well throughout his term in office, we must give him full credit for it. (Applause.)

Our task is to draw into leading Party and government work younger comrades who have proved their worth in work. Guided by the theory of Marxism-Leninism and the experience of generations of revolutionaries and builders of socialism, the new forces, in co-operation with the seasoned cadres, will successfully strengthen the might of our country, advance its economy, science, technology and culture. If we take into account that there are hundreds of thousands of elected bodies in our ramified system of primary and higher Party organisations, of our government bodies and public organisations, it will be clear that every regular election will bring millions of new people into the leadership.

The regular renewal of cadres, the promotion of new comrades who have proved their worth, the combination in our Party and state orchestra of young workers and workers mature in experience, is a law of development of the Marxist-Leninist party. In this the Party proceeds, in particular, from the lessons derived from the consequences of the cult of Stalin's person. I have spoken on this subject on more than one occasion, and in particular in the Central Committee's Report to the present Congress. The drafts of the Programme and the Rules, these basic documents of the Party, formulate propositions that should provide a safeguard against any recurrence of the cult of the individual, and raise a dependable barrier against it. We declare from the rostrum of the Congress: the Party must take all the necessary measures to bar the way to the cult of the individual for all time. *(Prolonged applause.)*

Regular renewal of elected bodies must henceforth become an implicit rule of Party life, of government and public life. This will open new opportunities for effecting the principles of collective leadership still more consistently.

The Party relies on the collective experience and collective thought of the Communists, of the entire people; it gives every encouragement to the initiative displayed by mass organisations, by all Soviet people. Every good innovation, every good idea, every valuable proposal should be given the most thoughtful consideration and active support, and should be realised. But we have officials who ignore the diverse manifestations of initiative displayed by the masses. To them the only important thing is what they themselves think or say. This is not a communist, but a bureaucratic point of view. It is the duty of all leading workers, all Party organisations, to apply the talents and abilities of every citizen for the good of communist construction. (*Applause.*)

The proposed system of forming elective bodies opens new opportunities for developing criticism and self-criticism aimed at resolutely rooting out cases where individuals are personally dependent on the whims of their superiors, doing away with elements of nepotism, and the mutual concealing of shortcomings and mistakes in work. The principle of renewal will make it possible to clear the elective bodies of people who are not inclined to consider the opinion and will of the leading collective of the given organisation and of the masses, who have lost their sense of responsibility to the Party and the people. Henceforth the elective bodies must be regularly renewed and must absorb the most capable people who have proved their worth and are devoted to communism.

It is in the best interests of our work to ensure a proper combination of old and new cadres and continuity in leadership, especially in the higher bodies. Without continuity it would be difficult to pursue a correct home and foreign policy and to direct economic and cultural development with success. Continuity of leadership is one of the basic Leninist principles. Lenin teaches us: "That, in fact, is one of the functions of a Party organisation and of Party leaders worthy of the calling, namely, through the prolonged, persistent, variegated and comprehensive efforts of all thinking representatives of the given class, to evolve the knowledge, the experience and—in addition to knowledge and experience—the political instinct necessary for the speedy and correct solution of intricate political problems."[*]

The prestige of Party workers, of its leaders is a valuable asset of the Party. While we reject the cult of the individual, we do not by any means waive the need of training leading Party workers and enhancing their prestige.

---

[*] V. I. Lenin, *Collected Works*, 4th Russ. ed., Vol. 31, p. 50.

The whole point is that Party leaders should be promoted from among the Party rank and file on the merits of their talents, and their political and business capacity, that they should have close ties with the Communists, with the people. That is how the development of Party leaders proceeded in Lenin's lifetime. That is how it should be today. *(Stormy applause.)*

We must implicitly observe and develop the Leninist standards of Party life and the principle of collective leadership, ensure strict supervision by the Party rank and file of the activities of the leading bodies and their officials, encouragement of the activity and initiative of all Communists, their really constructive participation in the elaboration and implementation of Party policy, the development of criticism and self-criticism.

If a party always looks ahead, if it always turns to the people and draws on their intelligence, enriching and broadening its experience, it can weather all trials. Our Party, founded and reared by Lenin, is just such a party. *(Stormy applause.)* So let us, comrades, always sacredly cherish and ever more consistently put the behests of our immortal leader and teacher into effect. Our successes will then be all the greater. *(Prolonged applause.)*

At the new stage of our development it is especially important to improve Party leadership of government and economic bodies, and trade union, Komsomol, co-operative and other mass organisations. This is an essential condition for enhancing the organisation of the people and for mobilising their creative powers. While bearing responsibility for the state of work in all spheres of communist construction, the Party organisations must not assume functions assigned to government bodies and public organisations. The main thing in the Party's leadership of the mass organisations is to mobilise their efforts to build communism; regularly to improve the composition of their leading bodies; to promote, properly place and train cadres.

At the present stage the role and responsibility of the Party member are particularly great. The name of Communist is a high one. Today, as never before, he is expected to be in the van of the struggle for the implementation of the Party's policy. In his devoted service to the people, and in his behaviour in public and in private life, a Communist should set an example of observing the communist moral code and thereby contribute to the development and strengthening of communist relations. (*Applause.*)

A cardinal source of the Party's strength and invincibility lies in its unshakable ideological and organisational solidity. In its arsenal the Party retains organisational guarantees against all manifestations of factionalism and group activity incompatible with Leninist party principles.

The measures envisaged in the draft Programme concerning renewal of cadres, prevention of the cult of the individual, and an extensive promotion of inner-Party democracy are truly revolutionary measures. They are organically connected with the Party's general plan, its tactics and strategy in the struggle for communism. Realisation of these measures will make it possible to develop on a still broader scale the training of capable cadres devoted to communism, to promote the activity of the Party, of all the mass organisations, of the whole people. This means that the development of the economy and culture, the building of communism will proceed still more successfully.

Comrades, the elaboration of the programme for the full-scale building of communism is evidence of the tremendous theoretical strength of our Party and its Central Committee. Armed with the Programme, we Soviet Communists shall, as it were, rise to new heights affording a clearer view of our communist future. (*Applause.*) What gives us this strength? First and foremost, Marxism-Leninism—our ever victorious and constantly developing doctrine. The process of socialist and communist construction is, at the same time, a process enriching Marxist-Leninist theory through the practical experience of the millions of working people. The new Programme is an outstanding theoretical and political document containing both the basic principles of Marxist-Leninist theory on communism and the new conclusions drawn from the experience gained in implementing these principles in socialist and communist construction.

We are advancing along uncharted paths. We have to elaborate a large variety of problems arising in the course of communist construction, to develop and give concrete expression to theoretical propositions. Just as a living organism cannot grow normally without sunlight, so communist construction cannot succeed unless its course is illumined by Marxist-Leninist science. The task of our Party is to show constant concern for the development of our Marxist-Leninist theory, a most reliable compass indicating the way to new victories for communism. *(Prolonged applause.)*

*　*　*

Comrades, we the delegates to the Twenty-Second Congress have the great honour of considering and adopting the new Programme of the C.P.S.U.—the programme of communist construction. The realisation of this Programme will usher in the happiest era in the history of mankind.

For centuries mankind dreamt of a society without exploitation, without social and national oppression, a society where the bloody scourge of war would no longer threaten people. Many died the death of heroes in the struggle for the people's cause. But happiness remained no more than a dream, and sorrow and tears, the lot of the peoples. The greatness of the Marxist-Leninist doctrine is that it has shown the realistic way to realising the aspirations of the people of labour. To our Party has fallen the good fortune of translating into reality the first phase of communism, socialism, and of leading the Soviet people to the higher phase of communism. *(Stormy applause.)*

By raising the torch of liberty, the banner of socialism and communism over the world, our Party has glorified the twentieth century as the century of revolutionary, sweeping changes in the destinies of man. The heroic struggle of the great army of Communists of all countries who have carried the masses along with them, has accelerated the course of history, has brought closer the realisation of mankind's finest ideals. But how much faster history will advance when a communist society has been built in the Soviet Union!

The communist cause is advancing with giant strides. The standard-bearers of communism, the Marxist-Leninist parties, have demonstrated that they are parties of revolutionaries and innovators, the makers of the people's happiness. Progressives in all countries associate with Communists all that is most fine and most radiant. The forces of communism are legion. The truth of life, the truth of history is on the side of communism. *(Prolonged applause.)*

The triumph of communism has always been the cherished ultimate aim of the Leninist Party. This dream of communism is now becoming a reality. Not only our descendants, comrades, but we as well, our generation of Soviet people, shall live under communism! Knowledge of this inspires every Soviet citizen, spurs him on to live and work with unparalleled enthusiasm. *(Prolonged applause.)*

The Programme shows everyone the place he should occupy in the ranks of the builders of communism, how to work and study for the good of communism, how to prepare oneself to live in a communist society. So let us, comrades, devote all our efforts, all our energies to hastening the day when the sun of communism will shine over our land! *(Stormy applause.)*

The banner of Lenin inspired us in the struggle for the triumph of socialism. And we were victorious! *(Stormy applause.)*

The banner of Lenin inspires us in the new historic stage of our country's development—the stage of communist construction. *(Stormy applause.)*

Under the banner of Marxism-Leninism, under the leadership of the Communist Party, forward to the triumph of communism! *(Stormy, prolonged applause, ovation. All rise. Cheers. Shouts of "Long live the Communist Party!", "Long live Leninism!", "Long live the Leninist Central Committee!", "Long live Communism!")*

N. S. KHRUSHCHOV

CONCLUDING SPEECH
AT THE 22nd CONGRESS OF THE C.P.S.U.

October 27, 1961

Comrade Delegates, we have come to the end of our discussion of the Central Committee's Report and the Report on the Programme of the Communist Party of the Soviet Union which has proceeded at a high political level. Many delegates to the Congress have spoken from this rostrum. What may be said of these speeches? I think you will agree with me that each speech may be described as a report, as an account to the Party. Everyone who ascended this rostrum spoke of the most agitating, the most essential things that have been accomplished or have still to be accomplished. The speeches were imbued with indomitable faith in the triumph of communism. (*Prolonged applause.*)

All the speakers unanimously approved both the Central Committee's political line and practical activities, and the draft of our Party Programme, a programme for the building of communism. The Twenty-Second Congress is a most vivid demonstration of the unity of our Leninist Party, of the fact that all the Soviet people are lined up squarely behind it. (*Applause.*)

The entire content of the Twenty-Second Congress has reaffirmed our Party's unwavering fidelity to the line worked out by the Twentieth Congress. (*Applause.*) It is now still more evident that the Twentieth Congress has, by removing all the after-effects of the period of the personality cult, opened a new chapter in the history of our

Party and exercised a beneficial influence on the development of our country and of the world Communist and working-class movement as a whole. (*Applause.*)

The attention of our Congress is focussed on the Party Programme, a programme for the building of a communist society. All the delegates to the Congress who spoke from this rostrum approved the draft Programme submitted by the Central Committee, and discussed in a business-like manner concrete practical ways of translating it into reality. They expressed deep confidence that the new Programme will be successfully realised, and the readiness of Soviet people to apply all their energies to fulfilling the third Programme as successfully as the first and second. (*Prolonged applause.*)

Our Programme derives its strength and vitality from the devoted labour of the Soviet people. What joy and pride one feels when listening to the speeches of such wonderful innovators as Valentina Gaganova, Alexander Kolchik, Maria Rozhneva, Vasily Kavun, Vasily Smirnov, Alexander Gitalov and many others! How much initiative, inventiveness, skill and perseverance in labour our foremost men and women show in fulfilling their duty to their country and people! It is the millions of such innovators that are the flower and pride of our Soviet society. (*Applause.*)

It is very important at present that all working people at each factory, each building project, each collective and state farm, should concentrate on fulfilling and over-fulfilling the production plans. The higher the productivity and the higher the quality, the more values will we create; and the more values there are, the more rapid will be the Soviet people's advance towards the great goal, the building of a communist society. (*Applause.*)

Representatives of all the republics and of many territories and regions of our country—Party and government officials, people prominent in industry and agriculture—our wonderful beacons, as they are figuratively called, have spoken at the Congress; so have scientists, writers and art workers, and representatives of our glorious Armed Forces.

The delegates spoke of the key questions of communist construction. They spoke of the ways and means of building the material and technical basis of communism; of the urgent questions concerning the work of industry and the further development of agriculture; of the outlook for still greater progress in science, culture, education, art and literature in our country; of the tasks of moulding the man of the new communist society. All these matters were deeply and thoroughly examined by the Congress. Now, at the Twenty-Second Congress, we can see still more clearly that communist construction has become the practical task of the Party, the cause of all the Soviet people. (*Applause.*)

The delegates' speeches were highly principled, businesslike and intolerant of shortcomings. The comrades rightly called attention to the need for developing to the utmost the productive forces of Soviet society, for better planning and organisation of production, more efficient economic management, and for properly utilising the potentialities of industry and agriculture. The submitted proposals aimed at obtaining the maximum economic results at a minimum outlay of labour.

Important questions concerning the further improvement of economic management were raised during the debate on the Central Committee Report and the draft Programme. The Congress has shown that the Party unanimously approves of the measures effected in that field by the Central Committee and the Government in the last few years. In particular, everybody welcomed the creation of economic administration areas and of councils for the co-ordination and planning of the work of economic councils in the enlarged economic administration areas.

The delegates to the Congress unanimously approved the measures taken in recent years by the Central Committee of the Party and by the Government in the field of agriculture.

We have heard many vivid and purposeful speeches here. The proposals made at the Congress on various aspects of economic, scientific and cultural development, and concerning the work and the living conditions of Soviet people, merit every support. It is difficult to so much as enumerate all the valuable proposals made during the debate.

Comrade Keldysh was quite right, for example, when he stressed the need for organising joint scientific institutions in the economic administration areas and the Union republics.

Comrade Rozhneva raised the question of abolishing night shifts for women. That is a big problem. You will realise that its complete solution will take time and require the necessary conditions. The Central Committee and the Government will look into the problem and do everything possible to solve it. (*Applause.*)

Comrade Gitalov stressed very appropriately that we need to promote far and wide the experience of the comprehensive mechanisation of agricultural operations.

A number of other important proposals was made during the debate. Their implementation will unquestionably help to accomplish the tasks we confront. The Central Committee, the Council of Ministers, and the local Party and government bodies should study all these proposals closely and take the necessary measures.

Comrades, delegations from nearly all the Communist and Workers' parties of the world are attending our Congress. The speeches made from this rostrum by our dear guests and the salutatory messages the Congress has received from the fraternal parties express the great unity of the world Communist movement, and confirm once more that all the Marxist-Leninist parties approve and support the Leninist policy of our Party. (*Prolonged applause.*)

Allow me, on behalf of the Congress and of our Party and the Soviet people, to express profound and heartfelt gratitude to the Communist and Workers' parties of the world for their high evaluation of the activities of the Soviet Communist Party and of its role in the international Communist and working-class movement, for their confidence and their wishes of success in the implementation of our new Programme. (*Stormy applause.*)

May I assure you, dear foreign comrades and brothers, that the Communist Party of the Soviet Union will continue to bear aloft the great banner of Marxism-Leninism, that, with added energy, it will build communism, where Peace, Labour, Freedom, Equality, Fraternity and Happiness for all peoples will reign supreme. (*Prolonged applause.*)

The speeches made at our Congress by the leaders of the Communist and Workers' parties of the socialist countries have shown that the fraternal parties abide unanimously by the 1957 Declaration and the 1960 Statement. The socialist camp has again demonstrated the solid unity of its ranks, the growth and the increased cohesion of the forces of world socialism. (*Applause.*)

The presence at the Twenty-Second Congress of delegations from eighty Marxist-Leninist parties, and the speeches they have made here, indicate the powerful growth of the world Communist and working-class movement, of the national-liberation movement, and the unshakable loyalty of the Communists of all countries to the principles of proletarian internationalism, bequeathed to us by Marx, Engels and Lenin. (*Prolonged applause.*) All of us rejoice that the world over the forces of fighters for the people's happiness, for peace and social progress, for communism, are maturing and becoming steeled. (*Applause.*)

Allow me, comrades, on behalf of this Congress to cordially thank the representatives of the democratic national parties of the independent African states of Guinea, the Republic of Ghana and the Mali Republic. These parties are not Communist, but we are glad that they have accepted our invitation and sent their delegations to the Twenty-Second Congress. Representatives of these parties are attending our Congress; they can see and hear what the Communists are engaged in, and what tasks they set themselves.

We ask these delegations, when they return home, to convey to their parties and their peoples the best wishes of our Congress, of the Soviet people. (*Prolonged applause.*) All Soviet people wish the independent African states that have taken or are taking the path of independent economic and political development, much success and prosperity. (*Applause.*)

Comrades, in their speeches at the Congress the delegates voiced approval of the foreign policy of the Soviet Government. The matters raised in the Central Committee Report and in the Report on our Party Programme are also being discussed outside this auditorium. It is not only our friends, but our opponents as well, who are taking part in the debate. They, too, voice their opinion about the domestic and foreign policy of our Party, and assess it from the point of view of their class.

The successes of the Soviet Union and the other socialist countries have tremendous appeal. Like the rising sun, they illumine the right road for other peoples to achieve victory for the most just social system in the shortest historical space of time.

Being aware of this, the imperialists would like to retard our swift advance. It is this that accounts for the aggressive nature of the policy pursued by the ruling circles of the United States, Britain, France, West Germany and the other imperialist powers. Their policy is not determined by the interests of peace and the tranquility of people, but by the profit-seeking interests of the monopolists, by the desire to preserve the domination of the imperialists. It is for these ends that they strive to step up international tension and obstruct a peaceful settlement of pressing international problems.

Take the problem of abolishing the survivals of the Second World War in Europe. Any further delay in solving it may have grave consequences to the cause of peace.

The Soviet Union has long been proposing that a peace treaty be signed with Germany and that the situation in West Berlin be normalised on that basis, ending the occupational regime in that city. The Soviet Union wants to create the conditions for peaceful coexistence in the heart of Europe.

What could be more just than this aim? Do we threaten anyone? Do we want to take something from the West? We do not. After the peace treaty is signed, the relations between the European countries will be normalised and the peoples will have a better opportunity to develop good-neighbour relations.

But in reply to our peaceful proposals, the Western Powers openly threaten to take up arms against us.

Today, the Western Powers "explain" condescendingly that the Soviet Union may, just imagine it, conclude a peace treaty with the German Democratic Republic, but has no right to abandon commitments undertaken by the allied victor-countries when Hitler Germany was defeated.

What commitments do they have in mind? Is it the commitments to root out German militarism and revanchism, to which the Soviet Government is indeed applying its efforts, and which the Allies undertook after the Second World War had ended? No, they do not refer to the commitments assumed jointly by the Western Powers and ourselves in Yalta and Potsdam, and which they have long since forsaken in favour of the NATO military plans. By threatening war they want to make us perpetuate the rights of the United States, Britain and France to occupy West Berlin.

It may be asked why they need these rights now, more than 16 years after the war ended? The Western Powers pretend to need these rights "to safeguard the freedom" of West Berlin. But neither the Soviet Union, the German Democratic Republic, nor the other socialist countries have any designs upon the freedom of West Berlin.

The Western Powers speak of "freedom", but what they mean by it is the occupation of West Berlin. They want to keep their armed forces and intelligence centres there, that is, they want to continue using West Berlin for their hostile, subversive activities against the German Democratic Republic, against the Soviet Union, against all the socialist countries. This is their real purpose and it is for this purpose that they cling to the rights of occupation, which have outlived their day. What is more, they want us to help them in this.

They want us to ensure, like traffic police, the unintermittent transportation to West Berlin of their military supplies, spies and saboteurs, to be used for subversive acts against ourselves and our allies.

Who do these gentlemen take us for? Do they actually imagine that they may do anything they please and that they can make us act against our vital interests and the interests of world peace and security?

It is time—high time—they realised the simple fact that today the only way in which they can negotiate with the Soviet Union, and the socialist community as a whole, is from a position of common sense, not of strength. (*Prolonged applause.*) And common sense and justice are on our side, not on theirs.

No sensible person will understand why or agree that the Western Powers have a legal or moral right to attack us if we sign a German peace treaty and the occupation regime in West Berlin is ended. Millions of Americans, Britons and Frenchmen, in fact all peoples, will bitterly condemn anyone who ventures to start a war in reply to the conclusion of a German peace treaty. (*Applause.*)

The policy of the Western Powers on the German question is not prompted by the interests of peace but primarily by the interests of the militarist and revenge-seeking forces in West Germany. The chief demon shaping that policy is Chancellor Adenauer.

The aggressive militarist circles do not conceal their hatred for the Soviet state and our peace policy. Nor does that surprise us in the least. The imperialists cannot be expected ever to grow fond of our social system. But whatever their feelings for socialism, let them give up all hope of ever imposing their capitalist system on the socialist countries. (*Applause.*) Today we can say to them once again: Don't lose your senses, gentlemen, don't try to test the strength and durability of our system. (*Prolonged applause.*) Everyone knows that our enemies have tried it more than once in the past, and knows what came of it. (*Applause.*)

As has been pointed out in the Central Committee Report, the Soviet Government holds that if the Western Powers show a readiness to settle the German problem, the issue of dates will not be so important. In that case we will not insist on a treaty being signed before December 31. We are not superstitious and we believe that both the 31st and the 13th may be lucky days. (*Animation. Applause.*) The important thing is not the date but a businesslike and fair solution of the problem. We want the Western Powers to acknowledge the necessity of doing away with the vestiges of the Second World War for the sake of preserving peace on earth, in the interests of all countries, of all mankind. (*Applause.*)

We are willing to meet with Western representatives, to exchange views with them, in order to prepare the ground for fruitful negotiations. But it is essential to really prepare for negotiations and seek agreement in order to find, at a conference attended by all the countries concerned, mutually acceptable solutions to the issues relating to the elimination of the vestiges of the Second World War.

But the Soviet Union will not have negotiations for their own sake, negotiations which the Western Powers could take advantage of to delay a peaceful settlement in Europe. If anyone is counting on this, let him know in advance that his expectations will never materialise. Such is our stand. We have adhered to it, and we abide by it firmly. (*Prolonged applause.*)

Bourgeois propaganda has been most vociferous lately over the Soviet Union's forced resumption of nuclear weapons tests. It became quite hysterical after the forthcoming test of a 50-megaton nuclear weapon was announced at this Congress. Some people assert that such tests run counter to moral principles.

Strange logic, that. When the United States first made an atom bomb, it found it legally and morally justifiable to drop such bombs on the defenceless people of Hiroshima and Nagasaki. Those were acts of senseless cruelty, acts utterly unwarranted from the military point of view. Hundreds of thousands of women, children and old men were burned alive in the atomic blasts. And it was done merely to frighten the peoples into bowing their heads to America's might. Some U.S. politicians were proud of that massacre, and strange as it may seem, they still are.

No U. S. Government or President has ever declared since the end of the war that those were immoral acts. Why? For the simple reason that they are guided by the imperialist moral principle that might is right. They thought their monopoly in nuclear weapons would enable them to gain world dominion.

But it was not long before the Soviet Union developed a powerful thermonuclear weapon and thereby ended the U.S. monopoly in this field. (*Prolonged applause.*)

When we launched our first sputniks, when Soviet ships blazed the first trails into space and Comrades Gagarin and Titov accomplished their unprecedented flights round the earth, the world saw that the Soviet Union was far ahead of the United States in important fields of science and technology. Even President Kennedy had to admit that the United States is faced with the arduous task of overtaking the Soviet Union in this sphere. You will observe that the word *overtake* has now appeared in the American vocabulary as well. (*Animation. Applause.*)

I have said on more than one occasion that the Soviet Union will overtake the United States in maize production, though Americans have been rather sceptical of it. But overtaking a country in maize production is easier than in space exploration. Space is so much tougher to handle! (*Animation. Applause.*) The facts show that the situation has changed considerably in favour of socialism.

But while the U.S. President speaks of the need of overtaking the Soviet Union, Secretary of State Rusk goes on calling for a policy "from positions of strength". A few days ago he said Mr. Khrushchov should know that the United States was strong. He made it clear that the Western Powers mean to go on talking to us "from positions of strength". It looks as if the right hand did not know what the left was doing.

The minds of some Western leaders are obviously working in the wrong direction. If peace is to be something more than a mere spell of calm, or a respite, between wars, it is indispensable to create a situation that would rule out war for ever.

The Soviet Union is far from seeking to dictate its will and terms to other countries. Even though we have achieved indisputable superiority in rocketry and nuclear arms, we have proposed general and complete disarmament and the destruction of nuclear weapons under the strictest international control. Moreover, the Soviet Union has unilaterally effected a considerable reduction of its Armed Forces, dismantled its military bases on foreign soil and carried out a series of other measures of a similar nature.

As we all know, the United States, Britain and France,

far from following the Soviet example, have lately been stepping up the arms race, increasing their armed forces and holding troop manoeuvres near our borders. They are openly threatening us with war over the German peace treaty.

In the face of outright threats and the danger of war, the Soviet Union was compelled to take appropriate steps to increase its defensive power so as to be able to defend the Soviet people and the peoples of the great commonwealth of socialist countries.

We were confronted with the necessity of improving our thermonuclear weapon and testing new types of it. The decision which the Soviet Government took on the matter in view of the serious aggravation of international tension had the understanding of all who cherish peace and refuse to shut their eyes to the dangerous intrigues of the enemies of peace. (*Prolonged applause.*)

In adopting that decision, the Soviet Government realised, of course, that the reasons which made us renew the tests would not be understood correctly and immediately by all. Indeed, today fair-minded people, too, express concern over the consequences of the nuclear explosions that are being carried out. I have been receiving letters and telegrams from some of them. We have no grounds to question the sincerity of those people, who fear that the nuclear blasts may contaminate the atmosphere.

To those people we say: Dear friends, ladies and gentlemen, the peoples of the socialist countries would like nothing better than that the sky above our planet should be clear and serene. What we live and work for is to achieve a happy future for the peoples, to turn the earth into a flowering garden. We have children, grandchildren and even great-grandchildren just as you have. And we are thinking not only of their present but of their future as well. I must say that our scientists are doing everything necessary to reduce the harmful after-effects of the tests to a minimum.

But we cannot forgo those tests at a time when the U.S., British, French and West German imperialists are making preparations to destroy not only the socialist gains but also the peoples of our countries. For they do not merely threaten to contaminate the atmosphere but want to take the lives of millions of people.

In the face of a very real threat to our security, the Soviet people had to take measures to increase the defence might of the Soviet Union and the socialist commonwealth as a whole. We would be poor leaders if we did not improve all the means of defence required for the security of the Soviet state. (*Prolonged applause.*)

It is very regrettable indeed that certain fair-minded people abroad have so far been unable to grasp the complicated international situation. Imperialist propaganda is taking advantage of the humane sentiments of those people as it seeks to prevent us through them from improving the necessary means of defence and to facilitate preparations for a new war against us.

In strengthening the defences of the Soviet Union, we act not only in our own interests but in the interests of all the peace-loving peoples, of all mankind. When the enemies of peace threaten us with force, they must and will be countered with force, and greater force too. (*Stormy applause.*) If there is still anyone today who cannot understand this, he is certain to understand it tomorrow. (*Applause.*)

We again draw the attention of the leaders of the United States, Britain, France, West Germany and other countries to the fact that the most sensible thing to do would be to discard the policy "from positions of strength" and of "cold war". (*Applause.*) In international relations, it is necessary to pursue the realistic policy of peaceful co-existence. (*Applause.*)

And this means taking into consideration the reality that developing successfully on our planet, side by side with the capitalist world, and growing stronger year by year, are the countries of the world socialist system. In our times it would be simply ridiculous and short-sighted not to see this, or to ignore it.

The imperialists are not pleased that the socialist countries are growing and developing. They would like to limit us and to teach us like children how to live on earth. For they regard Soviet power as an illegitimate child. And they simply cannot resign themselves to the fact that we are now so grown up that we are not only learning but can also teach many things to others. Here, too, there is a contradiction between the old and the new, as you see. It stands to reason that we cannot, and will not, live as the imperialists want us to. And they don't like it, they threaten us and say they will use the stick on us. But if they try, we shall go for them with a full-sized broom-stick. (*Stormy applause.*)

Speaking seriously, the wisest thing for states with different systems would be to coexist peacefully, to build up good-neighbour relations. A neighbour is not a husband or wife that can choose a partner by mutual consent. We cannot choose our neighbours; their presence does not depend on our desires. Our country, for instance, has as its neighbour in the south present-day Iran, whose rulers are pursuing a policy that is anything but good-neighbourly. If it were up to us, we would probably choose a more pleasant neighbour. I suppose the rulers of Iran would also prefer a different neighbour. But historical development has placed our countries side by side, as neighbours. And there is nothing to be done about it, we have to take account of the situation as it really is. You must not interfere in the affairs of your neighbours or allow them to interfere in yours. (*Applause.*)

I should like to deal in somewhat greater detail with such an important theoretical and political question as the character of modern imperialism, and the peaceful coexistence of states with different social systems.

The peaceful coexistence of countries with different social and political systems is the cardinal issue of our times. The states existing on the globe make up two different world systems—the socialist and the capitalist. For all the power of modern science, it is impossible to cut the globe in two and allot each of the two systems a definite area, to disengage them if I may say so. And this means that the coexistence of countries with different social and political systems is a historical fact.

There is a grim struggle, a debate, going on between the two social systems as to which system is better and which provides more benefits for man. Should this debate between the two different systems be settled through war or through peaceful economic competition? Unless one proposes to resort to armed conflict as a means of settling the disputes arising between states, one must accept the peaceful coexistence of countries with different social systems. The socio-political system of each country is the internal affair of its people, and the people themselves should and do decide this issue as they see fit.

Some people attack us, accusing us of oversimplifying or toning down the appraisal of the international situation when we stress the necessity of peaceful coexistence in present-day conditions. We are told that whoever lays emphasis on peaceful coexistence shows an underestimation of the nature of imperialism and, indeed, comes into conflict with the Leninist appraisal of imperialism.

The classical definition of imperialism given by Lenin is well known. Lenin's definition of imperialism reveals the reactionary, aggressive character of imperialism, the last stage of capitalism. Imperialism is inseparably bound up with wars, with the struggle to divide and redivide the world, to enslave the peoples and bring them under the rule of monopoly capital. It is capable of any adventurous undertaking.

This appraisal of the nature of imperialism fully retains its validity. Our Party, far from denying the accuracy of this appraisal, reaffirms it, and proceeds from it always in shaping its policy, in elaborating the strategy and tactics of the revolutionary struggle, as our draft Programme clearly shows. At the same time the Party must, if it is to adhere to creative Marxism-Leninism, take account of the important changes that have come about in the world since Lenin furnished his analysis of imperialism.

We are passing through a time when there exist two world systems, when the world socialist system is making rapid progress and the day is not far off when it will also surpass the world capitalist system in the production of material benefits. As regards science and culture, in a number of spheres the countries in the world socialist system have already outstripped the capitalist countries considerably. Today the world socialist system is more powerful than the imperialist countries in the military sphere as well.

That being so, it is no use saying that nothing has happened or changed in the world within recent decades. Those who say so are out of touch with reality and see nothing of the important changes taking place in the balance of the world forces.

It is true that the nature of imperialism, its aggressive character, has not changed. But the possibilities it now has are different from those it had at the time of its undivided rule. As matters stand, imperialism can no longer dictate its will to all, or pursue its policy of aggression without hindrance.

The predatory aspirations of the imperialists, who are intent on redividing the world and enslaving other peoples, are checked by the invincible forces of the world socialist system, above all of the Soviet Union. (Prolonged applause.) These forces subdue the wolfish appetites of the imperialists. Hundreds of millions of people in the peace-loving countries, and in fact all the peoples, are championing peace. This is the important thing, and it has to be understood. (Applause.)

Here is an example to make clear the idea I have just expressed. The tiger is a beast of prey and will be one as long as it lives. But a tiger will never attack an elephant. Why? After all, the flesh of an elephant is hardly less tasty than that of any other animal, and a tiger would probably not mind feasting on it. But it is afraid to attack the elephant because the elephant is stronger than the tiger. If a tiger were mad enough to attack an elephant, it would be sure to lose its life—the elephant would trample it to death. (*Animation. Applause.*)

In films on Africa or Asia, you must have seen kings, princes, rajahs and other notables go tiger shooting on elephants. They do so because they know that it is safe to hunt tigers in that way. To continue the simile, it must be said that the Soviet Union and the socialist world are today a tougher proposition for the imperialists than the elephant is for the tiger. (*Animation. Applause.*)

Imperialism is much in the same position as the tiger. Today the imperialists are compelled to bear in mind—not so much because they are reasonable as because, if I may say so, their instinct of self-preservation suggests it—that they cannot crush, plunder and enslave everyone with impunity. The imperialists are forced to take into account the mighty forces blocking their road. They realise that if they start a world war, the imperialist system, which is so hated by the people, is bound to fall. (*Prolonged applause.*)

The might of the world socialist system is now greater than ever. That system already constitutes more than one-third of mankind, and its forces are growing fast; it is the great bulwark of world peace. (*Applause.*) The principle of the peaceful coexistence of countries with different social systems is of vital importance today.

This is not seen only by hopeless dogmatists who have learned general formulas on imperialism by heart and obstinately ignore reality. And this is the stand which the hard-headed Molotov still takes. He and his like do not understand the changes that have occurred in the world, nor the new phenomena of life. They are trailing behind developments, and have long since been a handicap and a deadweight. (*Applause.*)

*　*　*

Comrades, the Central Committee Report, as well as speeches by delegates to this Congress, dealt with the erroneous stand of the leaders of the Albanian Party of Labour, who have set out to fight against the course adopted by the Twentieth Congress of our Party and to undermine the foundations of friendship with the Soviet Union and other socialist countries.

The representatives of fraternal parties who spoke here said that they share our concern over the state of affairs in the Albanian Party of Labour and emphatically condemn the dangerous actions of its leaders, which prejudice the basic interests of the Albanian people and the unity of the socialist commonwealth as a whole. The speeches made by delegates and by the representatives of fraternal parties show convincingly that the Central Committee of our Party was absolutely correct in reporting to this Congress, frankly and from a standpoint of principle, that Soviet-Albanian relations are in an abnormal state.

It was our duty to do so because, unfortunately, our numerous attempts to normalise relations with the Albanian Party of Labour yielded no results. I should like to stress that the Central Committee of our Party has shown the greatest patience and done all in its power to restore good relations between our two parties.

Members of the Presidium of the C.C. C.P.S.U. made repeated attempts to meet the Albanian leaders to discuss the questions that had arisen. As far back as August 1960 we twice proposed a meeting to the Albanian leaders, but they evaded it. And they just as stubbornly rejected talks with us during the Moscow Meeting of the fraternal parties in November 1960.

When a meeting was finally arranged at the instance of the C.C. C.P.S.U., Enver Hoxha and Mehmet Shehu wrecked it, and began actions that may only be described as provocative. The leaders of the Albanian Party of Labour withdrew arrogantly from the November Meeting, thus showing that they refused to take the collective opinion of the fraternal parties into consideration. They rudely turned down our subsequent proposals for meeting to exchange views and remove the differences, and stepped up their campaign of slanderous attacks against our Party and its Central Committee.

The leaders of the Albanian Party of Labour do not mind using any methods to conceal from their people the truth as to what our Party and our people are doing. Albania is the only country in the socialist community not to have published the full text of the draft Programme of the C.P.S.U. The Albanian press carried only some parts of the draft, deliberately creating a distorted picture of the activities of our Party. That fact speaks for itself. Indeed, even the opponents of communism were unable to keep silent about our Programme.

We are aware why the Albanian leaders are concealing the Programme of the C.P.S.U. from their Party and their people. They fear the truth like death. The Party Programme is our sacred cause, it is our lodestar in communist construction.

Had the Albanian leaders published it in full, Albania's working people would have seen who lies and who speaks the truth; they would have seen that all the activities of our Party, and all its plans, are in keeping with the vital interests of the peoples, including the interests of the Albanian people who are friendly to us. (Prolonged applause.)

Our great Party has more than once been a target for bitter and foul attacks on the part of overt and covert enemies of communism. But we must say in so many words that we do not recall anyone passing at so giddy a speed as the Albanian leaders have done from professions and vows of everlasting friendship to unbridled anti-Soviet calumny.

They apparently expect in this manner to clear the ground for winning the right to receive hand-outs from the imperialists. The imperialists are always ready to pay thirty pieces of silver to those who split the Communist ranks. But pieces of silver have never brought anyone anything but dishonour and ignominy. (*Applause.*)

Obviously, the Central Committee of our Party had to tell this Congress the whole truth about the pernicious stand of the leadership of the Albanian Party of Labour. Had we not done so, the Albanian leaders would have continued to insinuate that the Central Committee of the Soviet Communist Party was afraid to inform the Party of the differences it had with the leadership of the Albanian Party of Labour. Our Party and the Soviet people should know about the conduct of the Albanian leaders. And let this Congress, which is entitled to speak on behalf of the entire Party, take its stand on the matter, let it pass its weighty judgement.

This Congress emphasised the readiness there is to normalise relations with the Albanian Party of Labour on the basis of Marxist-Leninist principle. But what was the Albanian leaders' reaction? They came out with a clamorous statement slinging mud at our Party and its Central Committee.

Comrade Chou En-lai, leader of the Delegation of the Communist Party of China, voiced in his speech concern over the open discussion, at this Congress, of the issue of Albanian-Soviet relations. The main point in his statement was, as we see it, the anxiety that the present state of our relations with the Albanian Party of Labour might affect the unity of the socialist camp.

We share the anxiety expressed by our Chinese friends, and appreciate their concern for greater unity. If the Chinese comrades wish to apply their efforts towards nor-

malising the relations between the Albanian Party of Labour and the fraternal parties, there is hardly anyone who
can contribute to the solution of this problem more than
the Communist Party of China. That would really benefit
the Albanian Party of Labour, and would meet the interests of the entire socialist commonwealth. (*Prolonged applause.*)

It is true, of course, that Communists should shape their
inter-Party relations in such a way as to leave no loop-
hole for the enemy. Unfortunately, the Albanian leaders
have grossly flouted this principle. They have long since
been openly assailing the policy of the Twentieth Congress, thereby furnishing the bourgeois press with food
for all kinds of speculation. None other than the Albanian
leaders have been shouting from the house-tops about their
special stand and their special views, as distinct from
those of our Party and other fraternal parties. This became
evident at the Fourth Congress of the Albanian Party of
Labour, and has been even more so of late.

Why did the Albanian leaders launch a campaign against
the decisions of the Twentieth Congress of our Party?
What is the heresy they espy in those decisions?

To begin with, the Albanian leaders resent the emphatic
condemnation of the cult of Stalin's person and its harmful consequences. They disapprove of our having firmly
condemned the arbitrary methods and the abuses of power which hit many innocent people, including prominent
representatives of the old guard, who together with Lenin
founded the world's first proletarian state. The Albanian
leaders cannot speak without annoyance and rancour of
the fact that we have for ever put an end to a situation in
which one man was able to decide at will highly important
questions bearing on our Party and our country. (*Prolonged applause.*)

Stalin is no longer among the living, but we considered
it necessary to brand the disgraceful methods of leadership that flourished in the atmosphere of the cult of his

person. Our Party does this to ensure that such practices never recur.

One would think that the Leninist course adopted by the Twentieth Congress of the C.P.S.U. and supported by the fraternal parties should also have been backed by the leadership of the Albanian Party of Labour, since the cult of the individual is incompatible with Marxism-Leninism. What happened, however, was that the Albanian leaders began to extol the cult of Stalin's person and launched a bitter struggle against the decisions of the Twentieth Congress of the C.P.S.U., in an effort to divert the socialist countries from this correct course. Needless to say that that was no accident. All that was pernicious in our country at the time of the cult of the individual manifests itself in even worse form in the Albanian Party of Labour. It is no longer a secret to anyone that the Albanian leaders maintain their power by resorting to force and arbitrary methods.

The situation in the Albanian Party of Labour has been abnormal and harmful for a long time now. In that situation, anyone whom the leadership does not favour may be subjected to a cruel repression.

Where are the Albanian Communists who founded the Party and fought against the Italian and German fascist invaders? Almost all of them have fallen victim to the bloody crimes committed by Mehmet Shehu and Enver Hoxha.

The C.C. C.P.S.U. has received more than one letter from Albanian Communists asking us to prevent the Albanian leaders from doing injustice to the finest sons and daughters of the Albanian Party of Labour. Delegates to this Congress can form an idea of the moral make-up of the Albanian leaders by reading some of those letters.

The Albanian leaders accuse us of interfering in the internal affairs of the Albanian Party of Labour. I should like to say what they mean by this so-called interference.

A few years ago the C.C. C.P.S.U. pleaded with the Albanian leaders for Liri Gega, former member of the Political Bureau of the C.C. of the Albanian Party of Labour, who was sentenced to death together with her husband. For a number of years she had been a member of leading bodies of the Albanian Party of Labour, and had taken part in the liberation struggle of the Albanian people. In appealing at that time to the Albanian leaders, we were prompted by humane considerations, by the desire to prevent the shooting of a woman who, moreover, was pregnant. We considered, and still consider, that as a fraternal party we had a right to express our opinion on the matter. Indeed, even in the blackest periods of reaction the tsar's satraps, who tortured revolutionaries, could not bring themselves to execute pregnant women. And here is a socialist country where a woman about to become a mother was sentenced to death and executed. It was an utterly unwarranted act of cruelty. (*Commotion. Voices*: "Shame!")

Today honest people are being cruelly persecuted in Albania merely because they make bold to speak out for Soviet-Albanian friendship, of which the Albanian leaders like to talk in such pompous and florid terms.

Comrades Liri Belishova and Koço Tashko, prominent functionaries of the Albanian Party of Labour, were expelled from the Central Committee of the Albanian Party of Labour; what is more, they are now being openly branded enemies of the Party and the people. And this just because Liri Belishova and Koço Tashko had the courage honestly and openly to voice their disagreement with the policy of the Albanian leaders, and called for unity between Albania, the Soviet Union and the other socialist countries.

Those who today advocate friendship with the Soviet Union and the C.P.S.U. are regarded as enemies by the Albanian leaders.

How are we to reconcile these facts with the vows and assurances of friendship for the C.P.S.U. and the Soviet Union that came from Shehu and Hoxha? It seems that their talk about friendship was so much hypocrisy and eyewash.

That is the situation in the Albanian Party of Labour, and that is why the Albanian leaders are opposing the Leninist course adopted by the Twentieth Party Congress. For Shehu, Hoxha and others, putting an end to the cult of the individual would mean, in effect, relinquishing key posts in Party and government, and that is something they do not want to do. We are confident, however, that the time will come when the Albanian Communists and the Albanian people will have their say, and then the Albanian leaders will have to answer for the damage they have done to their country, their people, and the cause of socialist construction in Albania. (*Stormy, prolonged applause.*)

Comrades, our Party will continue to fight against revisionists of all hues as it has done so far. In strict accordance with the principles of the Declaration and the Statement of the meetings of Marxist-Leninist parties, we have exposed, and shall continue untiringly to expose, the revisionism that found expression in the Programme of the League of Communists of Yugoslavia. We shall also struggle perseveringly against dogmatism and all other deviations from Marxism-Leninism. (*Applause.*)

* * *

Comrades, the Twenty-Second Congress may in all truth be called a congress of the Leninist Party's solid unity, a congress of complete unanimity and cohesion. Our enemies are frightened by the growing unity of our ranks. They are speculating on the fact that this Congress has paid considerable attention to the harmful consequences of the personality cult, and also to the final exposure of the anti-

Party factional group. But the enemies of communism are wasting their efforts—it will get them nowhere.

What distinguishes the Marxist-Leninist parties from all other political parties is that Communists do not hesitate to boldly expose the shortcomings and faults in their work and eliminate them. Criticism, no matter how severe, helps us make progress. This is a sign of the Communist Party's strength, an indication of its unshakable faith in its cause. *(Prolonged applause.)*

Many comrades who have spoken here have wrathfully condemned the subversive, anti-Party activities of the handful of factionalists headed by Molotov, Kaganovich and Malenkov. Our entire Party and the whole people have rejected these renegades who opposed everything new, who strove to re-establish the harmful methods prevailing at the time of the personality cult. They wanted matters to go back to those trying times for our Party and our country when nobody was safe from violence and repressions. Yes, that is precisely what Molotov and the others wanted.

We definitely reject such methods of so-called leadership. We stand for the decision of inner-Party matters according to Leninist standards, by methods of persuasion and broad democracy, and we shall remain firm in this respect. *(Applause.)* The Party's strongest weapon is its ideology, the great doctrine of Marxism-Leninism, which has brought many splendid victories to our Party, the Soviet people and the international Communist movement. *(Prolonged applause.)*

Is it possible for different opinions to arise within the Party at various periods in its activities, especially at turning points? Yes, it is. What is to be done with those who express opinions differing from those of the others? We are against repressions in such cases; we stand for Leninist methods of persuasion and explanation. *(Applause.)*

Let me remind you of an episode from the history of our Party. On the eve of October, at the decisive moment when the question was whether there was to be a great socialist revolution or not, Zinoviev and Kamenev attacked in the press the Party's intention to begin an armed uprising and thus revealed the plans of the Central Committee of the Bolshevik Party to its enemies. It was a betrayal of the cause of the revolution.

Lenin exposed Zinoviev and Kamenev and demanded their expulsion from the Party. The subsequent development of the revolution fully bore out the correctness of Lenin's policy of armed uprising. When Zinoviev and Kamenev later announced that they had been mistaken, and admitted their guilt, Lenin displayed great magnanimity towards them and himself raised the question of their reinstatement in the Party leadership.

Lenin pursued a firm policy aimed at developing inner-Party democracy. He always relied on the mass of Communists and non-Party people.

In the years that followed Lenin's death, the Leninist standards of Party life were grossly distorted in the conditions of the cult of Stalin's person. Stalin elevated curtailments of inner-Party and Soviet democracy to the level of standards of inner-Party life and the life of the state. He grossly violated the Leninist principles of leadership and permitted arbitrary methods and abuses of power.

Stalin could look at a comrade sitting at the same table with him and say: "There's something shifty about your eyes today." After that you could consider that the comrade whose eyes had supposedly been shifty had become a suspect.

Comrade Delegates, I wish to inform the Congress of the reaction of the anti-Party group to the proposal to discuss at the Twentieth Congress the question of the abuses of power in the period of the personality cult.

Molotov, Kaganovich, Malenkov, Voroshilov and others raised categorical objections. In answer to their objections, they were told that if they opposed the raising of the question we would let the Congress delegates decide. We did not doubt that the Congress would be in favour of discussing the question. Only then did they agree, and the question of the personality cult was submitted to the Twentieth Party Congress. But the factionalists did not cease their struggle even after the Congress; they did their utmost to hamper an investigation of the abuses of power, fearing that their role as accomplices in mass repressions would be revealed.

Mass repressions began after the assassination of Kirov. Considerable effort will still be required to establish who was guilty of Kirov's death. The deeper we look into the records concerning Kirov's death, the greater the number of questions that crop up. There is the outstanding fact that Kirov's assassin had on two previous occasions been detained by security people in the vicinity of Smolny and had been found to be carrying a weapon. But someone had ordered his release on both occasions. Then this armed man turned up in Smolny, in the very corridor along which Kirov usually passed. And it somehow happened that at the moment of the assassination the chief of Kirov's bodyguard was far behind him, although, according to his instructions, he had no right to lag so far behind the man he was guarding.

There is another very strange fact. When the chief of Kirov's bodyguard was being taken for interrogation—he was to have been interrogated by Stalin, Molotov and Voroshilov—an accident was deliberately staged on the way, as the driver of the car afterwards said, by those who should have taken the guard chief for interrogation. They then reported that the chief of the bodyguard had been killed in the accident, although he was actually killed by those escorting him.

That is how the man who guarded Kirov was killed. Afterwards the people who had killed him were shot. This was obviously not an accident but a deliberate crime. Who could have committed it? A thorough study of this complicated case is now being made.

It turned out that the driver of the vehicle in which the chief of Kirov's bodyguard was taken for interrogation is still alive. He has said that when they drove to the interrogation, a Commissariat of the Interior officer sat in the cab with him. The vehicle used was a lorry. (Of course, it is very strange that the man should have been taken to be interrogated in a lorry, as though in that particular case no other vehicle could be found. Apparently everything had been pre-arranged in detail.) Two other Commissariat of the Interior officers were in the back of the lorry with the chief of Kirov's bodyguard.

The driver further relates: As they were driving along the street, the man sitting in the cab with him suddenly wrenched the wheel from his hands and headed the lorry straight into a house. The driver snatched the wheel back and turned the lorry, so that only the side struck the wall of the house. He was later told that the chief of Kirov's bodyguard had been killed in that accident.

How was it that he was killed and yet none of those travelling with him were hurt? Why was it that the two Commissariat of the Interior officers who were escorting the commander of Kirov's guard were themselves shot? Apparently somebody had to have them killed in order to cover up all traces.

There is still very, very much that has not been cleared up concerning the circumstances of this and other cases.

Comrades, it is our duty to make a thorough, all-round examination of cases of this sort that are due to abuse of power. The time will come when we shall die, for we are all mortal, but as long as we continue working, we can and must find out a great deal and tell the truth to the Party and the people. It is our duty to do all in our power to establish the truth now, because the longer the time that passes since those events, the more difficult it will be to re-establish the truth. You cannot bring back the dead, but the facts must be faithfully recorded in the history of the Party. And it must be done to prevent for ever the recurrence of similar cases. (*Stormy, prolonged applause.*)

You may imagine how difficult it was to solve such problems when there were people on the Presidium of the Central Committee who had themselves been guilty of abusing power, of mass repressions. They stubbornly opposed all measures for the exposure of the personality cult and then began a struggle against the Central Committee. They wanted to change the composition of its leading body and revise the Leninist policy of the Party, the course mapped out by the Twentieth Congress.

Naturally, they did not want to examine such matters. You have heard Comrade Shelepin's speech. He said a lot at this Congress, but it stands to reason he did not at all tell you everything that has now been revealed. Thousands of absolutely innocent people perished, and, remember, every person is a story. Many leading Party, government and army people lost their lives.

Of course, those people on the Presidium of the Central Committee who were responsible for breaches of legality, for mass repressions, tried hard to prevent the exposure of the arbitrary acts perpetrated in the period of the cult of the individual. Then they launched an anti-Party factional struggle against the Central Committee leadership, concentrating their fire mainly against me as First Secretary of the Central Committee, since I, by virtue of my duties, was the one who had to raise those questions. I had to take their blows and counter them. (*Stormy, prolonged applause.*)

The members of the anti-Party factional group wanted to seize the leadership in the Party and the country and remove those comrades who had made exposures of the criminal acts committed in the period of the personality cult. The anti-Party group wanted to put Molotov in the leadership. If they had done so, there would certainly have been no exposures of those abuses of power.

Even after the Twentieth Congress, which condemned the cult of the individual, the anti-Party group did everything it could to prevent the exposures from going any further. Molotov said that in big matters good and bad things occur. He tried to justify the acts that had taken place at the time of the personality cult, and claimed that such acts are possible and may yet recur. Such was the line taken by the anti-Party factional group. It was not just an error. It was a calculated, criminal, adventurous position. They wanted to divert the Party and the country from the Leninist path, they wanted to revert to the policy and methods of leadership of the period of the personality cult. They miscalculated, however. The Central Committee, our entire Party, the whole Soviet people, firmly rebuffed the anti-Party group, exposed and defeated the factionalists. (*Stormy, prolonged applause.*)

Delegates have spoken here with pain in their hearts of many innocent victims among prominent Party officials and statesmen.

Such prominent army leaders as Tukhachevsky, Yakir, Uborevich, Kork, Yegorov, Eideman and others were victims of the repressions. They were military men who had great services to their credit, especially Tukhachevsky, Yakir and Uborevich, who were outstanding soldiers. Later Blücher and other prominent army leaders suffered from the repressions.

A rather curious report once found its way into the foreign press to the effect that when Hitler was preparing his assault on our country he had his secret service fabricate a document describing Comrades Yakir, Tukhachevsky and others as agents of the German General Staff. This "document", allegedly secret, fell into the hands of President Beneš of Czechoslovakia, and he, presumably prompted by good intentions, forwarded it to Stalin. Yakir, Tukhachevsky and other comrades were arrested and were then killed.

Many splendid commanders and political officers of the Red Army met their deaths. Here among the delegates there are comrades—I withhold their names in order not to cause them pain—who spent many years in prison. They were "persuaded", persuaded by certain methods, that they were either German, British, or some other spies. Some of them "confessed". There were even cases when some of those people, on being told that the charge of espionage had been withdrawn, themselves insisted on their previous depositions; they thought it better to stick to their false depositions in order the sooner to put an end to their torment, the sooner to go to their death.

That is what the personality cult means. That was the meaning of the actions of Molotov and the others who wanted to restore the evil practices of the period of the personality cult. That is what the anti-Party group wanted to bring the Party back to, and that is why the struggle against them was so acute and so difficult. Everybody realised what it meant.

I knew Comrade Yakir very well. I also knew Tukhachevsky, but not as well as I knew Yakir. During a conference in Alma Ata this year his son, who is working in Kazakhstan, came to me. He asked me about his father. What could I say to him? When we were examining these cases in the Presidium of the Central Committee and were informed that neither Tukhachevsky, Yakir, nor Uborevich had committed any crimes against the Party and the state, we asked Molotov, Kaganovich and Voroshilov:

"Are you in favour of their rehabilitation?"

"Yes, we are," they answered.

"But it was you who executed those people," we said indignantly. "When were you following the dictates of your conscience, then or now?"

They did not answer that question. And they never will. You have heard what kind of resolutions they wrote on letters addressed to Stalin. So what can they say?

In his speech to this Congress, Comrade Shelepin told you how these fine representatives of the Communist Party in the Red Army were killed. He also quoted a letter from Comrade Yakir to Stalin, and read to you the resolutions on that letter. It should be said that at one time Stalin had a lot of respect for Yakir.

I can add that at the moment Yakir was shot he shouted, "Long live the Party, long live Stalin!"

He had so much faith in the Party, in Stalin, that it never occurred to him that the lawlessness was deliberate. He thought that enemies had infiltrated the organs of the People's Commissariat of the Interior.

When Stalin was told how Yakir had behaved before his death, he cursed Yakir.

Let us recall Sergo Orjonikidze. I was present at his funeral. I believed it when I was told at the time that he had died suddenly, because we knew that he had heart trouble. Much later, after the war, I learnt quite by accident that he had committed suicide. His brother had been arrested and shot. Comrade Orjonikidze realised that he could no longer work with Stalin, although he had been one of his closest friends. Orjonikidze held a key post in the Party. Lenin had known and valued him, but things had come to a pass where Orjonikidze could no longer work normally, and in order not to have encounters with Stalin and not to share responsibility for his abuses of power, he decided to commit suicide.

The fate of the brother of Stalin's first wife, Alyosha Svanidze, who was less known to the bulk of our Party membership, was also a tragic one. He was a veteran Bolshevik, but Beria, by means of various machinations, made a case to the effect that Svanidze had been planted near Stalin by the German secret service, although he was Stalin's very close friend. And Svanidze was shot. Before he was shot, he was told that Stalin had said that if he asked forgiveness he would be pardoned. When Stalin's words were repeated to Svanidze, he asked: "Why should I ask forgiveness? I have not committed any crime." He was shot. After Svanidze's death Stalin said: "See how proud he is, he died but wouldn't ask forgiveness." It never occurred to Stalin that Svanidze was, above all, an honest man.

And that is how many absolutely innocent people died.

That is what the cult of the individual means. That is why we cannot show the slightest tolerance towards abuses of power.

Comrades, the presidium of this Congress has received letters from veteran Bolsheviks, who write that in the period of the personality cult outstanding Party leaders and statesmen, such true Leninists as Comrades Chubar, Kosior, Rudzutak, Postyshev, Eiche, Voznesensky, Kuznetsov and others, were done to death although they were innocent.

The comrades propose perpetuating the memory of those prominent Party and Government leaders who fell victim to the unwarranted repressions in the period of the personality cult.

We consider this a fit and proper proposal. (*Stormy, prolonged applause.*) It would be advisable to instruct the Central Committee that will be elected by the Twenty-Second Congress to take a positive decision on this question. Perhaps a monument should be erected in Moscow to perpetuate the memory of comrades who fell victim to arbitrary practices. (*Applause.*)

At the time of the personality cult, the Party was deprived of normal conditions of life. People who usurp power cease to be accountable to the Party—they put themselves beyond its control. That is the chief danger of the personality cult.

It is indispensable always to maintain in the Party a situation in which every leader is accountable to the Party and its bodies, and in which the Party can replace any leader when it sees fit. (*Applause.*)

Since the Twentieth Congress, the Leninist principles of Party life and collective leadership have been restored in the Party. The new Party Programme and the Rules reaffirm the provisions restoring the Leninist standards of Party life and precluding recurrences of the personality cult.

The Twentieth Congress of our Party condemned the cult of the individual, restored justice and demanded the elimination of the distortions that had taken place. The Central Committee adopted decisive measures to prevent a return to arbitrary and unlawful practices. The anti-Party group consisting of Molotov, Kaganovich, Malenkov and others tried hard to prevent the implementation of these measures.

The factionalists made an attempt to seize the leadership and divert the Party from the Leninist path. They intended to deal harshly with those who upheld the policy mapped out by the Twentieth Congress. When the anti-Party group was defeated, its members thought they would be dealt with as they had dealt with people at the time of the personality cult, and as they would have liked to deal with those who approved of the restoration of Leninist standards in Party life.

A conversation I had with Kaganovich was typical. It took place the day after the June Plenary Meeting of the C.C., which expelled the anti-Party group from the Central Committee, completed its work. Kaganovich telephoned me and said:

"Comrade Khrushchov, I have known you for many years. Please do not let me be dealt with as people were dealt with under Stalin."

Kaganovich knew very well how people were dealt with at the time, because he himself had taken part in dealing with them.

I replied:

"Comrade Kaganovich, your words are further proof of the methods by which you intended to achieve your infamous aims. You wanted to turn the country back to the methods that prevailed at the time of the cult of the individual. You wanted to use violence against people. You measure others with your own yardstick. But you are making a mistake. We act, and shall continue to act, strictly in conformity with Leninist principles. You will be given a job," I said to Kaganovich, "and you will have the opportunity of working and living in peace if you work honestly as all Soviet people do."

That was the kind of conversation I had with Kaganovich. It shows that when the factionalists had failed they thought they would be dealt with in the same way as they would have dealt with Party cadres had they succeeded in carrying out their treacherous designs. But we Communists-Leninists must never allow ourselves to abuse power. We firmly adhere to Party, Leninist positions and believe in the strength and unity of our Party, and that the people are solid behind the Party. (*Stormy applause.*)

Many delegates spoke indignantly of the members of the anti-Party group and produced facts to expose the group members' criminal activity. The indignation of the speakers is understandable and justified.

I should like specially to say a few words about Comrade Voroshilov. He approached me several times and spoke of what his feelings were. One can, of course, understand the state he is in. But we political leaders must not go by feelings alone. Feelings differ and they may be misleading. Here at the Congress Voroshilov listens to criticism levelled at him and goes about like a broken man. But you should have seen him when the anti-Party group raised its hand against the Party. At that time he displayed activity, and appeared in full armour and with all his medals on, so to say—all but riding on a horse.

The anti-Party group used Comrade Voroshilov in its struggle against the Central Committee. It was not accidental that the factionalists chose him to speak to members of the C.C. who insisted on a plenary meeting of the Central Committee. The anti-Party group expected that Voroshilov would be able through his prestige to influence members of the Central Committee and shake their determination in their struggle against the anti-Party group. To help Voroshilov in his talks with members of the Central Committee, the anti-Party group also detailed Bulganin. But Bulganin did not enjoy the prestige that Voroshilov had. They therefore pinned more of their hopes on Voroshilov as one of the oldest Party officials. But even that did not help the factionalists.

The question arises how Comrade Voroshilov got himself mixed up with that group? Some comrades know of the personal dislike there was between Voroshilov and Molotov, between Voroshilov and Kaganovich, and between Malenkov and Voroshilov.

Yet, in spite of these relations, they joined forces. Why? On what basis? Because after the Twentieth Congress they were afraid of further exposures of their unlawful actions in the period of the personality cult, afraid they would have to answer before the Party. After all, it is no secret that all the abuses at that time were committed with their backing and that, moreover, they took an active part in them. Fear of responsibility and a desire to revive the practices that had prevailed in the period of the personality cult united the members of the anti-Party group despite the personal dislike between them.

Comrade Voroshilov has made grave mistakes. But I consider, comrades, that we must not approach him in the same way as we would other active members of the anti-Party group, such as Molotov, Kaganovich or Malenkov. It must be said that during the sharp struggle against the factionalists at the beginning of the June Plenary Meeting of the C.C., when Comrade Voroshilov saw the solidarity of the members of the Central Committee in their struggle against the anti-Party group, he evidently realised that he had overstepped the mark. Voroshilov saw that he had leagued himself with men who were opposing the Party; he condemned the actions of the anti-Party group and admitted his mistakes. He thereby helped the Central Committee to some extent. We must not underrate that step on his part, comrades, because at the time it came as support for the Party.

Kliment Yefremovich Voroshilov is widely known among the people. For that reason his participation in the anti-Party group together with Molotov, Kaganovich, Malenkov and the others strengthened the group, as it were, and made a certain impression on people inexperienced in politics. By leaving that group, Comrade Voroshilov helped the Central Committee in its struggle against the factionalists. So let us repay that good deed of his with good and make his position easier. (*Prolonged applause.*)

Comrade Voroshilov was sharply criticised. This criticism was correct because he made grave mistakes which Communists cannot forget. But I think that our approach to Comrade Voroshilov should be considerate and that we must show magnanimity. I am sure he sincerely condemns what he did and repents. (*Applause.*)

Kliment Yefremovich Voroshilov has lived a long life and has done a lot of good for our Party and people. I wish to say that when the Central Committee was considering Comrade Voroshilov's request to release him from his duties as President of the Presidium of the Supreme Soviet because of ill health, the members of the Central Committee spoke warmly of him despite the mistakes he had made. In May 1960, in recognition of his services to the Party and state, the Presidium of the Supreme Soviet awarded Kliment Yefremovich Voroshilov the title of Hero of Socialist Labour. (*Applause.*)

I think Kliment Yefremovich will, together with us, work actively for the cause of our Party. (*Stormy applause.*)

* * *

Comrades, the Twenty-Second Congress has forcefully confirmed that the course of the Twentieth Party Congress, a course to restore and further develop the Leninist standards of Party and state life, to heighten the leading role of the Party and promote the creative initiative of the masses, is the only correct course. The Twenty-Second Congress reaffirms this beneficial course. The Programme and Rules of the Party, and the decisions of the Congress provide further guarantees against recurrences of the cult of the individual. The role of the Party as the great inspiring and organising force in communist construction is rising still higher.

I should also like to say a few words about the following. In many of the speeches at this Congress, and not infrequently in the press as well, when mention is made of the activities of the Central Committee of our Party, special emphasis is placed on my person, and my role is stressed in the implementation of major measures of the Party and the Government.

I appreciate the kind feelings these comrades are prompted by. But allow me to state most emphatically that everything said about me should be credited to the Central Committee of our Leninist Party, to the Presidium of the Central Committee. (*Stormy, prolonged applause.*) In fact, not a single important measure, nor a single responsible speech, was undertaken in our country on anyone's personal instructions. They are all the result of collective discussion and collective decision. (*Prolonged applause.*) This concluding speech, too, has been considered and approved by the leading collective. (*Prolonged applause.*) Our great strength, comrades, lies in collective leadership, in a joint decision of all matters of principle. (*Stormy applause.*)

Whatever abilities a leader may possess, and no matter how much energy he puts into the work, no real, lasting success can be achieved without the support of the collective, without the most active participation of the entire Party and the broad masses in the implementation of the measures planned. That is something all of us must understand well and constantly bear in mind. (*Applause.*)

Communist leaders owe their strength to the activity of the masses they lead. Leaders who correctly understand and express the interests of the Party, the interests of the people, who struggle for these interests without stinting their strength, energy and even life, and who, in big and small things alike, are inseparable from the Party as the Party is inseparable from the people, will always have the support of the Party and the people. And the cause that such leaders champion is bound to triumph. (*Prolonged applause.*)

Naturally, one must possess the qualities needed for the struggle for the cause of the Party, for the vital interests of the people. After all, our ideological adversaries, our enemies, concentrate their fire first and foremost against leaders who, rallying the active, and through it the entire people, round the directing bodies, carry on along the only true, the Leninist, path.

Here at the Congress much has been said, for example, about the furious energy with which the anti-Party factionalists Molotov, Kaganovich, Malenkov and others attacked the Leninist Central Committee of the Party and myself. In opposing the Party line charted by the Twentieth Congress, the splitters concentrated their main fire against Khrushchov, who did not suit them. Why against Khrushchov? For the simple reason that, by the will of the Party, Khrushchov had been elected First Secretary of the Central Committee. The factionalists sorely miscalculated. The Party defeated them both ideologically and organisationally. (*Stormy applause.*)

The Central Committee of our Party displayed an exceptionally high degree of political maturity and a truly Leninist understanding of the situation. It is characteristic that not a single member or candidate member of the Central

Commission, nor a single member of the Auditing Committee supported the miserable handful of splitters. (*Prolonged applause.*)

While firmly opposing the revolting practices of the cult of the individual, Marxists-Leninists have always recognised the authority of leaders, and will continue to do so.

But it would be wrong to single out any leader, to set him apart in any way from the leading collective, to indulge in praising him excessively. This is contrary to the principles of Marxism-Leninism. It may be recalled how uncompromisingly Marx, Engels and Lenin spoke out against people who indulged in extolling their merits. Yet it is truly difficult to overrate the great role of Marx, Engels and Lenin, the founders of scientific communism, and the services they rendered the working class and all mankind. (*Prolonged applause.*)

Any inclination to self-praise and to special accentuation or excessive exaggeration of the role of individual leaders is thoroughly alien to true Marxists-Leninists. It is simply insulting to them when anyone importunately tries to set them apart, to isolate them, from the leading nucleus of comrades. (*Stormy applause.*)

We Communists value highly and support the prestige of correct and mature leadership. We must safeguard the prestige of leaders recognised by the Party and the people. But every leader must bear in mind the other side of the matter—never to plume himself on his position, to remember that by holding an office he merely performs the will of the Party, of the people, who have invested him with, albeit supreme, power, but never lose control over him. (*Applause.*) The leader who forgets this pays severely for such mistakes. I would say that he pays for it during his lifetime, or the people do not forgive him even after his death, as was the case with the condemnation of the cult of Stalin's person. (*Applause.*) One who forgets that it is his duty to perform the will of the Party, of the people, cannot really be called a leader. We must have no such "leaders" either in the Party or in the machinery of the state. (*Applause.*)

To be sure, for many reasons a great deal of power is concentrated in the hands of the individual holding a high office. A leader appointed by the Party and the people must not abuse his power. In the Reports to the Congress, mention has already been made of the measures we have effected, and will continue to effect, in order to ensure that the ugly practices of the personality cult are never revived. But there is one thing no clause in the Rules can provide for—the collective of leaders must understand well that a situation must not be allowed to arise where any one authority, however deserving, may cease to heed the opinion of those who promoted him. (*Applause.*)

Comrades, we must not—we simply cannot—allow a situation to arise and develop in which the merited prestige of an individual may assume such forms that he will get the notion that he may do anything he pleases and no longer needs the collective. In that case the individual concerned may stop heeding the voice of other comrades put in the leadership, like himself, and may start to suppress them. Lenin, our great teacher, was firmly opposed to that, and the Party has paid too high a price for not having heeded his wise counsel in the past.

So let us be worthy pupils of Lenin in this important matter as well. (*Stormy, prolonged applause.*)

* * *

Comrades, for more than a hundred years a struggle has been going on between the two ideologies—the ideology of the working class as expressed in the Marxist theory of scientific communism, and the ideology of the exploiting classes, bourgeois ideology.

With the appearance of the theory of Marx and Engels the working class, the most revolutionary class, acquired a powerful ideological weapon in the struggle for its emancipation, for the revolutionary transformation of society, for the dictatorship of the proletariat.

At first the ideas of scientific communism were comprehensible only to the more progressive intelligentsia and the foremost section of the working class. The development of revolutionary consciousness was no easy task. The spreading of the new ideas and their assimilation encountered considerable difficulties because these ideas called for waging a revolutionary struggle to destroy the capitalist system, the system of brutal exploitation.

That struggle required sacrifices and privations, and called for great deeds in the name of the future to be built on the ruins of capitalism. It called for a grim revolutionary class struggle, a struggle that only the most courageous people were equal to, people who had instilled in themselves hatred for the exploiting system and were confident of the inevitable victory of the working class. It was the best of the best who took this path, the finest of the revolutionaries, and they emerged victorious after overcoming incredible difficulties. (*Applause.*)

It was most fortunate for the working class of our country that more than half a century ago the leadership of their revolutionary struggle was assumed by the Party founded by Vladimir Ilyich Lenin. At its Second Congress, the Party adopted its first Programme, which had been drawn up with the close collaboration of Lenin. The chief task proclaimed by that Programme was to overthrow the power of the capitalists and landlords and establish the power of the working class and all working people.

Under the banner of the great ideas of Marxism, the working people of Russia accomplished a socialist revolution in October 1917 and took power into their own hands.

But on taking power, the working people received as their heritage an economy ruined by the world war. They had to overcome serious difficulties, suffer great privations and make many sacrifices. They had to repel the invasion of the interventionists, suppress internal counter-revolution, build up an industry, put a disrupted and neglected agriculture on its feet, rehabilitate the transport services, organise trade, and overcome havoc and hunger. The working class had to have a clear understanding of the need to work devotedly for the sake of the morrow, of the future.

It was a very complicated and difficult but noble task. Only people who were willing to make sacrifices today in order to provide a better future for their children and grandchildren could be drawn into the struggle to fulfil that task.

After the establishment of the dictatorship of the proletariat our Party adopted its second Programme, a programme of socialist construction, drawn up by Lenin. The paramount result of the implementation of the second Programme was the final and complete victory of socialism in our country, which became a country with a mighty industry, a large-scale agriculture, and advanced science and culture.

We have now entered the third stage of the great struggle, comrades. We are adopting the third Programme of the Leninist Party, a programme of communist construction. How far we have advanced, and how different conditions are today from those in which the second Programme of the Party was adopted, to say nothing of the first!

Socialist economy has built up such strength and possesses such energy that, from the heights we have now reached, we can challenge the most powerful capitalist country, the United States of America, to a peaceful economic competition.

Today the struggle between the two ideologies is quite different from what it was at the dawn of Marxism. The ideas of scientific socialism have conquered the minds of the masses and become a tremendous material force. They have become reality, and the material and technical basis of the new society is being created by the labour of peoples. The struggle has spread from the sphere of ideology alone to that of material production.

Today it is not only the foremost section of society but also the peoples of our country and other socialist countries that are conducting a struggle to achieve the great ideals of communism. The Soviet Union is now storming the heavens, both literally and figuratively, and in translating the ideas of communism into reality is demonstrating the superiority of the socialist over the capitalist system. (*Stormy applause.*)

Today socialism is not merely an idea for the sake of which the Party calls upon the working people to struggle. Socialism has become a reality. We say—look at the Soviet Union, at the socialist countries, and you will see what the working class and all working people are capable of accomplishing when they are in power and are carrying the ideas of scientific communism into practice. See what they have achieved in a brief historical period! Their successes and their example exert a powerful influence on the masses of the working people, on the peoples of the whole world. (*Applause.*)

Socialism is already today, and not somewhere in the future, giving great material and spiritual benefits to the peoples who have set out to build a new life. The example of the socialist countries is becoming more and more attractive to the working people of all countries. The ideas of communism are spreading far and wide, are taking deeper root, and are inspiring hundreds of millions of people to become the makers of their own history.

The powerful, and ever more rapid, movement towards communism will sweep aside everything that bars the way to our cherished goal, the building of the most just society on earth. (*Prolonged applause.*) It is not a struggle of some individuals against others with the object of legalising their rule over the others; it is a struggle against oppression, slavery and exploitation, a struggle for the happiness of all. We firmly believe that the time will come when the children and grandchildren of those who today do not understand and do not accept communism will live under communism. (*Stormy applause.*)

* * *

Comrades, the tasks which the Twenty-Second Congress sets the Party and the people are truly great. It will require immense effort on the part of the entire Party and the entire people to translate our majestic Programme into reality. But we have all that is needed to fulfil this Programme. (*Applause.*)

The task now is to direct, without wasting a single day, all our efforts, the whole of the tireless, inexhaustible energy of our people, towards accomplishing the practical tasks of communist construction. (*Applause.*)

The Programme has been unanimously endorsed by this Congress. The task now is to realise it, with the fervour characteristic of Bolsheviks. (*Applause.*)

Our Congress is splendid evidence of the readiness and determination of the Party, of all Soviet people, to achieve their great aim, the construction of communism in our country. And there is no doubt whatsoever that communism will be built in the Soviet Union, for such is the will of the Party, of the people. (*Stormy, prolonged applause.*)

After the Twenty-Second Congress the delegates equipped with the programme for building a communist society, will be returning to various parts of our great country. Our aims are clear, our course is charted. And we shall start fulfilling our Programme, not in the distant future but today. (*Prolonged applause.*)

Comrades, never before have our forces, the forces of world socialism, been as great as they are today. The new Programme opens before the Party and the people the most radiant, breath-taking vistas. The sun of communism is rising over our country. Let us do everything to hasten, by our tireless labour, the day when this sun will flood with its light the boundless spaces of our wonderful country! Let us devote all our forces, all our Bolshevik energy, to the triumph of communism! (*Stormy applause.*)

Under the leadership of the glorious Leninist Party—forward to the victory of communism! (*Stormy, prolonged applause. Ovation. All rise. Voices: "Long live our Communist Party!", "Glory to the Soviet people!", "Long live communism!", "Long live friendship among the peoples!", "Glory to the fraternal Parties!" Representatives of the fraternal parties of other countries can be heard saluting the Communist Party of the Soviet Union and the peoples of the U.S.S.R. The hall resounds with thunderous hurrahs.*)

F. R. KOZLOV

AMENDMENTS TO THE RULES
OF THE COMMUNIST PARTY
OF THE SOVIET UNION

REPORT TO THE 22nd CONGRESS OF THE C.P.S.U.

October 28, 1961

Comrades, our great Leninist Communist Party is experiencing joyous and exciting days. The eyes of the Soviet people, the eyes of all mankind, are fixed on the hall in the Kremlin where this Congress is taking place. (*Applause.*)

The Twenty-Second Congress of the Communist Party of the Soviet Union, a congress of builders of communism, has discussed with tremendous enthusiasm the Report of the Central Committee of the C.P.S.U. and the Report on the draft of the new Party Programme, which were delivered by Nikita Sergeyevich Khrushchov, First Secretary of the Central Committee. (*Prolonged applause.*)

In his historic reports to the Congress, Comrade Khrushchov has summed up the gigantic creative activity of our Party and the entire Soviet people since the Twentieth Congress of the C.P.S.U. Those reports reveal the chief trends and laws of the development of society in the present epoch and define the magnificent tasks of the Communist Party and the Soviet people for the whole period of full-scale communist construction. (*Applause.*)

Every Congress of our great Leninist Party reflects a certain stage in its history, in its work of revolutionary transformation. The Twenty-Second Congress will occupy a special place in the heroic annals of the Communist Party and in the development of Soviet society. It will go down in history as an outstanding event of our day, as the congress that adopted the great Programme for the building of communist society. (*Applause.*)

In an atmosphere of unprecedented ideological unity, the Congress, expressing the will of the entire Party and of the whole people, has voiced its complete approval of the political line and practical activity of the Central Committee of the C.P.S.U. in the spheres of home and foreign policy, and has unanimously endorsed the new Party Programme. (*Applause.*)

The years will pass, glorious new pages will be written into the history of our Party, many wonderful events will occur in the life of the Soviet country, but the adoption of the Programme of the C.P.S.U. by the Twenty-Second Congress will for ever remain an event of great historic significance. (*Applause.*)

The Programme of the Communist Party of the Soviet Union is a fruit of the collective creative thought of the entire Party and of its Leninist Central Committee headed by Comrade Khrushchov. A creative attitude to theory, contact with real life, and an ability to express correctly the basic interests of the people characterise Comrade Khrushchov as a true Leninist, an outstanding political leader and a Marxist-Leninist theoretician. (*Stormy applause.*)

The entire content of the work of the Twenty-Second Congress of the Party is a majestic anthem to the all-conquering ideas of Marxism-Leninism. The new Party Programme and the decisions of the Congress provide a sound basis for the solution of highly important theoretical and practical problems of communist construction in the U.S.S.R. and of the consolidation of the world socialist system; they furnish a thorough analysis of present-day world development.

The new Programme of the C.P.S.U. puts forward the construction of a communist society in the U.S.S.R. as the immediate practical task of the Party and the Soviet people. Comrade Khrushchov has said that our Programme *"is a concrete, scientifically substantiated programme for the building of communism.* The draft shows clearly how the bright edifice of communism is to be erected. We see how it should be built, how it will look from within and without, what kind of people will live in it, and what they will do to make it still more comfortable and attractive. We can proudly tell those who want to know what communism is: 'Read our Party Programme'." (*Stormy applause.*)

In the Party Programme and in Comrade Khrushchov's reports, the Marxist-Leninist theory of the Party has been further developed, and a theoretical basis to its growing role in the life of society in the period of the full-scale construction of communism has been given.

"There must be a new, higher stage in the development of the Party itself and of its political, ideological, and organisational work that is in conformity with the full-scale building of communism," says the Programme. "The Party will continuously improve the forms and methods of its work, so that its leadership of the masses, of the building of the material and technical basis of communism, of the development of society's spiritual life will keep pace with the growing requirements of the epoch of communist construction."

Our Party has grown from the small Marxist circles and groups that emerged in Russia at the end of the last century into a ten-million-strong army of advanced fighters for the revolutionary transformation of society, into a party that guides a great socialist state, a party of builders of communism. The Communist Party of the Soviet Union is a great force of our times, and its policy exerts a tremendous influence on the whole course of world history. (*Applause.*)

It was our Party that led the working people of Russia to victory over tsarism and capitalism, to the creation of the Soviet Union, the world's first socialist state. It was under the Party's tried and tested leadership that the Soviet people achieved the final and complete victory of socialism. Today the Party is confidently leading the 220-

million-strong Soviet people to the victory of communism and for the first time in history is breaking man's path to a happy future. (*Applause.*)

Comrades, the question of amendments to the Rules of the C.P.S.U. is presented for the consideration of the Twenty-Second Congress. The Rules of the Party constitute the basic law of inner-Party life. They determine the standards of Party life, the organisational principles of the Party's structure, and the methods of its practical activities.

It is in the order of things that our Congress should discuss amendments to the Rules of the C.P.S.U. The new Programme confronts the Party and all Communists with the new and higher demands that arise out of the tasks of the full-scale construction of a communist society. With these gigantic tasks in hand, the Party will increase its militancy and continuously perfect the forms and methods of its organisational and educational work.

The great Lenin taught us that whenever the Party is faced with new tasks it should elaborate organisational forms, rules and standards of internal Party life that are in accordance with the historical conditions of its activity and which ensure fulfilment of those tasks. This is the postulate that guided the Central Committee in drawing up the draft Rules of the C.P.S.U. that have now been submitted to this Congress.

The Rules now in force were, it will be remembered, adopted in 1952 at the Nineteenth Party Congress at which Comrade Khrushchov delivered his report "Amendments to the Rules of the C.P.S.U.(B)". The fundamental Leninist organisational principles of the structure and functioning of the Party embodied in the present Rules remain unchanged. The draft Rules presented for consideration to the Twenty-Second Congress develop these principles. They are based entirely on the requirements of the new Programme of the C.P.S.U. and reflect the great changes in the life of the country and the Party that have taken place in the interim; they reflect the requirements of our further development.

In these past years the Communist Party of the Soviet Union has grown numerically and has become stronger both ideologically and organisationally. The Party, having eliminated the consequences of the cult of Stalin's person, has fully restored the Leninist standards of Party life and the principle of collective leadership, and has mustered still more closely around its Leninist Central Committee. The role of the Party as the guiding and directing force of the Soviet people has increased. The Party has become enriched by fresh experience in the political leadership of the masses. Never before has there been such a durable and indestructible Leninist unity of the Party's ranks as in our days. (*Prolonged applause.*)

The Rules of the C.P.S.U. that our Congress is to approve will place in the hands of the Party a reliable organisational weapon in the struggle for the victory of communism; they will enhance the role of the Party as the inspirer and organiser of communist construction.

As a result of the victory of socialism in the U.S.S.R., and the strengthening of the moral and political unity of Soviet society, the Communist Party, the party of the working class, has become the party of the entire Soviet people. This is the great result of the historical development of our Party, of the final and complete victory of socialism in the U.S.S.R. (*Applause.*)

The Party's guiding star in all its activities is the theory of Marxism-Leninism, a powerful ideological weapon of cognition, a weapon for the revolutionary transformation of society on communist lines. While developing Marxism-Leninism creatively, our Party resolutely combats all manifestations of revisionism, dogmatism, and sectarianism which are profoundly alien to revolutionary theory.

The Communist Party of the Soviet Union is an inseparable, integral part of the international Communist and working-class movement. It firmly upholds the tried and tested principles of proletarian internationalism. Its long history and its manifold activities show that the Party fulfils its internationalist duty to the international Communist and working-class movement. The C.P.S.U. actively contributes to further consolidating the unity of the international Communist movement and fraternal relations with the great army of Communists of all countries; it co-ordinates its activities with the efforts of the other contingents of the world Communist movement to promote the joint struggle for peace, democracy and socialism. This is a most important condition ensuring the victory of socialism and communism, the triumph of the Marxist-Leninist theory on a world-wide scale. (*Applause.*)

Our struggle for the victory of communism in the U.S.S.R. is a great contribution to the cause of the world Communist and working-class movement, the highest manifestation of our internationalist duty.

All the amendments and addenda to the Rules are designed to raise the organisational work of the Party to the level of the great tasks of communist construction as laid down in the new Programme of the C.P.S.U. The indestructible ideological and organisational unity of the Party is a most important factor guaranteeing its invincibility. (*Prolonged applause.*)

COMMUNIST CONSTRUCTION
AND ENHANCEMENT OF THE PRESTIGE
OF THE NAME OF PARTY MEMBER

Comrades, in the conditions now obtaining, the role played by each Communist and his responsibility to the Party and the people have grown immensely, and the prestige of the name of Party member has increased. "It is the duty of a Communist in production, in social and personal life," says the Programme, "to be a model in the struggle for the development and consolidation of communist relations, and to observe the principles and norms of communist morality."

The draft Rules, proceeding from these propositions of the Programme, lay down the basic duties and rights of a Communist, and outline the organisational principles that govern admission into and expulsion from the C.P.S.U.

The question of Party membership is one of the fundamental questions of Party construction. The successful fulfilment of the Party's responsible role as the vanguard of the Soviet people, its strength and militancy, depend primarily on the composition of its membership. The Party will continue to reinforce its ranks by admitting into them the most politically conscious and active members of our society, and will keep the name of Communist immaculate and hold it high.

Article One of the draft Rules reads:

"Membership of the C.P.S.U. is open to any citizen of the Soviet Union who accepts the Programme and the Rules of the Party, takes an active part in communist construction, works in one of the Party organisations, carries out all Party decisions, and pays membership dues."

This article retains Lenin's principle of Party membership in full. What is new in the definition is the statement that membership of the Party is open to any Soviet citizen who *"takes an active part in communist construction."* This requirement is in accordance with the new conditions of Party life; it is the surest criterion of a citizen's worthiness to hold the title of Party member in the period of the full-scale construction of communist society. (*Applause.*)

Communism makes man's life secure, joyous and happy. For all the springs of public wealth to flow more abundantly, however, labour for the benefit of society must become the prime necessity of life for all Soviet people. It is with this in view that the duties of a Party member in respect of social labour, production and the creation of the material and technical basis of communism have been brought into the foreground in the draft Rules of the C.P.S.U.

A Party member must serve as an example of the communist attitude to labour, must raise productivity of labour and be an innovator, must support and popularise everything progressive. A Communist must be knowledgeable in the technical field, must continuously improve his qualifications and take an active part in economic and cultural development. It is above all the way in which a Communist carries out these obligations that indicates his political maturity and his devotion to the great cause of Marxism-Leninism. (*Applause.*)

The Soviet people are in the forefront of the revolutionary transformation of human society. Their world outlook is the most progressive theory of our times—Marxism-Leninism. A Communist must untiringly perfect his knowledge of that theory; he must be guided by it in his day-to-day work and must be an active propagandist of the Marxist-Leninist theory among the working people. The high political consciousness of Soviet people is the fundamental condition for their creative activity and for the development and strengthening of communist forms of labour and new, communist social relations.

We know, however, that in our society survivals of the past have not yet been completely eradicated from the minds and the conduct of people. These survivals manifest themselves in the scornful attitude of some people towards labour, in their striving to live at the expense of society, in private-property psychology, in improper behaviour at work and at home, and in religious prejudices. These survivals are constantly encouraged by the bourgeois propaganda that through various channels finds its way into our country and has a harmful influence on some Soviet citizens.

It is the duty of a Communist to be persistent in helping form and train the man of communist society, to struggle resolutely against all manifestations of bourgeois ideology, against the vestiges of private-property psychology and other survivals of the past; he must set an example in observing the norms of communist morality and always and in everything place social interests before his own.

Comrades, for a Marxist-Leninist party that is in power there is no more reliable and sure means of perfecting its work, training cadres, rectifying errors and removing shortcomings than the tried and tested method of criticism and self-criticism.

When a functionary ceases to be aware of his own shortcomings and blunders, when he does not assess the results of his own work critically, he becomes smug, conceited and complacent, he lives in the past and loses sight of perspectives. When his shortcomings and blunders are pointed out, he takes an incorrect stand unworthy of a Party member, and often resorts to suppression of criticism.

It happens at times that some conceited leaders regard even an appeal for criticism to be an encroachment on their authority. For instance, Comrade Gasparyan, former First Secretary of the Artashat District Committee of the Communist Party of Armenia, ordered the destruction of an issue of the district newspaper only because it contained a leading article that in the most general form called on the delegates to a district Party conference to criticise shortcomings in the work of the District Party Committee. Gasparyan considered that this appeal undermined his personal authority as Secretary of the District Committee. What sort of Party leader is that? He is no leader; he is a misfortune! (*Animation.*)

The Rules of the Party to be adopted by the Congress are intended to arm Communists in the struggle against such intolerable practices. It is one of the most important duties of a Party member to develop criticism and self-criticism, and to struggle against ostentation, conceit, complacency, bureaucratic methods, and parochialism.

A Communist must oppose resolutely all attempts to suppress criticism and any actions that are detrimental to the Party and the state. Proper conditions must be provided everywhere to ensure Party members the unhampered exercise of the right to criticise any Communist, irrespective of the post he holds. The draft Rules of the C.P.S.U. not only proclaim this right, but guarantee it: "Those who commit the offence of suppressing criticism or victimising anyone for criticism are responsible to and will be penalised by the Party, to the point of expulsion from the C.P.S.U."

Our Party exists for the people; it regards service to the people to be its supreme duty, the purpose of its activities. The Party is always guided by Lenin's proposition that the Party must not only teach the people but must learn from them, must study and make use of the experiences of the masses. It is the duty of a Communist to explain Party policy to the masses, to help strengthen and extend the Party's ties with the people, to be tactful and considerate to people, and respond in good time to their needs and requests. The further strengthening of the bonds between the Party and the masses is an essential condition for the successful realisation of the great plans for communist construction. (*Applause.*)

The draft Rules regard the education of Soviet people in the spirit of proletarian internationalism and socialist patriotism as one of the most important duties of a Party member. A Communist must fight against survivals of nationalism and chauvinism, and he must promote in word and deed the friendship of the peoples of the U.S.S.R., promote fraternal relations between the Soviet people and the peoples of the socialist countries and the proletarians and working people of all countries. (*Applause.*)

The strength and invincibility of our Party lie in the monolithic unity of its ranks, in conscious iron discipline. A Party member must actively defend the ideological and organisational unity of the Party, must display vigilance and safeguard the Party against infiltration by people unworthy of the lofty name of Communist.

What the Party demands of every Communist, of every Party functionary, is that he should be truthful and honest, that he should observe Party and state discipline strictly and serve his people faithfully.

Unfortunately we still meet with cases of certain functionaries forgetting that indisputable truth, and resorting to deception of the Party and the state.

Take, for example, the former leaders of the Tajik Party organisation, Uljabayev, Dodkhudoyev and Obnosov. When they proved incapable of ensuring the further development of the republic's economy, mainly cotton-growing, they resorted to anti-Party actions that amounted in effect to swindling. To conceal their political bankruptcy and at the same time to create the impression that they were keeping pace with reality, these pseudo-leaders falsified figures and doctored accounts. The republic did not fulfil its plan for cotton sales to the state, but its leaders, having lost all sense of shame, reported that the plan had been fulfilled ahead of schedule. They implanted servility and toadyism in the organisation, trampled inner-Party democracy underfoot, and violated Soviet laws.

It must be said that the Tajik Party organisation proved equal to the situation. With the help of the Central Committee of the C.P.S.U., it looked into the state of affairs in the republic, and sharply condemned the anti-Party conduct of the former leaders; as you know, a plenary meeting of the Central Committee of the Communist Party of Tajikistan removed them from their posts, and expelled them from the Party.

The Rules of the C.P.S.U. make it the duty of a Communist to oppose any act that is detrimental to the Party or the state, to be principled everywhere and in everything, and to display Bolshevik intolerance of facts of deception, lying and hypocrisy.

Our Party is of the flesh and blood of our great people.

It is strong in its ties with the people, its loyalty to the people and its profound understanding of their interests. The people will never stand for deception and falsehoods. They will recognise only that Communist, that Party leader, who is honest and truthful. Only such a leader can work boldly and confidently. He does not fear just criticism of his actions and, indeed, appreciates it as help and support from the masses. (*Applause.*)

Thus, the duties of a Party member as outlined in the draft Rules are prompted by the necessity of increasing the responsibility of every Communist for our great cause. The Party member's clear understanding of the duties imposed on him by the Rules and his full exercise of the extensive rights envisaged in the Rules should encourage initiative and independent activity on the part of Communists, should enhance the militancy of all Party organisations.

Comrades, in the period since the Twentieth Congress the Party has been substantially reinforced by the admission to its ranks of advanced workers, collective farmers and intellectuals. Party organisations have been paying greater attention to growth and composition of their membership.

This, however, does not mean that we have no shortcomings in the admission of new members. Not infrequently Party organisations fail to observe the principle of individual selection; when a comrade seeks admission to the Party, they show interest in his professional record, which, of course, is correct, but not in his social work nor his behaviour in the family, in private life.

A number of points have been added to the Rules of the C.P.S.U. to increase the responsibility of Party organisations for the admission of new members into the Party, for observation of the principle of individual selection for Party membership of the more politically conscious, advanced people of Soviet society. Party organisations must pay greater attention to the training and ideological moulding of newly-admitted members and candidate members.

The point on an extended probationary period has been removed from the draft Rules. This measure was introduced after the Nineteenth Party Congress, because at that time there were many candidate members whose term of probation had run out; there were then in the Party over 300,000 people who had been candidate members for more than five years. There are in the Party today about 10,000 people who have been candidate members for two or three years.

There is no doubt that the extension of the probationary period has played a positive role. As the above-quoted figures show, there is no need for it now. Furthermore, the leaders of some Party organisations who misinterpreted the right to extend the term of candidate membership did little to prepare candidate members for full membership within one year. The draft Rules envisage a different procedure. If, in the course of his term as candidate member, an applicant has not shown his abilities and, on account of his personal qualities, cannot be admitted into full membership of the C.P.S.U., the Party organisation passes a decision to refuse admission into the Party. The probationary period must actually serve as a school preparing candidate members for full membership of the C.P.S.U.

More active ideological work in the Party, the strengthening of Party discipline and greater political consciousness on the part of Communists have led to a sharp fall in the number of expulsions in recent years. In future, too, we must proceed from the principle that expulsion from the Party, as the highest Party penalty, should be applied only to those who are really unworthy of membership in the Party.

To establish a guarantee against any unwarranted application of the highest Party penalty and to make Party organisations more strictly accountable for their members, the draft Rules include a new point: a decision by a primary Party organisation to expel a member becomes valid only if it is passed not by a simple majority but by at least two-thirds of the Party members present at the meeting.

Primary Party organisations are entitled to discuss the question of calling to account and penalising Communists elected to district, city, area, regional and territorial committees and to the central committees of the Communist parties of the Union republics, as well as members of auditing commissions at those levels.

We must give careful attention to everything that concerns the fate of a Party member. But we must not be less exacting of Communists for it. Party organisations must be intolerant and principled in respect of those whose actions and practices cause detriment to the Party.

THE FURTHER DEVELOPMENT
OF INNER-PARTY DEMOCRACY

Comrades, the draft Rules are imbued with the idea of broader Party democracy as an essential condition for the further encouragement of the activity and initiative of all Party organisations and the drawing of all Communists into constructive Party work. The Party must organise its internal activities in a form that will serve as a model of communist public self-government.

The Leninist principle of democratic centralism has been the invariable foundation of Party organisational structure. It combines harmoniously sound organisation and the strictest discipline with the most extensive inner-Party democracy. On the basis of the experience accumulated by the Party, the draft Rules develop this inviolable Leninist principle of Party construction.

Of exceptional significance is the proposition in the draft Rules that collective leadership is the supreme principle of Party leadership, one that guarantees the Party and all its bodies against unilateral, subjective decisions and actions. Only collective leadership provides conditions for the development of the activity and initiative of Communists and ensures the proper training of cadres. It goes without saying that collective leadership does not in any way reduce the personal responsibility of a Party functionary for whatever is entrusted to him, for fulfilment of a decision adopted collectively.

Leninist standards in Party life, the principle of collective leadership and the regular renewal of the composition of Party bodies preclude the concentration of excessive power in the hands of individual functionaries, and prevent their placing themselves above the control of the collective; they ensure an ample influx of fresh forces into Party bodies and the proper blending of old and young cadres. (*Applause.*)

In conformity with the C.P.S.U. Programme, the draft Rules provide for a periodical renewal of the composition of Party committees and continuity of leadership.

It is envisaged that at each regular election the composition of the Central Committee of the C.P.S.U. and of its Presidium shall be renewed by not less than one quarter; the composition of the Central Committees of the Communist parties of the Union republics, territorial and regional Party committees, by not less than one-third; that of area, city and district Party committees and the Party committees or bureaus of primary Party organisations, by one half. In his report on the draft Programme of the C.P.S.U., Nikita Sergeyevich Khrushchov has given thorough and profound substantiation of the necessity for the introduction of this new, important principle.

It must be said, comrades, that we have every possibility of giving effect to this principle. Party cadres have grown numerically and have become stronger ideologically and politically. Thousands of Communists annually reinforce the ranks of Party activists. Regular renewal of the composition of leading Party bodies has, in recent years, become the rule in Party work.

Here are some figures. The composition of the Central Committees of the Communist parties of the Union republics, territorial and regional Party committees was renewed at the last elections by forty-five per cent, and that of city and district committees by forty per cent. Renewal of the composition of leading bodies must become a standard of Party life. It is, therefore, embodied in the Programme and the Rules, and thus made a law of Party life. (*Applause.*)

Formerly, a certain number of leading functionaries in many Party bodies remained in office for a very long period. The draft Rules preclude this. It is now laid down that members of the Presidium of the Central Committee of the C.P.S.U. shall, as a rule, be elected for not more than three successive terms. Communists shall not be elected for more than three terms to the Central Committees of the Communist parties of the Union republics, territorial, regional, area, city and district Party committees or the Party committees or bureaus of primary Party organisations. A Party member may not be elected secretary of a primary Party organisation for more than two successive terms.

The advisability of such a system of election to Party bodies is obvious. We need a steady flow of new, promising people with initiative coming into the leadership. At the same time the leading Party bodies must be rid with a firm hand of people who have been longer on the job than is good for it, who have come to believe that there is no one who can replace them, have stopped in their progress and, although unable to cope with the work entrusted to them, cling to their leading positions.

Take Comrade Dolgatov, the former Secretary of the Sergokala Party District Committee, Daghestan A.S.S.R. Having got it into his head that he was irreplaceable, he began to disregard the opinion of the Party organisation. When Communists brought this to the attention of the District Committee, and it raised the question of his work at a plenary meeting, Dolgatov announced: "No king ever surrendered power voluntarily, and I don't intend to give it up without a battle." (*Laughter.*) The Communists of the district removed this self-opinionated bureaucrat from the post of district secretary. (*Applause.*)

Such "leaders" sometimes establish themselves at higher levels than district committees. There was, for example, the former Secretary of the Tyumen Regional Committee, Comrade Kosov, who decided that nothing was taboo to him. He began to abuse his power and committed breaches of socialist legality. Kosov was removed from his post as Regional Secretary, and severely punished.

The proposed arrangement for the regular renewal of the Party bodies provides for an influx of fresh forces to and continuity in leadership and is, at the same time, directed against those conceited people who do not abide by the standards of inner-Party life, and also against weak-willed functionaries lacking in initiative, who may be said to have nothing but failures to boast of.

It must be made clear that the principle of the regular renewal of Party bodies is closely linked up with the principle of continuity in leadership. It does not by any means refute the important role played by experienced leaders enjoying high esteem. There can be no continuity in leadership, and experience cannot be properly passed on, unless there is a more or less stable group of leaders. For this reason, the draft Rules provide that some Party leaders and functionaries may, in consideration of their recognised prestige and outstanding political and organisational abilities, be elected to leading bodies for a longer period. In that case, however, the given candidate for election must obtain at least three-quarters of the votes tendered by secret ballot.

In the course of the discussion of the draft Rules the opinion has been expressed that the election of functionaries to leading Party bodies for a longer period than is envisaged by the draft Rules should be allowed only with regard to the Central Committee of the C.P.S.U. and its Presidium. This proposal cannot be accepted. Let us suppose that the secretary of a primary Party organisation is elected to the district committee for two successive terms. At the third election he is elected second secretary of the district committee. He shows himself an able functionary deserving promotion to first secretary. He cannot, however, be elected to the district committee for a fourth time if the Rules do not provide for the possible extension of the term of office in an elected body for a competent Communist enjoying great prestige. There must be no obstacles to the growth and promotion of competent and energetic functionaries.

Every leading Party functionary must, in all his actions, be an example of service to the people, a model for all Communists and non-Party people. (*Applause.*) The higher the Party post held by a Communist, the greater his responsibility. This has been stressed in the draft Rules of the C.P.S.U., specifically by the introduction of the following clause:

"A member or alternate member of the Central Committee of the C.P.S.U. must, by his entire activity, justify the great trust placed in him by the Party. A member or alternate member of the Central Committee of the C.P.S.U. who degrades his honour and dignity cannot remain a member or alternate member of the Central Committee."

This clause in the draft Rules shows how exacting our Party is towards those who have been found worthy to be members of its militant Leninist general staff. (*Prolonged applause.*)

The draft Rules envisage a change in the way in which the results of balloting at elections to Party bodies are decided. It has been the practice until now to consider a candidate elected to a Party body if he has won more votes than the other candidates and more than half the votes of those with the right to vote, present at the meeting, conference or congress.

In practice this not infrequently leads to experienced and valuable Party workers who have obtained an absolute majority of votes being rejected because there have been from three to five votes cast against them. This in no way accords with the policy of fully developing inner-Party democracy since it permits of an insignificant minority imposing its will on an absolute majority.

The draft Rules, therefore, say that a candidate is considered elected if more than half the participants in the meeting, conference or congress have voted for him.

The objection may be made that such a system of voting may in some cases lead to more people being elected to a Party body than was intended. Yes, there may be such cases. But then the draft Rules do not define the numerical strength of elective Party bodies. The meeting of a Party organisation, a conference or congress have the right to decide for themselves on the number of Communists to be elected to a leading body. It stands to reason that Party bodies should not be made too large. Details of the methods of elections to Party bodies must, as previously, be laid down in relevant instructions from the Central Committee of the C.P.S.U.

The draft Rules provide for a further development of inner-Party democracy by making it incumbent on Party bodies to give regular information on their work to Party organisations. This will help strengthen the ties between the leading Party bodies and the rank and file, will strengthen the supervision of the activities of elective bodies by the Party active, by all Communists.

The strength of the Party lies in the active work of its members. A Communist not only carries out the decisions of higher Party bodies, but himself, to the best of his ability, participates in the elaboration of those decisions. That is why every possibility must be ensured for a free and business-like discussion of questions of Party policy and for discussion on controversial or insufficiently clear questions, both in individual organisations and in the

Party as a whole. This, too, is reflected in the draft Rules.

An important feature of the draft Rules is the greater role allotted to local Party bodies and the extension of their initiative and independence in solving the economic and political problems confronting a region, territory or republic.

At the same time it must be pointed out that the C.P.S.U. is not a federation of parties or party committees. It is a centralised organisation. The Communist parties of the Union republics and the territorial and regional organisations are parts of a single whole, the Communist Party of the Soviet Union. (*Prolonged applause.*) The strict subordination of individual Party organisations to the centre, and of lower organisations to higher, is an indispensable condition for the Party's fulfilment of its historic tasks.

The Party fights against all manifestations of parochialism, against all attempts to approach problems of Party policy from a narrow departmental standpoint, for it considers them to be alien to Marxist-Leninist party principles. Lenin stressed that "refusal to accept the direction of the central bodies is tantamount to refusing to remain in the Party, it is tantamount to disrupting the Party...".

Centralism is not the antithesis of inner-Party democracy. It implies encouragement of local initiative and creative effort, and the promotion of a high degree of conscious discipline. Democratic centralism guarantees unity of will and action of the Party; it lends the Party mobility and enables it rapidly to re-form its ranks with due regard to the changing situation and to concentrate all its efforts on fulfilling the historic tasks of communist construction. (*Applause.*)

The C.P.S.U. is a voluntary alliance of the advanced, politically most conscious members of Soviet society. Freedom of opinion, freedom to discuss any matters concerning the policy or practical activity of the Party, is a standard of Party life. As a general rule, the more important the issue, the wider must be the range of Communists taking part in its discussion. And it is only natural that different opinions should be voiced. In the course of an exchange of views, a common, correct point of view is elaborated that is then set down in a Party decision binding on all.

Of course, we must not allow the Party to be involved in fruitless debate at the whim of a small group of confused or immature people, must not give anti-Party elements an opportunity to undertake actions tending to undermine Party unity. The Party must not discard any weapons that can be used in the struggle for the ideological and organisational unity of its ranks. (*Prolonged applause.*) That is why the Rules retain guarantees against attempts by a negligible minority to impose its will on the majority, as well as against attempts to form factional groups and split the Party.

Among the questions asked in the course of the discussion of the draft Rules were these: Does not the solid unity of the C.P.S.U. and Soviet society as a whole preclude all disruptive activity within the Party? Do we need, in present-day conditions, any formal statutory guarantees against factionalism and group activities?

We do need such guarantees, comrades.

It is true enough that in Soviet society there no longer exists a social basis on which any opportunist trends could thrive in the Party. But the causes of ideological waverings on the part of individuals or groups have not yet been fully removed. Some people may yield to the influence of bourgeois propaganda from without; others, who fail to understand the dialectics of social development and who have turned into smouldering embers, as Comrade Khrushchov so aptly put it, may keep on rejecting all that is new and clinging to old dogmas defeated by the realities of life.

We know well how bitterly the anti-Party factional group, made up of Molotov, Kaganovich, Malenkov, Voroshilov, Bulganin, Pervukhin, Saburov and of Shepilov who later joined them, resisted the implementation of the Leninist course charted by the Twentieth Party Congress.

The members of the group betrayed the Leninist principles of Party activity. They were bent on carrying out their anti-Party designs at all costs, and went to the point of holding clandestine gatherings and hatching plans to seize the leadership in the Party and the country and change Party policy. Molotov and the others wanted to turn the clock back to the times that were so hard for our Party and country, the times when the harmful methods and practices bred by the cult of the individual were current, and when no one was safe from arbitrary and repressive measures. They ignored the fact that the Leninist course of our Party, adopted by the Twentieth Congress, had the fullest approval of the entire Party, of all Soviet people and the fraternal Marxist-Leninist parties. (*Applause.*)

It stands to reason that the factional group, which tried to impose its anti-Party, anti-Leninist views on the Party, could have done serious damage to the cause of communist construction.

I fully agree with Comrade Khrushchov in that had those renegades gained the upper hand, they would have stopped at nothing to achieve their infamous ends, and would have begun dealing summarily with honest, absolutely innocent people. It is most fortunate for us, comrades, that the anti-Party group was rendered harmless and that we have been able, strictly in keeping with the Leninist course, to bring about tremendous changes in the country and raise the prestige of our Party and the Soviet state to an unprecedented height in the international arena. (*Prolonged applause.*)

Nikita Sergeyevich Khrushchov, First Secretary of the Central Committee of our Party, displayed Bolshevik firmness and fidelity to principle in the struggle against the anti-Party factional group, in the defence of the Leninist line of our Party. (*Applause.*) The whole of the Central Committee rallied round Comrade Khrushchov. In that complicated situation, the Central Committee of our Party adhered firmly to its Marxist-Leninist stand; it exposed the factional, anti-Party group with merciless determination, and defeated it completely. *(Applause.)* These actions of the C.C. C.P.S.U. and Comrade Khrushchov won the approval of the entire Party and the people as a whole. *(Stormy, prolonged applause.)*

From the lofty rostrum of the Twenty-Second Congress, many delegates indignantly condemned the foul deeds of the anti-Party group as a whole and of its individual members.

Facts were established and disclosed which indicate that Molotov, Kaganovich and Malenkov took a hand in exterminating many absolutely innocent people, including prominent Party leaders and statesmen, and that by their careerist policy and their departure from Leninism they contributed to the rise and flourishing of the cult of the individual.

The facts indicate that the organisers of the anti-Party group are still trying to uphold their harmful views. Molotov shows particular zeal in this respect. He has gone so far as to describe the new Programme of the C.P.S.U. as anti-revolutionary in spirit. He, Molotov, does not care at all that in the course of its nation-wide discussion the Programme won the unqualified approval of the Party and the people and of the fraternal Marxist-Leninist parties, and that all fair-minded people on earth describe it as the Communist Manifesto of our epoch. That statement of Molotov's is in effect a challenge to our Party as a whole, and to the Twenty-Second Congress of the C.P.S.U., which has unanimously approved the new Programme. I share the opinion of the delegates who spoke here and who said that Molotov, Kaganovich and Malenkov must be called to strict account by the Party and the people for all their anti-Party, criminal deeds.

The anti-Party group, above all Molotov, Kaganovich and Malenkov, resisted with might and main the elimination of the after-effects of the personality cult. They were afraid that they would be called to account for the abuses of power perpetrated at the time of the cult of Stalin's person.

Violations of Lenin's behests by Stalin, the abuses of power, and wholesale repression of honest Soviet people have been condemned by our Party and all Soviet people. (*Prolonged applause.*)

Comrades, in the Central Committee Report to the Congress and in his Concluding Speech yesterday, N. S. Khrushchov said that lately the leaders of the Albanian Party of Labour have, without any cause given by the Communist Party of the Soviet Union and its leadership, radically altered their political course and adopted the path of sharply worsening relations with our Party, with the Soviet Union and other socialist countries. The actions of the leaders of the Albanian Party of Labour, primarily those of Mehmet Shehu and Enver Hoxha, show clearly what may result from recurrences of the cult of the individual, violations of the Leninist principles of party leadership and the introduction of anti-democratic practices in the party and the country.

The Albanian leaders have forgotten what the aid and support of the Soviet Union and of the other socialist countries have meant to Albania. While continuing to pay lip-service to Soviet-Albanian friendship, they are, in effect, violating that friendship and persecuting the true friends of the Soviet Union. They have gone so far in their actions as to openly attack our Party and its Leninist Central Committee, and the leadership of the fraternal parties of the socialist countries. As for themselves, they pose as almost the sole consistent Marxists-Leninists. In reality, however, they are reviving in their Party and their country all that was bad in our country at the time of the cult of the individual, and are maintaining their power by force and arbitrary methods.

The pernicious policy of the Albanian leadership may lead to Albania's detachment from the socialist camp and to the political isolation of the Albanian Party of Labour within the ranks of the international Communist movement. This anti-Leninist course may, at the same time, do grave damage to the building of socialism in Albania, which has cost her heroic people so much effort and labour, and impair the country's position on the world scene.

The Moscow Meeting of Communist and Workers' Parties, held in November 1960, has said in its Statement: "A resolute defence of the unity of the world Communist movement on the principles of Marxism-Leninism and proletarian internationalism, and the prevention of any actions which may undermine that unity, are a necessary condition for victory in the struggle for national independence, democracy and peace, for the successful accomplishment of the tasks of the socialist revolution and of the building of socialism and communism. Violation of these principles would weaken the forces of communism."

As you know, the Albanian Party of Labour has affixed its signature to that historic Statement. But of late all the actions of its leaders indicate that they have begun to deviate from the agreed common line of the international Communist movement on the principal questions of our time. What is more, the leaders of the Albanian Party of Labour turned down the repeated attempts of the C.C. C.P.S.U. and other fraternal parties aimed at overcoming the divergences that had arisen. They replied to these steps with a rude refusal, and resorted to what were in effect provocative actions.

What was the Central Committee to do after the numerous attempts to persuade the Albanian leadership to abandon its sectarian actions proved futile and after, through the fault of this leadership, its harmful policy of deviation from the principles of proletarian internationalism came to be known to our ideological adversaries? Obviously, principled censure of the anti-Leninist conduct of the Albanian leaders and an open appeal to look for ways and means of surmounting the differences was, in the circumstances, the only correct and sound Marxist-Leninist approach to the matter. (*Prolonged applause.*) That is why the Central Committee, in its Report to this Congress, told the whole truth about the harmful attitude of the leadership of the Albanian Party of Labour.

Comrade Khrushchov has cited facts which show that Mehmet Shehu, Enver Hoxha and other Albanian leaders have in the last few days, even while the Twenty-Second Congress of the C.P.S.U. has been in session, committed acts which indicate that they are drifting still more towards nationalism and sectarianism, that they are departing still further from the agreed line of the international Communist movement and have adopted a course of outright slander against the C.P.S.U. and its Central Committee, a course of deceiving their Party and their people. Is it not a disgrace, comrades, that the Albanian leaders consider enemies all those who today advocate friendship with the Soviet Union!

We must state emphatically that genuine unity of the fraternal Communist and Workers' parties is possible only on a principled Marxist-Leninist basis, and not through hushing up the pernicious policy of the Albanian leadership. (*Applause.*) In this case, hushing up matters would be tantamount to encouraging people to continue their wrong, anti-Leninist actions. Our Party cannot adopt such an attitude. (*Prolonged applause.*)

We Soviet Communists will continue to expose resolutely all who depart from Leninism, all revisionists and dogmatists. The cause of the socialist revolution, of Marx and Lenin, is a great cause, and it is the sacred duty of every Soviet Communist and the whole of our Leninist Party to uphold the purity of Marxism-Leninism, to promote its creative development and the ideological unity of the world Communist movement. (*Stormy, prolonged applause.*)

THE GROWING ROLE OF LOCAL PARTY BODIES AND PRIMARY ORGANISATIONS

Comrades, the policy of the Party is put into practice through the effort of millions of Soviet people. Lead by the Party, by its local bodies and primary organisations at factories, on collective and state farms, in offices and research institutions, Soviet people are enthusiastically carrying out the magnificent tasks of communist construction.

The chief component of the work of district, city, area, regional and territorial Party organisations, the Communist parties of the Union republics and their leading bodies is to implement the policy of the Party, to organise the execution of decisions adopted by Party congresses and directives given by the C.C. C.P.S.U. The draft Rules specify this general task in a list of the basic duties of local Party organisations and their leading bodies.

The most important of these duties are the all-round promotion of industrial and agricultural production, and work to continuously improve the living and cultural standards of the people. The Party bodies can ensure the fulfilment of these duties by a higher standard of political and organisational work among the masses, better selection and education of personnel, and more efficient leadership of government and non-government organisations.

The selection and placing of leading personnel and their education in a communist spirit, in a spirit of awareness of their great responsibility to the Party and the people for the job entrusted to them, constitute the chief organisational task of the Party, of its local bodies and primary organisations.

The Party organisations have done much to improve the selection, placing and education of personnel, and have achieved positive results. The overwhelming majority of the Party cadres possess adequate knowledge and organisational experience. Over nine-tenths of the secretaries of regional and territorial Party committees and central committees of the Communist parties of the Union republics, and almost three-quarters of the secretaries of city and district Party committees, have received a higher education. In the last five years the number of secretaries of district and city Party committees who have received a higher education has more than trebled. The number of engineers, economists, agronomists, livestock-breeding experts and other specialists among Party officials is growing from year to year.

In these circumstances, it is particularly impermissible that some sectors of Party, government, economic and cultural activity should still be headed by people lacking adequate knowledge or who are simply unqualified for the job. The reason for this is the careless selection, placing and education of personnel.

Party bodies sometimes substitute the mechanical filling of vacancies and rash promotion for a thoughtful policy of selecting and placing personnel, a policy that would take into account the nature of the task in hand. Here is an example. The Strommashina Factory in Kuibyshev needed a director. How do you think the problem was solved? The economic council concerned telephoned the Regional Party Committee, and the decision was taken, without looking properly into the matter, to appoint to the post Comrade Kuroyedov, shop chief at a factory. No one seemed to be embarrassed by the fact that Kuroyedov had shortly before been found guilty of falsification and doctoring reports, offences for which he had been called to account at Party and administrative level. Small wonder that after becoming director of the factory, Kuroyedov indulged in doctoring reports on an even larger scale, with the result that it soon became necessary to remove him. It is characteristic, however, that neither the economic council nor the Kuibyshev City Party Committee had the courage, in relieving Kuroyedov of the office of director, to admit their error and say in so many words that they were relieving him for falsification. They covered their decision with the elastic formula: "Relieved in view of his transfer to another job." (*Animation.*)

It should be obvious that such unsound practices give rise to an irresponsible attitude to the selection and promotion of personnel, and breed more errors.

It is the duty of Party committees to be highly exacting with regard to officials. They must work patiently with people and educate them in the spirit of the utmost fidelity to our ideas and principles. But there are still Party committees whose sole means of influencing people seem to be threats and high-handed methods. This style of leadership was typical, for example, of the Kardymovo District Committee in Smolensk Region. That district saw 32 collective-farm chairmen replaced in a short period of time. One of the collective-farm chairmen, speaking at a district Party conference, gave a very apt description of such methods of would-be leadership. "The District Committee," he said, "guided the collective farms from positions of strength and brinkmanship between a severe Party penalty and expulsion from the Party." (*Laughter.*)

We must put an end to such treatment of personnel. It is at variance with the policy of promoting inner-Party democracy adopted by the Party. The Rules of the C.P.S.U. direct Party bodies towards improving their work with personnel, towards making officials more strictly accountable to the Party and the people, and improving the methods of Party leadership.

In recent years important measures have been taken to extend the rights of the local government and economic bodies. These measures have removed the restrictions shackling independence and initiative in planning, in industrial and agricultural management, and in the use of funds and materials at local level. Thereby greater opportunities have been provided for the effective utilisation of the resources of regions, territories and republics. Local Party committees, too, now have extensive rights in settling organisational and other Party matters.

This course, aimed at promoting socialist democracy, has had a beneficial effect on the activities of local bodies. Party organisations undoubtedly take a more responsible attitude to the manner in which government and public affairs are managed. This does not mean, however, that Party committees must assume functions assigned to government and economic bodies.

Unfortunately, Party committees sometimes deal with matters which can perfectly well be taken care of by other bodies. This is evident from the fact that certain Party and government bodies adopt numerous joint decisions on matters of secondary importance. Indeed, was it really necessary for the Buryat Regional Committee of the Party to adopt, jointly with the Council of Ministers of the Buryat Autonomous Republic, a decision on the use of the sea buckthorn shrubs in Selenga District? Such practices give rise to an irresponsible attitude and get government and economic executives into the habit of securing the endorsement of Party bodies on any matter, however unimportant.

Government and economic bodies should be released from petty tutelage. The draft Rules of the C.P.S.U. state: "Party organisations must not assume the functions assigned to government, trade union, co-operative or other mass organisations of the working people; they must not mix the functions of Party bodies with those of other bodies, must not allow unnecessary parallelism in work."

Strict observance of these requirements as laid down in the Rules will enable Party bodies to concentrate on more effective work among the masses. We must draw the working people more actively into the administration of government and public affairs, must improve our work in the selection, placing and education of personnel, and organise the effective supervision and check-up of work done. All this has been dealt with comprehensively in the Central Committee's Report to the Congress.

The promotion of the voluntary principle in Party activity is of vast importance in improving the work of local Party organisations. The variety and scope of the application of this principle may be gathered from the following: there are now more than 230,000 non-staff functionaries, lecturers and members of various standing commissions of the district, city, area, regional and territorial Party committees and of the central committees of the Communist parties of the Union republics. Over 600,000 Communists are working on commissions of primary Party organisations, specially set up to check the work of the respective managements. Thousands of political education centres, Party study rooms and libraries are successfully working on the voluntary principle in the various Party organisations, and the press has some editorial boards and departments functioning on a voluntary basis. Another new way in which the help of Party activists is enlisted, is the voluntary commissions set up by district Party committees in Moscow and Leningrad for the preliminary examination of questions of admission into the Party and also of personal matters. These commissions are doing useful work. We should examine their activities carefully, study their experience and think of ways of applying it on a larger scale.

We must see to it that the paid apparatus of Party bodies is reduced and the number of unpaid Party functionaries increased. The Party bodies, says Nikita Sergeyevich Khrushchov, should have more and more commissions and departments, with district committee and city committee secretaries and other functionaries all working on a voluntary principle.

Comrades, the primary organisation is the basic Party unit where the Communist is moulded as a person of ideological integrity, as a socially conscious and active fighter. Nothing can take the place of the schooling the Communist receives in the Party collective. The primary organisations carry on their activities in the midst of the masses.

The Party gives leadership to the masses, carries out its policy and its decisions through the primary Party organisations.

During the past few years the primary Party organisations have grown stronger, have increased numerically. There are nearly 300,000 primary organisations in the Party today. In view of the growing demands being made on all aspects of Party work, the section on the primary organisations in the draft Rules has been considerably revised in the light of the tasks outlined in the Programme of the C.P.S.U.

The primary Party organisations should today focus their attention on questions concerning the creation of the material and technical basis of communism, the development of communist social relations and the education of the working people in the spirit of communism. (*Applause.*)

As stated in the draft Rules, the primary Party organisation acts as organiser of the working people in carrying out the current tasks of communist construction, heads the socialist emulation movement for the fulfilment of state plans and of obligations undertaken by the working people. One of its cardinal tasks is to rally the masses to find and make the best use of untapped resources at enterprises and collective farms and to introduce in production, on a broad scale, the achievements of science and engineering, and the experience of front-rankers. It is the duty of the primary Party organisations to work for better labour discipline, the steady increase of labour productivity and improvement of the quality of production, and to see to it that the social wealth at enterprises and at state and collective farms is taken proper care of and increased.

To enable primary Party organisations at industrial enterprises and trading establishments, state and collective farms to cope with these tasks they have been empowered to use such an effective means as supervision of the work of the relevant management. The draft Rules now extend this right to the primary Party organisations of designing and drafting offices and research institutes directly related to production.

The primary Party organisation helps the working people to acquire proficiency in administering state and public affairs, and through extensive criticism and self-criticism, to put a stop to red tape, parochialism, and violations of state discipline. It is the duty of the primary Party organisation to enhance the vanguard role of Communists in the field of labour and in the socio-political and economic life of the country, and to improve agitational and propaganda work among the masses.

Comrades, the Communist Party—the spokesman of the finest aspirations of the Soviet people—is the standard-bearer of communist morality. On its banners are inscribed the most lofty and radiant ideals. The Party will be able to accomplish its majestic tasks only if it educates all its members and all Soviet people in the spirit of communist morality, to cultivate in them ideological integrity, a high sense of social consciousness and civic duty, industriousness and discipline. The moral code of the builder of communism, as formulated in the C.P.S.U. Programme and included in the draft Rules, will play a significant part in this. This code will become the standard of behaviour for every Party member, the yardstick by which every Communist and Party organisation will measure and assess the moral qualities of their Party comrades. (*Prolonged applause.*)

All the clauses in the draft Rules concerning the primary Party organisations are therefore designed to enhance their role, their activity and militancy when carrying out the grand tasks of communist construction.

In the period of the full-scale building of communism the Soviets, trade unions, co-operatives and other mass organisations of the working people play an ever bigger role in the life of the country. The Party will continue, through these organisations, to extend and strengthen its ties with the masses, to consult the people on cardinal questions of its policy, and to enlist the working people on a bigger scale in the administration of state and public affairs. The draft Rules stress that the Party guides the mass organisations through the Party groups in them, by encouraging the initiative and activity of the masses as an essential condition for the gradual transition from socialist state organisation to communist self-administration by the people.

The Party groups in the non-Party organisations must enhance in every possible way the influence of the Party, and carry out its policy among the non-Party masses, strengthen Party and state discipline, combat red tape, verify the execution of Party and state directives.

The importance of the Young Communist League is growing. The Party regards the youth as a big constructive and creative force in building communism, and the Komsomol as an independently-acting mass organisation of young people, an active helper and reserve of the Party. (*Applause.*) The Komsomol is called upon to help the Party educate the youth in the communist spirit, to draw it into the work of building a new society, and to train a generation of harmoniously developed people who will live and work, and govern public affairs under communism.

The Communist Party considers it as its sacred duty to strengthen the defensive might of the U.S.S.R., and regards Party guidance as basic in the building up and the organisation of the country's Armed Forces. The draft Rules state that in their work, the Party organisations in the Soviet Army take guidance from the Programme and the Rules of the C.P.S.U. They outline the principal tasks of the Party organisations in the Armed Forces. An important clause is the one that the guidance of Party work in the Armed Forces is exercised by the Central Committee of the C.P.S.U. through the Chief Political Administration of the Soviet Army and Navy, which functions as a department of the C.C. C.P.S.U.

RESULTS OF THE DISCUSSION
OF THE DRAFT RULES OF THE C.P.S.U.

Comrades, the draft Rules have been widely discussed at meetings of primary Party organisations, at district, city, area, regional, and territorial Party conferences and at congresses of the Communist parties of the Union republics, attended by over 9,000,000 Communists. More than one and a half million people have taken part in the discussion on the draft Rules; over 120,000 letters containing various suggestions and additions to the draft Rules have been received by Party bodies and the editorial offices of newspapers and magazines.

We may say with good reason that the whole Party, its entire membership has participated in the discussion of the draft Rules. The draft Rules have been unanimously endorsed at all the Party meetings, conferences and congresses without exception. (*Prolonged applause.*)

The very active part taken by Communists in the discussion, and the suggestions, amendments and additions made in the course of the discussion show that the many-million-strong army of Communists of the Soviet Union have at heart the further strengthening of the Party's ranks, the raising of its militancy and organisation, and the enhancing of the role of every Party organisation, of every Communist, in accomplishing the historic tasks outlined in the new Programme.

The proposals and remarks made by Communists concern the further development of the Party, the promotion of inner-Party democracy, the Leninist standards and principles of Party life, Party membership and the duties and rights of Communists.

The various proposals sent in may be divided into three groups.

The *first* group covers proposals which supplement or enlarge on one or another of the clauses in the draft Rules. They include proposals for greater stress on the necessity to continuously improve the forms and methods of the Party's activities, develop inner-Party democracy, and raise the level of leadership of the masses. All these proposals have been thoroughly studied by the Central Committee, and the relevant additions and more precise formulations have been introduced, in generalised form, in the text of the draft Rules distributed among the delegates.

I think it necessary to dwell in brief on some of these proposals.

In the course of the discussion many Communists expressed the wish that, in the period between conferences and congresses, the local Party committees should inform the Party organisations more extensively on their work. This fully accords with the Party's demand that there be stricter supervision by the rank and file of the Party over the work of their elective bodies. This proposal is a fitting one, and it is reflected in the draft Rules.

Many consider it necessary to include in the Rules a clause stating that it is the duty of every Communist to help in every possible way to increase the defensive might of the U.S.S.R., and to fight unflaggingly for peace. It is common knowledge that our Party regards defence of the socialist Motherland, the strengthening of the defence power of the U.S.S.R. as a sacred duty of the Party and the entire Soviet people, as an essential condition for the preservation and promotion of world peace; it regards the struggle for peace among nations as its cardinal task. (*Applause.*) This is also reflected in the draft Rules.

It has been proposed to put it down in the Rules that to be an active atheist, a propagandist of the scientific-materialist world outlook, is one of the Communist's duties. This proposal should be considered. Religious prejudices and superstition are tenacious and are still current among a certain section of the population. Who, if not the Communist, is in duty bound to explain the anti-scientific nature of religious ideas.

Besides the proposals and additions spoken of earlier, amendments of an editorial nature that improve certain formulations in the draft Rules, have also been suggested. Some of them have been introduced into the draft.

The *second* group covers proposals, additions and remarks which, in the main, are to the effect that various clauses contained in the draft Rules of the C.P.S.U. be elaborated in greater detail.

The proposal has been made, for instance, that the range of the Communists' duties should be expanded. But if this proposal were accepted there would be little distinction in the Rules between the important and unimportant, the essential and unessential. We believe that this should not be done. The duties of a Party member formulated in the draft Rules give a complete and exhaustive answer to the question what is required of a Communist in the period of the full-scale building of communist society.

It has also been proposed that the new Rules should retain the numerous points to the effect that non-fulfilment by a Party member of one or another of the duties laid down in the Rules is incompatible with Party membership. But the draft Rules contain special clauses defining the responsibility of a Communist for non-fulfilment or violation of the Rules. That is quite sufficient.

Many suggestions and additions have been submitted regarding admission into the Party and the probationary period. Some propose placing higher demands on those joining the Party: an increase of the probationary period up to two years and the Party standing of Party members giving recommendations up to five years; admission of new members by secret ballot; submission by applicants for Party membership of recommendations from the collectives they work in, their trade union organisations, etc. Others, on the contrary, believe that the existing rules of admission into the C.P.S.U. should be relaxed; for instance, that members of the Komsomol should be admitted into the Party without having to pass through the established probationary period; that the probationary period should be reduced to six months and the required number of recommendations decreased.

We believe that the procedure of admission into the C.P.S.U., as laid down in the draft Rules, conforms to the present period in the development of our Party, and should not, therefore, be changed. (*Applause.*)

Many proposals deal with the question of communist morality. Suggestions have been made that the Rules should give in fuller detail the duty of Party organisations in combating the manifestations of a private-property psychology, the tendencies towards personal enrichment, and the anti-social behaviour of some Communists. In the section on the duties of a Communist and in the moral code of the builder of communism, the draft Rules outline the respective demands on Party members. It stresses that a Party member must be implacable to injustice, parasitism, dishonesty and money-grubbing. The Party's position on the question of the moral make-up of the Communist has been comprehensively dealt with by Comrade Khrushchov in his reports to our Congress, and all Party organisations will be guided unswervingly by the propositions made. (*Prolonged applause.*)

The *third* group concerns proposals and additions which do not take into account the present-day conditions in the Party's activities.

It has been proposed, for instance, that the secretaries of district, city, regional, and territorial committees and of the central committees of the Communist parties of the Union republics should be elected not at plenary meetings but directly at conferences and congresses, and the secretaries of Party bureaus at Party meetings. But if this proposal were accepted and if the secretaries of Party bureaus and committees were elected directly at meetings and conferences, it would mean that the secretaries would be invested with greater powers than the rest of the bureau or committee members, and placed above the bureau or the committee. This proposal runs counter to the principle of collective leadership, and its acceptance is inadvisable. (*Applause*.)

We cannot agree for that matter with the proposal that the secret ballot be replaced by open ballot at election of Party bodies. The authors of this proposal give as their reason that open voting, more so than secret, tends to foster in Party members a spirit of fidelity to principles, promotes the development of criticism. This kind of argument is unconvincing. As you know, the secret ballot is preceded by preliminary open discussion of the candidate nominated to the Party body. Every Party member has the unrestricted right to criticise and challenge any candidate. There is, therefore, every opportunity for principled discussion of the merits and demerits of the candidates put forward, and hence for fostering in Communists a spirit of fidelity to Party principles. Rejection of the secret ballot would be a step back in the development of inner-Party democracy, would mean narrowing and restricting the right of Party members to express their will fully and freely. (*Applause*.)

Then there is the proposal to abolish candidate membership. The argument is that the political and cultural level of the people has risen considerably, that the primary Party organisations are working in the midst of the masses and so are in a position to judge of the merits of every working person who wants to join the Party, and that, therefore, the probationary period can be dispensed with.

The Communist must be in the van of Soviet society; he must be an example to non-Party people. The probationary period is an important way of checking whether the person who is joining the Party is fitted to carry out the lofty and complex duties of a Communist. It is precisely in the Party organisation, in working together with Party members, that all the qualities of the prospective Party member become apparent. To abolish the probationary period would mean reducing the demands made on those joining the Party.

The proposal has been made that the Rules provide for the restoration of periodical Party purges. It will be remembered that the Eighteenth Party Congress already considered it necessary to abandon the practice of mass purges. The resolution of that Congress stated: "The method of mass purges, introduced at the beginning of NEP, in the period of the revival of capitalist elements, to safeguard the Party against infiltration into its ranks of people who had become corrupted under NEP, is no longer needed in the present situation when the capitalist elements have been liquidated."

Twenty-two years have passed since then. The victory of socialism in our country is complete and final. The U.S.S.R. has entered the period of the full-scale building of communism. Is there any need in these circumstances to restore Party purges?

The purges were necessary in conditions of the acute class struggle within the country. Now, in the period of full-scale communist construction, when complete moral and political unity of the whole people has been welded, such a measure is unnecessary. The Party is strong enough, ideologically and organisationally, to clear its ranks of those who violate the Programme or the Rules, without recourse to purges. (*Prolonged applause.*)

There are also proposals and additions which, while essentially correct, do not, however, come under the Rules. They mostly concern the organisation and holding of Party election meetings and Party conferences, the method of determining ballot results, and other such questions. These proposals and remarks, as I have earlier mentioned, should be taken into account when the relevant instructions of the C.C. C.P.S.U. are being worked out.

In conclusion, during the discussion of the draft Rules Communists and non-Party people made a number of critical remarks concerning the activities of local Party bodies. They pointed out particular shortcomings in the way the Party's political and organisational work was conducted, facts of violation of the Leninist standards of Party life, of an incorrect attitude to criticism, distortions of the Party's line in the selection of cadres. The Central Committees of the Communist parties of the Union republics, and the territorial and regional committees of the Party should carefully consider all the critical remarks and concrete proposals made by Communists with regard to local Party bodies, and take the necessary measures to eliminate these shortcomings.

* * *

Comrades, the Central Committee's Report and the Report on the draft Party Programme delivered by Comrade Khrushchov, and the Programme of the C.P.S.U. that has been unanimously and enthusiastically approved by the Congress, open up wide new vistas before the Party and the entire Soviet people. The path to our great goal, communism, is now outlined with the utmost clarity and scientific authenticity. (*Applause.*)

This is an inspiration to the members of the great Party of Communists, to all Soviet people, it gives them fresh strength and calls on them to accomplish further exploits for the triumph of communism. The tremendous creative activity and initiative displayed by Soviet people in the days preceding the Twenty-Second Congress of the C.P.S.U. and during it, show their readiness to fulfil, under the Party's leadership, the great plans envisaged in the new Party Programme. (*Prolonged applause.*)

At the new stage in the historical development of our country, the great Communist Party of the Soviet Union will continue to march at the head of our heroic people and will raise still higher the level of its political and organisational leadership of the masses.

The Rules of the C.P.S.U., which are to be adopted by the Twenty-Second Congress of the Party, will help every

Party organisation, every Communist, to define its or his place in the constructive endeavour of the entire people, to work with redoubled energy for the realisation of the Congress decisions. "The organisational principles laid down in the Rules," said Comrade Khrushchov, "must ensure the successful implementation of the Programme, must strengthen the unity and cohesion of the Party, the militant vanguard of the Soviet people in the struggle for communism." (*Prolonged applause.*)

Guided by the Programme of the C.P.S.U.—that great document of our era which defines the aims and tasks of our Party and the Soviet people for many years to come—and undeviatingly observing the Leninist standards and principles embodied in the Rules, the Party will unite its ranks still more closely, it will extend and strengthen its bonds with the working people and lead our people along the straight and bright road to the triumph of communism. (*Prolonged applause.*)

The time is not far distant when the Soviet people, under the leadership of the Party, under the banner of Marxism-Leninism, will build a communist society, which will put into effect the great principle "From each according to his ability, to each according to his needs", and the sun of communism will shine over the whole world. Communism establishes throughout the world Peace, Labour, Freedom, Equality, Fraternity and Happiness for all peoples. (*Prolonged applause.*)

Long live Marxism-Leninism, the mighty ideological weapon of the working people of the whole world! (*Stormy applause.*)

Long live the Communist Party of the Soviet Union, the guiding and directing force of Soviet society in the struggle to build communism! (*Stormy applause.*)

Long live communism! (*Stormy, prolonged applause.*)

RESOLUTION OF THE 22nd CONGRESS OF THE COMMUNIST PARTY OF THE SOVIET UNION ON THE REPORT OF THE CENTRAL COMMITTEE OF THE C.P.S.U.

(Adopted Unanimously on October 31, 1961)

The Twenty-Second Congress of the Communist Party of the Soviet Union has met at a time when our country has entered the period of the full-scale construction of communist society, when socialism has been firmly established in the People's Democracies and the forces of peace and progress are vigorously growing throughout the world.

The years since the Twentieth Congress of the C.P.S.U. were of extreme importance in the life of our Party, the Soviet people and the whole of mankind. Implementing its Leninist general line, the Party rallied all the working people for the fulfilment of the tasks of communist construction along the entire front of great undertakings. An important landmark on the road of development of the U.S.S.R. towards communism was the extraordinary Twenty-First Congress of the C.P.S.U., which adopted the Seven-Year Economic Development Plan.

With great satisfaction the Twenty-Second Congress of the C.P.S.U. has summed up the historic victories of the Soviet people. The Land of Soviets has travelled a road of heroic struggle and is now at the full height of its creative powers. The might of the Soviet Union has become still greater, its international prestige as a fighter for the cause of peace and progress, for the friendship of peoples, for the happiness of mankind, has immeasurably increased.

The entire course of events confirms the correctness of the theoretical conclusions and political line of our Party. The course taken by the Twentieth Congress, which was dictated by life itself, by concern for the well-being of the people, and which was imbued with the Leninist creative revolutionary spirit, has completely triumphed.

Having heard and discussed the report of the First Secretary of the Central Committee, Comrade Khrushchov —the Report of the Central Committee of the C.P.S.U., the Twenty-Second Congress of the Communist Party of the Soviet Union resolves:

Wholly and fully to approve the political course and practical work of the Central Committee of the C.P.S.U. in the fields of foreign and internal policy. To approve the conclusions and proposals contained in the Report of the Central Committee of the C.P.S.U.

I

The Twenty-Second Congress notes that the further growth of the forces of socialism, democracy and peace throughout the world is the decisive feature of the present international situation. Life has confirmed the correctness of the Party's foreign policy aimed at preventing war and stabilising peace. This policy accords with the fundamental interests of the Soviet people and has the support of the peace-loving forces of all countries. The Congress highly appreciates the consistency, flexibility and initiative of the foreign policy, and fully approves the measures of the Central Committee and the Soviet Government aimed at strengthening political, economic and cultural ties with all states.

The fact that it has been possible to avert war and that the Soviet people and peoples of other countries have been able to enjoy the benefits of a peaceful life should be regarded as the main result of the activity of the Party and its Central Committee in augmenting the might of the Soviet state and implementing the Leninist foreign policy, and as the result of the activity of the fraternal parties of the socialist countries and the enhanced activity of the peace-loving forces of all countries.

The Soviet Union, the People's Republic of China and all the countries of the world socialist system are advancing confidently along the road of socialist and communist construction. Backed by their increased might, and with the support of the peace-loving forces throughout the world, the socialist countries have not allowed the imperialists to divert the world from the path of peaceful economic competition of the two systems on to one leading to a universal world catastrophe. The peaceful competition of the two opposing social systems, which is the backbone of contemporary international life, has entered a decisive phase. The policy of friendship and peace among the peoples is winning ever greater recognition and support, and gaining the upper hand over the imperialist policy of aggression and war.

The world socialist system is successfully developing, growing in strength and becoming the determining factor of the progress of human society. The Soviet Union has entered the period of the full-scale construction of communism; in the majority of the People's Democracies the multiplicity of economic forms has been eliminated and the building of socialism is being completed; the standard of living of the peoples is steadily rising; fraternal co-operation and mutual assistance among the socialist states is increasing. The Congress warmly welcomes the outstanding successes of the fraternal parties and of the peoples of the socialist countries and wishes them further glorious victories.

The Twenty-Second Congress approves the line of the Central Committee and the Soviet Government towards steadily strengthening economic, political and cultural co-operation among the socialist states based on the principles of proletarian internationalism, equality and comradely mutual assistance. The Congress notes in particular the great and fruitful work of the Central Committee to develop and strengthen co-operation between the C.P.S.U. and the fraternal Communist and Workers' parties on the basis of Marxism-Leninism and in the interests of the unity and solidarity of the international Communist movement. The Congress emphatically rejects as unfounded and slanderous the attacks of the leaders of the Albanian Party of Labour against the C.P.S.U. and its Leninist Central Committee. The actions of the Albanian leaders go against the Declaration and the Statement of the meetings of representatives of the Communist and Workers' parties in 1957 and 1960, and can only be appraised as splitting actions that aim at undermining the friendship and solidarity of the socialist countries and that play into the hands of imperialism. The Congress expresses the hope that the Albanian leaders, if they value the interests of their people and truly desire friendship with the C.P.S.U. and all the fraternal parties, will renounce their erroneous views and return to the path of unity and co-operation with all the socialist countries and with the international Communist movement.

The further strengthening of the unity of the socialist camp, the increasing of its might and defence capacity, remains one of the most important tasks. Combining the efforts to develop the national economy of each socialist country with the common efforts to consolidate and extend economic co-operation and mutual assistance—this is the way that leads to the further flourishing and rapid progress of all the countries of the socialist community, of world socialist economy.

The successes of the socialist countries have an increasing, all-round effect on the peoples of the non-socialist states, revolutionising and accelerating the development of mankind on progressive lines. *Today it is socialism, not imperialism, that determines the main trend of world development.*

The conclusion drawn by the Twentieth Congress that the general crisis of capitalism would inevitably deepen has been fully confirmed. During the past few years there has been a further weakening of the economic, political and ideological positions of imperialism. Its basic contradictions have become still sharper, and the revolutionary struggle of the working class and the democratic and national-liberation movement of the peoples have assumed tremendous proportions. The capitalist system is becoming more and more discredited in the eyes of the people as a system of savage exploitation of the working people, of national and colonial oppression, of the armaments race and wars of annihilation.

Under the powerful blows of the national-liberation movement the colonial system has virtually collapsed. The imperialist forces—and in the first place American imperialism, the main bulwark of world reaction and the international gendarme—are endeavouring to retain their positions by using new, more subtle forms of colonial enslavement. But the experience of history is increasingly convincing the peoples of the former colonies that only emancipation once and for all from every form of economic and political dependence, only the non-capitalist path of development, can bring their countries to true freedom, prosperity and happiness.

Despite the prophesies of the imperialist ideologists and their henchmen, the Right-wing Socialists and revisionists, the class struggle in the capitalist countries is not dying down but broadening in scope and becoming more and more acute. Side by side with the revolutionary actions of the working class, the peasant and the general democratic movements are growing in strength. It is becoming urgently necessary to unite all the anti-imperialist forces and decisively overcome the ideology and practice of anti-communism and reformism.

The entire course of social development, the incessant growth of the forces working for socialism and against imperialism confirm the correctness of the conclusion drawn by the Twentieth Congress on the variety of forms of transition of countries to socialism. This conclusion, which was supported by the international Communist movement, was embodied and developed in the 1957 Declaration and the 1960 Statement adopted at the meetings of the Marxist-Leninist parties.

The Marxist-Leninist parties are heading the struggle of the working class and all the working people of their countries for the realisation of the socialist revolution and the establishment of the dictatorship of the proletariat in one form or another.

The forms and paths of development of the socialist revolution will depend on the actual relationship of class forces in the country concerned, the organisation and maturity of the working class and its vanguard and the degree of resistance of the ruling classes. Irrespective of the forms in which the dictatorship of the proletariat will be established, it will always represent a broadening of democracy, a transition from formal, bourgeois democracy to genuine democracy, democracy for the working people. The working class and its vanguard—the Marxist-Leninist party—are striving to achieve the socialist revolution by peaceful means. The realisation of this possibility would be in accord with the interests of the working class and the whole people, the national interests of the country.

In a number of capitalist countries today it is possible for the working class headed by its vanguard, on the basis of a workers' and people's front and other possible forms of agreement and political co-operation among various parties and mass organisations, to unite the majority of the people, win state power without civil war and ensure the transfer of the basic means of production into the hands of the people.

Backed by the majority of the people and administering a decisive rebuff to opportunist elements incapable of rejecting a policy of conciliation with the capitalists and landlords, the working class is able to defeat the reactionary, anti-popular forces, win a stable majority in parliament, convert parliament from an instrument serving the class interests of the bourgeoisie into one serving the working people, launch a broad mass struggle outside parliament, break down the resistance of the reactionary forces and create the necessary conditions for the peaceful achievement of the socialist revolution. All this will be possible only through the broad, continuous development of the class struggle of the workers, peasants and middle urban sections against big monopoly capital, against reaction, and for far-reaching social reforms, for peace and socialism. Under conditions where the exploiting   classes resort to violence against the people, the other possibility, that of non-peaceful transition to socialism, has to be taken into account. Leninism teaches, and the experience of history confirms it, that ruling classes do not voluntarily relinquish power. The degree of ferocity and the forms of the class struggle under these conditions will depend not so much on the proletariat as on the strength of the resistance of the reactionary forces to the will of the overwhelming majority of the people, and on the use of violence by these forces at a particular stage of the struggle for socialism.

Communism has become the most influential political force of our day. There is no longer any country with a more or less well-developed working-class and a liberation movement, where the influence is not felt of the Communists, the most consistent, steadfast and courageous fighters for the interests of the peoples. Of tremendous importance for the further consolidation of the ranks of the international Communist movement were the historic meetings of representatives of the Communist and Workers' parties in 1957 and 1960 and the documents drawn up by these meetings. The Congress highly appreciates and fully approves the work of the C.P.S.U. delegation at the meetings of representatives of the Communist and Workers' parties.

An uncompromising, consistent struggle on two fronts—against revisionism as the chief danger and against dogmatism and sectarianism—is of decisive importance for the triumph of Marxism-Leninism. The C.P.S.U. regards it as its internationalist duty to strengthen in every way the monolithic character of the international Communist movement, to wage a struggle against all those who try to weaken the unity of the Communists of all countries. It is necessary to continue to expose the theory and practice of modern revisionism, which has found expression in its most concentrated form in the programme of the League of Communists of Yugoslavia.

The issue of war and peace has been and remains the most burning issue of our time, arousing the anxiety of all mankind.

The events of recent years have confirmed the correctness of the conclusion of the Twentieth and Twenty-First Congresses that in the present epoch wars between states are not inevitable, that they can be prevented. In our day the powerful forces on guard for peace have at their disposal all the necessary means for curbing the imperialist warmongers. The world socialist system is becoming an ever more reliable shield protecting not only the peoples of the socialist countries but all mankind against imperialist military adventures. The ever-growing might of the Soviet Union and the other socialist countries is an important guarantee of peace throughout the world.

The countries of Asia, Africa and Latin America that have freed themselves from colonial oppression, and the working class and all working people of the capitalist countries, are fighting for peace side by side with the socialist states; the Peace Movement is growing throughout the world. The people are the decisive force in the struggle for peace. The greater the might of the socialist camp, the more actively the struggle for peace develops in the capitalist countries, the more difficult will it be for the imperialists to unleash a new world war. The struggle of the socialist countries and all peace-loving forces against preparations for a new war forms the main content of world politics today.

As a result of the radical change in favour of socialism of the world balance of forces, the policy of peaceful coexistence of states with differing social systems has acquired a still more solid basis. Lenin's principles of the peaceful coexistence of states with differing social systems, which are the basis of the foreign policy of the Soviet Union, have won wide recognition as the way to safeguard peace and prevent a new world war. Today, prospects have opened up for achieving peaceful coexistence during the whole period in which the social and political problems now dividing mankind should find their solution. Developments show that even before the complete global victory of socialism, with capitalism remaining in part of the world, a real possibility will arise for banishing world war from the life of society.

It has to be taken into account, however, that the foreign policy of the imperialist states is determined by the class interests of monopoly capital, an inherent characteristic of which is aggression and war. As long as imperialism survives, the ground for aggressive wars will remain. International imperialism, and American imperialism first and foremost, is the main danger to the cause of world peace. It is preparing the most terrible crime against humanity—a world nuclear war. The imperialists have created a dangerous situation in the heart of Europe, threatening war in reply to the proposal of the Soviet Union and other peace-loving countries to eliminate the remnants of the Second World War, conclude a peace treaty with Germany and normalise the West Berlin situation. In the past few years the reactionaries have more than once imperilled universal peace, and do not cease their attempts to aggravate the international situation and bring mankind to the brink of war. Now as never before the peoples need to be highly vigilant.

The Congress regards as timely, correct and essential the measures adopted by the Central Committee and the Soviet Government for the further strengthening of the defence capacity of our country. As long as the imperialist aggressors continue to exist it is necessary to be on the alert, to keep our powder dry and to improve the defence of the socialist countries and their armed forces.

Consolidation of peace demands the immediate solution, on the basis of the principles of peaceful coexistence, of the fundamental international problems, and above all those of general and complete disarmament under the strictest international control; the final abolition of colonial oppression in all its forms and manifestations; real and effective assistance for the peoples that have recently won their independence; elimination of the remnants of the Second World War, a peaceful settlement with Germany; restoration of the legitimate rights of the People's Republic of China in the United Nations; fundamental improvement of the U.N. machinery; development of business relations among states, economic and cultural ties between all countries.

The Communist Party of the Soviet Union will do everything necessary to preserve and consolidate peace and friendship among the peoples, so that the lofty ideals of social progress and the happiness of the peoples should triumph.

The Twenty-Second Congress of the C.P.S.U. considers it essential in the future as well:

—unswervingly and consistently to implement the principle of the peaceful coexistence of states with differing social systems as the general line of the foreign policy of the Soviet Union;

—tirelessly to strengthen the unity of the socialist countries on the basis of fraternal co-operation and mutual assistance, to contribute to the strengthening of the might of the world socialist system;

—to develop and deepen co-operation with all the forces fighting for world peace;

—to strengthen proletarian solidarity with the working class and the working people of the whole world, to give

the utmost support to the peoples fighting for their liberation from imperialist and colonial oppression, and for the
consolidation of their independence;

—to develop still more extensively international business
relations, mutually advantageous economic co-operation
and trade with all countries;

—to conduct an active and flexible foreign policy in
order to settle urgent world issues through negotiations, to expose the intrigues and manoeuvres of the imperialist war-mongers, to consolidate world peace.

II

The Congress notes with satisfaction that during the
period under review great successes have been achieved
in the development of all branches of the national economy
as a result of the steady fulfilment of the *internal policy*
formulated by the Twentieth Congress. Industry and agriculture have advanced rapidly to high levels, the economic
might and defence potential of the country have been still
further strengthened, the material and spiritual needs of
the Soviet people have been more fully satisfied. The work
of creating the material and technical basis of communism
has been put on a firm foundation.

*The accelerated rate of communist construction is a
most important feature of the period after the Twentieth
Congress.*

During the last six years, industrial output has increased
by almost 80 per cent. The Seven-Year Plan is being
successfully fulfilled. The average annual increase of industrial output amounts to 10 per cent instead of the 8.3
per cent laid down for the first three years of the Seven-
Year Plan. New important potentialities of the socialist
economy have been revealed and brought into operation,
making possible an industrial output of approximately
19,000 million rubles in excess of the targets for the first
three years of the Seven-Year Plan. Much work has been

carried out on the technological re-equipment of all branches of material production. Thousands of the latest types of machines, lathes, apparatus, instruments and means of automation have been developed.

The Congress notes that thanks to the unremitting care of the Party and Government, and to the selfless labour of the Soviet people, the re-equipment of the Soviet Armed Forces with rocket and nuclear weapons has been completely accomplished. The powerful military equipment in the hands of our people reliably safeguards socialist gains and promotes the cause of peace throughout the world.

Since the Twentieth Congress important *qualitative changes* have taken place in industry, building and transport. There has been a radical improvement in the fuel balance; power engineering has been given a new technical basis; the rates of development of the chemical industry and of the technical reconstruction of all forms of transport have been considerably accelerated. Measures have been taken by the Party and Government to develop the light and food industries, and to increase the output of consumer goods, which is already having a favourable effect and will in the future still further contribute to raising the living standard of the Soviet people.

As a result of providing building sites with new equipment and making wide use of prefabricated concrete building elements, capital construction has expanded to unprecedented proportions. During 1956-61, 156,000 million rubles were invested in the national economy, an amount exceeding the volume of capital investment during all the years of Soviet power previous to the Twentieth Party Congress. About six thousand new state enterprises have been brought into operation, including the largest hydro-power stations in the world, metallurgical, chemical and engineering factories and textile mills; wide use is being made of such an economical and effective way of increasing industrial capacity as the reconstruction and enlargement of existing enterprises.

The course outlined by the Party for accelerating the development of the productive forces of the *Eastern areas of the country* is being consistently put into effect. Big power stations are being built on the basis of abundant hydro-power resources and cheap coal, very rich deposits of iron ores and natural gas are being exploited, a third metallurgical base is being successfully created, the non-ferrous metallurgical, chemical, engineering and building industries are developing, new towns and industrial centres are springing up.

The Congress fully approves the *reconstruction of management in industry and building* carried out by the Central Committee and the Soviet Government. This revolutionary, vitally necessary measure broke down the departmental barriers which had become a brake on the further development of the productive forces of the country, increased the part played by the Union republics and local Party, government and economic bodies in economic and cultural development, and stimulated the creative initiative of the masses. Following the reconstruction of management in industry and building, all branches of the national economy are working better and more efficiently, utilising more fully the existing productive potentials.

The task of overtaking and surpassing the most highly developed capitalist countries in per capita output is being successfully accomplished. The Soviet Union has already outstripped the most developed capitalist country—the U.S.A.—not only in rates of growth of production but in the absolute annual increase of production. At the present time the extraction of iron ore and coal is greater in the U.S.S.R. than in the U.S.A., as is the output of coke, prefabricated concrete building elements, electric and fuel locomotives, sawn timber, woollen fabrics, butter, sugar, fish and a number of other manufactured goods and foodstuffs.

The fulfilment of the Seven-Year Plan will bring the Soviet national economy to a stage at which only a little time will be needed for it to surpass the U.S.A. in per capita production as well. This will be a historic victory of socialism over capitalism.

The Congress notes the great work carried out by the Central Committee to advance *agriculture*. Owing to the effects of the war, and also owing to past mistakes and shortcomings in management, the situation in agriculture was a grave one. The low level of output of agricultural products could have retarded the development of the Soviet economy and seriously affected the well-being of the people.

The Central Committee laid bare the causes of the lag of agriculture and drew up and put into effect urgent measures for the further development of agricultural production. With the active participation of the whole people, the Party strengthened the material and technical basis of the collective and state farms, reorganised the machine and tractor stations, increased the role of the state farms in communist construction, introduced a new system of planning agricultural production, restored the Leninist principle of the material incentive of the collective and state farm workers in increasing the output of agricultural produce, strengthened the collective and state farms with leading personnel and specialists, reorganised the work of the agricultural bodies, and increased the part played by science in agriculture.

The cultivation of virgin and fallow lands, which now provide over 40 per cent of the country's grain deliveries, has played an outstanding part in increasing the production of grain and developing agriculture as a whole. *The cultivation of virgin lands is a great labour feat on the part of the Soviet people and will live through the ages!*

The measures adopted by the Party for the progress of agriculture have already yielded tangible results, and in the future these results will be still more considerable. In the five years gross agricultural output increased by 43 per cent compared with the preceding five-year period.

Whereas previously the state bought only about 2,000 million poods of grain annually, in recent years it has been buying 3,000 million poods or more. There has been a considerable increase in state purchases of other agricultural produce. Radical changes have been achieved in the development of livestock breeding, which for many long years was in a neglected state. In the past five years the number of cattle in collective and state farms has increased by 68 per cent, and of pigs by 150 per cent; there has been a considerable increase in the state purchases of livestock produce.

Noting the great importance of the decisions of the January Plenary Meeting of the Central Committee of the C.P.S.U. (1961), which condemned complacency and self-satisfaction, the diminished attention to agriculture in a number of regions and republics, as a result of which the rate of increase in the production of grain, meat and milk in 1959-60 fell, failing to reach the targets set by the Seven-Year Plan, the Congress fully approves the concrete measures devised by the Central Committee for a further increase in the output of agricultural produce. As the preliminary figures for the current year show, these measures yielded positive results. The collective and state farms have increased their grain output. This year the state will buy considerably more grain than last year. There has also been an increase in the production of cotton, sugar beet, sunflower and other crops. The number of cattle has increased, as well as the production and purchases of livestock products. Nevertheless, the rate of increase in the production of meat and milk is still far below the required level.

The collective and state farms should now, on the basis of their accumulated experience, take another big step forward and successfully fulfil the targets of the Seven-Year Plan. In solving the urgent problems of agriculture, particular importance attaches to the work of collective and state farms in revising the crop pattern and replacing low-yielding crops by more productive ones, primarily maize and legumes. It is essential to continue making the most persistent use of the potentialities available in agriculture in order successfully to solve one of the most important tasks of communist construction—the creation of an abundance of agricultural produce for the people.

The Party organisations and working people of the Russian Federation, the Ukraine and Kazakhstan have drawn up plans for securing a steep increase in grain production.

— The Russian Federation has set itself the task of bringing the production of grain up to 12,000 million poods and state purchases up to 4,000-5,000 million poods.

— The Ukrainian S.S.R. has undertaken to bring production up to 3,800 million poods and state purchases up to 1,500 million poods.

— The Kazakh S.S.R. has undertaken to bring production up to 3.500 million poods and state purchases up to more than 2,000 million poods.

The Congress approved the initiative of the Party and government organisations and of all workers in agriculture of the Russian Federation, the Ukraine and Kazakhstan, and wishes them success in attaining their planned levels.

The material well-being of the working people is steadily improving. On the basis of the growth of the national income of the U.S.S.R., the real incomes of workers and other employees (calculated per worker) have increased by 27 per cent in the five years, and the incomes of collective farmers by 33 per cent. The retail turnover of state-operated and co-operative trade has increased more than 50 per cent. All workers and other employees now have a seven- or six-hour working day. The adjustment of wage rates is being completed, wages have been increased, especially for the low-paid brackets of workers and other employees, and excessively high payment for the work of certain categories has been eliminated. Improved provision has been made for pensioners; the average old-age pension has been more than doubled. In 1960 the payment of taxes by the population began to be abolished. Public funds are playing an ever increasing role in the improvement of the well-being of the people. From these funds the population in 1960 received 24,500 million rubles in benefits and privileges, compared with 4,200 million in 1940, and by the end of the Seven-Year Plan the amount will increase to 40,000 million rubles. The programme of state housing construction for the years 1956-60 has been successfully carried out; more residential buildings were built in these five years than in the preceding 15 years, about 50 million people being allotted new homes.

The period between the Twentieth and Twenty-Second congresses is characterised by the outstanding achievements of *Soviet science and culture.* A new brilliant era in the development of the scientific knowledge of mankind was opened up by the victories of the Soviet Union in the conquest of space, the unexampled flights of Yuri Gagarin and Herman Titov, the first cosmonauts in history. Soviet scientists achieved considerable successes in the use of atomic energy for peaceful purposes, in cybernetics and the development of high-speed computers, in polymer chemistry, in the advancement of automation and telemechanics, radio engineering and electronics, in the sphere of the social sciences and other branches of science and technology.

The Congress regards as correct the measures adopted for *reorganising public education and strengthening the link between the school and life,* for organising boarding schools, day-care schools and groups, for developing the system of correspondence courses and evening schools, for preparing highly skilled specialists for all branches of economy and culture.

Recent years have seen the creation of a number of important works of *literature and art,* truthfully reflecting the realities of our life and depicting features of the character of the new man—the builder of communism.

On the basis of the development of the productive forces and of the increase of the material and spiritual wealth of Soviet society, a steady improvement of *socialist social relations* is taking place. The Congress approves the course towards strengthening and bringing closer together the national and kolkhoz-cooperative forms of socialist ownership, towards consistent realisation of the principle of material incentive, the development of socialist democracy, towards drawing closer together the cultures of the Soviet socialist nations and their all-round mutual enrichment, the consolidation of the moral and political unity of our society, towards the active development of communist principles in the labour, everyday life and consciousness of Soviet people.

The great successes achieved by our people under the leadership of the Party are a source of rejoicing for Soviet people and inspire confidence that in the future our country will advance still more successfully and rapidly along the road to communism. The Party, faithful to Leninism, will never tolerate conceit and complacency; it sees not only the successes but also the shortcomings in the work of the Party, government and economic bodies, and concentrates its efforts on achieving tasks as yet unaccomplished. All efforts must be directed towards securing a still more rapid growth of the economy, towards raising the well-being of the people and strengthening the might of the Soviet state. The more active the support given to all that is new and progressive, the more widely it is introduced into production, the more sharply shortcomings are revealed and the more rapidly they are removed, the more successfully will the tasks confronting us be fulfilled. The cause of building communism is the cause of millions, the cause of the whole people.

The Congress instructs the Central Committee to continue to direct the efforts of the Party and the people towards an acceleration of the rate of communist construction, towards a still fuller utilisation of the vast untapped potentialities available in all the branches of the socialist national economy.

The attention of the Party and the people must be concentrated above all on effecting the following major tasks:

— *to ensure the fulfilment and over-fulfilment of the targets of the Seven-Year Plan, which will be of decisive significance for creating the material and technical basis of communism, for our victory in the peaceful economic competition with capitalism.* The development of heavy industry must be continued at an accelerated pace, in the first place the power engineering, metallurgical, chemical, mechanical engineering, fuel and building industries. The Congress makes it binding on all Party organisations to mobilise the working people for the struggle to fulfil the Seven-Year Plan targets that have been amended in an upward direction. An all-round expansion of the output of consumer goods must be regarded as essential. Funds that will accumulate as a result of the overfulfilment of planned targets by industry are to be directed mainly into agriculture and the light and food industries;

— on the basis of further technical progress *to work for the utmost increase of labour productivity in industry, building, agriculture and transport.* Raising labour productivity is a key question of the policy and practice of communist construction, an essential condition for the improvement of the well-being of the people and the creation of an abundance of material and cultural wealth for the working people;

— *persistently to improve organisational work in the management of the national economy,* to do things in such a way as to obtain the greatest increase of production with the least expenditure. For this purpose it is necessary to select the most progressive, economically advantageous directions in the development of branches of industry; to improve specialisation and co-operation; to carry out the comprehensive mechanisation and automation of production processes; to introduce more rapidly into industry the latest achievements of science and technology, progressive techniques and advanced experience; to make better use of the latent potentialities of economic areas, enterprises and building projects; to strengthen state discipline at all levels of the economic apparatus, to wage a relentless struggle against mismanagement, waste, inertia and conservatism. Lowering production costs and improving the quality of output, thrift and economy in everything, increased profitability and the growth of socialist accumulation, must be a law of the operation of every Soviet enterprise;

— decisively to improve the planning and organisation of capital construction, to secure a marked increase in the efficacy of capital investments, to put an end to the anti-state, parochial practice of scattering monetary funds and material, technical and labour resources. Special attention must continue to be devoted to the development of the productive forces of the Eastern areas, and the development and all-round utilisation of their natural wealth;

— concretely and competently to guide *agriculture*, persistently to put into effect scientific achievements and advanced experience, to make better use of land, to introduce a more efficient crop pattern, to make wide use of maize, peas, fodder legumes and other high-yielding crops, to increase sharply the stocks of fertilisers and to improve their utilisation, to raise the quality of agricultural work and on this basis achieve a considerable increase in the per-hectare yields, and in the total harvests of grain and other agricultural crops, a systematic expansion of the number of cattle and of the output of livestock products. The Congress regards as an urgent task the extension of mechanisation and electrification of agriculture, full satisfaction of the requirements of the collective and state farms in up-to-date technical equipment, increased output of mineral and organic fertilisers as well as of weed-killers and other chemical means of controlling weeds, plant diseases and agricultural pests. It is necessary to ensure increased labour productivity and lower production costs on the basis of comprehensive mechanisation. To produce the maximum output with the minimum expenditure of labour is the most important principle of communist development in the countryside. In the next few years annual state purchases of grain must be raised to 4,200 million poods, of meat to 13 million tons, of milk to 50 million tons, and the output of sugar beet, cotton, flax, potatoes and other vegetables, fruit, tea and other agricultural produce must be increased considerably. *The development of agriculture is the concern of the whole Party, the whole Soviet people;*

— on the basis of the further growth of industrial and agricultural output to ensure a steady rise in the *standard of living of the people.* The Congress considers it necessary to take further measures for a reduction of the working day and working week, as well as for abolishing taxes on the population; to complete the adjustment of the wage scale for all categories of workers; to carry out housing construction at a still higher rate, improving its quality and reducing its cost, to accelerate the construction of community service institutions, crèches and kindergartens, to improve the provision of pensions and the organisation of retail trade, public catering and medical and community services for the population; continuously to improve public education at all levels;

— to carry out purposeful scientific research, to open wider the way to science for young talent. The most important task the Congress sets Soviet scientists is to achieve such a level of development of Soviet science as will enable it to win leading positions in all the basic fields of world science and technology;

— *to develop the literature and art of socialist realism,* to raise their ideological and artistic level, to strengthen their link with the practical work of Communist construction, with the life of the people;

— *to maintain at the requisite level and to strengthen*

in every way the defence potential of our Motherland—the bulwark of world peace, to improve the armament of the Soviet Armed Forces, to raise the level of the military and ideological and political training of their personnel, to heighten the vigilance of our people, reliably to safeguard the creative labour and peaceful life of Soviet people—the builders of communism;

— *to develop and advance socialist social relations*: to strengthen national and kolkhoz-cooperative forms of socialist ownership; correctly to combine material and moral incentives to labour; to extend the participation of the masses of the people in the administration of all the affairs of the country; to strengthen the friendship of the peoples; to support in every way the endeavour of Soviet people to work and live in a communist way.

The creation of the material and technical basis of communism, the development of socialist social relations, the moulding of the man of communist society—such are the major tasks confronting the Party in the sphere of internal policy during the period of the full-scale construction of communism.

III

The successes of our country in the spheres of foreign and home policy are the result of the heroic labour of the Soviet people, the immense organisational and educational work of the Communist Party; they are the result of the consistent implementation of its Leninist policy that was profoundly and creatively embodied in the historic decisions of the Twentieth Congress of the C.P.S.U. The Party has still further strengthened its ties with the people. As a result of the victory of socialism in the U.S.S.R., and the enhanced unity of Soviet society the Communist Party, which arose as a party of the working class, has become the party of the whole people; it has extended its guiding influence to all spheres of social life. The Communist Party came to its Twenty-Second Congress united and solid, abounding in creative power and filled with the unconquerable will to advance under the banner of Marxism-Leninism to the complete triumph of communism.

The Congress notes that a major aspect of the Party's activity in the period under review was the *restoration and further development of the Leninist standards of Party life and the principle of collective leadership at all levels in the Party and the state.*

Of vast importance for socialist and communist construction, and for the whole international Communist movement, was the frank and bold condemnation of the cult of J. V. Stalin's personality by the Party and its Central Committee. The Party told the people the whole truth about the abuses of power in the period of the personality cult and vigorously condemned the mistakes, distortions and methods alien to the spirit of Leninism to which this cult had given rise. The Party severely criticised the cult of the individual, and overcame the distortions and mistakes of the past; it is now steadily carrying out measures that will rule out the possibility of such mistakes ever occurring in the future. These measures have found expression in the Party's Programme and Rules.

The Twenty-Second Congress wholly and fully approves the extensive and fruitful work performed by the Central Committee to restore and promote Leninist principles in all spheres of Party, state and ideological work, which has given full play to the creative initiative of the Party and the people, furthered the expansion and consolidation of the Party's ties with the masses, and heightened its efficiency.

The Congress considers as absolutely correct and fully approves the resolute measures adopted by the Central Committee for exposing and ideologically routing the anti-Party group of Molotov, Kaganovich, Malenkov, Bulganin, Pervukhin and Saburov, and also Shepilov, who had joined them, which opposed the Leninist course charted by the

Twentieth Congress, resisted the measures to eradicate the personality cult and its consequences, and tried to retain forms and methods of leadership that had been discredited, and to obstruct the development of the new in our life. At the time of the anti-Party group's factional struggle serious mistakes were committed by Comrade Voroshilov, who took part with this group in opposing the Party's Leninist policy. In the course of the June Plenary Meeting of the C.C. Comrade Voroshilov admitted his mistakes, condemned the factional actions of the anti-Party group, thereby helping in some measure to expose the anti-Party renegades. The Party swept out of its way the unprincipled factionalists, intriguers and careerists, and united its ranks still more solidly, strengthened its ties with the people and rallied all forces for successfully carrying out its general line.

The Twenty-Second Congress, in the name of the whole Party, indignantly condemns subversive, anti-Party factional activity as incompatible with the Leninist principle of Party unity. Any one who takes the path of factional struggle, of clandestine intriguing and scheming against the Leninist line of the Party and its unity, is acting against the interests of the entire people, against the interests of communist construction. Expressing the will of all Communists, the Congress declares that the Party will continue undeviatingly to observe the Leninist law of preserving the unity and purity of the Party ranks, will continue to wage a relentless struggle against all manifestations of clique activity and factionalism.

The restoration and development of the Leninist principle of collective leadership was of particular importance to the Party and the Soviet state. The regular holding of Party congresses, of plenary meetings of the Central Committee and of all elective Party bodies, nation-wide discussion of cardinal questions relating to state, economic and Party construction, the holding of conferences with workers in various fields of the national economy and culture, have become a rule of Party and state life. All major issues of home and foreign policy have been widely discussed in our Party, providing expression for its collective intelligence and experience.

The Party's indissoluble ties with the people are vividly reflected in the growth of its ranks, in the steady influx of fresh forces into the Party. In the period under review the membership of the Party increased by two and a half million and now totals nearly ten million.

The Twenty-Second Congress instructs the Central Committee to continue to strengthen the unity of the Party, to fight for the purity of its Marxist-Leninist world outlook, and to reinforce the ranks of the Party with the foremost representatives of the working class, collective-farm peasantry and intelligentsia, and to still further enhance the name of Communist—the active, staunch and conscious fighter for the happiness of the people, for communism.

The Congress notes that in the past few years the *Party made a decisive turn towards giving concrete leadership to the national economy*. The Central Committee focussed the attention of the Party organisations and leading personnel on fulfilment of the national economic plans, mobilisation of our economy's reserves, on studying and widely employing advanced methods of work; it taught, through concrete positive examples, proper conduct of the economy. The Congress stresses that strength of Party leadership lies in the ability to organise and concentrate the efforts of the masses on the principal tasks, in the art of combining the talent, knowledge and experience of many people for the accomplishment of great things. Always mindful of Lenin's precepts that our Party's strength is in the consciousness and activity of the masses, we must still more energetically heighten the Communist consciousness and political activity of the working people, still more solidly unite them round the Party.

The Congress draws particular attention to *the neces-*

sity for improving matters with regard to cadres, their selection and training, for properly combining old, experienced personnel with young, energetic and competent organisers. People who are lagging behind, who have grown conceited and have lost touch with life, who are devoid of principles and ideals must not be allowed to hold executive positions. The Party is waging, and will continue to wage, an implacable fight against those who violate Party and state discipline, against people who set out to deceive the Party and the state, against sycophants, hosanna singers, humbugs and bureaucrats. In the struggle to eliminate shortcomings in work we must develop to the utmost criticism and self-criticism, our most effective weapon.

The Congress attaches great importance to the principle of renewal of the elective bodies; this will offer new opportunities for making wider use of the creative power of the Party and the people in the interests of communist construction. Regular renewal of the elective bodies must become an invariable rule of our Party, state and public life.

Life, practical activity, is the best school for training cadres, for steeling them politically. The Party leader and statesman of the Leninist type is moulded in the struggle to implement the Party's line, in practical work, in accomplishing the concrete tasks of communist construction. We must more boldly draw a broad active of Party members into work in the Party bodies on a voluntary basis.

In present conditions *paramount importance attaches to Party, state and public control over the proper organisation of things, over the strict fulfilment by every worker regardless of the position he holds of the demands laid down in the Programme and the Rules of the C.P.S.U., and the directives and instructions of the Party and the Soviet Government.* The system of control is an effective way of perfecting management in communist construction on truly democratic principles; it is a reliable weapon in fighting formalism and red-tape; it is a school of communist education of the masses.

With a view to strengthening the control and verification of the actual execution of assignments it is essential to establish a strict procedure of accountability by the local Party bodies to the higher Party bodies, and to the Communist membership, on the fulfilment of Party decisions. The Twenty-Second Congress instructs the Central Committee to work out effective measures to improve and perfect Party, state and public control.

The Congress attaches great importance to the *activity of the mass organisations of the working people*—the Soviets, trade unions, Y.C.L. and co-operatives. Now, when Communist self-administration is more and more widely developing, the role of these organisations in the life of socialist society will steadily increase.

It is necessary to enhance still further *the role of the Soviets* in the management of economic and cultural development, in drawing the masses into the administration of the socialist state. The further promotion of Soviet democracy is a most important requisite for gradual transition to communist self-administration by the people.

The Party will *in every possible way help the trade unions to play a bigger part* in running the economy, in organising emulation for communist labour, in teaching the masses how to manage socialist production and public affairs, in raising the communist consciousness of the working people. One of the important tasks of the trade unions is to show constant concern for the individual, for his work, education, living conditions, health and rest.

Our Party highly appreciates the activity of its militant helper, the *Leninist Young Communist League.* A chief task of the Y.C.L. is to educate the youth in the heroic traditions of the revolutionary struggle, through the example of the devoted labour of the workers, collective farmers and intellectuals, in the great ideas of Marxism-Leninism, to develop steadfast, highly-educated, industrious young builders of communism. It is the youth who will be opening up new natural resources, who will be building new factories, mines, state farms, new institutions of science and art, new cities. The future belongs to them, and it is they who will build and perfect communist society.

The further strengthening and raising of the level of *ideological work* is one of the basic tasks of the Party, a cardinal condition for the success of all its practical activity. The interests of communist construction demand that all Party organisations, the Soviet public as a whole, centre their activity on the communist education of the working people, and in the first place, the rising generation.

The principal lines of this ideological work in present conditions are: propaganda of the Marxist-Leninist theory and the shaping of a scientific world outlook in all members of society; combating the survivals of capitalism in the minds of people and the influence of hostile bourgeois ideology; education of the working people in the spirit of lofty moral principles, as embodied in the moral code of the builder of communism; the harmonious development of members of communist society. To prepare the individual for labour, to instil in him love and respect for labour as a prime necessity of life, is the essence, the core of all our work in communist education.

In the present period the main thing in ideological work is to thoroughly explain the Programme of the C.P.S.U., to equip the working people of Soviet society with the great plan of struggle for the triumph of communism, to mobilise all the working people for putting the new Programme of the Party into effect. All the media through which the Party exercises its ideological influence on the masses must be subordinated to the accomplishment of this task: propaganda and agitation, the press, radio, television, the cinema, cultural and educational work, literature and art.

Ideological work is a highly important medium in accomplishing the tasks of communist construction. It must help to promote political and labour activity, the communist consciousness of Soviet people. A paramount task of the Party in the sphere of propaganda and ideological work continues to be the deep study by Party and state cadres of the Marxist-Leninist theory and the epoch-making experience acquired by the Communist Party and the Soviet people in the struggle for the triumph of socialism and communism, the raising of the level of educational work and enhancement of its influence on the life and affairs of the people. Unity of ideological and organisational work must be a cardinal, guiding principle of the Party.

The scope and importance of the theoretical activity of the Party and its Central Committee have increased immensely in the past few years. While waging a struggle on two fronts—against revisionism, as the chief danger, and the dogmatic devitalising of revolutionary theory— the Party has firmly upheld and creatively developed the teachings of Marxism-Leninism. The period under review in the life of our Party has witnessed the creative solution of major theoretical problems of communist construction in our country, and urgent problems of the international Communist movement. The Twenty-Second Congress approves unanimously and with great satisfaction the fruitful theoretical work accomplished by the Central Committee of the C.P.S.U., which has found its most comprehensive expression in the new Programme of our Party.

The Congress stresses the necessity for continuing to hold high and keep pure the all-conquering banner of Marxism-Leninism, to develop and enrich theory with new conclusions and propositions that sum up the experience of communist construction. Guided by the Leninist principle of the unity of theory and practice, the Party must regard the defence and creative development of Marxism-Leninism as its prime duty.

The Twenty-Second Congress sets all Party organisations the following tasks in the field of organisational and ideological work:

— to continue to enhance the role of the Party in communist construction, to strengthen its ties with the working people, to give concrete leadership in all spheres of communist construction, to secure a still higher level of organisation and efficiency in work, to develop the initiative and the political and labour activity of the masses;

— to observe and develop the Leninist standards of Party life and the principle of collective leadership, to improve the selection, placing and education of personnel, to increase the responsibility of Party bodies and their personnel to the Party, to intensify the activity of Communists and their participation in elaborating and realising the policy of the Party, to develop inner-Party democracy, criticism and self-criticism;

— to enhance the role of the Soviets of Working People's Deputies, the trade unions and Y.C.L. in communist construction, and in the Marxist-Leninist education of the masses;

— to perfect Party, state and public control and make it really nation-wide control over the activity of all state and public organisations and officials;

— to broaden the scope and raise the level of ideological work, elaborate the new problems advanced by life, educate Soviet people in the spirit of fidelity to Marxism-Leninism, and implacability to all manifestations of bourgeois ideology;

— to promote fraternal contacts with all the Communist and Workers' parties, and, together with them, to wage a vigorous struggle for the purity of Marxism-Leninism and against revisionism, dogmatism and sectarianism, to strengthen the unity of the entire international Communist and working-class movement.

In the course of the discussion of the draft Programme and the draft Rules of the C.P.S.U. at Party meetings, conferences and congresses of the Communist parties of the Union republics, at meetings of working people, and in the press and letters received by the Central Committee and local Party bodies, Communists and non-Party working people made many practical proposals and suggestions regarding economic and cultural development, improving living standards and community services, eliminating existing shortcomings in the work of the Party, government, economic, trade union and Y.C.L. organisations and various institutions.

The Congress instructs the C.C. of the Communist parties of the Union republics, the territorial and regional Party committees to consider all remarks and proposals received in the course of the discussion of the draft Programme and the draft Rules, to take the necessary measures to eliminate shortcomings and to report on the measures taken to the plenary meetings of Party committees, to conferences and the Central Committee of the C.P.S.U.

* * *

The epoch-making victories achieved in building socialism and communism in our country are recognised by all mankind. They are the majestic results of the heroic labour and selfless struggle of the Leninist Party and the Soviet people, the triumph of the ideas of Marxism-Leninism.

Never before has the great vitality of the Marxist-Leninist doctrine revealed itself so forcefully as at the present time when socialism has triumphed in the Soviet Union, completely and finally, and is winning new victories in the People's Democracies, when the international Communist, working-class, democratic and national-liberation movements are developing apace. Sweeping social changes, profound revolutionary transformations are taking place in the world, and will continue to take place, under the impact of the successes of the international Communist movement.

The Twenty-Second Congress of the Communist Party of the Soviet Union calls on all Communists and Y.C.L. members, on all Soviet citizens, to fight actively for the fulfilment of the programme of communist construction. The Congress is fully confident that the workers, collective farmers and Soviet intelligentsia will spare no effort to realise the lofty ideals of communism.

Expressing the will of the whole Soviet people, the Twenty-Second Congress declares in the name of ten million Communists:

The Communist Party of the Soviet Union will continue to hold aloft the victorious banner of Marxism-Leninism, will perform its internationalist duty to the working people of all countries, will devote all its energies to the struggle for the interests of the people and to the achievement of the great historic goal—the building of communist society.

The Party solemnly proclaims: the present generation of Soviet people shall live under communism!

ON THE PROGRAMME
OF THE COMMUNIST PARTY
OF THE SOVIET UNION

RESOLUTION OF THE 22nd CONGRESS OF THE C.P.S.U.

(Adopted Unanimously on October 31, 1961)

The Twenty-Second Congress of the Communist Party of the Soviet Union, having heard Comrade N. S. Khrushchov's Report on the Programme of the C.P.S.U. and having examined the draft of the Programme submitted by the Central Committee, has resolved:

To adopt the Programme of the Communist Party of the Soviet Union.

PROGRAMME
OF THE COMMUNIST PARTY
OF THE SOVIET UNION

INTRODUCTION

The Great October Socialist Revolution ushered in a new era in the history of mankind, the era of the downfall of capitalism and the establishment of communism. Socialism has triumphed in the Soviet Union and has achieved decisive victories in the People's Democracies; socialism has become the practical cause of hundreds of millions of people, and the banner of the revolutionary movement of the working class throughout the world.

More than a hundred years ago Karl Marx and Frederick Engels, the great teachers of the proletariat, wrote in the Communist Manifesto: "*A spectre is haunting Europe, the spectre of communism.*" The courageous and selfless struggle of the proletarians of all countries brought mankind nearer to communism. First dozens and hundreds of people, and then thousands and millions, inspired by the ideals of communism, stormed the old world. The Paris Commune, the October Revolution, the socialist revolutions in China and in a number of European and Asian countries are the major historical stages in the heroic battles fought by the international working class for the victory of communism. A tremendously long road, a road drenched in the blood of fighters for the happiness of the people, a road of glorious victories and temporary reverses, had to be traversed before *communism, which was once no more than a dream, became the greatest force*

*of modern times, a society that is being built up over vast
areas of the globe.*

In the early twentieth century the centre of the international revolutionary movement shifted to Russia. Russia's heroic working class, led by the Bolshevik Party headed by Vladimir Ilyich Lenin, became its vanguard. The Communist Party inspired and led the socialist revolution; it was the organiser and leader of the first workers' and peasants' state in history. The brilliant genius of Lenin, the great teacher of the working people of the world, whose name will live for ever, illumines mankind's road to communism.

On entering the arena of political struggle, the Leninist Communist Party raised high the banner of revolutionary Marxism over the world. Marxism-Leninism became a powerful ideological weapon for the revolutionary transformation of society. At every historical stage the Party, taking guidance from the theory of Marx-Engels-Lenin, accomplished the tasks scientifically formulated in its Programmes.

In adopting its *first Programme* at its Second Congress in 1903, the Bolshevik Party called on the working class and all working people of Russia to fight for the overthrow of the tsarist autocracy and then of the bourgeois system and for the establishment of the dictatorship of the proletariat. In February 1917 the tsarist regime was swept away. In October 1917 the proletarian revolution abolished the capitalist system so hated by the people. *A socialist country came into being for the first time in history. The creation of a new world began.*

The first Programme of the Party had been carried out.

Adopting its *second Programme* at its Eighth Congress in 1919, the Party promulgated the task of building a socialist society. Treading on unexplored ground and overcoming difficulties and hardships, the Soviet people under the leadership of the Communist Party put into practice the plan for socialist construction drawn up by Lenin.

Socialism triumphed in the Soviet Union completely and finally.

The second Programme of the Party had likewise been carried out.

The gigantic revolutionary exploit accomplished by the Soviet people has roused and inspired the masses in all countries and continents. A mighty purifying thunderstorm marking the spring-time of mankind is raging over the earth. *The socialist revolutions in European and Asian countries have resulted in the establishment of the world socialist system.* A powerful wave of national-liberation revolutions is sweeping away the colonial system of imperialism.

One-third of mankind is building a new life under the banner of scientific communism. The first contingents of the working class to shake off capitalist oppression are facilitating victory for fresh contingents of their class brothers. The socialist world is expanding; the capitalist world is shrinking. Socialism will inevitably succeed capitalism everywhere. Such is the objective law of social development. Imperialism is powerless to check the irresistible process of emancipation.

Our epoch, whose main content is the transition from capitalism to socialism, is an epoch of struggle between the two opposing social systems, an epoch of socialist and national-liberation revolutions, of the breakdown of imperialism and the abolition of the colonial system, an epoch of the transition of more and more peoples to the socialist path, of the triumph of socialism and communism on a world-wide scale. The central factor of the present epoch is the international working class and its main creation, the world socialist system.

Today the Communist Party of the Soviet Union (C.P.S.U.) is adopting its third Programme, a programme for the building of communist society. The new Programme is a constructive generalisation of the experience of socialist development, it takes account of the experience of the revolutionary movement throughout the world and, giving expression to the collective opinion of the Party, defines the main tasks and principal stages of communist construction.

The supreme goal of the Party is to build a communist society on whose banner will be inscribed: "From each according to his ability, to each according to his needs". The Party's motto, "Everything for the sake of man, for the benefit of man", will be put into effect in full.

The Communist Party of the Soviet Union, true to proletarian internationalism, always follows the militant slogan "Workers of all countries, unite!". *The Party regards communist construction in the U.S.S.R. as the Soviet people's great internationalist task*, in keeping with the interests of the world socialist system as a whole and with the interests of the international proletariat and all mankind.

Communism accomplishes the historic mission of delivering all men from social inequality, from every form of oppression and exploitation, from the horrors of war, and proclaims *Peace, Labour, Freedom, Equality, Fraternity* and *Happiness* for all peoples of the earth.

PART ONE

THE TRANSITION
FROM CAPITALISM TO COMMUNISM
IS THE ROAD OF HUMAN PROGRESS

I. THE HISTORICAL NECESSITY OF THE TRANSITION
FROM CAPITALISM TO SOCIALISM

The epoch-making turn of mankind from capitalism to socialism, initiated by the October Revolution, is a natural result of the development of society. Marxism-Leninism discovered the objective laws of social development and revealed the contradictions inherent in capitalism, the inevitability of their bringing about a revolutionary explosion and of the transition of society to communism.

Capitalism is the last exploiting system. Having developed its productive forces to an enormous extent, it became a tremendous obstacle to social progress. Capitalism alone is responsible for the fact that the twentieth century, a century of colossal growth of the productive forces and of great scientific progress, has not yet put an end to the poverty of hundreds of millions of people, has not provided an abundance of material and spiritual values for all men on earth. The growing conflict between productive forces and production relations imperatively demands that mankind should break the decayed capitalist shell, release the powerful productive forces created by man and use them for the good of society as a whole.

Whatever the specific character of the rise and development of capitalism in any country, that system has everywhere common features and objective laws.

The development of world capitalism and of the revolutionary struggle of the working class has fully confirmed the correctness of the Marxist-Leninist analysis of capitalism and its highest stage, imperialism, given in the first and second Programmes of the Party. The basic propositions of this analysis are also given below in the present Programme.

Under capitalism, the basic and decisive means of production belong to the numerically small class of capitalists and landowners, while the vast majority of the population consists of proletarians and semi-proletarians, who own no means of production and are therefore compelled to sell their labour-power and by their labour create profits and riches for the ruling classes of society. The bourgeois state, whatever its form, is an instrument of the domination of labour by capital.

The development of large-scale capitalist production— production for profit, for the appropriation of surplus value—leads to the elimination of small independent producers, makes them wholly dependent on capital. Capitalism extensively exploits female and child labour. The economic laws of its development necessarily give rise to a huge army of unemployed, which is constantly replenished by ruined peasants and urban petty bourgeoisie. The exploitation of the working class and all working people is continuously increasing, social inequality is becoming more and more marked, the gulf between the haves and havenots is widening, and the sufferings and privations of the millions are growing worse.

Capitalism, by concentrating millions of workers in its factories, socialising the process of labour, imparts a social character to production; nevertheless it is the capitalists who appropriate the fruits of labour. This fundamental contradiction of capitalism—the contradiction between the social character of production and the private-capitalist form of appropriation—manifests itself in production anarchy and in the fact that the purchasing power of society falls short of the expansion of production and leads periodically to destructive economic crises. Crises and periods of industrial stagnation, in turn, are still more ruinous to small producers, increase the dependence of wage-labour on capital and lead more rapidly to a relative, and sometimes an absolute, deterioration of the condition of the working class.

The growth and development of the contradictions of bourgeois society are accompanied by the growing discontent of the working and exploited masses with the capitalist system, by an increase in the number of proletarians and their greater unity, and by a sharpening of their struggle against the exploiters. At the same time there is an accelerated *creation of the material conditions that make possible the replacement of capitalist by communist production relations, that is, the accomplishment of the social revolution which is the aim of the Communist Party, the politically conscious exponent of the class movement of the proletariat.*

The working class, which is the most consistent revolutionary class, is the chief motive force of the revolutionary transformation of the world. In the course of class struggles it becomes organised, sets up its trade unions and political parties, and wages an economic, political and theoretical struggle against capitalism. In fulfilling its historic mission as the revolutionary remaker of the old society and creator of a new system, the working class becomes the exponent, not only of its own class interests, but of the interests of all working people. It is the natural leader of all forces fighting against capitalism.

The dictatorship of the proletariat and the leadership of the Marxist-Leninist party are indispensable conditions for the triumph of the socialist revolution and the building of socialism. The firm alliance of the working class and the working peasant masses under the leadership of the working class is the supreme principle of the dictatorship of the proletariat.

The process of concentration and centralisation of capital, while destroying free competition, led in the early twentieth century to the establishment of powerful capitalist monopoly associations—syndicates, cartels, and trusts—which acquired decisive importance in the economy, led to the merging of bank capital and immensely concentrated industrial capital, and to intensive export of capital. The trusts, which encompassed entire groups of capitalist powers, began the economic division of a world already divided territorially among the wealthiest countries. Capitalism had entered its final stage, the stage of monopoly capitalism, of imperialism.

The period of a more or less smooth spread of capitalism all over the globe gave way to spasmodic, cataclysmic development causing an unprecedented growth and aggravation of all the contradictions of capitalism—economic, political, class, and national. The imperialist powers' struggle for markets, for spheres of capital investment, for raw materials and labour, and for world domination became more intense than ever. In an epoch of the undivided rule of imperialism, that struggle necessarily led to devastating wars.

Imperialism is decaying and moribund capitalism; it is the eve of the socialist revolution. *The world capitalist system as a whole is ripe for the social revolution of the proletariat.*

The exceedingly high degree of development of world capitalism in general; the replacement of free competition by state-monopoly capitalism; the establishment, by banks as well as associations of capitalists, of machinery for the social regulation of production and the distribution of products; the growing cost of living and the oppression of the working class by the syndicates, connected with the growth of capitalist monopolies; the enslavement of the working class by the imperialist state, and the immensely increased difficulty of the economic and political struggle of the proletariat; and the horrors, hardships, and ruination brought about by imperialist war have all made inevitable the downfall of capitalism and the transition to a higher type of social economy.

The revolutionary break-up of imperialism does not take place all over the world simultaneously. The uneven character of the economic and political development of the capitalist countries under imperialism leads to revolutions occurring at different periods in different countries. V. I. Lenin developed the theory of the socialist revolution in new historical conditions, elaborated the theory of the possibility of socialism triumphing first in one capitalist country taken singly.

Russia was the weakest link in the imperialist system and the focal point of all its contradictions. On the other hand, all the conditions necessary for the victory of socialism arose in her. Her working class was the most revolutionary and best organised in the world and had considerable experience of class struggle. It was led by a Marxist-Leninist party armed with an advanced revolutionary theory and steeled in class battles.

The Bolshevik Party brought together in one revolutionary torrent the struggle of the working class for socialism, the country-wide peace movement, the peasants' struggle for land, and the national-liberation movement of the oppressed peoples of Russia, and directed these forces to the overthrow of capitalism.

II. THE HISTORIC SIGNIFICANCE
OF THE OCTOBER REVOLUTION
AND OF THE VICTORY OF SOCIALISM
IN THE U.S.S.R.

The Great October Revolution breached the imperialist front in Russia, one of the world's largest countries, firmly established the dictatorship of the proletariat and created a new type of state—the Soviet socialist state, and a new type of democracy—democracy for the working people.

Workers' and peasants' power, born of the revolution, took Russia out of the bloodbath of the imperialist war, saved her from the national catastrophe to which the exploiting classes had doomed her, and delivered her peoples from the danger of enslavement by foreign capital.

The October Revolution undermined the economic basis of a system of exploitation and social injustice. Soviet power nationalised industry, the railways, banks, and the land. It abolished the landlord system and fulfilled the peasants' age-long dream of land.

The October Revolution smashed the chains of national oppression; it proclaimed and put into effect the right of nations to self-determination, up to and including the right to secede. The Revolution completely abolished the social-estate and class privileges of the exploiters. For the first time in history, it emancipated women and granted them the same rights as men.

The socialist revolution in Russia shook the entire structure of world capitalism to its very foundations; the world split into two opposing systems.

For the first time there emerged in the international arena a state which put forward the great slogan of peace and began carrying through new principles in relations between peoples and countries. Mankind acquired a reliable bulwark in its struggle against wars of conquest, for peace and the security of the peoples.

The October Revolution led the country on to the road of socialism. The path which the Soviet people were to traverse was an unexplored and arduous one. The reactionary forces of the old world did all they could to strangle the Soviet state at its birth. The young Soviet Republic had to cope with intervention and civil war, economic blockade and disruption, conspiracies, sabotage, subversion, terrorism, and numerous other trials. Socialist construction was rendered incredibly difficult by the socio-economic, technical and cultural backwardness of the country. The victorious workers and peasants lacked knowledge of state administration and the experience necessary for the construction of a new society. The difficulties of socialist construction were greatly increased by the fact that for almost thirty years the U.S.S.R. was the world's only socialist state, and was subjected to incisive attacks by the hostile capitalist encirclement. The class struggle in the period of transition from capitalism to socialism was therefore acute.

The enemies of Leninism maintained that Russia was not mature enough for a socialist revolution, that it was impossible to build socialism in one country. But the enemies of Leninism were put to shame.

A wise, discerning policy, the greatest staunchness, organisation, and deep faith in their own strength and in the strength of the people were required of the Party of the working class. It was necessary to steer the right course in socialist construction and ensure the victory of socialism, despite the highly complicated international situation and a relatively weak industrial basis, in a country whose economy had been badly ravaged by war and where small-commodity production was overwhelmingly predominant.

The Party proved equal to that historic task. Under the leadership of Lenin it worked out a plan for the radical transformation of the country, for the construction of socialism. On the basis of a thorough scientific analysis, Lenin elaborated the policy of the proletarian state for the entire period of transition from capitalism to socialism. He evolved the New Economic Policy (NEP), designed to bring about the victory of socialism. The main elements of the Lenin plan for the building of a socialist society were industrialisation of the country, agricultural co-operation, and the cultural revolution.

The Party upheld that plan in an acute struggle against sceptics and capitulators, against the Trotskyists, Right opportunists, nationalist-deviators, and other hostile groups. It rallied the whole of the Soviet people to the struggle to put Lenin's programme into practice.

The point at issue at the time was: either perish or

forge full steam ahead and overtake the capitalist countries economically.

The Soviet state had first of all to solve the problem of *industrialisation*. In a historically brief period, without outside help, the Soviet Union built up a large-scale modern industry. By the time it had fulfilled three five-year plans (1929-41) the Soviet Union had become a mighty industrial power that had achieved complete economic independence from the capitalist countries. Its defence capacity had increased immeasurably. *The industrialisation of the U.S.S.R. was a great exploit performed by the working class and the people as a whole,* for they spared no effort or means, and consciously made sacrifices to lift the country out of its backward state.

The destiny of socialism in a country like the U.S.S.R. largely depended on the solution of a most difficult problem, namely, the transition from a small-scale, dispersed peasant economy to *socialist co-operation.* Led by the Party, aided and fully supported by the working class, the peasantry took the road of socialism. Millions of small individual farms went into voluntary association to form collective farms. A large number of Soviet state farms and machine and tractor stations were established. The introduction in the Soviet countryside of large-scale socialist farming meant *a great revolution in economic relations, in the entire way of life of the peasantry.* Collectivisation for ever delivered the countryside from kulak bondage, from class differentiation, ruin, and poverty. The real solution of the eternal peasant question was provided by the Lenin co-operative plan.

To build socialism it was necessary to raise the cultural level of the people; this too was successfully accomplished. A *cultural revolution* was carried out in the country. It freed the working people from spiritual slavery and ignorance and gave them access to the cultural values accumulated by mankind. The country, the bulk of whose population had been illiterate, made breath-taking progress in science and culture.

Socialism, which Marx and Engels scientifically predicted as inevitable and the plan for the construction of which was mapped out by Lenin, has become a reality in the Soviet Union.

Socialism has done away for ever with the supremacy of private ownership of the means of production, that source of the division of society into antagonistic classes. Socialist ownership of the means of production has become the solid economic foundation of society. Unlimited opportunities have been afforded for the development of the productive forces.

Socialism has solved a great social problem—it has abolished the exploiting classes and the causes engendering the exploitation of man by man. There are now two friendly classes in the U.S.S.R.—the working class and the peasantry. And these classes, furthermore, have changed. The common character of the two forms of socialist property has brought the working class and the collective-farm peasantry close together; it has strengthened their alliance and made their friendship indestructible. A new intelligentsia, coming from the people and devoted to socialism, has emerged. The one-time antithesis between town and countryside, between labour by hand and by brain, has been abolished. The indestructible sociopolitical and ideological unity of the Soviet people has been built on the basis of the common vital interests of the workers, peasants and intellectuals.

The socialist principle "From each according to his abilities, to each according to his work" has been put into effect in the Soviet Union. This principle ensures that the members of society have a material interest in the fruits of their labour; it makes it possible to harmonise personal and social interests in the most effective way and serves as a powerful stimulus for increasing productivity of labour, developing the economy and raising the people's standard of living. The awareness that they work for themselves and their society and not for exploiters inspires the working people with labour enthusiasm; it encourages their effort for innovation, their creative initiative, and mass socialist emulation. Socialism is creative effort by the working masses. The growing activity of the people in the building of a new life is a law of the socialist epoch.

The aim of socialism is to meet the growing material and cultural requirements of the people ever more fully by continuously developing and improving social production.

The entire life of socialist society is based on the principle of broad *democracy*. Working people take an active part, through the Soviets, trade unions, and other mass organisations, in managing the affairs of the state and in solving problems of economic and cultural advancement. Socialist democracy includes both political freedoms— freedom of speech, of the press and of assembly, the right to elect and to be elected, and also social rights— the right to work, to rest and leisure, to free education and free medical services, to material security in old age and in case of illness or disability; equality of citizens of all races and nationalities; equal rights for women and men in all spheres of political, economic and cultural activity. Socialist democracy, unlike bourgeois democracy, does not merely proclaim the rights of the people, but guarantees that they are really implemented. Soviet society ensures the real liberty of the individual. The highest manifestation of this liberty is man's emancipation from exploitation, which is what primarily constitutes genuine social justice.

Socialism has created the most favourable conditions for the rapid progress of science. The achievements of Soviet science clearly show the superiority of the socialist system and testify to the unlimited possibilities of scientific progress and to the growing role of science under socialism. It is only logical that the country of victorious socialism should have ushered in the era of the utilisation of atomic energy for peaceful purposes, and that it should have blazed a trail into outer space. The man-made satellites of the earth and the sun, powerful space rockets and interplanetary spaceships, atomic power stations and the first triumphal orbitings of the globe, accomplished by Soviet citizens, which are a source of pride to all mankind, have become symbols of the creative energy of ascendant communism.

The solution of the *national question* is one of the greatest achievements of socialism. This question is of especial importance to a country like the Soviet Union, inhabited by more than a hundred nations and nationalities. Socialist society has not only guaranteed the political equality of nations and created Soviet national statehood, but has also abolished the economic and cultural inequality inherited from the old system. With reciprocal fraternal assistance, primarily from the great Russian people, all the Soviet non-Russian republics have set up their own modern industries, trained their own national working class and intelligentsia and developed a culture that is national in form and socialist in content. Many peoples which in the past were backward have achieved socialism by-passing the capitalist stage of development. The union and consolidation of equal peoples on a voluntary basis in a single multinational state—the Union of Soviet Socialist Republics—their close co-operation in state, economic and cultural development, their fraternal friendship and flourishing economy and culture constitute the most important result of the Leninist national policy.

To the Soviet people fell the historic role of starting on a new road, of blazing a new path of social development. This required special efforts of them, a continuous quest for forms and methods of building the new society that had to be tested in the crucible of life. For nearly two out of little more than four decades, the Soviet people were compelled to devote their energies to the repulsion of invasions by the imperialist powers and to post-war economic rehabilitation. The Soviet system was put to a particularly severe test during the Great Patriotic War, the most trying war in history. By winning that war, the Soviet people proved that there are no forces in the world capable of stopping the progress of socialist society.

What are the principal lessons to be learned from the experience of the Soviet people?

Soviet experience has shown that the peoples are able to achieve socialism only as a result of *the socialist revolution and the establishment of the dictatorship of the proletariat*. Despite certain specific features due to the concrete historical conditions of socialist construction in the Soviet Union, then in a hostile capitalist encirclement, this experience has fully confirmed the fundamental principles of socialist revolution and socialist construction, principles which are of universal significance.

Soviet experience has shown that socialism alone can put an end to the exploitation of man by man, production anarchy, economic crises, unemployment and the poverty of the people, and ensure planned, continuous and rapid development of the economy and steady improvement of the people's standard of living.

Soviet experience has shown that the working class can fulfil its historic mission as the builder of a new society only in a firm *alliance with the non-proletarian working masses*, primarily the peasantry.

Soviet experience has shown that the victory of the socialist revolution alone provides all possibilities and conditions for the abolition of all national oppression, *for the voluntary union of free and equal nations and nationalities in a single state*.

Soviet experience has shown that *the socialist state* is the main instrument for the socialist transformation of society. The state organises and unites the masses, exercises planned leadership of economic and cultural construction, and safeguards the revolutionary gains of the people.

Soviet experience has shown that *socialism and peace are inseparable*. The might of socialism serves peace. The

Soviet Union saved mankind from fascist enslavement. The Soviet state, which champions peace and implements the Leninist principle of the peaceful coexistence of states with different social systems, is a mighty barrier to imperialist aggression.

Soviet experience has fully borne out the Marxist-Leninist theory that *the Communist Party plays a decisive role* in the formation and development of socialist society. Only a party that steadfastly pursues a class, proletarian policy, and is equipped with progressive, revolutionary theory, only a party solidly united and closely linked with the masses, can organise the people and lead them to the victory of socialism.

Soviet experience has shown that fidelity *to the principles of Marxism-Leninism, of proletarian internationalism*, their firm and unswerving implementation and defence against all enemies and opportunists, are imperative conditions for the victory of socialism.

The world's greatest revolution and the socialist reorganisation of society, which has attained unprecedented heights in its development and prosperity, have confirmed in practice *the historical truth of Leninism* and have delivered a crushing blow to social-reformist ideology.

As a result of the devoted labour of the Soviet people and the theoretical and practical activities of the Communist Party of the Soviet Union, *there exists in the world a socialist society that is a reality and a science of socialist construction that has been tested in practice. The highroad to socialism has been paved.* Many peoples are already marching along it, and it will be taken sooner or later by all peoples.

III. THE WORLD SOCIALIST SYSTEM

The Soviet Union is not pursuing the tasks of communist construction alone but in fraternal community with the other socialist countries.

The defeat of German fascism and Japanese militarism in the Second World War, in which the Soviet Union played the decisive part, created favourable conditions for the overthrow of capitalist and landlord rule by the peoples in a number of European and Asian countries. The peoples of Albania, Bulgaria, China, Czechoslovakia, the Democratic Republic of Vietnam, the German Democratic Republic, Hungary, the Korean People's Democratic Republic, Poland and Rumania, and still earlier the people of the Mongolian People's Republic, adopted the path of socialist construction and, together with the Soviet Union, have formed the socialist camp. Yugoslavia likewise took the socialist path. But the Yugoslav leaders by their revisionist policy contraposed Yugoslavia to the socialist camp and the international Communist movement, thus threatening the loss of the revolutionary gains of the Yugoslav people.

The socialist revolutions in Europe and Asia dealt imperialism a further powerful blow. The victory of the revolution in China was of special importance. The revolutions in European and Asian countries are the biggest event in world history since October 1917.

A new form of political organisation of society, *people's democracy*, a variety of the dictatorship of the proletariat, emerged. It reflected the distinctive development of socialist revolution at a time when imperialism had been weakened and the balance of forces had tilted in favour of socialism. It also reflected the distinctive historical and national features of the various countries.

There emerged a world socialist system, a social, economic and political community of free sovereign peoples pursuing the socialist and communist path, united by an identity of interests and goals and the close bonds of international socialist solidarity.

In the People's Democracies socialist production relations are dominant and the socio-economic possibility of capitalist restoration has been eliminated. The successes

of these countries have conclusively proved that true progress in all lands, irrespective of the level of their economic development, their area and population, is feasible
only under socialism.

The combined forces of the socialist camp are a sure
guarantee for each socialist country against encroachments by imperialist reaction. The consolidation of the
socialist countries in a single camp, its increasing unity
and steadily growing strength, ensures the complete victory of socialism and communism within the framework
of the system as a whole.

The countries of the socialist system have accumulated
considerable collective experience in the remodelling of
the lives of hundreds of millions of people and have contributed many new and specific features to the forms of
political and economic organisation of society. This experience is a most valuable asset to the international revolutionary movement.

It has been borne out in practice and recognised by all
Marxist-Leninist parties that the processes of socialist
revolution and construction are founded on a number of
basic objective laws applicable to all countries entering
upon the socialist path.

The world socialist system is *a new type of economic
and political relationship between countries.* The socialist
countries have the same type of economic basis—social
ownership of the means of production; the same type of political system—rule of the people with the working class
at their head; a common ideology—Marxism-Leninism;
common interests in the defence of their revolutionary
gains and national independence from encroachments by
the imperialist camp; and a great common goal—communism. This socio-economic and political community
constitutes the objective groundwork for lasting and
friendly inter-governmental relations within the socialist
camp. The distinctive features of the relations existing
between the countries of the socialist community are

complete equality, mutual respect for independence and sovereignty and fraternal mutual assistance and co-operation. In the socialist camp or, which is the same thing, in the world community of socialist countries, none have, nor can have, any special rights or privileges.

The experience of the world socialist system has confirmed the need for the *closest unity* of countries that fall away from capitalism, for their united effort in the building of socialism and communism. The line of socialist construction in isolation, detached from the world community of socialist countries, is theoretically untenable because it conflicts with the objective laws governing the development of socialist society. It is harmful economically because it causes waste of social labour, retards the rates of growth of production and makes the country dependent upon the capitalist world. It is reactionary and dangerous politically because it does not unite, but divides the peoples in face of the united front of imperialist forces, because it nourishes bourgeois-nationalist tendencies and may ultimately lead to the loss of the socialist gains.

As they combine their effort in the building of a new society, the socialist states give active support to and extend their political, economic and cultural co-operation with countries that have cast off colonial rule. They maintain—and are prepared to maintain—broad, mutually advantageous trade relations and cultural contacts with the capitalist countries.

The development of the world socialist system and of the world capitalist system is governed by diametrically opposed laws. The world capitalist system emerged and developed in fierce struggle between the countries composing it, through the subjection and exploitation of the weaker countries by the strong, through the enslavement of hundreds of millions of people and the reduction of entire continents to the status of colonial appendages of the imperialist metropolitan countries. The formation and development of the world socialist system, on the other hand, proceeds on the basis of sovereignty and free will and in conformity with the fundamental interests of the working people of all the countries of that system.

Whereas the world capitalist system is governed by the law of uneven economic and political development that leads to conflicts between countries, the world socialist system is governed by opposite laws, which ensure the steady and balanced growth of the economies of all countries belonging to that system. Growth of production in a country belonging to the capitalist world deepens the contradictions between countries and intensifies competitive rivalries. The development of each socialist country, on the other hand, promotes the general progress and consolidation of the world socialist system as a whole. The economy of world capitalism develops at a slow rate, and goes through crises and upheavals. Typical of the economy of world socialism, on the other hand, are high and stable rates of growth and the common unintermittent economic progress of all socialist countries.

All the socialist countries make their contribution to the building and development of the world socialist system and the consolidation of its might. The existence of the Soviet Union greatly facilitates and accelerates the building of socialism in the People's Democracies. The Marxist-Leninist parties and the peoples of the socialist countries proceed from the fact that the successes of the world socialist system as a whole depend on the contribution and effort made by each country, and therefore consider the greatest possible development of the productive forces of their country an internationalist duty. The cooperation of the socialist countries enables each country to use its resources and develop its productive forces to the full and in the most rational manner. *A new type of international division of labour* is taking shape in the process of the economic, scientific and technical cooperation of the socialist countries, the co-ordination of their economic plans, the specialisation and combination of production.

The establishment of the Union of Soviet Socialist Republics and, later, of the world socialist system is the commencement of the historical process of all-round association of the peoples. With the disappearance of class antagonisms in the fraternal family of socialist countries, national antagonisms also disappear. The rapid cultural progress of the peoples of the socialist community is attended by a progressive mutual enrichment of the national cultures and an active moulding of the internationalist features typical of man in socialist society.

The experience of the peoples of the world socialist community has confirmed that their fraternal *unity and co-operation* conform to the supreme national interests of each country. The strengthening of the unity of the world socialist system on the basis of proletarian internationalism is an imperative condition for the further progress of all its member countries.

The socialist system has to cope with certain difficulties, deriving chiefly from the fact that most of the countries in that system had a medium or even low level of economic development in the past, and also from the fact that world reaction is doing its utmost to impede the building of socialism.

The experience of the Soviet Union and the People's Democracies has confirmed the accuracy of Lenin's thesis that the class struggle does not disappear in the period of the building of socialism. The general trend of class struggle within the socialist countries in conditions of successful socialist construction leads to consolidation of the position of the socialist forces and weakens the resistance of the remnants of the hostile classes. But this development does not follow a straight line. Changes in the domestic or external situation may cause the class struggle to intensify in specific periods. This calls for constant vigilance in order to frustrate in good time the designs of hostile forces within and without, who persist in their attempts to undermine people's power and sow strife in the fraternal community of socialist countries.

Nationalism is the chief political and ideological weapon used by international reaction and the remnants of the domestic reactionary forces against the unity of the socialist countries. Nationalist sentiments and national narrow-mindedness do not disappear automatically with the establishment of the socialist system. Nationalist prejudice and survivals of former national strife are a province in which resistance to social progress may be most protracted and stubborn, bitter and insidious.

The Communists consider it their prime duty to educate working people in a spirit of internationalism, socialist patriotism, and intolerance of all possible manifestations of nationalism and chauvinism. Nationalism is harmful to the common interests of the socialist community and, above all, the people of the country where it obtains, since isolation from the socialist camp holds up that country's development, deprives it of the advantages deriving from the world socialist system and encourages the imperialist powers to make the most of nationalist tendencies for their own ends. Nationalism can gain the upper hand only where it is not consistently combated. The Marxist-Leninist internationalist policy and determined efforts to wipe out the survivals of bourgeois nationalism and chauvinism are an important condition for the further consolidation of the socialist community. Yet while they oppose nationalism and national egoism, Communists always show utmost consideration for the national feelings of the masses.

The world socialist system is advancing steadfastly towards decisive victory in its economic competition with capitalism. It will shortly surpass the world capitalist system in aggregate industrial and agricultural production. Its influence on the course of social development in the interests of peace, democracy and socialism is growing more and more.

The magnificent edifice of the new world being built by the heroic labours of the free peoples on vast areas of Europe and Asia is a prototype of the new society, of the future of all mankind.

IV. CRISIS OF WORLD CAPITALISM

Imperialism has entered the period of decline and collapse. An inexorable process of decay has seized capitalism from top to bottom—its economic and political system, its politics and ideology. Imperialism has for ever lost its power over the bulk of mankind. The main content, main trend and main features of the historical development of mankind are being determined by the world socialist system, by the forces fighting against imperialism, for the socialist reorganisation of society.

The First World War and the October Revolution ushered in the general crisis of capitalism. The second stage of this crisis developed at the time of the Second World War and the socialist revolutions that took place in a number of European and Asian countries. World capitalism has now entered a new, third stage of that crisis, the principal feature of which is that its development was not connected with a world war.

The break-away from capitalism of more and more countries; the weakening of imperialist positions in the economic competition with socialism; the break-up of the imperialist colonial system; the intensification of imperialist contradictions with the development of state-monopoly capitalism and the growth of militarism; the mounting internal instability and decay of capitalist economy evidenced by the increasing inability of capitalism to make full use of the productive forces (low rates of production growth, periodic crises, continuous undercapacity operation of production plant, and chronic unemployment); the mounting struggle between labour and capital;

an acute intensification of contradictions within the world capitalist economy; an unprecedented growth of political reaction in all spheres, rejection of bourgeois freedoms and establishment of fascist and despotic regimes in a number of countries; and the profound crisis of bourgeois policy and ideology—all these are manifestations of the *general crisis of capitalism.*

In the imperialist stage *state-monopoly capitalism* develops on an extensive scale. The emergence and growth of monopolies leads to the direct intervention of the state, in the interests of the financial oligarchy, in the process of capitalist reproduction. It is in the interests of the financial oligarchy that the bourgeois state institutes various types of regulation and resorts to the nationalisation of some branches of the economy. World wars, economic crises, militarism, and political upheavals have accelerated the development of monopoly capitalism into state-monopoly capitalism.

The oppression of finance capital keeps growing. Giant monopolies controlling the bulk of social production dominate the life of the nation. A handful of millionaires and multimillionaires wield arbitrary power over the entire wealth of the capitalist world and make the life of entire nations mere small change in their selfish deals. The financial oligarchy is getting fabulously rich. The state has become a committee for the management of the affairs of the monopoly bourgeoisie. The bureaucratisation of the economy is rising steeply. State-monopoly capitalism combines the strength of the monopolies and that of the state into a single mechanism whose purpose is to enrich the monopolies, suppress the working-class movement and the national-liberation struggle, save the capitalist system, and launch aggressive wars.

The Right-wing Socialists and revisionists are making out state-monopoly capitalism to be almost socialism. The facts give the lie to this contention. State-monopoly capitalism does not change the nature of imperialism. Far from altering the position of the principal classes in the system of social production, it widens the rift between labour and capital, between the majority of the nation and the monopolies. Attempts at state regulation of the capitalist economy cannot eliminate competition and anarchy of production, cannot ensure the planned development of the economy on a nation-wide scale, because capitalist ownership and exploitation of wage-labour remain the basis of production. The bourgeois theories of "crisis-free" and "planned" capitalism have been laid in the dust by the development of contemporary capitalist economy. The dialectics of state-monopoly capitalism is such that instead of shoring up the capitalist system, as the bourgeoisie expects, it aggravates the contradictions of capitalism and undermines its foundations. State-monopoly capitalism is the fullest material preparation for socialism.

The new phenomena in imperialist development corroborate the accuracy of Lenin's conclusions on the principal objective laws of capitalism in its final stage and on its increasing decay. Yet this decay does not signify complete stagnation, a palsy of its productive forces, and does not rule out growth of capitalist economy at particular times and in particular countries.

All in all, capitalism is increasingly impeding the development of the contemporary productive forces. Mankind is entering the period of a scientific and technical revolution bound up with the conquest of nuclear energy, space exploration, the development of chemistry, automation and other major achievements of science and engineering. But the relations of production under capitalism are much too narrow for a scientific and technical revolution. Socialism alone is capable of effecting it and of applying its fruits in the interests of society.

Technical progress under the rule of monopoly capital is turning against the working class. By using new forms, the monopolies intensify the exploitation of the working class. Capitalist automation is robbing the worker of his daily bread. Unemployment is rising, the living standard is dropping. Technical progress is continuously throwing more sections of small producers overboard. Imperialism is using technical progress chiefly for military purposes. It is turning the achievements of human genius against humanity. As long as imperialism exists, mankind cannot feel secure about its future.

Modern capitalism has made the *market problem* extremely acute. Imperialism is incapable of solving it, because lag of effective demand behind growth of production is one of its objective laws. Moreover, it retards the industrial development of the underdeveloped countries. The world capitalist market is shrinking relative to the more rapidly expanding production capacity. It is partitioned by countless customs barriers and restrictive fences and split into exclusive currency and finance zones. An acute competitive struggle for markets, spheres of investment and sources of raw materials is under way in the imperialist camp. It is becoming doubly acute since the territorial sphere of capitalist domination has been greatly narrowed.

Monopoly capital has, in the final analysis, doomed bourgeois society to low rates of production growth that in some countries barely keep ahead of the growth of population. A considerable part of the production plant stands idle, while millions of unemployed wait at the factory gates. Farm production is artificially restricted, although millions are underfed in the world. People suffer want in material goods, but imperialism is squandering material resources and social labour on war preparations.

Abolition of the capitalist system in a large group of countries, the developing and strengthening of the world socialist system, the disintegration of the colonial system and the collapse of old empires, the commencing reorganisation of the colonial economic structure in the newly-free countries and the expanding economic connections between the latter and the socialist world—all these factors intensify *the crisis of the world capitalist economy*.

State-monopoly capitalism stimulates militarism to an unheard-of degree. The imperialist countries maintain immense armed forces even in peacetime. Military expenditures devour an ever-growing portion of the state budgets. The imperialist countries are turning into militarist, military-police states. Militarisation pervades the life of bourgeois society.

While enriching some groups of the monopoly bourgeoisie, militarism leads to the exhaustion of nations, to the ruin of the peoples languishing under an excessive tax burden, mounting inflation, and a high cost of living. Within the lifetime of one generation imperialism plunged mankind into the abyss of two destructive world wars. In the First World War the imperialists annihilated ten million and crippled twenty million people. The Second World War claimed nearly fifty million human lives. In the course of these wars entire countries were ravaged, thousands of towns and villages were demolished and the fruits of the labour of many generations were destroyed. The new war being hatched by the imperialists threatens mankind with unprecedented human losses and destruction. Even the preparations for it bring suffering and privation to millions of people.

The progress achieved in the development of the productive forces and the socialisation of labour is being usurped by the contemporary capitalist state in the interests of the monopolies.

The monopoly bourgeoisie is a useless growth on the social organism, one unneeded in production. The industries are run by hired managers, engineers, and technicians. The monopolists lead a parasitical life and with their menials consume a substantial portion of the national income created by the toil of proletarians and peasants.

Fear of revolution, the successes of the socialist countries, and the pressure of the working-class movement compel the bourgeoisie to make partial concessions with respect to wages, labour conditions, and social security. But more often than not mounting prices and inflation reduce these concessions to nought. Wages lag behind the daily material and cultural requirements of the worker and his family, which grow as society develops. Even the relatively high standard of living in the small group of capitalistically developed countries rests upon the plunder of the Asian, African and Latin American peoples, upon non-equivalent exchange, discrimination of female labour, brutal oppression of Negroes and immigrant workers, and also upon the intensified exploitation of the working people in those countries. The bourgeois myth of "full employment" has proved to be sheer mockery, for the working class is suffering continuously from mass unemployment and insecurity. In spite of some successes in the economic struggle, the condition of the working class in the capitalist world is, on the whole, deteriorating.

The development of capitalism has dissipated the legend of the stability of small peasant farming once and for all. The monopolies have seized dominant positions in agriculture as well. Millions of farmers and peasants are being driven off the land, and their farms are being brought under the hammer. Small farms survive at the price of appalling hardships, the peasants' underconsumption and excessive labour. The peasantry is groaning under the burden of mounting taxes and debts. Agrarian crises are bringing ever greater ruin to the countryside. Unspeakable want and poverty fall to the lot of the peasantry in the colonial and dependent countries; it suffers the dual oppression of the landlords and the monopoly bourgeoisie.

The monopolies are also ruining small urban proprietors. Handicrafts are going under. Small-scale industrial and commercial enterprises are fully dependent upon the monopolies.

Life has fully confirmed the Marxist thesis of increasing proletarisation in capitalist society. The expropriated masses have no other prospect of acquiring property than the revolutionary establishment of the social ownership of means of production, that is, making them the property of the whole people.

The uneven development of capitalism alters the balance of forces between countries and makes the contradictions between them more acute. The economic and with it the political and military centre of imperialism, has shifted from Europe to the United States. U.S. monopoly capital, gorged on war profits and the arms race, has seized the most important sources of raw materials, the markets and the spheres of investment, has built up a unique kind of colonial empire and become the biggest *international exploiter*. Taking cover behind spurious professions of freedom and democracy, U.S. imperialism is in effect performing the function of *world gendarme*, supporting reactionary dictatorial regimes and decayed monarchies, opposing democratic, revolutionary changes and launching aggressions against peoples fighting for independence.

The U.S. monopoly bourgeoisie is the mainstay of international reaction. It has assumed the role of "saviour" of capitalism. The U.S. financial tycoons are engineering a "holy alliance" of imperialists and founding aggressive military blocs. American troops and war bases are stationed at the most important points of the capitalist world.

But the facts reveal the utter incongruity of the U.S. imperialist claims to world domination. Imperialism has proved incapable of stemming the socialist and national-liberation revolutions. The hopes which American imperialism pinned on its atomic-weapons monopoly fell through. The United States has not been able to retain its share in the economy of the capitalist world, although it is still capitalism's chief economic, financial and military force. The United States, the strongest capitalist power, is past its zenith and has entered the stage of decline. Imperialist countries such as Great Britain, France, Germany, and Japan have also lost their former power.

The basic contradiction of the contemporary world, that between socialism and imperialism, does not eliminate the *deep contradictions* rending the capitalist world. The aggressive military blocs founded under the aegis of the U.S.A. are time and again faced with crises. The international state-monopoly organisations springing up under the motto of "integration", the mitigation of the market problem, are in reality new forms of the redivision of the world capitalist market and are becoming seats of acute strain and conflict.

The contradictions between the principal imperialist powers are growing deeper. The economic rehabilitation of the imperialist countries defeated in the Second World War leads to the revival of the old and the emergence of new knots of imperialist rivalry and conflict. The Anglo-American, Franco-American, Franco-West German, American-West German, Anglo-West German, Japanese-American, and other contradictions are becoming especially acute. Fresh contradictions will inevitably arise and grow in the imperialist camp.

The American monopolies and their British and French allies are openly assisting the West-German imperialists who are cynically advocating aggressive aims of revenge and preparing a war against the socialist countries and other European states. A dangerous centre of aggression, imperilling the peace and security of all peoples, is being revived in the heart of Europe. In the Far East the American monopolies are reviving Japanese militarism, which is in a certain way dependent on them. This constitutes another dangerous hotbed of war threatening the countries of Asia and, above all, the socialist countries.

The interests of the small group of imperialist powers are incompatible with the interests of all other countries, the interests of all peoples. Deep-rooted antagonism divides the imperialist countries from the countries that have won national independence and those that are fighting for their liberation.

Contemporary capitalism is inimical to the vital interests and progressive aspirations of all mankind. Capitalism with its exploitation of man by man, with its chauvinist and racist ideology, with its moral degradation, its rampage of profiteering, corruption and crime is defiling society, the family, and man.

The bourgeois system came into being with the alluring slogans of liberty, equality, fraternity. But the bourgeoisie made use of these slogans merely to elbow out the feudal gentry and to assume power. Instead of equality a new gaping abyss of social and economic inequality appeared. Not fraternity but ferocious class struggle reigns in bourgeois society.

Monopoly capital is revealing its reactionary, antidemocratic substance more and more strikingly. It does not tolerate even the former bourgeois-democratic freedoms, although it proclaims them hypocritically. In the current stage of historical development it is getting harder for the bourgeoisie to propagate slogans of equality and liberty. The upswing of the international labour movement restricts the manoeuvres of finance capital. Finance capital can no longer squash the revolutionary sentiments of the masses and cope with the inexorably growing revolutionary, anti-imperialist movement by means of the old slogans and by bribing the labour bureaucracy.

Having taken full possession of the principal material values, monopoly capital refuses to share political power with anyone. It has established a dictatorship, the dictatorship of the minority over the majority, the dictatorship of the capitalist monopolies over society. The ideologists of imperialism hide the dictatorship of monopoly capital behind specious slogans of freedom and democracy. They declare the imperialist powers to be countries of the "free world" and represent the ruling bourgeois circles as opponents of all dictatorship. In reality, however, freedom in the imperialist world signifies nothing but freedom to exploit the working class, the working people, not only at home, but in all other countries that fall under the iron heel of the monopolies.

The bourgeoisie gives extensive publicity to the allegedly democratic nature of its election laws, singing special praise to its multi-party system and the possibility of nominating many candidates. In reality, however, the monopolists deprive the masses of the opportunity to express their will and elect genuine champions of their interests. Being in control of such potent means as capital, the press, radio, cinema, television, and using their henchmen in the trade unions and other mass organisations, they mislead the masses and impose their own candidates upon the electorate. The different bourgeois parties are usually no more than different factions of the ruling bourgeoisie.

The dictatorship of the bourgeoisie also grossly violates the will of the electorate. Whenever the bourgeoisie sees that the working people are likely, by using their constitutional rights, to elect a considerable number of the champions of their interests to the legislative organs, it brazenly alters the election system and arbitrarily limits the number of working people's representatives in parliament.

The financial oligarchy resorts to the establishment of fascist regimes, banking on the army, police, and gendarmerie as a last refuge from the people's wrath, especially when the masses try to make use of their democratic rights, albeit curtailed, to uphold their interests and end the all-pervading power of the monopolies. Although the vicious German and Italian fascism has crashed, fascist regimes still survive in some countries and fascism is being revived in new forms in others.

Thus, *the world imperialist system is rent by deep-rooted and acute contradictions*. The antagonism of labour and capital, the contradictions between the people and the monopolies, growing militarism, the break-up of the colonial system, the contradictions between the imperialist countries, conflicts and contradictions between the young national states and the old colonial powers, and—most important of all—the rapid growth of world socialism, are sapping and destroying imperialism, leading to its weakening and collapse.

Not even nuclear weapons can protect the monopoly bourgeoisie from the unalterable course of historical development. Mankind has learned the true face of capitalism. Hundreds of millions of people see that capitalism is a system of economic anarchy and periodical crises, chronic unemployment, poverty of the masses, and indiscriminate waste of productive forces, a system constantly fraught with the danger of war. Mankind does not want to, and will not, tolerate the historically outdated capitalist system.

V. THE INTERNATIONAL REVOLUTIONARY MOVEMENT OF THE WORKING CLASS

The international revolutionary movement of the working class has achieved epoch-making victories. *Its chief gain is the world socialist system.* The example of victorious socialism is revolutionising the minds of the working people of the capitalist world; it inspires them to fight against imperialism and greatly facilitates their struggle.

Social forces that are to ensure the victory of socialism are taking shape, multiplying and becoming steeled in the womb of capitalist society. A new contingent of the world proletariat—the young working-class movement of the newly-free, dependent and colonial countries of Asia, Africa, and Latin America—has entered the world arena. Marxist-Leninist parties have arisen and grown. They are becoming a universally recognised national force enjoying ever greater prestige and followed by large sections of the working people.

The international revolutionary movement has accumulated vast experience in the struggle against imperialism and its placemen in the ranks of the working class. It has become more mature ideologically and possesses great organised strength and a militantly dynamic spirit. The trade union movement, which unites vast masses of working people, is playing an increasing role.

The capitalist countries are continuously shaken by class battles. Militant actions of the working class in defence of its economic and political interests are growing in number. The working class and all working people have frequently imperilled the class rule of the bourgeoisie. In an effort to maintain its power, the finance oligarchy, in addition to methods of suppression, uses diverse ways of deceiving and corrupting the working class and its organisations, and of splitting the trade union movement on a national and international scale. It bribes the top stratum of trade unions, co-operatives and other organisations and swells the labour bureaucracy, to which it allots lucrative positions in industry, the municipal bodies and the government apparatus. Anti-communist and anti-labour legislation, the banning of Communist parties, wholesale dismissal of Communists and other progressive workers, blacklisting in industry, "loyalty" screening of employees, police reprisals against the democratic press, and the suppression of strikes by military force have all become routine methods of action for the governments of the imperialist bourgeoisie in its efforts to preserve its dictatorship.

The reactionary forces in individual capitalist countries can no longer cope with the growing forces of democracy and socialism. Struggle and competition between the capitalist states do not preclude, however, a certain unity among them in the face of the increasing strength of socialism and the working-class movement. The imperialists form reactionary alliances; they enter into mutual agreements and set up military blocs and bases spearheaded not only against the socialist countries, but also against the revolutionary working-class and national-liberation movement. The reactionary bourgeoisie in a number of European states have in peacetime opened the doors of their countries to foreign troops.

The bourgeoisie seeks to draw definite lessons from the October Revolution and the victories of socialism. It is using new methods to cover up the ulcers and vices of the capitalist system. Although all these methods render the activities of the revolutionary forces in the capitalist countries more difficult, they cannot reduce the contradictions between labour and capital.

The world situation today is more favourable to the working-class movement. The achievements of the U.S.S.R. and the world socialist system as a whole, the deepening crisis of world capitalism, the growing influence of the Communist parties among the masses, and the ideological breakdown of reformism have brought about a substantial change in the conditions of class struggle that is to the advantage of the working people. Even in those countries where reformism still holds strong positions, appreciable shifts to the Left are taking place in the working-class movement.

In the new historical situation, the working class of many countries can, even before capitalism is overthrown, compel the bourgeoisie to carry out measures that transcend ordinary reforms and are of vital importance to the working class and the progress of its struggle for the victory of the revolution, for socialism, as well as to the majority of the nation. By uniting the democratic and peace-loving forces, the working class can make ruling circles cease preparations for a new world war, renounce the policy of starting local wars, and use the economy for peaceful purposes. By uniting the working people, the masses, the working class can beat back the offensive of fascist reaction and bring about the implementation of a national programme for peace, national independence, democratic rights, and a certain improvement of the living conditions of the people.

The capitalist monopolies are the chief enemy of the working class. They are also the chief enemy of the peasants, handicraftsmen, and other small urban proprietors, of most office workers and intellectuals, and even of a section of the middle capitalists.

The working class directs its main blow against the capitalist monopolies. All the main sections of a nation have a vital interest in abolishing the unlimited power of the monopolies. This makes it possible to unite all the democratic movements opposing the oppression of the finance oligarchy in a mighty *anti-monopoly torrent*.

The proletariat advances a programme for combating the power of the monopolies with due regard to the present as well as the future interests of its allies. It advocates broad nationalisation on terms most favourable to the people. It backs the peasants' demands for radical land reforms and works for the realisation of the slogan, "The land to those who till it".

The proletariat, together with other sections of the people, wages a resolute struggle for broad democracy. It mobilises the masses for effective action against the policy of the finance oligarchy, which strives to abolish democratic freedoms, restrict the power of parliament, revise the constitution with the aim of establishing the personal power of monopoly placemen, and to go over from the parliamentary system to some variety of fascism.

It is in this struggle that the alliance of the working class and all working people is shaped. The working class unites the peasantry, its chief ally, to combat the survivals of feudalism and monopoly domination. Large sections of the office workers and a considerable section of the intelligentsia, whom capitalism reduces to the status of proletarians and who realise the need of changes in the social sphere, become allies of the working class.

31*

General democratic struggles against the monopolies do not delay the socialist revolution but bring it nearer. *The struggle for democracy is a component of the struggle for socialism.* The more profound the democratic movement, the higher becomes the level of the political consciousness of the masses and the more clearly they see that only socialism clears for them the way to genuine freedom and well-being. In the course of this struggle, Right socialist, reformist illusions are dispelled and a political army of the socialist revolution is brought into being.

Socialist revolutions, anti-imperialist national-liberation revolutions, people's democratic revolutions, broad peasant movements, popular struggles to overthrow fascist and other despotic regimes, and general democratic movements against national oppression—all these merge in a single world-wide revolutionary process undermining and destroying capitalism.

The proletarian revolution in any country, being part of the world socialist revolution, is accomplished by the working class of that country and the masses of its people. The revolution is not made to order. It cannot be imposed on the people from without. It results from the profound internal and international contradictions of capitalism. The victorious proletariat cannot impose any "felicity" on another people without thereby undermining its own victory.

Together with the other Marxist-Leninist parties, the Communist Party of the Soviet Union regards it as its internationalist duty to call on the peoples of all countries to rally, muster all internal forces, take vigorous action, and drawing on the might of the world socialist system, forestall or firmly repel imperialist interference in the affairs of the people of any country risen in revolt and thereby prevent imperialist export of counter-revolution. It will be easier to prevent export of counter-revolution if the working people, defending the national sovereignty of their country, strive to bring about the abolition of foreign military bases on their territory and to make their country dissociate itself from aggressive military blocs.

Communists have never held that the road to revolution lies necessarily through wars between countries. Socialist revolution is not necessarily connected with war. Although both world wars, which were started by the imperialists, culminated in socialist revolutions, revolutions are quite feasible without war. The great objectives of the working class can be realised without world war. Today the conditions for this are more favourable than ever.

The working class and its vanguard—the Marxist-Leninist parties—seek to accomplish the socialist revolution *by peaceful means*. This would meet the interests of the working class and the people as a whole, it would accord with the national interests of the country.

In the conditions prevailing at present, in some capitalist countries the working class, headed by its forward detachment, has an opportunity to unite the bulk of the nation, win state power without a civil war and achieve the transfer of the basic means of production to the people upon the basis of a working-class and popular front and other possible forms of agreement and political co-operation between different parties and public organisations. The working class, supported by the majority of the people and firmly repelling opportunist elements incapable of renouncing the policy of compromise with the capitalists and landlords, can defeat the reactionary, anti-popular forces, win a solid majority in parliament, transform it from a tool serving the class interests of the bourgeoisie into an instrument serving the working people, launch a broad mass struggle outside parliament, smash the resistance of the reactionary forces and provide the necessary conditions for a peaceful socialist revolution. This can be done only by extending and continuously developing the class struggle of the workers and peasants and the middle strata of the urban population against big monopoly capital and reaction, for far-reaching social reforms, for peace and socialism.

Where the exploiting classes resort to violence against the people, the possibility of a *non-peaceful transition to socialism* should be borne in mind. Leninism maintains, and historical experience confirms, that the ruling classes do not yield power of their own free will. Hence, the degree of bitterness of the class struggle and the forms it takes will depend not so much on the proletariat as on the strength of the reactionary groups' resistance to the will of the overwhelming majority of the people, and on the use of force by these groups at a particular stage of the struggle for socialism. In each particular country the actual applicability of one method of transition to socialism or the other depends on concrete historical conditions.

It may well be that as the forces of socialism grow, the working-class movement gains strength and the positions of capitalism are weakened, there will arise in certain countries a situation in which it will be preferable for the bourgeoisie, as Marx and Lenin foresaw, to agree to the basic means of production being purchased from it and for the proletariat to "pay off" the bourgeoisie.

The success of the struggle which the working class wages for the victory of the revolution will depend on how well the working class and its party master the use of *all forms* of struggle—peaceful and non-peaceful, parliamentary and extra-parliamentary—and how well they are prepared for any swift and sudden replacement of one form of struggle by another form of struggle. While the principal law-governed processes of the socialist revolution are common to all countries, the diversity of the national peculiarities and traditions that have arisen in the course of history creates specific conditions for the revolutionary process, the variety of forms and rates of the proletariat's advent to power. This predetermines the possibility and necessity, in a number of countries, of *transi-*

tion stages in the struggle for the dictatorship of the proletariat, and a *variety of forms* of political organisation of the society building socialism. But whatever the form in which the transition from capitalism to socialism is effected, that transition can come about only through revolution. However varied the forms of a new, people's state power in the period of socialist construction, their essence will be the same—*dictatorship of the proletariat*, which represents genuine democracy, democracy for the working people.

A bourgeois republic, however democratic, however hallowed by slogans purporting to express the will of the people or nation as a whole, or extra-class will, inevitably remains in practice—owing to the existence of private capitalist ownership of the means of production—a dictatorship of the bourgeoisie, a machine for the exploitation and suppression of the vast majority of the working people by a handful of capitalists. In contrast to the bourgeoisie, which conceals the class character of the state, the working class does not deny the class character of the state.

The dictatorship of the proletariat is a dictatorship of the overwhelming majority over the minority; it is directed against the exploiters, against the oppression of peoples and nations, and is aimed at abolishing all exploitation of man by man. The dictatorship of the proletariat expresses not only the interests of the working class, but also those of all working people; its chief content is not violence but creation, the building of a new, socialist society, and the defence of its gains against the enemies of socialism.

Overcoming the split in its ranks is an important condition for the working class to fulfil its historic mission. No bastion of imperialism can withstand a closely-knit working class that exercises unity of action. The Communist parties favour co-operation with the Social-Democratic parties not only in the struggle for peace, for better living conditions for the working people, and for the preservation and extension of their democratic rights and freedoms, but also in the struggle to win power and build a socialist society.

At the same time Communists criticise the ideological positions and Right-wing opportunist practice of Social-Democracy and expose the Right Social-Democratic leaders, who have sided openly with the bourgeoisie and renounced the traditional socialist demands of the working class.

The Communist parties are the vanguard of the world revolutionary movement. They have demonstrated the vitality of Marxism-Leninism and their ability not only to propagate the great ideals of scientific communism, but also to put them into practice. Today the international Communist movement is so powerful that the combined forces of reaction cannot crush it.

The Communist movement grows and becomes steeled as it fights against various opportunist trends. Revisionism, Right opportunism, which is a reflection of bourgeois influence, is the chief danger within the Communist movement today. The revisionists, who mask their renunciation of Marxism with talk about the necessity of taking account of the latest developments in society and the class struggle, in effect play the role of pedlars of bourgeois-reformist ideology within the Communist movement. They seek to rob Marxism-Leninism of its revolutionary spirit, to undermine the faith which the working class and all working people have in socialism, to disarm and disorganise them in their struggle against imperialism. The revisionists deny the historical necessity of the socialist revolution and of the dictatorship of the proletariat. They deny the leading role of the Marxist-Leninist party, undermine the foundations of proletarian internationalism, and drift to nationalism. The ideology of revisionism is most fully embodied in the programme of the League of Communists of Yugoslavia.

Another danger is dogmatism and sectarianism, which cannot be reconciled with a creative development of revolutionary theory, which lead to the dissociation and isolation of Communists from the masses, doom them to passive expectation or incite them to Leftist adventurist actions in the revolutionary struggle, and hinder a correct appraisal of the changing situation and the use of new opportunities for the benefit of the working class and all democratic forces. Dogmatism and sectarianism, unless steadfastly combated, can also become the chief danger at particular stages in the development of individual parties.

The Communist Party of the Soviet Union holds that an uncompromising struggle against revisionism, dogmatism and sectarianism, against all departures from Leninism, is a necessary condition for the further strengthening of the unity of the world Communist movement and for the consolidation of the socialist camp.

The Communist parties are independent and they shape their policies with due regard to the specific conditions prevailing in their own countries. They base relations between themselves on equality and the principles of proletarian internationalism. They co-ordinate their actions, consciously and of their own free will, as components of a single international army of labour. The Communist Party of the Soviet Union, like all the other Communist parties, regards it as its internationalist duty to abide by the appraisals and conclusions which the fraternal parties have reached jointly concerning their common tasks in the struggle against imperialism, for peace, democracy and socialism, and by the Declaration and the Statement adopted by the Communist parties at their international meetings.

Vigorous defence of the unity of the world Communist movement in line with the principles of Marxism-Leninism and proletarian internationalism, and prevention of any action likely to disrupt that unity are an essential condition for victory in the struggle for national independence, democracy and peace, for the successful accomplishment of the tasks of the socialist revolution, for the construction of socialism and communism.

The C.P.S.U. will continue to concentrate its efforts on strengthening the unity and cohesion of the ranks of the great army of Communists of all countries.

VI. THE NATIONAL-LIBERATION MOVEMENT

The world is experiencing a period of stormy national-liberation revolutions. Imperialism suppressed the national independence and freedom of the majority of the peoples and put the fetters of brutal colonial slavery on them, but *the rise of socialism marks the advent of the era of emancipation of the oppressed peoples.* A powerful wave of national-liberation revolutions is sweeping away the colonial system and undermining the foundations of imperialism. Young sovereign states have arisen, or are arising, in one-time colonies or semi-colonies. Their peoples have entered a new period of development. They have emerged as makers of a new life and as active participants in world politics, as a revolutionary force destroying imperialism.

But the struggle is not yet over. The peoples who are throwing off the shackles of colonialism have attained different degrees of freedom. Many of them, having established national states, are striving for economic and durable political independence. The peoples of those formally independent countries that in reality depend on foreign monopolies politically and economically are rising to fight against imperialism and reactionary pro-imperialist regimes. The peoples who have not yet cast off the chains of colonial slavery are conducting a heroic struggle against their foreign enslavers.

The young sovereign states do not belong either to the

system of imperialist states or to the system of socialist states. But the overwhelming majority of them have not yet broken free from world capitalist economy even though they occupy a special place in it. They constitute that part of the world which is still being exploited by the capitalist monopolies. As long as they do not put an end to their economic dependence on imperialism, they will be playing the role of a "world countryside", and will remain objects of semi-colonial exploitation.

The existence of the world socialist system and the weakening of imperialism offer the peoples of the newly-free countries the prospect of a national renascence, of ending age-long backwardness and poverty, and achieving economic independence.

The interests of a nation call for the eradication of the remnants of colonialism, the elimination of the roots of imperialist power, the ousting of foreign monopolies, the founding of a national industry, the abolition of the feudal system and its survivals, the implementation of radical land reforms with the participation of the entire peasantry and in its interests, the pursuit of an independent foreign policy of peace, the democratisation of the life of society and the strengthening of political independence. All patriotic and progressive forces of the nation are interested in the solution of national problems. That is the basis on which they can be united.

Foreign capital will retreat only before a broad union of patriotic, democratic forces pursuing an anti-imperialist policy. The pillars of feudalism will crumble only under the impact of a general democratic movement. Only far-reaching agrarian reforms and a broad peasant movement can sweep away the remnants of medievalism that fetter the development of the productive forces, and solve the acute food problem that faces the peoples of Asia, Africa, and Latin America. Political independence can be made secure only by a people that has won democratic rights and freedoms and is taking an active part in governing the state.

Consistent struggle against imperialism is a paramount condition for the solution of national tasks. Imperialism seeks to retain one-time colonies and semi-colonies within the system of capitalist economy and perpetuate their underprivileged position in it. *U.S. imperialism is the chief bulwark of modern colonialism.*

The imperialists are using new methods and new forms to maintain colonial exploitation of the peoples. They resort to whatever means they can (colonial wars, military blocs, conspiracies, terrorism, subversion, economic pressure, bribery) to control the newly-free countries and to reduce the independence they have won to mere form, or to deprive them of that independence. Under the guise of "aid", they are trying to retain their old positions in those countries and capture new ones, to extend their social basis, lure the national bourgeoisie to their side, implant military despotic regimes and put obedient puppets in power. Using the poisoned weapon of national and tribal strife, the imperialists seek to split the ranks of the national-liberation movement; reactionary groups of the local exploiting classes play the role of allies of imperialism.

Imperialism thus remains the chief enemy and the chief obstacle to the solution of the national problems facing the young sovereign states and all dependent countries.

A national-liberation revolution does not end with the winning of political independence. Independence will be unstable and will become fictitious unless the revolution brings about radical changes in the social and economic spheres and solves the pressing problems of national rebirth.

The working class is the most consistent fighter for the consummation of this revolution, for national interests and social progress. As industry develops, its ranks will swell and its role on the socio-political scene will increase.

The alliance of the working class and the peasantry is the fundamental condition for the success of the struggle to carry out far-reaching democratic changes and achieve economic and social progress. This alliance must form the core of a broad national front. The extent to which the national bourgeoisie will take part in the anti-imperialist and anti-feudal struggle will depend in considerable measure on the solidity of the alliance of the working class and the peasantry. The national front embraces the working class, the peasantry, the national bourgeoisie and the democratic intelligentsia.

In many countries, the liberation movement of the peoples that have awakened proceeds under the flag of nationalism. Marxists-Leninists draw a distinction between the nationalism of the oppressed nations and that of the oppressor nations. The nationalism of an oppressed nation contains a *general democratic element* directed against oppression, and Communists support it because they consider it historically justified at a given stage. That element finds expression in the striving of the oppressed peoples to free themselves from imperialist oppression, to gain national independence and bring about a national renascence. But the nationalism of an oppressed nation has yet another aspect, one expressing the ideology and interests of the reactionary exploiting top stratum.

The national bourgeoisie is dual in character. In modern conditions the national bourgeoisie in those colonial, one-time colonial and dependent countries where it is not connected with the imperialist circles is objectively interested in accomplishing the basic tasks of an anti-imperialist and anti-feudal revolution. Its progressive role and its ability to participate in the solution of pressing national problems are, therefore, not yet spent.

But as the contradictions between the working people and the propertied classes grow and the class struggle inside the country becomes more acute, the national bourgeoisie shows an increasing inclination to compromise with imperialism and domestic reaction.

The development of the countries which have won their freedom may be a complex multi-stage process. By virtue of varying historical and socio-economic conditions in the newly-free countries, the revolutionary effort of the masses will impart many distinctive features to the forms and rates of their social progress.

One of the basic questions confronting these peoples is, which road of development the countries that have freed themselves from colonial tyranny are to take, whether the capitalist road or the non-capitalist.

What can capitalism bring them?

Capitalism is the road of suffering for the people. It will not ensure rapid economic progress nor eliminate poverty; social inequality will increase. The capitalist development of the countryside will ruin the peasantry still more. The workers will be fated either to engaging in back-breaking labour to enrich the capitalists, or to swelling the ranks of the disinherited army of the unemployed. The petty bourgeoisie will be crushed in competition with big capital. The benefits of culture and education will remain out of reach of the people. The intelligentsia will be compelled to sell its talent.

What can socialism bring the peoples?

Socialism is the road to freedom and happiness for the peoples. It ensures rapid economic and cultural progress. It transforms a backward country into an industrial country within the lifetime of one generation and not in the course of centuries. Planned socialist economy is an economy of progress and prosperity by its very nature. Abolition of the exploitation of man by man does away with social inequality. Unemployment disappears completely. Socialism provides all peasants with land, helps them to develop farming, combines their labour efforts in voluntary co-operatives and puts modern agricultural machinery and agronomy at their disposal. Peasant labour is made more productive and the land is made more fertile. Socialism provides a high material and cultural standard of living for the working class and all working people. Socialism lifts the people out of darkness and ignorance and gives them access to modern culture. The intelligentsia is offered ample opportunities for creative effort for the benefit of the people.

It is for the peoples themselves to decide which road they will choose. In view of the present balance of the world forces and the actual feasibility of powerful support from the world socialist system, the peoples of the former colonies can decide this question in their own interest. Their choice will depend on the balance of the class forces. The non-capitalist road of development is ensured by the struggle of the working class and the masses of the people, by the general democratic movement, and meets the interests of the absolute majority of the nation.

The establishment and development of *national democracies* opens vast prospects for the peoples of the economically underdeveloped countries. The political basis of a national democracy is a bloc of all the progressive, patriotic forces fighting to win complete national independence and broad democracy, and to consummate the anti-imperialist, anti-feudal, democratic revolution.

A steady growth of the class and national consciousness of the masses is a characteristic of the present stage of social development. The imperialists persist in distorting the idea of national sovereignty, in emasculating it of its main content and in using it as a means of fomenting national egoism, implanting a spirit of national exclusiveness and increasing national antagonisms. The democratic forces establish the idea of national sovereignty in the name of equality for the peoples, of their mutual trust, friendship and assistance and of closer relations between them, in the name of social progress. The idea of national sovereignty in its democratic sense becomes more and more firmly established; it acquires increasing significance and becomes an important factor in the progressive development of society.

The Communist parties are steadfastly carrying on an active struggle to consummate the anti-imperialist, anti-feudal, democratic revolution, to establish a state of national democracy and achieve social progress. *The Communists' aims are in keeping with the supreme interests of the nation.* The attempts of reactionary circles to disrupt the national front under the guise of anti-communism and their persecution of Communists lead to the weakening of the national-liberation movement and run counter to the national interests of the peoples; they imperil the gains achieved.

The national states become ever more active as an independent force on the world scene; objectively, this force is in the main a *progressive, revolutionary and anti-imperialist force.* The countries and peoples that are now free from colonial oppression are to play a prominent part in the prevention of a new world war—the focal problem of today. The time is past when imperialism could freely use the manpower and material resources of those countries in its predatory wars. The time has come when the peoples of those countries, breaking the resistance of the reactionary circles and those connected with the colonialists, and overcoming the vacillation of the national bourgeoisie, can put their resources at the service of universal security and become a new bulwark of peace. This is what their own fundamental interests and the interests of all peoples demand.

The joining of the efforts of the newly-free peoples and of the peoples of the socialist countries in the struggle against the war danger is a cardinal factor of world peace. This mighty front, which expresses the will and strength of two-thirds of mankind, can force the imperialist aggressors to retreat.

The socialist countries are sincere and true friends of peoples fighting for their liberation and of those that have freed themselves from imperialist tyranny, and render them all-round support. They stand for the abolition of all forms of colonial oppression and vigorously promote the strengthening of the sovereignty of the states rising on the ruins of colonial empires.

The C.P.S.U. considers fraternal alliance with the peoples who have thrown off colonial or semi-colonial yoke to be a corner-stone of its international policy. This alliance is based on the common vital interests of world socialism and the world national-liberation movement. The C.P.S.U. regards it as its internationalist duty to assist the peoples who have set out to win and strengthen their national independence, all peoples who are fighting for the complete abolition of the colonial system.

VII. THE STRUGGLE AGAINST BOURGEOIS AND REFORMIST IDEOLOGY

A grim struggle is going on between two ideologies—communist and bourgeois—in the world today. This struggle is a reflection, in the spiritual life of mankind, of the historic process of transition from capitalism to socialism.

The new historical epoch has brought the revolutionary world outlook of the proletariat a genuine triumph. Marxism-Leninism has gripped the minds of progressive mankind.

Bourgeois doctrines and schools have failed in the test of history. They have been and still are unable to furnish scientific answers to the questions posed by life. The bourgeoisie is no longer in a position to put forward ideas that will induce the masses to follow it. More and more people in the capitalist countries are renouncing the bourgeois world outlook. *Bourgeois ideology is experiencing a grave crisis.*

A revolutionary change in the minds of vast masses is a long and complex process. The more victories the world socialist system achieves, the deeper the crisis of world capitalism and the sharper the class struggle, the more important becomes the role of Marxist-Leninist ideas in unifying and mobilising the masses to fight for communism. The ideological struggle is a most important element of the class struggle of the proletariat.

Imperialist reaction mobilises every possible means to exert ideological influence on the masses as it attempts to denigrate communism and its noble ideas and to defend capitalism. The chief ideological and political weapon of imperialism is *anti-communism*, which consists mainly in slandering the socialist system and distorting the policy and objectives of the Communist parties and Marxist-Leninist theory. Under the false slogans of anti-communism, imperialist reaction persecutes and hounds all that is progressive and revolutionary; it seeks to split the ranks of the working people and to paralyse the proletarians' will to fight. Rallied to this black banner today are all the enemies of social progress: the finance oligarchy and the military, the fascists and reactionary clericals, the colonialists and landlords and all the ideological and political supporters of imperialist reaction. Anti-communism is a reflection of the extreme decadence of bourgeois ideology.

The defenders of the bourgeois system, seeking to keep the masses in spiritual bondage, invent new "theories" designed to mask the exploiting character of the bourgeois system and to embellish capitalism. They assert that modern capitalism has changed its nature, that it has become "people's capitalism" in which property is "diffused" and capital becomes "democratic", that classes and class contradictions are disappearing, that "incomes are being equalised" and economic crises eliminated. In reality, however, the development of modern capitalism confirms the accuracy of the Marxist-Leninist theory of the growing contradictions and antagonisms in capitalist society and of the aggravation of the class struggle within it.

The advocates of the bourgeois state call it a *"welfare state"*. They propagate the illusion that the capitalist state opposes monopolies and can achieve social harmony and universal well-being. But the masses see from their own experience that the bourgeois state is an obedient tool of the monopolies and that the vaunted "welfare" is welfare for the magnates of finance capital, and suffering and torture for hundreds of millions of workingmen.

The "theoreticians" of anti-communism describe the imperialist countries as the "free world". In reality the "free world" is a world of exploitation and lack of rights, a world where human dignity and national honour are trampled underfoot, a world of obscurantism and political reaction, of rabid militarism and bloody reprisals against the working people.

Monopoly capital engenders *fascist ideology*—the ideology of extreme chauvinism and racism. Fascism in power is an overt terroristic dictatorship of the most reactionary, most chauvinistic and most imperialist elements of finance capital. Fascism begins everywhere and always with vicious anti-communism to isolate and rout the parties of the working class, to split the forces of the proletariat and defeat them piecemeal, and then to do away with all the other democratic parties and organisations and turn the people into the blind tool of the policy of the capitalist monopolies. Fascism strikes first of all at the Communist parties since they are the most consistent, staunch and incorruptible defenders of the interests of the working class and all working people.

Imperialist reaction makes extensive use of *chauvinism and racism* to incite nationalist and racial conflicts, persecute entire nationalities and races (anti-Semitism, racial discrimination against Negroes and the peoples of the underdeveloped countries), blunt the class consciousness of the working people and divert the proletariat and its allies from the class struggle.

Clericalism is acquiring ever greater importance in the political and ideological arsenal of imperialism. The clericals do not confine themselves to using the Church and its ramified machinery. They now have their own big polit-ical parties which in many capitalist countries are in power. By setting up its own trade union, youth, women's and other organisations clericalism splits the ranks of the working class and all working people. The monopolies lavishly subsidise clerical parties and organisations, which exploit the religious sentiments of the working people and their superstitions and prejudices.

Bourgeois ideology assumes a variety of forms and uses the most diverse methods and means of deceiving the working people. But they all boil down to the same thing—defence of the declining capitalist system. The ideas run-ning through the political and economic theories of the modern bourgeoisie, through its philosophy and sociology, through its ethics and aesthetics, substantiate monopoly domination, justify exploitation, defame social property and collectivism, glorify militarism and war, whitewash colonialism and racism, and foment enmity and hatred among the peoples.

Anti-communism is becoming the main instrument of reaction in its struggle against the democratic forces of Asia, Africa and Latin America. It is the meeting ground of imperialist ideology and the ideology of the feudal, pro-imperialist elements and the reactionary groups of the bourgeoisie of the countries which have gained their free-dom from colonial tyranny.

The anti-popular circles of those countries seek to tone down the general democratic content of nationalism, to play up its reactionary aspect, to push aside the democ-ratic forces of the nation, to prevent social progress, and to hinder the spread of scientific socialism. At the same time they advance theories of "socialism of the national type", propagate socio-philosophical doctrines that are, as a rule, so many variations of the petty-bourgeois illusion of socialism, an illusion which rules out the class struggle. These theories mislead the people, hamper the development of the national-liberation movement and imperil its gains.

National-democratic, anti-imperialist ideas are becoming widespread in the countries which have liberated themselves from colonial oppression. The Communists and other proponents of these ideas patiently explain to the masses the untenability of the illusion that national independence and social progress are possible without a determined struggle against imperialism and internal reaction. They come out actively against chauvinism and other manifestations of reactionary ideology, which justifies despotic regimes and the suppression of democracy. At the same time the Communists act as exponents of the socialist ideology, rallying the masses under the banner of scientific socialism.

The ideological struggle of the imperialist bourgeoisie is spearheaded primarily against the working class and its Marxist-Leninist parties. Social-Democratism in the working-class movement and revisionism in the Communist movement reflect the bourgeois influence on the working class.

The contemporary Right-wing Social-Democrats are the most important ideological and political prop of the bourgeoisie within the working-class movement. They eclectically combine old opportunist ideas with the "latest" bourgois theories. The Right Wing of Social-Democracy has completely broken with Marxism and contraposed so-called democratic socialism to scientific socialism. Its adherents deny the existence of antagonistic classes and the class struggle in bourgeois society; they forcefully deny the necessity of the proletarian revolution and oppose the abolition of the private ownership of the means of production. They assert that capitalism is being "transformed" into socialism.

The Right-wing Socialists began by advocating social reforms in place of the socialist revolution and went as far as to defend state-monopoly capitalism. In the past they impressed on the minds of the proletariat that their differences with revolutionary Marxism bore not so much on the ultimate goal of the working-class movement as on the ways of achieving it. Now they openly renounce socialism. Formerly the Right-wing Socialists refused to recognise the class struggle to the point of recognising the dictatorship of the proletariat. Today they deny, not only the existence of the class struggle in bourgeois society, but also the very existence of antagonistic classes.

Historical experience has shown the bankruptcy of both the ideology and the policy of Social-Democracy. Even when reformist parties come to power they limit themselves to partial reforms that do not affect the rule of the monopoly bourgeoisie. Anti-communism has brought social reformism to an ideological and political impasse. This is one of the main reasons for the crisis of Social-Democracy.

Marxism-Leninism is winning more and more victories. It is winning them because it expresses the vital interests of the working class, of the vast majority of mankind, which seeks peace, freedom and progress, and because it expresses the ideology of the new society succeeding capitalism.

VIII. PEACEFUL COEXISTENCE
AND THE STRUGGLE FOR WORLD PEACE

The C.P.S.U. considers that the chief aim of its foreign-policy activity is to provide peaceful conditions for the building of a communist society in the U.S.S.R. and developing the world socialist system, and together with the other peace-loving peoples to deliver mankind from a world war of extermination.

The C.P.S.U. maintains that forces capable of preserving and promoting universal peace have arisen and are growing in the world. Possibilities are arising for essentially new relations between states.

Imperialism knows no relations between states other than those of domination and subordination, of oppression of the weak by the strong. It bases international relations on diktat and intimidation, on violence and arbitrary rule. It regards wars of aggression as a natural means of settling international issues. For the imperialist countries diplomacy has been, and remains, a tool for imposing their will upon other nations and preparing wars. At the time of the undivided rule of imperialism the issue of war and peace was settled by the finance and industrial oligarchy in the utmost secrecy from the peoples.

Socialism contrasts imperialism with *a new type of international relations*. The foreign policy of the socialist countries, which is based on the principles of peace, the equality and self-determination of nations, and respect for the independence and sovereignty of all countries, as well as the fair, humane methods of socialist diplomacy, are exerting a growing influence on the world situation. At a time when imperialism no longer plays a dominant role in international relations, while the socialist system is playing an increasing role, and when the influence of the countries that have won national independence and of the masses of the people in the capitalist countries has grown very considerably, it is becoming possible for the new principles advanced by socialism to gain the upper hand over the principles of aggressive imperialist policy.

For the first time in history, a situation has arisen in which not only the big states, but also the small ones, the countries which have chosen independent development, and all the states which want peace, are in a position, irrespective of their strength, to pursue an independent foreign policy.

The issue of war and peace is the principal issue of today. Imperialism is the only source of the war danger. The imperialist camp is making preparations for the most terrible crime against mankind—a world thermonuclear war that can bring unprecedented destruction to entire countries and wipe out entire nations. The problem of war and peace has become a life-and-death problem for hundreds of millions of people.

The peoples must concentrate their efforts on curbing the imperialists in good time and preventing them from making use of lethal weapons. *The main thing is to ward off a thermonuclear war, to prevent it from breaking out.* This can be done by the present generation.

The consolidation of the Soviet state and the formation of the world socialist system were historic steps towards the realisation of mankind's age-old dream of banishing wars from the life of society. In the socialist part of the world there are no classes or social groups interested in starting a war. Socialism, outstripping capitalism in a number of important branches of science and technology, has supplied the peace-loving peoples with powerful material means of curbing imperialist aggression. Capitalism established its rule with fire and sword, but socialism does not require war to spread its ideals. Its weapon is its superiority over the old system in social organisation, political system, economy, the improvement of the standard of living and spiritual culture.

The socialist system is a natural centre of attraction for the peace-loving forces of the globe. The principles of its foreign policy are gaining ever greater international recognition and support. A vast *peace zone* has taken shape on earth. In addition to the socialist countries, it includes a large group of non-socialist countries that for various reasons are not interested in starting a war. The emergence of those countries in the arena of world politics has substantially altered the balance of forces in favour of peace.

There is a growing number of countries that adhere to a policy of neutrality and strive to safeguard themselves against the hazards of participation in aggressive military blocs.

In the new historical epoch the masses have a far greater opportunity of actively intervening in the settlement of international issues. The peoples are taking the solution of the problem of war and peace into their own hands more and more vigorously. The anti-war movement of the masses, which takes various forms, is a major factor in the struggle for peace. The international working class, the most uncompromising and most consistent fighter against imperialist war, is the great organising force in this struggle of the people as a whole.

It is possible to avert a world war by the combined efforts of the mighty socialist camp, the peace-loving non-socialist countries, the international working class and all the forces championing peace. The growing superiority of the socialist forces over the forces of imperialism, of the forces of peace over those of war, will make it actually possible to banish world war from the life of society even before the complete victory of socialism on earth, with capitalism surviving in a part of the world. The victory of socialism throughout the world will do away completely with the social and national causes of all wars. *To abolish war and establish everlasting peace on earth is a historic mission of communism.*

General and complete disarmament under strict international control is a radical way of guaranteeing a durable peace. Imperialism has imposed an unprecedented burden of armaments on the peoples. Socialism sees its duty towards mankind in delivering it from this absurd waste of national wealth. The solution of this problem would have historical significance for mankind. By an active and determined effort the peoples can and must force the imperialists into disarmament.

Socialism has offered mankind the only reasonable principle of maintaining relations between states at a time when the world is divided into two systems—the principle of the peaceful coexistence of states with different social systems, put forward by Lenin.

Peaceful coexistence of the socialist and capitalist countries is an *objective necessity* for the development of human society. *War cannot and must not serve as a means of settling international disputes.* Peaceful coexistence or disastrous war—such is the alternative offered by history. Should the imperialist aggressors nevertheless venture to start a new world war, the peoples will no longer tolerate a system which drags them into devastating wars. They will sweep imperialism away and bury it.

Peaceful coexistence implies renunciation of war as a means of settling international disputes, and their solution by negotiation; equality, mutual understanding and trust between countries; consideration for each other's interests; non-interference in internal affairs; recognition of the right of every people to solve all the problems of their country by themselves; strict respect for the sovereignty and territorial integrity of all countries; promotion of economic and cultural co-operation on the basis of complete equality and mutual benefit.

Peaceful coexistence serves as a basis for the peaceful competition between socialism and capitalism on an international scale and constitutes a specific form of class struggle between them. As they consistently pursue the policy of peaceful coexistence, the socialist countries are steadily strengthening the positions of the world socialist system in its competition with capitalism. Peaceful coexistence affords more favourable opportunities for the struggle of the working class in the capitalist countries and facilitates the struggle of the peoples of the colonial and dependent countries for their liberation. Support for the principle of peaceful coexistence is also in keeping with the interests of that section of the bourgeoisie which realises that a thermonuclear war would not spare the ruling classes of capitalist society either. The policy of peaceful coexistence is in accord with the vital interests of all mankind, except the big monopoly magnates and the militarists.

The Soviet Union has consistently pursued, and will continue to pursue, the policy of the peaceful coexistence of states with different social systems.

The Communist Party of the Soviet Union advances the following *tasks in the field of international relations*:

to use, together with the other socialist countries, peaceful states and peoples, every means of preventing world war and providing conditions for the complete banishment of war from the life of society;

to pursue a policy of establishing sound international relations, and work for the disbandment of all military blocs opposing each other, the discontinuance of the "cold war" and the propaganda of enmity and hatred among the nations, and the abolition of all air, naval, rocket, and other military bases on foreign territory;

to work for general and complete disarmament under strict international control;

to strengthen relations of fraternal friendship and close co-operation with the countries of Asia, Africa, and Latin America which are fighting to attain or consolidate national independence, with all peoples and states that advocate the preservation of peace;

to pursue an active and consistent policy of improving and developing relations with all capitalist countries, including the United States of America, Great Britain, France, the Federal Republic of Germany, Japan, and Italy, with a view to safeguarding peace;

to contribute in every way to the militant solidarity of all contingents and organisations of the international working class, which oppose the imperialist policy of war;

steadfastly to pursue a policy of consolidating all the forces fighting against war. All the organisations and parties that strive to avert war, the neutralist and pacifist movements and the bourgeois circles that advocate peace and normal relations between countries will meet with understanding and support on the part of the Soviet Union;

to pursue a policy of developing international co-operation in the fields of trade, cultural relations, science, and technology;

to be highly vigilant with regard to the aggressive circles, which are intent on violating peace; to expose, in good time, the initiators of military adventures; to take all necessary steps to safeguard the security and inviolability of our socialist country and the socialist camp as a whole.

The C.P.S.U. and the Soviet people as a whole will continue to oppose all wars of conquest, including wars between capitalist countries, and local wars aimed at strangling people's emancipation movements, and consider it their duty to support the sacred struggle of the oppressed peoples and their just anti-imperialist wars of liberation.

The Communist Party of the Soviet Union will hold high the banner of peace and friendship among the nations.

PART TWO

THE TASKS
OF THE COMMUNIST PARTY OF THE SOVIET UNION
IN BUILDING A COMMUNIST SOCIETY

Communism—the Bright Future of All Mankind

The building of a communist society has become an immediate practical task for the Soviet people. The gradual development of socialism into communism is an objective law; it has been prepared by the development of Soviet socialist society throughout the preceding period.

What is communism?

Communism is a classless social system with one form of public ownership of the means of production and full social equality of all members of society; under it, the all-round development of people will be accompanied by the growth of the productive forces through continuous progress in science and technology; all the springs of co-operative wealth will flow more abundantly, and the great principle "From each according to his ability, to each according to his needs" will be implemented. Communism is a highly organised society of free, socially conscious working people in which public self-government will be established, a society in which labour for the good of society will become the prime vital requirement of everyone, a necessity recognised by one and all, and the ability of each person will be employed to the greatest benefit of the people.

A high degree of communist consciousness, industry, discipline, and devotion to the public interest are qualities typifying the man of communist society.

Communism ensures the continuous development of social production and rising labour productivity through rapid scientific and technological progress; it equips man with the best and most powerful machines, greatly increases his power over nature and enables him to control its elemental forces to an ever greater extent. The social economy reaches the highest stage of planned organisation, and the most effective and rational use is made of the material wealth and labour reserves to meet the growing requirements of the members of society.

Under communism there will be no classes, and the socio-economic and cultural distinctions, and differences in living conditions, between town and countryside will disappear; the countryside will rise to the level of the town in the development of the productive forces and the nature of work, the forms of production relations, living conditions and the well-being of the population. With the victory of communism mental and physical labour will merge organically in the production activity of people. The intelligentsia will no longer be a distinct social stratum. Workers by hand will have risen in cultural and technological standards to the level of workers by brain.

Thus, communism will put an end to the division of society into classes and social strata, whereas the whole history of mankind, with the exception of its primitive period, was one of class society. Division into opposing classes led to the exploitation of man by man, class struggle, and antagonisms between nations and states.

Under communism all people will have equal status in society, will stand in the same relation to the means of production, will enjoy equal conditions of work and distribution, and will actively participate in the management of public affairs. Harmonious relations will be established between the individual and society on the basis of the unity of public and personal interests. For all their diversity, the requirements of people will express the sound, reasonable requirements of the fully developed person.

The purpose of communist production is to ensure uninterrupted progress of society and to provide all its members with material and cultural benefits according to their growing needs, their individual requirements and tastes. People's requirements will be satisfied from public sources. Articles of personal use will be in the full ownership of each member of society and will be at his disposal.

Communist society, which is based on highly organised production and advanced technology, alters the character of work, but it does not release the members of society from work. It will by no means be a society of anarchy, idleness and inactivity. Every able-bodied person will participate in social labour and thereby ensure the steady growth of the material and spiritual wealth of society. Thanks to the changed character of labour, its better technical equipment and the high degree of consciousness of all members of society, the latter will work willingly for the public benefit according to their own inclinations.

Communist production demands high standards of organisation, precision and discipline, which are ensured, not by compulsion, but through an understanding of public duty, and are determined by the whole pattern of life in communist society. Labour and discipline will not be a burden to people; labour will no longer be a mere source of livelihood—it will be a genuinely creative process and a source of joy.

Communism represents the highest form of organisation of public life. All production units and self-governing associations will be harmoniously united in a common planned economy and a uniform rhythm of social labour.

Under communism the nations will draw closer and closer together in all spheres on the basis of a complete identity of economic, political and spiritual interests, of fraternal friendship and co-operation.

Communism is the system under which the abilities and talents of free man, his best moral qualities, blossom forth and reveal themselves in full. Family relations will be freed once and for all from material considerations and will be based solely on mutual love and friendship.

In defining the basic tasks to be accomplished in building a communist society, the Party is guided by Lenin's great formula: *"Communism is Soviet power plus the electrification of the whole country."*

The C.P.S.U. being a party of scientific communism, proposes and fulfils the tasks of communist construction in step with the preparation and maturing of the material and spiritual prerequisites, considering that it would be wrong to jump over necessary stages of development, and that it would be equally wrong to halt at an achieved level and thus check progress. The building of communism must be carried out by successive stages.

In the current decade (1961-70) the Soviet Union, in creating the material and technical basis of communism, will surpass the strongest and richest capitalist country, the U.S.A., in production per head of population; the people's standard of living and their cultural and technical standards will improve substantially; everyone will live in easy circumstances; all collective and state farms will become highly productive and profitable enterprises; the demand of Soviet people for well-appointed housing will, in the main, be satisfied; hard physical work will disappear; the U.S.S.R. will have the shortest working day.

The material and technical basis of communism will be built up by the *end of the second decade* (1971-80), ensuring an abundance of material and cultural values for the whole population; Soviet society will come close to a stage where it can introduce the principle of distribution according to needs, and there will be a gradual transition to one form of ownership—public ownership. Thus, *a communist society will in the main be built in the U.S.S.R.* The construction of communist society will be fully completed in the subsequent period.

The majestic edifice of communism is being erected by the persevering effort of the Soviet people—the working class, the peasantry and the intelligentsia. The more successful their work, the closer the great goal—communist society.

I. THE TASKS OF THE PARTY
IN THE ECONOMIC FIELD
AND IN THE CREATION AND PROMOTION
OF THE MATERIAL AND TECHNICAL BASIS OF COMMUNISM

The main economic task of the Party and the Soviet people is to create *the material and technical basis of communism* within two decades. This means complete electrification of the country and perfection on this basis of the techniques, technologies, and organisation of social production in all the fields of the national economy; comprehensive mechanisation of production operations and a growing degree of their automation; widespread use of chemistry in the national economy; vigorous development of new, economically effective branches of production, new types of power and new materials; all-round and rational utilisation of natural, material and labour resources; organic fusion of science and production, and rapid scientific and technical progress; a high cultural and technical level for the working people; and substantial superiority over the more developed capitalist countries in productivity of labour, which constitutes the most important prerequisite for the victory of the communist system.

As a result, the U.S.S.R. will possess productive forces of unparalleled might; it will surpass the technical level of the most developed countries and occupy first place in the world in per capita production. This will serve as a basis for the gradual transformation of socialist social relations into communist relations and for a development of production that will make it possible to meet in abundance the requirements of society and all its members.

In contrast to capitalism, the planned socialist system of economy combines accelerated technical progress with the full employment of all able-bodied citizens. Automation and comprehensive mechanisation serve as a material basis for the gradual development of socialist labour into communist labour. Technical progress will require higher standards of production and a higher level of the vocational and general education of all working people. The new machinery will be used to improve radically the Soviet people's working conditions, and make them much easier, to reduce the length of the working day, to improve living conditions, eliminate hard physical work and, subsequently, all unskilled labour.

The material and technical basis will develop and improve continuously together with the evolution of society towards the complete triumph of communism. The level of development of science and technology, and the degree of mechanisation and automation of production operations, will steadily rise.

The creation of the material and technical basis of communism will call for huge investments. The task is to utilise these investments most rationally and economically, with the maximum effect and gain of time.

1. THE DEVELOPMENT OF INDUSTRY, BUILDING, TRANSPORT, AND THEIR ROLE IN CREATING THE PRODUCTIVE FORCES OF COMMUNISM

The creation of the material and technical basis of communism, the task of making Soviet industry technologically the best and strongest in the world call for the further development of heavy industry. On this basis, all the other branches of the national economy—agriculture, the consumer goods industries, the building industry, transport and communications, as well as the branches directly concerned with services for the population—trade, public catering, health, housing, and communal services—will be technically re-equipped.

A first-class heavy industry, the basis for the country's technical progress and economic might has been built up in the Soviet Union. The C.P.S.U. will continue to devote unflagging attention to the growth of heavy industry and its technical progress. The main task of heavy industry is to meet all the needs of the country's defence and to ensure the development of industries producing consumer goods, so as to satisfy better and in full the requirements of the people, the vital demands of Soviet man, and to effect the development of the country's productive forces.

With these aims in view, the C.P.S.U. plans the following increases in *total industrial output*:

within the current 10 years, approximately 150 per cent, thus exceeding the level of U. S. industrial output;

within 20 years, not less than 500 per cent, thus leaving the present overall volume of U.S. industrial output far behind.

To achieve this, it is necessary to raise *productivity of labour* in industry by more than 100 per cent within 10 years, and by 300-350 per cent within 20 years. In 20 years' time labour productivity in Soviet industry will exceed the present level of labour productivity in the U.S.A. by roughly 100 per cent, and considerably more in terms of per-hour output, due to the reduction of the working day in the U.S.S.R.

Such an intensive development of industry will call for major progressive changes in its *structure*. The role of new branches ensuring the greatest technical progress will grow very considerably. The less effective fuels, types of power, raw and semi-manufactured materials will be increasingly superseded by highly effective ones, and their comprehensive use will increase greatly. The share of synthetic materials, metals and alloys with new properties will increase considerably. New types of automatic and electronic machinery, instruments and apparatus will be rapidly introduced on a large scale.

Electrification, which is the pivot of the economic construction of communist society, plays a key role in the development of all economic branches and in the effecting of all modern technological progress. It is therefore important to ensure the priority development of *electric power* output. The plan for the electrification of the country provides for an almost threefold increase in the power capacity per industrial worker within the present decade; a considerable expansion of industries with a high rate of power consumption through the supply of cheap power; and extensive electrification of transport, agriculture and the household in town and countryside. The electrification of the country will in the main be completed in the course of the second decade.

The annual output of electricity must be brought up to about 900,000-1,000,000 million kwh by the end of the first decade, and to 2,700,000-3,000,000 million kwh by the end of the second decade. For this it will be necessary in the course of 20 years to increase accordingly the installed capacities of electric power plants and to build hundreds of thousands of kilometres of high-tension transmission and distribution lines throughout the country. A single power grid for the whole U.S.S.R. will be built and will have sufficient capacity reserves to transmit electric power from the eastern regions to the European part of the country; it will link up with the power grids of other socialist countries.

As atomic energy becomes cheaper, the construction of atomic power stations will be expanded, especially in areas poor in other power sources, and the use of atomic energy for peaceful purposes in the national economy, in medicine and science will increase.

The further rapid expansion of the output of *metals and fuels*, the basis of modern industry, remains one of the major economic tasks. Within 20 years metallurgy will develop sufficiently to produce about 250 million tons of steel a year. Steel output must cover fully the growing requirements of the national economy in accordance with the technological progress achieved in that period. The output of light, non-ferrous and rare metals will grow very appreciably; the output of aluminium and its use in electrification, engineering, building, and the household will considerably increase. A steady effort will be made to ensure priority development of oil and gas production as these items will be used increasingly as raw materials for the chemical industry. Coal, gas, and oil extraction must meet the requirements of the national economy in full. The most progressive and economic methods of extracting mineral fuels are to be applied extensively.

One of the most important tasks is the all-round development of the *chemical* industry, and the full use in all economic fields of the achievements of modern chemistry. This provides greater opportunities to increase the national wealth and the output of new, better and cheaper capital and consumer goods. Metal, wood, and other materials will be increasingly replaced by economical, durable, light synthetic materials. The output of mineral fertilisers and chemical weed and pest killers will rise sharply.

Of primery importance for the technical re-equipment of the entire national economy is the development of *mechanical engineering*, with special stress laid on the accelerated production of automated production lines and machines, automatic, telemechanic and electronic devices and precision instruments. The designing of highly efficient machines consuming less raw materials and power and leading to higher productivity of labour will make rapid progress. The requirements of the national economy in all types of modern machines, machine tools and apparatus, as well as spare parts and instruments, will be met in full.

The development of mechanical engineering in the first decade will serve as the basis for *comprehensive mechanisation* in industry, agriculture, building, transport, and in the municipal economy. Comprehensive mechanisation will exclude manual loading and unloading jobs and strenuous labour in both the basic and auxiliary operations.

In the 20 years comprehensive *automation* will be effected on a mass scale, with increasing emphasis on fully automated shops and factories, making for high technical and economic efficiency. Introduction of the very latest systems of automated control will be speeded up. Cybernetics, electronic computer and control systems will be widely applied in production processes in industry, building and transport, in scientific research, planning, designing, accounting, statistics, and management.

The vast scope of capital construction calls for the rapid development and technological modernisation of the *building and building materials industry* up to a level meeting the requirements of the national economy, for a maximum reduction of building schedules and costs, and an improvement of the quality of building through its continuous industrialisation; it is essential to go over completely at the earliest possible time to erecting wholly prefabricated buildings and structures of standard design made of large prefabricated elements.

The C.P.S.U. will concentrate its efforts on ensuring a rapid increase in the output of *consumer goods*. The growing resources of industry must be used more and more to fully meet all the requirements of Soviet people and to build and equip enterprises and establishments catering to the household and cultural needs of the population. Along with the accelerated development of all branches of the light and food industries, the share of consumer goods in the output of heavy industry will also increase. More electricity and gas will be supplied to the population.

The growth of the national economy will call for the accelerated development of *all transport facilities*. The most important tasks in the sphere of transport are: expansion of transport and road construction to meet in full the requirements of the national economy and the population in all modes of transport; further modernisation of the railways and other transport systems; a considerable increase of the speed of rail, sea and river trafic; the coordinated development of all types of transport as components of a single transport network. The share of pipe transport will increase.

A single deep-water system will link the main inland waterways of the European part of the U.S.S.R.

A ramified network of modern roads will be built throughout the country. The automobile fleet will increase sufficiently to fully meet freight and passenger requirements; car hire centres will be organised on a large scale. Air transport will become a means of mass passenger traffic extending to all parts of the country.

Up-to-date *jet* engineering will develop rapidly, above all in air transport, as well as in space exploration.

All means of *communication* (post, radio and television, telephone and telegraph) will be developed still more. All regions of the country will have reliable communications and a link-up system of television stations.

Full-scale communist construction calls for a more rational *geographic distribution* of the industries in order to save social labour and ensure the comprehensive development of areas and the specialisation of their industries, do away with the overpopulation of big cities, facilitate the elimination of essential distinctions between town and countryside, and further even out the economic levels of different parts of the country.

To gain time, priority will be given to developing easily exploited natural resources that provide the greatest economic effect.

The industry in the areas to the *east of the Urals,* where there are immense natural riches, raw material and power resources, will expand greatly.

The following must be achieved within the next 20 years: in Siberia and Kazakhstan—the creation of new power bases using deposits of cheap coal or the water-power resources of the Angara and Yenisei rivers; the organisation of big centres of power-consuming industries, the development of new rich ore, oil, and coal deposits; and the construction of a number of new large machine-building centres; in areas along the Volga, in the Urals, North Caucasus, and Central Asia—the rapid development of the power, oil, gas, and chemical industries and the development of ore deposits. Alongside the development of the existing old metallurgical centres in the Urals and the Ukraine, the completion is envisaged of the country's third metallurgical base in Siberia, and the building of two new ones: in the central European part of the U.S.S.R., utilising the iron ore of the Kursk ironfields, and in Kazakhstan. Soviet people will be able to carry out daring plans to change the courses of some northern rivers and regulate their discharge for the purpose of utilising vast water resources for the irrigation and watering of arid areas.

The economy in the European part of the U.S.S.R. which contains the bulk of the population and where there are great opportunities for increased industrial output, will make further substantial progress.

The maximum acceleration of scientific and engineering progress is a major national task which calls for daily effort to reduce the time spent on designing new machinery and introducing it in industry. It is necessary to promote in every way the initiative of economic councils, enterprises, social organisations, scientists, engineers, designers, workers and collective farmers in creating and applying new technical improvements. Of utmost importance is the material and moral stimulation of mass invention and rationalisation movements, of enterprises, shops, state and collective farms, teams, and innovators who master the production of new machinery and utilise it skilfully.

The Party will do everything to *enhance the role of science* in the building of communist society; it will encourage research to discover new possibilities for the development of the productive forces, and the rapid and extensive application of the latest scientific and technical achievements; a decisive advancement in experimental work, including research directly at enterprises, and the efficient organisation of scientific and technical information and of the whole system of studying and disseminating progressive Soviet and foreign methods. Science will itself in full measure become a direct productive force.

The constant *improvement in the technology* of all industries and production branches is a requisite for their development. Technological progress will make man's labour easier, facilitate substantial intensification and acceleration of production and give it the highest degree of precision, will facilitate the standardisation of mass production items and maximum use of production lines. Machining will be supplemented and, when necessary, replaced by chemical methods, the technological use of electricity, electrochemistry, etc.; radio-electronics, semiconductors and ultrasound will occupy a more and more important place in production techniques. The construction of new, technically up-to-date enterprises will proceed side by side with the reconstruction of those now in existence and the replacement and modernisation of their equipment.

The development of the *specialisation and co-operation, and appropriate combination of related enterprises* is a most important condition for technical progress and the rational organisation of social labour. Articles of similar type should be manufactured mainly at large specialised plants, with provision for their most rational geographic distribution.

New techniques and the reduction of the working day call for *a higher level in the organisation of work.* Technical progress and better organisation must be fully utilised to increase labour productivity and reduce production costs at every enterprise. This implies a higher rate of increase in labour productivity as compared with the rate of growth of wages, better rate-fixing, prevention of loss of working time, and operation on a profitable basis in all sectors of production.

Most important will be systematic improvement of the qualifications of those working in industry and other branches of the economy in connection with technical progress. The planned training, instruction and rational employment of those released from various jobs and transferred to other jobs due to mechanisation and automation are essential.

Existing enterprises will be improved and developed into enterprises of communist society. Typical of this process will be new machinery, high standards of production organisation and efficiency through increased automation of production operations and the introduction of automation into control; an improvement of the cultural and technical standards of the workers, the increasing fusion of physical and mental labour and the growing proportion of engineers and technicians in every industrial enterprise; the expansion of research, and closer links between enterprises and research institutes; promotion of the emulation movement, the application of the achievements of science and the best forms of labour organisation and best methods of raising labour productivity, the extensive participation of workers' collectives in the management of enterprises, and the spreading of communist forms of labour.

2. THE DEVELOPMENT OF AGRICULTURE
AND SOCIAL RELATIONS IN THE COUNTRYSIDE

Along with a powerful industry, a flourishing, versatile and highly productive agriculture is an imperative condition for the building of communism. The Party organises a great development of productive forces in agriculture, which will make it possible to accomplish two basic, closely related tasks: (a) to build up an abundance of high-quality food products for the population and of raw materials for industry, and (b) to effect the gradual transition of social relations in the Soviet countryside to communist relations and eliminate, in the main, the distinctions between town and country.

The chief means of achieving progress in agriculture and satisfying the growing needs of the country in farm produce are comprehensive mechanisation and consistent *intensification:* high efficiency of crop farming and stock-breeding based on science and progressive experience in all kolkhozes and state farms, a steep rise in the yielding capacity of all crops and greater output per hectare with the minimum outlay of labour and funds. On this basis, it is necessary to achieve an unintermittent growth of agricultural production in keeping with the needs of society. Agriculture will approach the level of industry in technical equipment and the organisation of production; farm labour will turn into a variety of industrial labour, and the dependence of agriculture upon the elements will decrease considerably, and ultimately drop to a minimum.

The development of virgin and disused land and establishment of new large-scale state farms, the reorganisation of the machine and tractor stations, the sale of implements of production to the collective farms, introduction of new planning procedures, and the enhancement of material incentives for agricultural workers—all constituted an important stage in the development of agriculture. The Party will continue to devote considerable attention to the development of agriculture in the virgin and disused land development areas.

The further advance of the countryside to communism will proceed through the development and improvement of the two forms of socialist farming—the kolkhozes and state farms.

The *kolkhoz system* is an integral part of Soviet socialist society. It is a way charted by V. I. Lenin for the gradual transition of the peasantry to communism; it has stood the test of history and conforms to the distinctive features of the peasantry.

Kolkhoz farming accords in full with the level and needs of the development of modern productive forces in the countryside, and makes possible effective use of new machinery and the achievements of science, and rational employment of manpower. The kolkhoz blends the personal interests of the peasants with common, nation-wide interests, individual with collective interest in the results of production, and offers extensive opportunities for raising the incomes and the well-being of peasants on the basis of growing labour productivity. It is essential to make the most of the possibilities and advantages of the kolkhoz system. By virtue of the social form of its economy—its organisational structure and its democratic groundwork— which will develop more and more, the kolkhoz ensures that production is run by the kolkhoz members themselves, that their creative initiative is enhanced and that the collective farmers are educated in the communist spirit. The kolkhoz is a school of communism for the peasantry.

Economic advancement of the kolkhoz system creates conditions for the gradual *rapprochement* and, in the long run, also for the merging of kolkhoz property and the property of the whole people into one communist property.

The *state farms*, which are the leading socialist agricultural enterprises, play an ever increasing role in the development of agriculture. The state farms must serve the kolkhozes as a model of progressive, scientifically-managed, economically profitable social production, of high efficiency and labour productivity.

The C.P.S.U. proceeds from the fact that the further consolidation of the *unbreakable alliance of the working class and the kolkhoz peasantry* is of crucial political and socio-economic importance for the building of communism in the U.S.S.R.

A. Building up an abundance of agricultural produce.

In order fully to satisfy the requirements of the entire population and of the national economy in agricultural produce, the task is to increase the *aggregate volume of agricultural production* in 10 years by about 150 per cent, and in 20 years by 250 per cent. Agricultural output must keep ahead of the growing demand. In the first decade the Soviet Union will outstrip the United States in output of the key agricultural products per head of population.

Accelerated growth of *grain* production is the chief link

in the further development of all agriculture and a basis for the rapid growth of stock-breeding. The aggregate grain crops will more than double in twenty years, and their yielding capacity will double. The output of wheat, maize, cereal and leguminous crops will increase substantially.

Livestock breeding will develop at a rapid rate. The output of animal products will rise: meat about threefold in the first ten years and nearly fourfold in twenty years, and milk more than double in the first decade and nearly threefold in twenty years. The planned increase in the output of animal products will be achieved by increasing the cattle and poultry population, improving stock and productivity, and building up reliable fodder resources, chiefly maize, sugar-beet, fodder beans, and other crops.

Productivity of labour in agriculture will rise not less than 150 per cent in ten years, and five- to sixfold in twenty years. The rapid rise of the productivity of farm labour—at a higher rate than in industry—will serve to eliminate the lag of agriculture behind industry and will turn it into a highly developed branch of the economy of communist society.

The further mechanisation of agriculture, introduction of *comprehensive mechanisation* and use of automatic devices and highly efficient and economical machinery adapted to the conditions of each zone will be the basis for the growth of productivity of farm labour.

The Party considers rapid *electrification* of agriculture one of the most important tasks. All state farms and kolkhozes will be supplied electric power for production and domestic purposes, from the state power grid and from power stations to be built in the countryside.

The technical re-equipment of agriculture must combine with the most progressive forms and methods of the organisation of labour and production and the maximum improvement of the cultural and technical education of farm workers. There will be increasingly more qualified workers with special agricultural training and proficient in the use of new machinery in the kolkhozes and state farms. Good care and maintenance of agricultural machinery and its highly efficient use are extremely important.

To ensure high, stable, steadily increasing harvests, to deliver agriculture from the baneful effects of the elements, especially droughts, to steeply raise land fertility, and to rapidly advance livestock breeding, it is necessary:

to effect a scientifically expedient distribution of agriculture by natural-economic zones and districts, and a more thorough and stable *specialisation* of agriculture with priority given to the type of farm product where the best conditions for it exist and the greatest saving in outlay is achieved;

to introduce on all collective and state farms a *scientifically motivated system of land cultivation and animal husbandry* consistent with local conditions and with the specialisation of each farm, ensuring the most effective use of the land and the most economically expedient combination of branches, the best structure of crop acreage with the substitution of high-yielding and valuable crops for crops of little value and those giving low yields; to ensure that every kolkhoz and state farm master the most advanced methods of crop farming with the application of efficient crop rotation and sow high-grade seed only; to build up reliable fodder resources in all districts and to introduce the foremost stock-breeding techniques in kolkhozes and state farms;

to effect a rational *introduction of chemicals* in all branches of agriculture, to meet all its needs in mineral fertilisers and chemical and biological means of combating weeds, blights, diseases and plant and animal pests, and to ensure the best use of local fertilisers in all collective and state farms;

to apply broadly biological achievements, and especially microbiology, which is assuming ever greater importance for the improvement of soil fertility;

to carry through a far-flung *irrigation programme*: to irrigate and water millions of hectares of new land in the arid areas and improve existing irrigated farming; to expand field-protective afforestation, building of water reservoirs, watering of pastures and melioration of overmoist land; and to combat systematically the water and wind erosion of soil. Considerable attention will be devoted to the conservation and rational use of forests, water reservoirs, and other natural resources, and to their re-stocking and development.

The Party will promote the development of *agricultural science*, focus the creative efforts of scientists on the key problems of agricultural progress, and work for the practical application and extensive introduction of the achievements of science and progressive production experience in crop farming and stock-breeding. Research institutions and experimental stations are to become important links in agricultural management, and scientists and specialists must become the direct organisers of farm production. Each region or group of regions of the same zonal type should have agricultural research centres, with their own large-scale farms and up-to-date material and technical resources, to work out recommendations for collective and state farms applicable to the given district. Agricultural research and educational establishments and institutions must be chiefly located in rural areas and be directly associated with farm production, so that students may learn while working and work while learning.

B. Kolkhozes and state farms on the road to communism; remoulding social relations in the countryside.

The economic basis for the development of kolkhozes and state farms lies in the continuous growth and best use of their productive forces, improvement of the organisation of production and methods of management, steady rise of labour productivity and strict observance of the principle: higher payment for good work, for better results. On this basis the kolkhozes and state farms will become to an increasing degree enterprises of the communist type in production relations, character of labour, and the living and cultural standards of their personnel.

The policy of the Party in relation to the *kolkhozes* is based on blending country-wide interests with the material interest of the kolkhozes and their members in the results of their labour. The state will promote the growth of the productive forces of the kolkhoz system and the economic advancement of all kolkhozes; concurrently, the kolkhoz peasantry must contribute more widely to the building of communist society.

The state will ensure the full satisfaction of the needs of the kolkhozes in modern machinery, spare parts, chemicals, and other means of production, will train new hundreds of thousands of skilled farm workers, and will considerably increase capital investments in the countryside, in addition to the greater investments which the collective farms will themselves make. The amount of manufactured goods made available to the countryside will increase greatly.

Strict observance of their contracted commitments to the state by the kolkhozes and their members is an inviolable principle of their participation in the development of the national economy.

The system of state purchasing must aim at increasing the amount and improving the quality of the agricultural products bought, on the basis of an all-round advancement of kolkhoz farming. It is essential to co-ordinate the planning of state purchases and the production plans of the kolkhozes, with utmost consideration for the interests of agricultural production, its proper distribution and specialisation.

The policy in the sphere of state purchasing prices of agricultural produce and state selling prices of means of production for the countryside must take account of the interests of extended reproduction in both industry and agriculture and of the need to accumulate funds in the kolkhozes. It is essential that the level of state purchasing prices encourage the kolkhozes to raise labour productivity and reduce production expenses, since greater farm output and lower production costs are the basis of greater incomes for the kolkhozes.

The proper ratio of *accumulation and consumption* in the distribution of incomes is a prerequisite of successful kolkhoz development. The kolkhozes cannot develop without continuously extending their commonly-owned assets for production, insurance, cultural and community needs. At the same time, it must be a standing rule for every kolkhoz to raise its members' incomes from collective farming and to enhance their living standard as labour productivity rises.

Great importance attaches to improved methods of rate setting and labour remuneration at kolkhozes, supplementary remuneration of labour, and other incentives to obtain better production results. Increasingly equal economic conditions must be provided to improve the incomes of kolkhozes existing under unequal natural-economic conditions in different zones, and also within the zones, in order to put into effect more consistently the principle of equal pay for equal work on a scale embracing the entire kolkhoz system. Farming on all collective farms must be based on the principle of profitability.

In its organisational work and economic policy, the Party will strive to overcome the lag of the economically weak kolkhozes and to turn all kolkhozes into economically strong, high-income farms in the course of the next few years. The Party sets the task of continuously improving and educating kolkhoz personnel, of ensuring the further extension of kolkhoz democracy and promoting the principle of collectivism in management.

As the kolkhozes develop, their basic production facilities will expand, and modern technical means will become dominant.

The economic advancement of the kolkhozes will make it possible to perfect *kolkhoz internal relations*: to raise the degree to which production is socialised; to bring the rate setting, organisation and payment of labour closer to the level and the forms employed at state enterprises and effect a transition to a guaranteed monthly income; to develop community services more broadly (public catering, kindergartens and nurseries, and other services).

At a certain point the collective production at kolkhozes will achieve a level at which it will fully satisfy members' requirements. On this basis, supplementary individual farming will gradually become economically unnecessary. When collective production at the kolkhozes is able to replace in full production on the supplementary individual plots of the kolkhoz members, when the collective farmers see for themselves that their supplementary individual farming is unprofitable, they will give it up of their own accord.

As the productive forces increase, inter-kolkhoz production ties will develop and the socialisation of production will transcend the limits of individual kolkhozes. The building, jointly by several kolkhozes, of enterprises and cultural and welfare institutions, state-kolkhoz power stations and enterprises for the primary processing, storage, and transportation of farm products, for various types of building, the manufacture of building materials and elements, etc., should be encouraged. As the commonly-owned assets increase, the kolkhozes will participate more and more in establishing enterprises and cultural and welfare institutions for general public use, boarding-schools, clubs, hospitals and holiday homes. All these developments, which must proceed on a voluntary basis and when the necessary economic conditions are available, will gradually impart to kolkhoz-co-operative property the nature of public property.

The *state farms* have a long way to travel in their development—to increase production and improve its quality continuously, to concentrate on attaining high rates of growth of labour productivity, to steadily reduce production costs and raise farm profitability. This calls for the economically expedient specialisation of state farms. Their role in supplying food to the urban population will grow. They must become mechanised and well-organised first-class factories of grain, cotton, meat, milk, wool, vegetables, fruit, and other products, and must develop seed farming and pure-strain animal husbandry to the utmost.

The material and technical basis of the state farms will be extended and improved, and the living and cultural conditions at the state farms will approach those in towns. State-farm management should follow a more and more democratic pattern which will allot a greater role to the personnel, to general meetings and production conferences, in deciding production, cultural and other community issues.

As the kolkhozes and state farms develop, their production ties with each other and with local industrial enterprises will grow stronger. The practice of jointly organising various enterprises will expand. This will ensure a fuller and more balanced use of manpower and production resources throughout the year, raise the productivity of social labour and enhance the living and cultural standards of the population. Agrarian-industrial associations will gradually emerge wherever economically expedient, in which, given appropriate specialisation and co-operation of agricultural and industrial enterprises, agriculture will combine organically with the industrial processing of its produce.

As production in collective and state farms develops and social relations within them advance, agriculture rises to a higher level, affording the possibility of transition to communist forms of production and distribution. The kolkhozes will draw level in economic conditions with the nationally-owned agricultural enterprises. They will turn into highly developed mechanised farms. By virtue of high labour productivity all kolkhozes will become economically powerful. Kolkhoz members will be adequately provided and their requirements fully satisfied out of collective-farm production. They will have the services of catering establishments, bakeries, laundries, kindergartens and nurseries, clubs, libraries, and sports grounds. The payment of labour will be the same as at nationally-owned enterprises; they will enjoy all forms of social security (pensions, holidays, etc.) out of kolkhoz and state funds.

Gradually, the kolkhoz villages will grow into amalgamated urban communities with modern housing facilities, public amenities and services, and cultural and medical institutions. The rural population will ultimately draw level with the urban population in cultural and living conditions.

Elimination of socio-economic and cultural distinctions between town and country and of differences in their living conditions will be one of the greatest gains of communist construction.

3. MANAGEMENT OF THE NATIONAL ECONOMY AND PLANNING

The building of the material and technical basis of communism calls for a continuous improvement in economic management and planning. Chief emphasis at all levels of planning and economic management must be laid on the most rational and effective use of the material, labour and financial resources and natural wealth and on the elimination of excessive expenditure and of losses. The immutable law of economic development is to achieve in the interests of society the highest results at the lowest cost. In the improvement of economic management utmost stress is to be laid on making the apparatus of management simpler and cheaper to run.

Planning must at all levels concentrate on the rapid development and introduction of new techniques. It is essential that progressive, scientifically substantiated norms for the use of means of production be continuously improved and strictly observed in all sectors of the national economy.

The Party attaches prime importance to more *effective investments,* the choice of the most profitable and economical trends in capital construction, achievement of the maximum growth of output per invested ruble, and reduction of the time lapse between investment and return. It is necessary continuously to improve the structure of capital investments and to expand that portion of them which is spent on equipment, machinery, and machine tools.

It should be an immutable condition of planning and economic organisation to concentrate investments in the decisive sectors of industry, to eliminate scattering of allocations and to accelerate the commissioning of projects in construction.

Continuous improvement of the *quality of output* is an imperative requirement of economic development. The quality of goods produced by Soviet enterprises must be considerably higher than that of the best capitalist enterprises. For this purpose, it is necessary to apply a wide range of measures, including public control, and to enhance the role of quality indexes in planning, in the assessment of the work of enterprises and in socialist emulation.

Communist construction presupposes the maximum development of *democratic principles of management* coupled with a strengthening and improvement of *centralised economic management by the state.* The economic independence and the rights of local organs and enterprises will continue to expand within the framework of the single national economic plan. Plans and recommendations made at lower levels, beginning with enterprises, must play an increasing role in planning.

Centralised planning should chiefly concentrate on working out and ensuring the fulfilment of the key targets of the economic plans with the greatest consideration paid to recommendations made at lower levels; on co-ordinating and dovetailing plans drawn up locally; on spreading scientific and technical achievements and advanced production experience; on enforcing a single state policy in the spheres of technical progress, capital investment, distribution of industry, payment of labour, prices, and finance, and a unified system of accounting and statistics.

It is essential that the national economy develop on a strictly *proportionate* basis, that economic disproportions are prevented in good time, ensuring sufficient economic reserves as a condition for stable high rates of economic development, uninterrupted operation of enterprises and continuous improvement of the people's well-being.

The growing scale of the national economy, the rapid development of science and technology call for an improvement of the scientific level of planning, designing, accounting and statistics. A better scientific, technical and economic substantiation of the plans will ensure their greater stability, which also presupposes timely correction and amendment of plans in the course of their fulfilment. Planning must be continuous, the annual and long-term plans must be organically integrated, and the funds and material and technical resources must be provided for.

Firm and consistent discipline, day-to-day control, and determined elimination of elements of parochialism and of a narrow departmental approach in economic affairs are necessary conditions for successful communist construction.

There must be a further expansion of the role and responsibility of *local bodies* in economic management. The transfer of a number of functions of economic management by the all-Union bodies to those of the republics, by republican bodies to those of the regions and by regional bodies to those of the districts should be continued. It is necessary to improve the work of the economic councils as the most viable form of management in industry and building conforming to the present level of the productive forces. The improvement of the work of economic councils within the economic administration areas will also be accompanied by greater co-ordination of the work of the economic bodies, in order better to organise the planned, comprehensive economic development of such major economic areas as the Urals, the Volgaside area, West Siberia, East Siberia, the Far East, Transcaucasia, the Baltic area, Central Asia, etc.

Extension of the operative independence and *initiative of enterprises* on the basis of the state-plan targets is essential in order to mobilise untapped resources and make more effective use of capital investments, production facilities and finances. It is necessary to enhance the role of enterprises and stimulate their interest in introducing the latest machinery and using the production capacities to the utmost.

The selection, training and promotion of people who directly head enterprises and kolkhozes, who organise and manage production, are of decisive importance in economic management. The sphere of material production is the main sphere in the life of society; the most capable people must, therefore, be given leading posts at enterprises.

The direct and most active participation of *trade unions* in elaborating and realising economic plans, in matters concerning the labour of factory and office workers, in setting up organs of economic administration and of management of enterprises, must be extended more and more at the big centres and the localities. The role of the collectives of factory and office workers in matters concerning the work of enterprises must be enhanced.

In the process of communist construction economic management will make use of material and moral incentives for high production figures. Proper combination of material and moral labour incentives is a great creative factor in the struggle for communism. In the course of the advance to communism the importance of moral labour incentives, public recognition of achieved results and the sense of responsibility of each for the common cause will become continuously greater.

The entire system of planning and assessing the work of central and local organisations, enterprises and collective farms must stimulate their interest in higher plan targets and the maximum dissemination of progressive production experience. Initiative and successes in finding and using new ways of improving the quantitative and qualitative indexes of production should be specially encouraged.

There must be a continuous improvement in rate setting, the system of labour payments and bonuses, in the financial control over the quantity and quality of work, in the elimination of levelling, and the stimulation of collective forms of material incentives raising the interest of each employee in the high efficiency of the enterprise as a whole.

It is necessary in communist construction to make full use of commodity-money relations in keeping with their new content in the socialist period. In this, such instruments of economic development as cost accounting, money, price, production cost, profit, trade, credit, and finance play a big part. With the transition to the single communist form of people's property and the communist system of distribution, commodity-money relations will become economically outdated and will wither away.

The important role of the state budget in distributing the social product and national income will prevail throughout the period of full-scale communist construction. There will be a further strengthening of the monetary and credit system, a consolidation of Soviet currency, a steady rise of the purchasing power of the ruble and an increase in the importance of the ruble in the international arena.

It is necessary to promote profitable operation of enterprises, to work for economy and thrift, reduction of losses, lower production costs and higher profitability. The price system should be continuously improved in conformity with the tasks of communist construction, technical progress, growth of production and consumption, and the reduction of production expenditures. Prices must, to a growing extent, reflect the socially-necessary outlays of labour, ensure return of production and circulation expenditures and a certain profit for each normally operating enterprise. Systematic, economically justified price reductions based on growth of labour productivity and reduction of production costs are the main trend of the price policy in the period of communist construction.

Soviet society possesses immense national assets. For this reason, the role of accounting and control over the maintenance and proper use of the national wealth increases. Thrift, the proper use of every ruble belonging to the people, competent expenditure of funds, the continuous improvement of planning and methods of management, improvement of organisation and conscious discipline, and development of the initiative of the people are powerful means of accelerating the advance of Soviet society to communism.

II. THE TASKS OF THE PARTY IN IMPROVING THE LIVING STANDARD OF THE PEOPLE

The heroic labour of the Soviet people has produced a powerful and versatile economy. There is now every possibility to improve rapidly the living standard of the entire population—the workers, peasants, and intellectuals. The C.P.S.U. sets the historically important task of *achieving in the Soviet Union a living standard higher than that of any of the capitalist countries.*

This task will be effected by: (a) raising individual payment according to the quantity and quality of work done, coupled with reduction of retail prices and abolition of taxes paid by the population; (b) increase of the public consumption fund intended for the satisfaction of the requirements of members of society irrespective of the quantity and quality of their labour, that is, free of charge (education, medical treatment, pensions, maintenance of children at children's institutions, transition to cost-free use of public amenities, etc.).

The rise of the real incomes of the population will be outstripped by a rapid increase in the amount of commodities and services, and by extensive construction of dwellings and cultural and service buildings.

Soviet people will be more prosperous than working people in the developed capitalist countries even if average incomes will be equal, because in the Soviet Union the national income is distributed in the interests of all members of society and there are no parasitical classes as in the bourgeois countries who appropriate and squander immense wealth plundered from millions of working people.

The Party acts upon Lenin's thesis that communist construction must be based upon the principle of material incentive. In the coming twenty years payment according to one's work will remain the principal source for satisfying the material and cultural needs of the working people.

The disparity between high and comparatively low incomes must be steadily reduced. Increasingly greater numbers of unskilled personnel will become skilled, and the diminishing difference in proficiency and labour productivity will be accompanied by a steady reduction of disparities in the level of pay. As the living standard of the entire population rises, low income levels will approach the higher, and the disparity between the incomes of peasants and workers, low-paid and high-paid personnel and of the populations of different parts of the country, will gradually shrink.

At the same time, as the country advances towards communism, personal needs will be increasingly met out of public consumption funds, whose rate of growth will exceed the rate of growth of payments for labour. The transition to communist distribution will be completed after the principle of distribution according to one's work will outlive itself, that it, when there will be an abundance of material and cultural wealth and labour will become a prime necessity of life for all members of society.

(a) Provision of a high level of income and consumption for the whole population. Expansion of trade.

The national income of the U.S.S.R. in the next ten years will increase nearly 150 per cent, and about 400 per cent in twenty years. The real income per head of population will increase by more than 250 per cent in twenty years. In the first decade already the real incomes of all factory, professional and office workers (including public funds) per employed person will, on the average, be almost doubled, and the incomes of the low-paid brackets of factory and office workers will increase approximately 3-fold. Thus, by the end of the first decade there will be no low-paid brackets of factory and office workers in the country.

By virtue of higher rates of growth of the labour productivity of collective farmers their real incomes will grow more rapidly than the incomes of factory workers, and will, on an average per employed person, more than double in the next ten years and increase more than fourfold in twenty years.

The wages of such numerically large sections of the Soviet intelligentsia as engineers and technicians, agronomists and stock-breeding experts, teachers, medical and cultural workers, will rise considerably.

As the incomes of the population grow, *the general level of popular consumption will rise rapidly*. The entire population will be able adequately to satisfy its need in high-quality and varied foodstuffs. The share of animal products (meat, fats, dairy produce), fruit, and high-grade vegetables in popular consumption will rise substantially in the near future. The demand of all sections of the population for high-quality consumer goods—attractive and durable clothes, footwear and goods improving and adorning the daily life of Soviet people, such as comfortable modern furniture, up-to-date domestic goods, a wide range of goods for cultural purposes, etc.—will be amply satisfied. Production of motor-cars will be considerably extended to service the population.

Output of consumer goods must meet the growing consumer demand in full, and must conform to its changes. Timely output of goods in accordance with the varied demand of the population, with consideration for local, national and climatic conditions, is an imperative requirement for all the consumer industries.

Soviet trade will be further developed as a necessary condition to meeting the growing requirements of the people. Good shopping facilities will be made available throughout the country, and progressive forms of trading will be widely applied. The material and technical basis of Soviet trade—the network of shops, warehouses, refrigerators and vegetable stores—will be extended.

Consumer co-operatives, which are to improve trade in the countryside and to organise sales of surplus agricultural produce, will develop. Collective-farm trade will lose none of its importance.

An abundance of material and cultural benefits for the whole population will be attained in the course of the second decade, and material prerequisites will be created for the transition in the period to follow to the communist principle of distribution according to need.

(b) Solution of the housing problem and improvement of living conditions. The C.P.S.U. sets the task of solving the most acute problem in the improvement of the well-being of the Soviet people—the housing problem. In the course of the first decade an end will be put to the housing shortage in the country. Families that are still housed in overcrowded and substandard dwellings, will get new flats. At the end of the second decade, every family, including newlyweds, will have a comfortable flat conforming to the requirements of hygiene and cultural living. Peasant houses of the old type will, in the main, give place to new modern dwellings, or—wherever possible—they will be rebuilt and appropriately improved. In the course of the second decade housing will gradually become rent-free for all citizens.

Town building, architecture and planning aimed at designing modern, comfortable towns and communities, industrial projects, dwellings and public buildings economical to build and to maintain, are acquiring great importance. Towns and communities must constitute a rational and comprehensive organisation of industrial zones, residential areas, public and cultural institutions, communal services, transport, engineering equipment and power sources ensuring the best possible conditions for labour, life and leisure.

An extensive programme of public-services construction and of improvements in all towns and workers' estates will be carried out in the coming period, which will involve completion of their electrification, the necessary gasification, provision of telephone communications, public transport facilities, waterworks, sewerage, and measures for the further improvement of sanitary conditions in towns and other populated localities, including tree planting, pond building, and effective measures to combat air, soil and water pollution. Well-appointed small and middle-size towns will be increasingly developed, making for better and healthier living conditions.

Public transport facilities (tramways, buses, trolley-buses, and subways) will become free in the course of the second decade, and at the end of it such public amenities as water, gas, and heating will also be free.

(c) Reduction of working hours and the further improvement of working conditions. In the coming ten years the country will go over to *a six-hour working day* with one day off a week, or *a 35-hour working week* with two days off, and on underground jobs and enterprises with harmful working conditions to a five-hour working day or a 30-hour five-day working week.

By virtue of a corresponding rise in labour productivity, transition to a still shorter working week will be begun in the second decade.

The Soviet Union will thus have the world's shortest and, concurrently, the most productive and highest-paid working day. Working people will have much more leisure time, and this will add to their opportunities of improving their cultural and technical level.

The length of the annual paid holidays of working people will be increased together with the reduction of the working day. Gradually the minimum leave for all industrial, professional and office workers will increase to three weeks and subsequently to one month. Paid holidays will be gradually extended also to collective farmers.

All-round measures to make working conditions healthier and lighter constitute an important task in improving the well-being of the people. Modern means of labour safety and hygiene designed to prevent occupational injuries and diseases will be introduced at all enterprises. Night shifts will be gradually abolished at enterprises, save those where round-the-clock operation is required by the production process or the need to service the population.

(d) Health services and measures for increased longevity. The socialist state is the only state which undertakes to protect and continuously improve the health of the whole population. This is provided for by a system of socio-economic and medical measures. There will be an extensive programme designed to prevent and sharply reduce diseases, wipe out mass infectious diseases and further increase longevity.

The needs of the urban and rural population in all forms of highly-qualified *medical services* will be met in full. This will call for the extensive building of medical institutions, including hospitals and sanatoria, the equipment of all medical institutions with modern appliances, and regular medical check-ups for the entire population. Special emphasis must be laid on extending in town and country the network of mother-and-child health institutions (maternity homes, medical consultation centres, children's health homes and hospitals, forest schools, etc.).

In addition to the existing free medical services, accommodation of sick persons at sanatoria and the dispensing of medicines will become gratuitous.

In order to afford the population an opportunity to rest in an out-of-town environment, holiday homes, boarding-houses, country hotels, and tourist camps will be built, where working people will be accommodated at a reasonable charge or by way of a bonus, as well as at a discount or gratis.

The Party considers it a most important task to ensure the education from early childhood of a sound young generation harmoniously developed physically and spiritually. This calls for utmost encouragement of all forms of mass sport and physical training, specifically at schools, and for drawing greater and greater sections of the population, particularly the youth, into sports.

(e) Improvement of family living conditions and of the position of women. Maintenance of children and incapacitated people at public expense. The remnants of the unequal position of women in domestic life must be totally eliminated. Social and living conditions must be provided to enable women to combine happy motherhood with increasingly active and creative participation in social labour and social activities, and in scientific and artistic pursuits. Women must be given relatively lighter and yet sufficiently well-paid jobs. Confinement leave will be extended.

It is essential to provide conditions to reduce and lighten the domestic work of women, and later to make possible the replacement of domestic work by public forms of satisfying the daily needs of the family. Up-to-date inexpensive domestic machines, appliances, and electrical devices will be made extensively available for this purpose;

the needs of the population in service establishments will be fully met in the next few years.

The extension of *public catering*, including canteens at enterprises, institutions, and in big dwelling houses, until it meets the demands of the population, calls for special attention. The service at catering establishments and the quality of catering must be radically improved, so that meals at public catering establishments should be tasty and nourishing and should cost the family less than meals cooked at home. Price reductions in public catering will keep ahead of price reductions for foodstuffs in the shops. By virtue of all this public catering will be able to take precedence over home cooking within 10-15 years.

The transition to free public catering (midday meals) at enterprises and institutions, and for collective farmers at work, will begin in the second decade.

A happy childhood for every child is one of the most important and noble aspects of communist construction. The development of a ramified network of children's institutions will make it possible for more and more families, and in the second decade for every family, to keep children and adolescents free of charge at children's establishments if they so desire. The Party considers it essential that everything should be done to fully meet in the next few years the demand in children's pre-school institutions.

In town and country there will be: full and cost-free satisfaction of the population's need in nurseries, kindergartens, playgrounds, day-care schools and Young Pioneer camps; the mass provision of an extensive network of boarding-schools with free maintenance of children; free hot meals at all schools, introduction of after-school hours with free dinners for school children, and free issue of uniforms and school supplies.

In keeping with the growth of the national income, the organs of state, the trade unions, and the kolkhozes will in the course of the twenty years gradually undertake maintenance of all citizens incapacitated through old age or some disability. Sickness and disability grants and old-age pensions will be extended to kolkhoz members; old-age and disability pensions will be steadily raised. The number of comfortable homes for old people and invalids providing free accommodation for all applicants will be greatly increased in town and country.

By fulfilling the tasks set by the Party for the improvement of the well-being of the people, the Soviet Union will make considerable headway towards the practical realisation of the communist principle of distribution according to need.

At the end of the twenty years public consumption funds will total about half of the aggregate real income of the population. This will make it possible to effect at public expense:

free maintenance of children at children's institutions and boarding-schools (if parents wish);

maintenance of disabled people;

free education at all educational establishments;

free medical services for all citizens, including the supply of medicines and the treatment of sick persons at sanatoria;

rent-free housing and free communal services;

free municipal transport facilities;

free use of some types of public services;

steady reduction of charges for, and, partially, free use of holiday homes, boarding-houses, tourist camps and sports facilities;

increasingly broad provision of the population with benefits, privileges and scholarships (grants to unmarried mothers, mothers of many children, scholarships for students);

gradual introduction of free public catering (midday meals) at enterprises and institutions, and for collective farmers at work.

The Soviet state will thus demonstrate to the world a truly full satisfaction of the growing material and cultural requirements of man. The living standard of Soviet people will improve all the faster, the faster the productive forces of the country develop and labour productivity grows, and the more broadly the creative energy of the Soviet people comes into play.

The set programme can be fulfilled with success under conditions of peace. Complications in the international situation and the resultant necessity to increase defence expenditures may hold up the fulfilment of the plans for raising the living standard of the people. An enduring normalisation of international relations, reduction of military expenditures and, in particular, the realisation of general and complete disarmament under an appropriate agreement between countries, would make it possible greatly to surpass the plans for raising the people's living standard.

The fulfilment of the grand programme of improving the living standard of the Soviet people will have a worldwide historic impact. The Party calls on the Soviet people to work perseveringly, with inspiration. Every one of the working people of the Soviet Union must do his duty in the building of a communist society and in the effort to fulfil the programme for the improvement of the people's living standard.

III. THE TASKS OF THE PARTY IN THE SPHERES OF STATE DEVELOPMENT AND THE FURTHER PROMOTION OF SOCIALIST DEMOCRACY

The dictatorship of the proletariat, born of the socialist revolution, played an epoch-making role by ensuring the victory of socialism in the U.S.S.R. In the course of socialist construction, however, it underwent changes. After the exploiting classes had been abolished, the function of suppressing their resistance ceased to exist. The chief functions of the socialist state—organisation of the economy, culture and education—developed in full measure. The socialist state entered a new period of its development. The state began to grow over into a nation-wide organisation of the working people of socialist society. Proletarian democracy was growing more and more into a socialist democracy of the people as a whole.

The working class is the only class in history that does not aim to perpetuate its power.

Having brought about the complete and final victory of socialism—the first phase of communism—and the transition of society to the full-scale construction of communism, the dictatorship of the proletariat has fufilled its historic mission and has ceased to be indispensable in the U.S.S.R. from the point of view of the tasks of internal development. The state, which arose as a state of the dictatorship of the proletariat, has, in the new, contemporary stage, become a state of the entire people, an organ expressing the interests and will of the people as a whole. Since the working class is the foremost and best organised force of Soviet society, it plays a leading role also in the period of the full-scale construction of communism. The working class will have completed its role of leader of society after communism is built and classes disappear.

The Party holds that the dictatorship of the working class will cease to be necessary before the state withers away. The state as an organisation of the entire people will survive until the complete victory of communism. Expressing the will of the people, it must organise the building up of the material and technical basis of communism, and the transformation of socialist relations into communist relations, must exercise control over the measure of work and the measure of consumption, promote the people's welfare, protect the rights and freedoms of Soviet citizens, socialist law and order and socialist property, instil in the people conscious discipline and a communist attitude to labour, guarantee the defence and security of the country, promote fraternal co-operation with the socialist countries, uphold world peace, and maintain normal relations with all countries.

All-round extension and perfection of socialist democracy, active participation of all citizens in the administration of the state, in the management of economic and cultural development, improvement of the government apparatus, and increased control over its activity by the people constitute the main direction in which socialist statehood develops in the period of the building of communism. As socialist democracy develops, the organs of state power will gradually be transformed into organs of public self-government. The Leninist principle of democratic centralism, which ensures the proper combination of centralised leadership with the maximum encouragement of local initiative, the extension of the rights of the Union republics and greater creative activity of the masses, will be promoted. It is essential to strengthen discipline, constantly control the activities of all the sections of the administrative apparatus, check the execution of the decisions and laws of the Soviet state and heighten the responsibility of every official for the strict and timely implementation of these laws.

1. THE SOVIETS AND DEVELOPMENT
OF THE DEMOCRATIC PRINCIPLES OF GOVERNMENT

The role of the Soviets, which are an all-inclusive organisation of the people embodying their unity, will grow as communist construction progresses. The Soviets, which combine the features of a government body and a mass organisation of the people, operate more and more like social organisations, with the masses participating extensively and directly in their work.

The Party considers it essential to perfect the forms of popular representation and promote the democratic principles of the Soviet electoral system.

In nominating candidates for election to the Soviets, it is necessary to guarantee the widest and fullest discussion of the personal qualities and suitability of the candidates at meetings and in the press to ensure the election of the worthiest and most authoritative of them.

To improve the work of the Soviets and bring fresh forces into them, it is advisable that at least one-third of the total number of deputies to a Soviet should be elected anew each time so that *fresh millions of working people may learn to govern the state.*

The Party considers *systematic renewal of the leading bodies* necessary to bring a wider range of able persons into them and rule out abuses of authority by individual government officials. It is advisable to introduce the principle that the leading officials of the Union, republican and local bodies should be elected to their offices, as a rule, for not more than three consecutive terms. In those cases when the personal gifts of the official in question are generally believed to make his further activity within a leading body useful and necessary, his re-election may be allowed. His election shall be considered valid if not a simple majority, but not less than three-quarters of the votes are cast in his favour.

The Party regards the perfection of the principles of socialist democracy and their rigid observance as a most important task. It is necessary to ensure in full: regular accountability of Soviets and Deputies to their constituents and the right of the electorate to recall ahead of term Deputies who have not justified the confidence placed in them; publicity and the free and full discussion of all important questions of government and of economic and cultural development at the meetings of Soviets; regular accountability of executive government bodies to meetings of Soviets—from top to bottom; checking the work of these bodies and control over their activity; systematic discussion by the Soviets of questions raised by Deputies; criticism of shortcomings in the work of government, economic and other organisations.

Every Deputy to a Soviet must take an active part in government affairs and carry on definite work. The role of the standing committees of the Soviets will become greater. The standing committees of the Supreme Soviets must systematically control the activities of ministries, departments, and economic councils; they must actively contribute to the implementation of the decisions adopted by the respective Supreme Soviets. To improve the work of the legislative bodies and increase control over the executive bodies, Deputies shall be periodically released from their regular employment for committee work.

An increasing number of questions which now come under the jurisdiction of the departments and sections of executive bodies must be gradually referred to the standing committees of the local Soviets for decision.

The rights of the local Soviets of Working People's Deputies (local self-government) will be extended. Local Soviets will make final decisions on all questions of local significance.

Special attention should be paid to the strengthening of government bodies at district level. As kolkhoz-co-operative and public property draw closer together, a single democratic body administering all enterprises, organisations and institutions at district level will gradually take shape.

The participation of social organisations and associations of the people in the legislative activity of the representative bodies of the Soviet state will be extended. The trade unions, the Y.C.L. and other mass organisations as represented by their all-Union and republican bodies must be given the right to take legislative initiative, that is, to propose draft laws.

Discussion by the people of draft laws and other decisions of both national and local significance must become the rule. The most important draft laws should be put to a nation-wide referendum.

The C.P.S.U. attaches great importance to improving the work of the government apparatus, which is largely responsible for the proper utilisation of all the resorces of the country and the timely settlement of all questions relating to the cultural and everyday needs of the people. The Soviet government apparatus must be simple, qualified, inexpensive, efficient and free of bureaucracy, formalism and red tape.

Constant state and public control is an important means of accomplishing this task. In keeping with Lenin's directions, control bodies must function permanenty to combine state control with public inspection at the centre and in the localities. The Party regards inspection by people's control bodies as an effective means of drawing large sections of the people into the management of state affairs and control over the strict observance of legality, as a means of perfecting the government apparatus, eradicating bureaucracy and promptly realising proposals made by the people.

The government apparatus of the socialist state serves the people and is accountable to them. Negligence, abuse of power and red tape by an official must be resolutely combated and the official concerned must be severely punished regardless of the position he holds. It is the duty of Soviet people to see to it that legality and law and order are rigidly enforced; they must not tolerate any abuses, and must combat them.

The Party holds that democratic principles in *administration* must be developed further. The principle of electivity and accountability to representative bodies and to the electorate will be gradually extended to all the leading officials of state bodies.

An effort should be made to ensure that the salaried government staffs are reduced, that ever larger sections of the people learn to take part in administration and that work on government staffs eventually cease to constitute a profession.

While every executive must be held strictly and personally responsible for the job entrusted to him, it is necessary consistently to exercise the principle of collective leadership at all levels of the government and economic apparatus.

The broadest democracy must go hand in hand with strict observance of comradely discipline by the working people, and should promote such discipline and control from above and from below. The important thing in the activity of all government bodies is organisational work among the masses, proper selection, testing and appraisal of officials on the strength of their practical work, and control over the actual fulfilment of the assignments and decisions of the leading bodies.

The further *promotion of socialist law and order* and the improvement of legal rules governing economic organisation, cultural and educational work and contributing to the accomplishment of the tasks of communist construction and to the all-round development of the individual are very important.

The transition to communism means the fullest extension of personal freedom and the rights of Soviet citizens. Socialism has brought the working people the broadest guaranteed rights and freedoms. Communism will bring the working people further great rights and opportunities.

The Party's objective is to enforce strict observance of socialist legality, eradicate all violations of law and order, abolish crime and remove all the causes of crime.

Justice in the U.S.S.R. is exercised in full conformity with the law. It is based on truly democratic lines: election and accountability of the judges and people's assessors, the right to recall them before expiry of their term, the publicity of court proceedings, and the participation of prosecutors and advocates from the general public in the work of the courts, with the courts and investigating and prosecuting bodies strictly observing legality and all the norms of judicial procedure. The democratic foundations of justice will be developed and improved.

There should be no room for law breakers and criminals in a society building communism. But as long as there are criminal offences, it is necessary severely to punish those who commit crimes dangerous to society, violate the rules of the socialist community and refuse to live by honest labour. Attention should be mainly focussed on crime prevention.

Higher standards of living and culture, and greater social consciousness of the people, pave the way to the abolition of crime and the ultimate replacement of judicial punishment by measures of public influence and education. Under socialism, anyone who has strayed from the path of the working man can return to useful activity.

The whole system of government and social organisations educates the people in a spirit of voluntary and conscientious fulfilment of their duties and leads to a natural fusion of rights and duties to form single standards of communist behaviour.

2. THE FURTHER HEIGHTENING OF THE ROLE OF SOCIAL ORGANISATIONS. THE STATE AND COMMUNISM

The role of social organisations increases in the period of the full-scale construction of communism. The *trade unions* acquire particular importance as schools of administration and economic management, as schools of communism. The Party will help the trade unions to take a growing share in economic management and to make the standing production conferences increasingly effective in improving the work of enterprises and exercising control over production. The trade unions shall:

work constantly to increase the communist consciousness of the masses; organise an emulation movement for communist labour and help the working people in learning to manage state and social affairs; take an active part in controlling the measure of labour and the measure of consumption;

encourage the activity of factory and office workers, enlisting their aid in the work for continuous technical progress, for higher productivity of labour, for the fulfilment and overfulfilment of state plans and assignments;

work steadfastly for the improvement of the skill of factory and office workers and their working and living conditions; protect the material interests and rights of the working people;

ensure that housing and cultural development plans are fulfilled and that public catering, trade, social insurance, and health resort services are improved;

ensure control over the spending of public consumption funds and over the work of all enterprises and institutions serving the people;

improve cultural services and recreation facilities for the working people; encourage physical training and sports.

The *Young Communist League,* an independently acting public organisation of the youth which helps the Party to educate young people in a communist spirit, enlist them in the practical job of building the new society and train a generation of harmoniously developed people who will live, work and manage public affairs under communism, will play a greater role. The Party regards the youth as a great creative force in the Soviet people's struggle for communism.

The Y.C.L. must display still greater initiative in all spheres of life, must encourage the activity and labour heroism of the youth. Y.C.L. organisations must concentrate on educating the youth in a spirit of utmost devotion to their country, the people, the Communist Party and the communist cause, constant preparedness for labour for the good of society and for overcoming all difficulties and improving the general education and technical knowledge of all young men and women. It is the sacred duty of the Y.C.L. to prepare young people for the defence of their socialist country, to educate them as selfless patriots capable of firmly repelling any enemy. The Y.C.L. educates the youth in a spirit of strict adherence to communist moral principles and standards. Its activities in the schools and Young Pioneer organisations must contribute to the moulding of a buoyant, industrious, and physically and morally sound generation.

A greater role will be played by *co-operatives*—kolkhozes, consumers', housing and other co-operative organisations—as a form of drawing the masses into communist construction, as media of communist education and schools of public self-government.

Other social associations of the working people—scientific, scientific-technical and popular-science societies, rationalisers' and inventors' organisations, associations of writers, art workers and journalists, cultural-education organisations, and sports societies—will likewise be developed.

The Party regards it as a major task of the social organisations to promote labour emulation in every possible way, and to encourage communist forms of labour, to stimulate the activity of working people in building a communist society, to work for the improvement of the living conditions of the people and the satisfaction of their growing spiritual requirements. Mass organisations should be given a greater part in managing cultural, health and social insurance institutions; within the next few years they should be entrusted with the management of theatres and concert halls, clubs, libraries, and other state-controlled cultural-education establishments; they should be encouraged to play a greater part in promoting law and order, particularly through the people's volunteer squads and comradely courts.

To extend the independent activities of mass organisations, the Party considers it necessary further to reduce their salaried staffs from top to bottom, to renew each elective body by roughly as many as one-half of its membership at the regular election. It is advisable for the leading functionaries of social organisations not to be elected, as a general rule, for more than two consecutive terms.

As socialist statehood develops, it will gradually become *communist self-government* of the people which will embrace the Soviets, trade unions, co-operatives, and other mass organisations of the people. This process will represent a still greater development of democracy, ensuring the active participation of all members of society in the management of public affairs. Public functions similar to those performed by the state today in the sphere of economic and cultural management will be preserved under communism and will be modified and perfected as society develops. But the character of the functions and the ways in which they are carried out will be different from those under socialism. The bodies in charge of planning, accounting, economic management, and cultural advancement, now government bodies, will lose their political character and will become organs of public self-government. Communist society will be a highly-organised community of working men. Universally recognised rules of the communist way of life will be established whose observance will become an organic need and habit with everyone.

Historical development inevitably leads to the withering away of the state. To ensure that the state withers away completely, it is necessary to provide both internal conditions—the building of a developed communist society—and external conditions—the victory and consolidation of socialism in the world arena.

3. THE STRENGTHENING OF THE ARMED FORCES AND THE DEFENCE POTENTIAL OF THE SOVIET UNION

With the wholehearted support of the entire Soviet people, the Communist Party of the Soviet Union steadfastly upholds and defends the gains of socialism and the cause of world peace, and works tirelessly to deliver mankind for all time from wars of aggression. The Leninist principle of peaceful coexistence of states with different social systems always has been, and remains, the general principle of the foreign policy of the Soviet state.

The Soviet Union perseveringly seeks to bring about the realisation of its proposals for general and complete disarmament under strict international control. But the imperialist countries stubbornly refuse to accept these proposals, and feverishly build up their armed forces. They refuse to reconcile themselves to the existence of the world socialist system, and openly proclaim their insane plans for the liquidation of the Soviet Union and the other socialist states through war. This obliges the Communist Party, the Armed Forces, the state security organs and all the peoples of the U.S.S.R. to be keenly vigilant with regard to the aggressive intrigues of the enemies of peace, always to protect peaceful labour, and to be constantly prepared to take up arms in defence of their country.

The Party maintains that as long as imperialism exists the threat of aggressive wars will remain. The C.P.S.U. regards the defence of the socialist motherland, and the strengthening of the defence potential of the U.S.S.R., of the might of the Soviet Armed Forces, as a sacred duty of the Party and the Soviet people as a whole, as a most important function of the socialist state. The Soviet Union sees it as its internationalist duty to guarantee, together with the other socialist countries, the reliable defence and security of the entire socialist camp.

In terms of internal conditions, the Soviet Union needs no army. But since the danger of war coming from the imperialist camp persists, and since complete and general disarmament has not been achieved, the C.P.S.U. considers it necessary to maintain the defensive power of the Soviet state and the combat preparedness of its Armed Forces at a level ensuring the decisive and complete defeat of any enemy who dares to encroach upon the Soviet land. The Soviet state will see to it that its Armed Forces are powerful, that they have the most up-to-date means of defending the country—atomic and thermonuclear weapons, rockets of every range, and that they keep all types of military equipment and all weapons up to standard.

The Party educates the Communists and all Soviet people in the spirit of constant preparedness for the defence of their socialist country, of love of their armed forces. It will promote in every way the further development of voluntary mass defence organisations. Defence of the country, and service in the Soviet Armed Forces, is the lofty and honourable duty of Soviet citizens.

The C.P.S.U. is doing everything to ensure that the Soviet Armed Forces are a well-knit and smoothly operating organism, that they have a high standard of organisation and discipline, carry out in exemplary fashion the tasks assigned them by the Party, the Government, the people, and are prepared at any moment to administer a crushing rebuff to imperialist aggressors. One-man leadership is a major principle of the organisation of the Soviet Armed Forces.

The Party will work indefatigably to train Army and Navy officers and political and technical personnel fully devoted to the communist cause and recruited among the finest representatives of the Soviet people. It considers it necessary for the officer corps tirelessly to master Marxist-Leninist theory, to possess a high standard of military-technical training, meet all the requirements of modern military theory and practice, strengthen military discipline. All Soviet soldiers must be educated in the spirit of unqualified loyalty to the people, to the communist cause, of readiness to spare no effort and, if necessary, to give their lives in the defence of their socialist country.

Party leadership of the Armed Forces and the increasing role and influence of the Party organisations in the Army and Navy are the bedrock of military development. The Party works unremittingly to increase its organising and guiding influence on the entire life and activity of the Army, Air Force and Navy, to rally the servicemen round the Communist Party and the Soviet Government, to strengthen the unity of the Armed Forces and the people, and to educate the soldiers in the spirit of courage, bravery, heroism and comradeship with the armies of the socialist countries, of readiness at any moment to take up the defence of their Soviet country, which is building communism.

IV. THE TASKS OF THE PARTY
IN THE FIELD OF NATIONAL RELATIONS

Under socialism the nations flourish and their sovereignty grows stronger. The development of nations does not proceed along lines of strengthening national strife, national narrow-mindedness and egoism, as it does under capitalism, but along lines of their association, fraternal mutual assistance and friendship. The appearance of new industrial centres, the prospecting and development of mineral deposits, virgin land development, and the growth of all modes of transport increase the mobility of the population and promote greater intercourse between the peoples of the Soviet Union. People of many nationalities live together and work in harmony in the Soviet republics. The boundaries between the Union republics of the U.S.S.R. are increasingly losing their former significance, since all the nations are equal, their life is based on a common socialist foundation, the material and spiritual needs of every people are satisfied to the same extent, and they are all united in a single family by common vital interests and are advancing together to the common goal—communism. Spiritual features deriving from the new type of social relations and embodying the finest traditions of the peoples of the U.S.S.R. have taken shape and are common to Soviet men and women of different nationalities.

Full-scale communist construction constitutes a new stage in the development of national relations in the U.S.S.R. in which the nations will draw still closer together until complete unity is achieved. The building of the material and technical basis of communism leads to still greater unity of the Soviet peoples. The exchange of material and spiritual values between nations becomes more and more intensive, and the contribution of each republic to the common cause of communist construction increases. Obliteration of distinctions between classes and the development of communist social relations make for a greater social homogeneity of nations and contribute to the development of common communist traits in their culture, morals and way of living, to a further strengthening of their mutual trust and friendship.

With the victory of communism in the U.S.S.R., the nations will draw still closer together, their economic and ideological unity will increase and the communist traits common to their spiritual make-up will develop. However, the obliteration of national distinctions, and especially of language distinctions, is a considerably longer process than the obliteration of class distinctions.

The Party approaches all questions of national relationships arising in the course of communist construction from the standpoint of proletarian internationalism and firm pursuance of the Leninist nationalities policy. The Party neither ignores nor over-accentuates national characteristics.

The Party sets the following tasks in the sphere of national relations:

(a) to continue the all-round economic and cultural development of all the Soviet nations and nationalities, ensuring their increasingly close fraternal co-operation, mutual aid, unity and affinity in all spheres of life, thus achieving the utmost strengthening of the Union of Soviet Socialist Republics; to make full use of, and advance the forms of, national statehood of the peoples of the U.S.S.R.;

(b) in the economic sphere, it is necessary to continue the line of comprehensive development of the economies of the Soviet republics, effect a rational geographic location of production and a planned working of natural wealth, and promote socialist division of labour among the republics, unifying and combining their economic efforts, and properly balancing the interests of the state as a whole and those of each Soviet republic. The extension of the rights of the Union republics in economic management having produced substantial positive results, such measures may also be carried out in the future with due regard to the fact that the creation of the material and technical basis of communism will call for still greater interconnection and mutual assistance between the Soviet republics. The closer the intercourse between the nations and the greater the awareness of the country-wide tasks, the more successfully can manifestations of parochialism and national egoism be overcome.

In order to ensure the successful accomplishment of the tasks of communist construction and the co-ordination of economic activities, inter-republican economic organs may be set up in some zones (notably for such matters as irrigation, power grids, transport, etc.).

The Party will continue its policy ensuring the actual equality of all nations and nationalities with full consideration for their interests and devoting special attention to those areas of the country which are in need of more rapid development. Benefits accumulating in the course of communist construction must be fairly distributed among all nations and nationalities;

(c) to work for the further all-round development of the socialist cultures of the peoples of the U.S.S.R. The big scale of communist construction and the new victories of communist ideology are enriching the cultures of the peoples of the U.S.S.R., which are socialist in content and national in form. There is a growing ideological unity among the nations and nationalities and a greater rapprochement of their cultures. The historical experience of socialist nations shows that national forms do not ossify; they change, advance and draw closer together, shedding all outdated traits that contradict the new conditions of life. An international culture common to all the Soviet nations is developing. The cultural treasures of each nation are increasingly augmented by works acquiring an international character.

Attaching decisive importance to the development of the socialist content of the cultures of the peoples of the

U.S.S.R., the Party will promote their further mutual enrichment and rapprochement, the consolidation of their international basis, and thereby the formation of the future single world-wide culture of communist society. While supporting the progressive traditions of each people, and making them the property of all Soviet people, the Party will in all ways further new revolutionary traditions of the builders of communism common to all nations;

(d) to continue promoting the free development of the languages of the peoples of the U.S.S.R. and the complete freedom for every citizen of the U.S.S.R. to speak, and to bring up and educate his children, in any language, ruling out all privileges, restrictions or compulsions in the use of this or that language. By virtue of the fraternal friendship and mutual trust of peoples, national languages are developing on a basis of equality and mutual enrichment.

The voluntary study of Russian in addition to the native language is of positive significance, since it facilitates reciprocal exchanges of experience and access of every nation and nationality to the cultural gains of all the other peoples of the U.S.S.R., and to world culture. The Russian language has, in effect, become the common medium of intercourse and co-operation between all the peoples of the U.S.S.R;

(e) to pursue consistently as heretofore the principles of internationalism in the field of national relations; to strengthen the friendship of peoples as one of the most important gains of socialism; to conduct a relentless struggle against manifestations and survivals of nationalism and chauvinism of all types, against trends of national narrow-mindedness and exclusiveness, idealisation of the past and the veiling of social contradictions in the history of peoples, and against customs and habits hampering communist construction. The growing scale of communist construction calls for the continuous exchange of trained personnel among nations. Manifestations of national aloofness in the education and employment of workers of different nationalities in the Soviet republics are impermissible. The elimination of manifestations of nationalism is in the interests of all nations and nationalities of the U.S.S.R. Every Soviet republic can continue to flourish and strengthen only in the great family of fraternal socialist nations of the U.S.S.R.

V. THE TASKS OF THE PARTY IN THE SPHERES OF IDEOLOGY, EDUCATION, INSTRUCTION, SCIENCE, AND CULTURE

Soviet society has made great progress in the socialist education of the masses, in the moulding of active builders of socialism. But even after the socialist system has triumphed there persist in the minds and behaviour of people survivals of capitalism, which hamper the progress of society.

In the struggle for the victory of communism, ideological work becomes an increasingly powerful factor. The higher the social consciousness of the members of society, the more fully and broadly their creative activities come into play in the building of the material and technical basis of communism, in the development of communist forms of labour and new relations between people, and, consequently, the more rapidly and successfully the building of communism proceeds.

The Party considers that the paramount task in the ideological field in the present period is to educate all working people in a spirit of ideological integrity and devotion to communism, and cultivate in them a communist attitude to labour and the social economy; to eliminate completely the survivals of bourgeois views and morals; to ensure the all-round, harmonious development of the individual; to create a truly rich spiritual culture. Special importance is attached by the Party to the moulding of the rising generation.

The moulding of the new man is effected through his own active participation in communist construction and the development of communist principles in the economic and social spheres, under the influence of the educational work carried out by the Party, the state, and various social organisations, work in which the press, radio, cinema, and television play an important part. As communist forms of social organisation are created, communist ideas will become more firmly rooted in life and work and in human relations, and people will develop the ability to enjoy the benefits of communism in a rational way. Joint planned labour by the members of society, their daily participation in the management of state and public affairs, and the development of communist relations of comradely co-operation and mutual support, recast the minds of people in a spirit of collectivism, industry, and humanism.

Increased communist consciousness of the people furthers the ideological and political unity of the workers, collective farmers, and intellectuals and promotes their gradual fusion in the single collective of the working people of communist society.

The Party sets the following tasks:

1. IN THE FIELD OF DEVELOPMENT OF COMMUNIST CONSCIOUSNESS

(a) The Shaping of a Scientific World Outlook. Under socialism and at a time when a communist society is being built, when spontaneous economic development has given way to the conscious organisation of production and social life as a whole, and when theory is daily translated into practice, it is of prime importance that a scientific world outlook be shaped in all working people of Soviet society on the basis of Marxism-Leninism, an integral and harmonious system of philosophical, economic and socio-political views. The Party calls for the education of the population as a whole in the spirit of scientific communism and strives to ensure that all working people fully understand the course and perspectives of world development, that they take a correct view of international and domestic events and consciously build their life on communist lines. Communist ideas and communist deeds should blend organically in the behaviour of every person and in the activities of all collectives and organisations.

The theoretical elaboration and timely practical solution of new problems raised by life are essential to the successful advance of society to communism. Theory must continue to illumine the road of practice, and help detect and eliminate obstacles and difficulties hindering successful communist construction. The Party regards it as one of its most important duties to further elaborate Marxist-Leninist theory by studying and generalising new phenomena in the life of Soviet society and the experience of the world revolutionary working-class and liberation movements, and creatively to combine the theory and the practice of communist construction.

(b) Labour Education. The Party sees the development of a communist attitude to labour in all members of society as its chief educational task. Labour for the benefit of society is the sacred duty of all. Any labour for society, whether physical or mental, is honourable and commands respect. Exemplary labour and management in the social economy should serve to educate all working people.

Everything required for life and human progress is created by labour. Hence every able-bodied man must take part in creating the means which are indispensable for his life and work and for the welfare of society. Anyone who received any benefits from society without doing his share of work, would be a parasite living at the expense of others.

It is impossible for a man in communist society not to work, for neither his social consciousness, nor public opinion would permit it. Work according to one's ability will become a habit, a prime necessity of life, for every member of society.

(c) The Affirmation of Communist Morality. In the course of transition to communism, the moral principles of society become increasingly important; the sphere of action of the moral factor expands and the importance of the administrative control of human relations diminishes accordingly. The Party will encourage all forms of conscious civic self-discipline leading to the assertion and promotion of the basic rules of the communist way of life.

The Communists reject the class morality of the exploiters; in contrast to the perverse, selfish views and morals of the old world, they promote communist morality, which is the noblest and most just morality, for it expresses the interests and ideals of the whole of working mankind. Communism makes the elementary standards of morality and justice, which were distorted or shamelessly flouted under the rule of the exploiters, inviolable rules for relations both between individuals and between peoples. Communist morality encompasses the fundamental norms of human morality which the masses of the people evolved in the course of millenniums as they fought against vice and social oppression. The revolutionary morality of the working class is of particular importance to the moral advancement of society. As socialist and communist construction progresses, communist morality is enriched with new principles, a new content.

The Party holds that *the moral code of the builder of communism* should comprise the following principles:

devotion to the communist cause; love of the socialist motherland and of the other socialist countries;

conscientious labour for the good of society—he who does not work, neither shall he eat;

concern on the part of everyone for the preservation and growth of public wealth;

a high sense of public duty; intolerance of actions harmful to the public interest;

collectivism and comradely mutual assistance: one for all and all for one;

humane relations and mutual respect between individuals—man is to man a friend, comrade and brother;

honesty and truthfulness, moral purity, modesty, and unpretentiousness in social and private life;

mutual respect in the family, and concern for the up-bringing of children;

an uncompromising attitude to injustice, parasitism, dishonesty, careerism and money-grubbing;

friendship and brotherhood among all peoples of the U.S.S.R.; intolerance of national and racial hatred;

an uncompromising attitude to the enemies of communism, peace and the freedom of nations;

fraternal solidarity with the working people of all countries, and with all peoples.

(d) The Promotion of Proletarian Internationalism and Socialist Patriotism. The Party will untiringly educate Soviet people in the spirit of proletarian internationalism and will vigorously promote the international solidarity of the working people. In fostering the Soviet people's love of their country, the Party maintains that with the emergence of the world socialist system the patriotism of the members of socialist society is expressed in devotion and loyalty to their own country and to the entire community of socialist countries. Socialist patriotism and socialist internationalism necessarily imply proletarian solidarity with the working class and all working people of all countries. The Party will continue perseveringly to combat the reactionary ideology of bourgeois nationalism, racism, and cosmopolitanism.

(e) All-Round and Harmonious Development of the Individual. In the period of transition to communism, there are greater opportunities of *educating a new man, who will harmoniously combine spiritual wealth, moral purity and a perfect physique.*

All-round development of the individual has been made possible by historic social gains—freedom from exploitation, unemployment and poverty, from discrimination on account of sex, origin, nationality or race. Every member of society is provided with equal opportunities for education and creative labour. Relations of dependence and inequality between people in public affairs and in family life disappear. The personal dignity of each citizen is protected by society. Each is guaranteed an equal and free choice of occupation and profession with due regard to the interests of society. As less and less time is spent on material production, the individual is afforded ever greater opportunities to develop his abilities, gifts, and talents in the fields of production, science, engineering, literature, and the arts. People will increasingly devote their leisure to public pursuits, cultural intercourse, intellectual and physical development, scientific, technical and artistic endeavour. Physical training and sports will become part and parcel of the everyday life of people.

(f) Elimination of the Survivals of Capitalism in the Minds and Behaviour of People. The Party considers it an integral part of its communist education work to combat manifestations of bourgeois ideology and morality, and the remnants of private-owner psychology, superstitions, and prejudices.

The general public, public opinion, and extensive criticism and self-criticism must play a big role in combating survivals of the past and manifestations of individualism and selfishness. Comradely censure of anti-social behaviour will gradually become the principal means of doing away with manifestations of bourgeois views, customs and habits. The power of example in public affairs and in private life, in the performance of one's public duty, acquires tremendous educational significance.

The Party uses ideological media to educate people in the spirit of a scientific materialist world conception, to overcome religious prejudices without insulting the sentiments of believers. It is necessary to conduct regularly broad atheistic propaganda on a scientific basis, to explain patiently the untenability of religious beliefs, which were engendered in the past when people were overawed by the elemental forces and social oppression and did not know the real causes of natural and social phenomena. This can be done by making use of the achievements of modern science, which is steadily solving the mysteries of the universe and extending man's power over nature, leaving no room for religious inventions about supernatural forces.

(g) The Exposure of Bourgeois Ideology. The peaceful coexistence of states with different social systems does not imply any easing of the ideological struggle. The Communist Party will go on *exposing the anti-popular, reactionary nature of capitalism* and all attempts to paint bright pictures of the capitalist system.

The Party will *steadfastly propagate the great advantages of socialism and communism over the declining capitalist system.*

The Party advances the scientific ideology of communism in contrast to reactionary bourgeois ideology. Communist ideology, which expresses the fundamental interests of the working class and all working people, teaches them to struggle, to live and work, for the happiness of all. It is the most humane ideology. Its ideals are to establish truly human relations between individuals and peoples, to deliver mankind from the threat of wars of extermination, and bring about universal peace and a free, happy life for all men on earth.

2. IN THE FIELD OF PUBLIC EDUCATION

The transition to communism implies training that will make people communist-minded and highly-cultured, people fitted for both physical and mental labour, for active work in various social, governmental, scientific, and cultural spheres.

The system of public education is so organised as to ensure that the instruction and education of the rising generation are closely bound up with life and productive labour, and that the adult population can combine work in the sphere of production with further training and education in keeping with their vocations and the requirements of society. Public education along these lines will make for the moulding of harmoniously developed members of communist society and for the solution of a cardinal social problem, namely, the elimination of substantial distinctions between mental and physical labour.

The main tasks in the field of instruction and education are:

(a) Introduction of Universal Compulsory Secondary Education. In the next decade compulsory secondary general and polytechnical eleven-year education is to be introduced for all children of school age, and eight-year education for young people engaged in the national economy who have not had the appropriate schooling; in the subsequent decade every one will have the opportunity to receive a complete secondary education. Universal secondary education is guaranteed by the development of general and polytechnical education, professional training combined with socially useful labour of school children to the extent of their physical capacity, and a considerable expansion of the network of all types of general schools, including evening schools, which provide a secondary education in off-work hours.

Secondary education must furnish a solid knowledge of the fundamentals of the basic sciences, an understanding of the principles of the communist world outlook, and a labour and polytechnical training in accordance with the rising level of science and engineering, with due regard to the needs of society and to the abilities and inclinations of the students, as well as the moral, aesthetic and physical education of a healthy rising generation.

In view of the rapid progress of science and engineering, the system of industrial, professional and vocational training should be improved continuously, so that the skills of those engaged in production may develop together with their better general education in the social and natural sciences and with the acquisition of specialised knowledge in engineering, agronomy, medicine, and other fields.

(b) The Public Upbringing of Children of Pre-School and

School Age. The communist system of public education is based on the public upbringing of children. The educational influence which the family exerts on children must be brought into ever greater harmony with their public upbringing.

The growing number of pre-school institutions and boarding-schools of different types will fully meet the requirements of all working people who wish to give their children of pre-school and school age a public upbringing. The importance of the school, which is to cultivate love of labour and knowledge in children and to raise the younger generation in the spirit of communist consciousness and morality, will increase. An honourable and responsible role in this respect falls to teachers, and to the Komsomol and Young Pioneer organisations.

(c) Creation of Conditions for High-Standard Instruction and Education of the Rising Generation. The Party plans to carry out an extensive programme for the construction of schools and cultural-education establishments to meet fully the needs of education and instruction. All schools will be housed in good buildings and will go over to a one-shift time-table. They will all have study workshops and chemical, physical and other laboratories; rural schools will also have their own farming plots; large factories will have production training shops for school children. Modern facilities—cinema, radio, and television—will be widely used in schools.

For physical training and aesthetic education, all schools and extra-scholastic establishments will have gymnasiums, sports grounds and facilities for the creative endeavour of children in music, painting, sculpture, etc. The network of sports schools, sports grounds, tourist camps, skiing centres, aquatic stations, swimming-pools, and other sports facilities will be expanded in town and countryside.

(d) Higher and Secondary Special Education. In step with scientific and technical progress, higher and secondary special education, which must train highly-skilled specialists with a broad theoretical and political background, will be expanded.

Shorter working hours and a considerable improvement in the standard of living of the entire population will provide everyone with an opportunity to receive a higher or secondary special education if he so desires. The number of higher and secondary specialised schools, evening and correspondence schools in particular, as well as higher schools at factories, agricultural institutes (on large state farms), studios, conservatoires, etc., must be increased in all areas of the country with the support of factories and trade unions and other social organisations. The plan is to considerably increase every year the number of students at higher and secondary specialised schools; special education will be afforded to tens of millions of people.

3. IN THE FIELD OF SCIENCE

Under the socialist system of economy, scientific and technical progress enables man to employ the riches and forces of nature most effectively in the interests of the people, to discover new forms of energy and to create new materials, to develop means of weather control, and to master outer space. Application of science in production becomes a decisive factor of rapid growth of the productive forces of society. Scientific progress and the introduction of scientific achievements into the economy will remain an object of special concern to the Party.

Most important are the following tasks:

(a) Development of Theoretical Investigations. The further perspectives of scientific and technical progress depend in the present period primarily on the achievements of *the key branches of natural science.* A high level of development in *mathematics, physics, chemistry, and biology* is a necessary condition for the advancement and the effectiveness of the technical, medical, agricultural, and other sciences.

Theoretical research will be promoted to the utmost, primarily in such decisive fields of technical progress as electrification of the whole country, comprehensive mechanisation and automation of production, transport and communications, the application of chemistry to the leading branches of the national economy, industrial uses of atomic energy. This applies to:

studying the power and fuel balance of the country, finding the best ways and means of utilising the natural sources of power, working out the scientific fundamentals of a single power grid, discovering new power sources and developing methods of direct conversion of thermal, nuclear, solar, and chemical energy into electric power, and solving problems related to control of thermonuclear reactions;

working out the theory and principles of designing new machines, automatic and telemechanical systems, intensively developing radioelectronics, elaborating the theoretical foundations of computing, control and information machines, and technically improving them;

investigating chemical processes, working out new, more efficient technologies and creating inexpensive high-quality artificial and synthetic materials for all branches of the national economy: mechanical engineering, building, the manufacture of household goods and mineral fertilisers, and creating new preparations for use in medicine and agriculture;

improving existing methods and devising new, more effective methods of prospecting minerals and making comprehensive use of natural wealth.

Big advances are to be made in the development of all the biological sciences in order successfully to solve medical problems and achieve further progress in agriculture. The main tasks to be solved by these sciences in the interests of mankind are: ascertainment of the essence of the phenomena of life, the biological laws governing the development of the organic world, study of the physics and chemistry of living matter, elaboration of various methods of controlling vital processes, in particular, metabolism, heredity and directed changes in organisms. It is essential to develop more broadly and deeply the Michurin line in biology, which is based on the proposition that conditions of life are primary in the development of the organic world. Medicine must concentrate on discovering means of preventing and conquering cancer, virulent, cardio-vascular, and other dangerous diseases. It is important to study and extensively use micro-organisms in the economy and the health services, among other things for the production of foods and feedstuffs, vitamins, antibiotics and enzymes, and for the development of new agricultural techniques.

Artificial earth satellites and spaceships have, by enabling man to penetrate into outer space, provided great opportunities of discovering new natural phenomena and laws and of investigating the planets and the sun.

In the age of rapid scientific progress, the elaboration of the philosophical problems of modern natural science on the basis of dialectical materialism, the only scientific method of cognition, becomes still more urgent.

There must be intensive development of research work in the *social sciences*, which constitute the scientific basis for the guidance of the development of society. Most important in this field is the study and theoretical generalisation of the experience gained in communist construction; investigation of the key objective laws governing the economic, political and cultural progress of socialism and its development into communism, and elaboration of the problems of communist education.

The task of economic science is to generalise new phenomena in the economic life of society, and to work out the national economic problems whose solution promotes successful communist construction. Economists must concentrate on finding the most effective ways of utilising material and labour resources in the economy, the best methods of planning and organising industrial and agricultural production, and elaborating the principles of a rational distribution of the productive forces and of the technical and economic problems of communist construction.

The investigation of the problems of world history and contemporary world development must disclose the law-governed process of mankind's advance towards communism, the change in the balance of forces in favour of socialism, the aggravation of the general crisis of capitalism, the break-up of the colonial system of imperialism and its consequences, and the upsurge of the national-liberation movement of peoples.

It is important to study the historical experience of the Communist Party and the Soviet people, tried and proved successful in practice, the objective laws of development of the world socialist system and the world Communist and working-class movement.

It is essential, in the future as well, to firmly defend and develop dialectical and historical materialism as the science of the most general laws of development of nature, society and human thinking.

The social sciences must continue to struggle with determination against bourgeois ideology, against Right-Socialist theory and practice, and against revisionism and dogmatism; they must uphold the purity of the principles of Marxism-Leninism.

(b) Ties Between Science and Production. Close ties with the creative labour of the people and the practice of communist construction are an earnest of a fruitful development of science.

In conformity with the requirements of economic and cultural development, it is essential to extend and improve the network of research institutions, including those attached to the central bodies directing economic development and those attached to the economic councils, and the network of research laboratories and institutes at the major industrial plants and in farming areas; to develop research at higher educational establishments; to improve the geographical distribution of research institutions and higher educational establishments, and to ensure the further development of science in all the Union republics and major economic areas.

The research institutions must plan and co-ordinate their work in the most important fields of research in accordance with the plans of economic and cultural development. The role of the collective opinion of scientists in directing scientific work will increase. Free comradely discussions promoting the creative solution of pressing problems are an essential condition for scientific development.

The Party will adopt measures to extend and improve the material facilities of science and to enlist the most capable creative forces in scientific pursuits.

It is a point of honour for Soviet scientists to consolidate the advanced positions which Soviet science has won in major branches of knowledge and to take *a leading place in world science* in all the key fields.

4. IN THE FIELD OF CULTURAL DEVELOPMENT, LITERATURE AND ART

Cultural development during the full-scale construction of communist society will constitute the closing stage of a great cultural revolution. At this stage all the necessary ideological and cultural conditions will be created for the victory of communism.

The growth of the productive forces, progress in engineering and in the organisation of production, increased social activity of the working people, development of the democratic principles of self-government, and a communist reorganisation of everyday life depend in very large measure on the cultural advancement of the population.

Absorbing and developing all the best that has been created by world culture, communist culture will be a new, higher stage in the cultural progress of mankind. It will embody the versatility and richness of the spiritual life of society, and the lofty ideals and humanism of the new world. It will be the culture of a classless society, a culture of the entire people, of all mankind.

(a) All-Round Advancement of the Cultural Life of Society. In the period of transition to communism, creative effort in all fields of culture becomes particularly fruitful and accessible to all members of society. Soviet literature, music, painting, cinema and theatre, television and all the other arts, will attain higher standards in their ideological make-up and artistry. People's theatres, mass amateur art, technical invention and other forms of creative endeavour by the people will become widespread. The advancement of artistic and creative activities among the masses will ensure the appearance of new gifted writers, artists, musicians and actors. The development and enrichment of the arts are based on a combination of mass amateur endeavour and professional art.

The Party will work unremittingly to ensure that literature, art, and culture flourish, that every individual is given full scope to apply his abilities, that the people are educated aesthetically and develop a fine artistic taste and cultural habits. The artistic element will ennoble labour still more, make living conditions more attractive, and lift man up spiritually.

To provide the material basis for cultural development on a grand scale:

book publishing and the press will be vigorously developed, and the printing and paper industries will be expanded accordingly;

there will be more libraries, lecture halls and reading-rooms, theatres, houses of culture, clubs, and cinemas;

the country-wide radio diffusion network will be completed; television stations covering all industrial and agricultural areas will be built;

people's universities, people's theatrical companies, and other amateur cultural organisations will be widely developed;

a large network of scientific and technical laboratories and of art and cinema studios will be provided for the use of all who have the inclination and ability.

The Party considers it necessary to distribute cultural institutions evenly throughout the country in order gradually to bring the cultural standard of the countryside level with that of the town and achieve rapid cultural progress in all the newly-developed areas.

(b) Enhancement of the Educational Role of Literature and Art. Soviet literature and art, imbued with optimism and dynamic communist ideas, are great factors in ideological education and cultivate in Soviet people the qualities of builders of a new world. They must be a source of joy and inspiration to millions of people, express their will, their sentiments and ideas, enrich them ideologically and educate them morally.

The high road of literature and art lies through the strengthening of their bond with the life of the people, through faithful and highly artistic depiction of the richness and versatility of socialist reality, inspired and vivid portrayal of all that is new and genuinely communist, and exposure of all that hinders the progress of society.

In the art of socialist realism, which is based on the principles of partisanship and kinship with the people, bold pioneering in the artistic depiction of life goes hand in hand with the cultivation and development of the progressive traditions of world culture. Writers, artists, musicians, theatrical workers, and film makers have every opportunity of displaying creative initiative and skill, using manifold forms, styles, and genres.

The Communist Party shows solicitude for the proper development of literature and art and their ideological and artistic standards, helps social organisations and literary and art associations in their activities.

(c) The Expansion of International Cultural Relations. The Party considers it necessary to expand the Soviet Union's cultural relations with the countries of the socialist system and with all other countries for the purpose of exchanging scientific and cultural achievements and of bringing about mutual understanding and friendship among the peoples.

VI. COMMUNIST CONSTRUCTION IN THE U.S.S.R. AND CO-OPERATION OF THE SOCIALIST COUNTRIES

The C.P.S.U. regards communist construction in the Soviet Union as a component of the building of communist society by the peoples of the entire world socialist system.

The fact that socialist revolutions took place at different times and that the economic and cultural levels of the countries concerned are dissimilar, predetermines the non-simultaneous completion of socialist construction in those countries and their non-simultaneous entry into the period of the full-scale construction of communism. Nevertheless, the fact that the socialist countries are developing as members of a single world socialist system and utilising the objective laws and advantages of this system *enables them to reduce the time necessary for the construction of socialism and offers them the prospect of effecting the transition to communism more or less simultaneously, within one and the same historical epoch.*

The first country to advance to communism facilitates and accelerates the advance of the entire world socialist system to communism. In building communism, the peoples of the Soviet Union are breaking new roads for mankind, testing their correctness by their own experience, bringing out difficulties, finding ways and means of overcoming them, and selecting the best forms and methods of communist construction.

Since the social forces—the working class, the co-operative peasantry and the people's intelligentsia—and the social forms of economy (enterprises based on the two forms of socialist property) in the Soviet Union and in the other socialist countries are of one type, there will be common basic objective laws for communist construction in the U.S.S.R. and in those countries, with due allowance made for the historical and national peculiarities of each country.

The construction of communism in the U.S.S.R. promotes the interests of every country of the socialist community, for it increases the economic might and defence potential of the world socialist camp and provides progressively favourable opportunities for the U.S.S.R. to expand its economic and cultural co-operation with the other socialist countries and increase the assistance and support it renders them.

The C.P.S.U. maintains that the existing forms of economic relations between the socialist countries—foreign trade, co-ordination of economic plans, and specialisation and combination of production—will be developed and perfected more and more.

The socialist system makes possible the abolition of the disparities in the economic and cultural development of countries inherited from capitalism, the more rapid development of the countries whose economy lagged behind under capitalism, the steady promotion of their economies and cultures with the purpose of evening up the general level of development of the countries of the socialist community. This is ensured by the advantages of the socialist economic system and by equality in economic relations; by mutual assistance and the sharing of experience, specifically, by reciprocal exchanges of scientific and technological achievements and by co-ordinated research; by the joint construction of industrial projects and by co-operation in the development of natural resources. All-round fraternal co-operation benefits every socialist country and the world socialist system as a whole.

It is in the best interest of socialist and communist construction that each socialist country combines the effort to strengthen and develop its national economy with the effort to expand economic co-operation of the socialist community as a whole. The development and levelling of the economy of the socialist countries must be achieved primarily by every country using its internal resources to the full, by improving the forms and methods of economic leadership, steadily applying the Leninist principles and methods of socialist economic management, and making effective use of the advantages of the world socialist system.

Material prerequisites for the construction of communism are created by the labour of the people of the country concerned and by its steadily growing contribution to the common cause—the consolidation of the socialist system. This purpose is served by the application in socialist construction of the law of planned, proportionate development; encouragement of the creative initiative and labour activity of the masses; continuous perfection of the system of the international division of labour through the co-ordination of national economic plans, specialisation and combination of production within the world socialist system on the basis of voluntary participation, mutual benefit and an overall improvement of the level of science and engineering; the study of collective experience; the promotion of co-operation and fraternal mutual assistance; strict adherence to the principles of material incentive and the all-round promotion of moral stimuli to work for the good of society; control over the measure of labour and rate of consumption.

Socialism brings peoples and countries together. In the course of extensive co-operation in all economic, socio-political and cultural fields, the common economic basis of world socialism will be consolidated.

The objective laws of the world socialist system, the growth of the productive forces of socialist society, and the vital interests of the peoples of the socialist countries predetermine an increasing affinity of the various national economies. As Lenin foresaw, tendencies develop toward the future creation of a world communist economy regulated by the victorious working people according to one single plan.

The C.P.S.U., in community with the Communist parties of the other socialist countries, regards the following as its tasks:

in the *political* field, the utmost strengthening of the world socialist system; promotion of fraternal relations with all the socialist countries on lines of complete equality and voluntary co-operation; political consolidation of the countries of the socialist community for joint struggle against imperialist aggressors, for universal peace and for the complete triumph of communism;

in the *economic* field, expansion of trade between the socialist countries; development of the international socialist division of labour; increasing co-ordination of long-range economic plans of the socialist countries to ensure a maximum saving of social labour and an accelerated development of the world socialist economy; the promotion of scientific and technical co-operation;

in the *cultural* field, steady development of all forms of cultural co-operation and intercourse between the peoples of the socialist countries; exchanges of cultural achievements; encouragement of joint creative effort by scientists, writers and artists; extensive measures to ensure the mutual enrichment of national cultures and bring the mode of life and the spiritual cast of the socialist nations closer together.

The C.P.S.U. and the Soviet people will do everything in their power to support all the peoples of the socialist community in the construction of socialism and communism.

VII. THE PARTY IN THE PERIOD OF FULL-SCALE COMMUNIST CONSTRUCTION

As a result of the victory of socialism in the U.S.S.R. and the consolidation of the unity of Soviet society, the Communist Party of the working class has become the vanguard of the Soviet people, a Party of the entire people, and extended its guiding influence to all spheres of social life. The Party is the brain, the honour and the conscience of our epoch, of the Soviet people, the people effecting great revolutionary transformations. It looks keenly into the future and shows the people scientifically-motivated roads along which to advance, arouses titanic energy in the masses and leads them to the accomplishment of great tasks.

The period of full-scale communist construction is characterised by a further *enhancement of the role and importance of the Communist Party* as the leading and guiding force of Soviet society.

Unlike all the preceding socio-economic formations, communist society does not develop spontaneously, but as a result of the conscious and purposeful efforts of the masses led by the Marxist-Leninist Party. The Communist Party, which unites the foremost representatives of the working class, of all working people, and is closely connected with the masses, which enjoys unbounded prestige among the people and understands the laws of social development, provides proper leadership in communist construction as a whole, giving it an organised, planned and scientifically based character.

The enhancement of the role of the Party in the life of Soviet society in the new stage of its development derives from:

the growing scope and complexity of the tasks of communist construction, which call for a higher level of political and organisational leadership;

the growth of the creative activity of the masses and the participation of fresh millions of working people in the administration of state affairs and of production;

the further development of socialist democracy, the enhancement of the role of social organisations, the extension of the rights of the Union republics and local organisations;

the growing importance of the theory of scientific communism, of its creative development and propaganda, the necessity for improving the communist education of the working people and struggling to overcome the survivals of the past in the minds of people.

There must be a new, higher stage in the development of the Party itself and of its political, ideological, and organisational work that is in conformity with the full-scale building of communism. The Party will continuously improve the forms and methods of its work, so that its leadership of the masses, of the building of the material and technical basis of communism, of the development of society's spiritual life will keep pace with the growing requirements of the epoch of communist construction.

Being the vanguard of the people building a communist society, the Party must also be in the van in the organisation of internal Party life and serve as an example and model in developing the most advanced forms of public communist self-government.

Undeviating observance of the Leninist standards of Party life and the principle of collective leadership, enhancement of the responsibility of Party organs and their personnel to the Party rank and file, promotion of the activity and initiative of all Communists and of their participation in elaborating and realising the policy of the Party, and the development of criticism and self-criticism, are a law of Party life. This is an imperative condition of the ideological and organisational strength of the Party itself, of the unity and solidarity of Party ranks, of an all-round development of inner-Party democracy and an activisation on this basis of all Party forces, and of the strengthening of ties with the masses.

The cult of the individual, and the violations of collectivism in leadership, of inner-Party democracy and socialist legality arising out of it, are incompatible with the Leninist principles of Party life. The cult of the individual belittles the role of the Party and the masses and hampers the development of the ideological life of the Party and the creative activity of the working people.

In order to effect the Leninist principle of collective leadership consistently, to ensure a greater influx of fresh Party forces into the leading Party organs, to properly combine old and young cadres, and to rule out the possibility of an excessive concentration of power in the hands of individual officials and prevent cases of their getting beyond the control of the collective, the Party considers it necessary to carry out the following measures:

(a) To introduce in practice a regular renewal, in certain proportions, of the members of all elected Party bodies—from primary organisations to the Central Committee, at the same time preserving continuity of leadership.

At all regular elections, not less than one-quarter of the members of the Central Committee of the C.P.S.U. and its Presidium shall be renewed. Presidium members may, as a rule, be elected for not more than three successive terms. Particular Party workers may, by virtue of their generally-recognised authority and high political, organisational and other abilities, be successively elected to the leading bodies for a longer period. In that case, the respective candidate is considered elected, provided not less than three-quarters of the votes are cast for him by secret ballot.

Members of the Central Committees of the Communist parties of Union republics, of territorial and regional committees shall be renewed by not less than one-third at each regular election, and those of area, city and district committees, and the committees and bureaus of primary Party organisations shall be renewed by one-half. Furthermore, members of these leading Party bodies may be elected consecutively for not more than three terms, and secretaries of the primary Party organisations for not more than two consecutive terms.

A Party organisation may, in consideration of the political and professional qualities of a person, elect him to its leading body for a longer period. In that case a candidate is considered elected if not less than three-quarters of the Communists attending vote for him.

Party members not re-elected to a leading Party body on the expiration of their term may be re-elected at subsequent elections.

A decision on the removal of a member from the C.C. C.P.S.U. and other leading organs shall be adopted solely by secret ballot, and is valid when not less than two-thirds of the members of the body concerned vote in favour of the decision.

(b) To extend the application of the elective principle and that of accountability in Party organisations at all levels, including Party organisations working under special conditions (Army, Navy).

(c) To enhance the role of Party meetings, conferences, congresses and plenary meetings of Party committees and other collective bodies. To provide favourable conditions for a free and business-like discussion within the Party of questions concerning its policy and practical activities, for comradely discussions of controversial or insufficiently clear matters.

(d) To reduce steadily the salaried Party staffs, enlisting Communists more extensively as non-salaried workers doing voluntary work.

(e) To develop criticism and self-criticism to the utmost as a tried and tested method of work and a means of disclosing and rectifying errors and shortcomings and properly educating cadres.

In the period of full-scale communist construction the role and responsibility of every Party member will steadily increase. It is the duty of a Communist, in production, in social and personal life, to be a model in the struggle for the development and consolidation of communist relations, and to observe the principles and norms of communist morality. The C.P.S.U. will reinforce its ranks with the most politically conscious and active working people, and keep pure and hold high the name of Communist.

The development of inner-Party democracy must ensure greater activity among Communists and enhance their responsibility for the realisation of the noble ideals of communism. It will promote the cultivation in them of an inner, organic need to act always and in all matters in full accordance with the principles of the Party and its lofty aims.

The Party will continue to strengthen the unity and solidarity of its ranks, and to maintain the purity of Marxism-Leninism. The Party preserves such organisational guarantees as are provided by the Rules of the C.P.S.U. against all manifestations of factionalism and group activity incompatible with Marxist-Leninist Party principles. *The unshakable ideological and organisational unity of the Party is the most important source of its invincibility, a guarantee for the successful solution of the great tasks of communist construction.*

The people are the decisive force in the building of communism. *The Party exists for the people, and it is in serving the people that it sees the purpose of its activity.* To further extend and deepen the ties between the Party and the people is an imperative condition of success in the struggle for communism. The Party considers it its duty always to consult the working people on the major questions of home and foreign policy, to make these questions an object of nation-wide discussion, and to attract more non-members to participating in all its work. The more socialist democracy develops, the broader and more versatile the work of the Party among the working people must be, and the stronger will be its influence among the masses.

The Party will in every way promote the extension and improvement of the work of the Soviets, the trade unions, the Y.C.L., and other mass organisations of working people, and the development of the creative energy and initiative of the masses, and will strengthen the unity and friendship of all the peoples of the U.S.S.R.

The C.P.S.U. is an integral part of the international Communist and working-class movement. The tried and tested Marxist-Leninist principles of proletarian internationalism will continue to be inviolable principles which the Party will follow undeviatingly.

The Communist Party of the Soviet Union will continue to strengthen the unity of the international Communist movement, to develop fraternal ties with all the Communist and Workers' parties and to co-ordinate its actions with the efforts of all the contingents of the world Communist movement in the joint struggle against the danger of a new world war, for the interests of the working people, for peace, democracy, and socialism.

* * *

Such is the programme of work for communist construction which the Communist Party of the Soviet Union has mapped out.

The achievement of communism in the U.S.S.R. will be the greatest victory mankind has ever won throughout its long history. Every new step made towards the bright peaks of communism inspires the working masses in all countries, renders immense moral support to the struggle for the liberation of all peoples from social and national oppression, and brings closer the triumph of Marxism-Leninism on a world-wide scale.

When the Soviet people will enjoy the blessings of communism, new hundreds of millions of people on earth will say: "We are for communism!" It is not through war with other countries, but by the example of a more perfect organisation of society, by rapid progress in developing the productive forces, the creation of all conditions for the happiness and well-being of man, that the ideas of communism win the minds and hearts of the masses.

The forces of social progress will inevitably grow in all countries, and this will assist the builders of communism in the Soviet Union.

The Party proceeds from the Marxist-Leninist proposition: history is made by the people, and communism is a creation of the people, of its energy and intelligence. The victory of communism depends on people, and communism is built for people. Every Soviet man brings the triumph of communism nearer by his labour. The successes of communist construction spell abundance and a happy life to all, and enhance the might, prestige and glory of the Soviet Union.

The Party is confident that the Soviet people will accept the new Programme of the C.P.S.U. as their own vital cause, as the greatest purpose of their life and as a banner of nation-wide struggle for the building of communism. The Party calls on all Communists, on the entire Soviet people—all working men and women, collective farmers and workers by brain—to apply their energies to the successful fulfilment of the historic tasks set forth in this Programme.

UNDER THE TRIED AND TESTED LEADERSHIP OF THE COMMUNIST PARTY, UNDER THE BANNER OF MARXISM-LENINISM, THE SOVIET PEOPLE HAVE BUILT SOCIALISM.

UNDER THE LEADERSHIP OF THE PARTY, UNDER THE BANNER OF MARXISM-LENINISM, THE SOVIET PEOPLE WILL BUILD COMMUNIST SOCIETY.

THE PARTY SOLEMNLY PROCLAIMS: THE PRESENT GENERATION OF SOVIET PEOPLE SHALL LIVE IN COMMUNISM!

ON THE RULES
OF THE COMMUNIST PARTY OF THE
SOVIET UNION

RESOLUTION OF THE 22nd CONGRESS OF THE C.P.S.U.

(Adopted Unanimously on October 31, 1961)

Having heard and discussed the report of the Secretary of the C.C. C.P.S.U., Comrade F. R. Kozlov, on the amendments to the Rules of the C.P.S.U., the Twenty-Second Congress of the Communist Party of the Soviet Union has resolved:

To endorse the Rules of the Communist Party of the Soviet Union submitted by the Central Committee of the C.P.S.U.

RULES
OF THE COMMUNIST PARTY
OF THE SOVIET UNION

The Communist Party of the Soviet Union is the tried and tested militant vanguard of the Soviet people, which unites, on a voluntary basis, the more advanced, politically more conscious section of the working class, collective-farm peasantry and intelligentsia of the U.S.S.R.

Founded by V. I. Lenin as the vanguard of the working class, the Communist Party has travelled a glorious road of struggle, and brought the working class and the working peasantry to the victory of the Great October Socialist Revolution and to the establishment of the dictatorship of the proletariat in the U.S.S.R. Under the leadership of the Communist Party, the exploiting classes were abolished in the Soviet Union, and the moral and political unity of Soviet society has taken shape and grown in strength. Socialism has triumphed completely and finally. The Communist Party, the party of the working class, has today become the party of the Soviet people as a whole.

The Party exists for, and serves, the people. It is the highest form of socio-political organisation, and is the leading and guiding force of Soviet society. It directs the great creative activity of the Soviet people, and imparts an organised, planned and scientifically-based character to their struggle to achieve the ultimate goal, the victory of communism.

The C.P.S.U. bases its work on unswerving adherence to the Leninist standards of Party life, the principle of collective leadership, the promotion, in every possible way, of inner-Party democracy, the activity and initiative of the Communists, criticism and self-criticism.

Ideological and organisational unity, monolithic cohesion of its ranks, and a high degree of conscious discipline on the part of all Communists are an inviolable law of the C.P.S.U. All manifestations of factionalism and group activity are incompatible with Marxist-Leninist Party principles, and with Party membership.

In all its activities, the C.P.S.U. takes guidance from Marxist-Leninist theory and the Programme based on it, which defines the fundamental tasks of the Party for the period of the construction of communist society.

In creatively developing Marxism-Leninism, the C.P.S.U. vigorously combats all manifestations of revisionism and dogmatism, which are utterly alien to revolutionary theory.

The Communist Party of the Soviet Union is an integral part of the international Communist and working-class movement. It firmly adheres to the tried and tested Marxist-Leninist principles of proletarian internationalism; it actively promotes the unity of the international Communist and working-class movement as a whole, and fraternal ties with the great army of the Communists of all countries.

I

PARTY MEMBERS, THEIR DUTIES AND RIGHTS

1. Membership of the C.P.S.U. is open to any citizen of the Soviet Union who accepts the Programme and the Rules of the Party, takes an active part in communist construction, works in one of the Party organisations, carries out all Party decisions, and pays membership dues.

2. It is the duty of a Party member:

(a) to work for the creation of the material and technical basis of communism; to serve as an example of the communist attitude towards labour; to raise labour productivity; to display the initiative in all that is new and progressive; to support and propagate advanced methods; to master techniques, to improve his skill; to protect and increase public socialist property, the mainstay of the might and prosperity of the Soviet country;

(b) to put Party decisions firmly and steadfastly into effect; to explain the policy of the Party to the masses; to help strengthen and multiply the Party's bonds with the people; to be considerate and attentive to people; to respond promptly to the needs and requirements of the working people;

(c) to take an active part in the political life of the country, in the administration of state affairs, and in economic and cultural development; to set an example in the fulfilment of his public duty; to assist in developing and strengthening communist social relations;

(d) to master Marxist-Leninist theory, to improve his ideological knowledge, and to contribute to the moulding and education of the man of communist society. To combat vigorously all manifestations of bourgeois ideology, remnants of a private-property psychology, religious prejudices, and other survivals of the past; to observe the principles of communist morality, and place public interests above his own;

(e) to be an active proponent of the ideas of socialist internationalism and Soviet patriotism among the masses of the working people; to combat survivals of nationalism and chauvinism; to contribute by word and by deed to the consolidation of the friendship of the peoples of the U.S.S.R. and the fraternal bonds linking the Soviet people with the peoples of the countries of the socialist camp, with the proletarians and other working people in all countries;

(f) to strengthen to the utmost the ideological and organisational unity of the Party; to safeguard the Party against the infiltration of people unworthy of the lofty name of Communist; to be truthful and honest with the

Party and the people; to display vigilance, to guard Party and state secrets;

(g) to develop criticism and self-criticism, boldly lay bare shortcomings and strive for their removal; to combat ostentation, conceit, complacency, and parochial tendencies; to rebuff firmly all attempts at suppressing criticism; to resist all actions injurious to the Party and the state, and to give information of them to Party bodies, up to and including the CC. C.P.S.U.;

(h) to implement undeviatingly the Party's policy with regard to the proper selection of personnel according to their political qualifications and personal qualities. To be uncompromising whenever the Leninist principles of the selection and education of personnel are infringed;

(i) to observe Party and state discipline, which is equally binding on all Party members. The Party has one discipline, one law, for all Communists, irrespective of their past services or the positions they occupy;

(j) to help, in every possible way, to strengthen the defence potential of the U.S.S.R.; to wage an unflagging struggle for peace and friendship among nations;

3. A Party member has the right:

(a) to elect and be elected to Party bodies;

(b) to discuss freely questions of the Party's policies and practical activities at Party meetings, conferences and congresses, at the meetings of Party committees and in the Party press; to table motions; openly to express and uphold his opinion as long as the Party organisation concerned has not adopted a decision;

(c) to criticise any Communist, irrespective of the position he holds, at Party meetings, conferences and congresses, and at the plenary meetings of Party committees. Those who commit the offence of suppressing criticism or victimising anyone for criticism are responsible to and will be penalised by the Party, to the point of expulsion from the C.P.S.U.;

(d) to attend in person all Party meetings and all bureau

and committee meetings that discuss his activities or conduct;

(e) to address any question, statement or proposal to any Party body, up to and including the C.C. C.P.S.U., and to demand an answer on the substance of his address.

4. Applicants are admitted to Party membership only individually. Membership of the Party is open to politically conscious and active workers, peasants and representatives of the intelligentsia, devoted to the communist cause. New members are admitted from among the candidate members who have passed through the established probationary period.

Persons may join the Party on attaining the age of eighteen. Young people up to the age of twenty may join the Party only through the Leninist Young Communist League of the Soviet Union (Y.C.L.).

The procedure for the admission of candidate members to full Party membership is as follows:

(a) Applicants for Party membership must submit recommendations from three members of the C.P.S.U. who have a Party standing of not less than three years and who know the applicants from having worked with them, professionally and socially, for not less than one year.

> *Note 1.* In the case of members of the Y.C.L. applying for membership of the Party, the recommendation of a district or city committee of the Y.C.L. is equivalent to the recommendation of one Party member.
> *Note 2.* Members and alternate members of the C.C. C.P.S.U. shall refrain from giving recommendations.

(b) Applications for Party membership are discussed and a decision is taken by the general meeting of the primary Party organisation; the decision of the latter takes effect after endorsement by the district Party committee, or by the city Party committee in cities with no district division.

The presence of those who have recommended an applicant for Party membership at the discussion of the application concerned is optional;

(c) citizens of the U.S.S.R. who formerly belonged to the Communist or Workers' Party of another country are admitted to membership of the Communist Party of the Soviet Union in conformity with the rules established by the C.C. C.P.S.U.

Former members of other parties are admitted to membership of the C.P.S.U. in conformity with the regular procedure, except that their admission must be endorsed by a regional or territorial committee or the C.C. of the Communist Party of a Union Republic.

5. Communists recommending applicants for Party membership are responsible to Party organisations for the impartiality of their description of the moral qualities and professional and political qualifications of those they recommend.

6. The Party standing of those admitted to membership dates from the day when the general meeting of the primary Party organisation decides to accept them as full members.

7. The procedure of registering members and candidate members of the Party, and their transfer from one organisation to another is determined by the appropriate instructions of the C.C. C.P.S.U.

8. If a Party member or candidate member fails to pay membership dues for three months in succession without sufficient reason, the matter shall be discussed by the primary Party organisation. If it is revealed as a result that the Party member or candidate member in question has virtually lost contact with the Party organisation, he shall be regarded as having ceased to be a member of the Party; the primary Party organisation shall pass a decision thereon and submit it to the district or city committee of the Party for endorsement.

9. A Party member or candidate member who fails to fulfil his duties as laid down in the Rules, or commits other

offences, shall be called to account, and may be subjected to the penalty of admonition, reprimand (severe reprimand), or reprimand (severe reprimand) with entry in the registration card. The highest Party penalty is expulsion from the Party.

Should the necessity arise, a Party organisation may, as a Party penalty, reduce a Party member to the status of candidate member for a period of up to one year. The decision of the primary Party organisation reducing a Party member to candidate membership is subject to endorsement by the district or city Party committee. On the expiration of his period of reduction to candidate membership his readmission to full membership of the Party will follow regular procedure, with retention of his former Party standing.

In the case of insignificant offences, measures of Party education and influence should be applied—in the form of comradely criticism, Party censure, warning, or reproof.

When the question of expelling a member from the Party is discussed, the maximum attention must be shown, and the grounds for the charges preferred against him must be thoroughly investigated.

10. The decision to expel a Communist from the Party is made by the general meeting of a primary Party organisation. The decision of the primary Party organisation expelling a member is regarded as adopted if not less than two-thirds of the Party members attending the meeting have voted for it, and is subject to endorsement by the district or city Party committee. The decision of the district or city committee expelling a member takes effect after endorsement by a regional or territorial committee or the C.C. of the Communist Party of a Union Republic.

Until such time as the decision to expel him is endorsed by a regional or territorial Party committee or the C.C. of the Communist Party of a Union Republic, the Party member or candidate member retains his membership card and is entitled to attend closed Party meetings.

An expelled Party member retains the right to appeal, within the period of two months, to the higher Party bodies, up to and including the C.C. C.P.S.U.

11. The question of calling a member or alternate member of the C.C. of the Communist Party of a Union Republic, of a territorial, regional, area, city or district Party committee, as well as a member of an auditing commission, to account before the Party is discussed by primary Party organisations.

Party organisations pass decisions imposing penalties on members or alternate members of the said Party committees, or on members of auditing commissions, in conformity with the regular procedure.

A Party organisation which proposes expelling a Communist from the C.P.S.U. communicates its proposal to the Party committee of which he is a member. A decision expelling from the Party a member or alternate member of the C.C. of the Communist Party of a Union Republic or a territorial, regional, area, city or district Party committee, or a member of an auditing commission, is taken at the plenary meeting of the committee concerned by a majority of two-thirds of the membership.

The decision to expel from the Party a member or alternate member of the Central Committee of the C.P.S.U., or a member of the Central Auditing Commission, is made by the Party congress, and in the interval between two congresses, by a plenary meeting of the Central Committee, by a majority of two-thirds of its members.

12. Should a Party member commit an indictable offence, he shall be expelled from the Party and prosecuted in conformity with the law.

13. Appeals against expulsion from the Party or against the imposition of a penalty, as well as the decisions of Party organisations on expulsion from the Party shall be examined by the appropriate Party bodies within not more than one month from the date of their receipt.

II

CANDIDATE MEMBERS

14. All persons joining the Party must pass through a probationary period as candidate members in order to more thoroughly familiarise themselves with the Programme and the Rules of the C.P.S.U. and prepare for admission to full membership of the Party. Party organisations must assist candidates to prepare for admission to full membership of the Party, and test their personal qualities.

The period of probationary membership shall be one year.

15. The procedure for the admission of candidate members (individual admission, submission of recommendations, decision of the primary organisation as to admission, and its endorsement) is identical with the procedure for the admission of Party members.

16. On the expiration of a candidate member's probationary period the primary Party organisation discusses and passes a decision on his admission to full membership. Should a candidate member fail, in the course of his probationary period, to prove his worthiness, and should his personal traits make it evident that he cannot be admitted to membership of the C.P.S.U., the Party organisation shall pass a decision rejecting his admission to membership of the Party; after endorsement of that decision by the district or city Party committee, he shall cease to be considered a candidate member of the C.P.S.U.

17. Candidate members of the Party participate in all the activities of their Party organisations; they shall have a consultative voice at Party meetings. They may not be elected to any leading Party body, nor may they be elected delegates to a Party conference or congress.

18. Candidate members of the C.P.S.U. pay membership dues at the same rate as full members.

III

ORGANISATIONAL STRUCTURE OF THE PARTY. INNER-PARTY DEMOCRACY

19. The guiding principle of the organisational structure of the Party is democratic centralism, which signifies:

(a) election of all leading Party bodies, from the lowest to the highest;

(b) periodical reports of Party bodies to their Party organisations and to higher bodies;

(c) strict Party discipline and subordination of the minority to the majority;

(d) the decisions of higher bodies are obligatory for lower bodies.

20. The Party is built on the territorial-and-production principle: primary organisations are established wherever Communists are employed, and are associated territorially in district, city, etc., organisations. An organisation serving a given area is higher than any Party organisation serving part of that area.

21. All Party organisations are autonomous in the decision of local questions, unless their decisions conflict with Party policy.

22. The highest leading body of a Party organisation is the general meeting (in the case of primary organisations), conference (in the case of district, city, area, regional or territorial organisations), or congress (in the case of the Communist Parties of the Union Republics and the Communist Party of the Soviet Union).

23. The general meeting, conference or congress, elects a bureau or committee which acts as its executive body and directs all the current work of the Party organisation.

24. The election of Party bodies shall be effected by secret ballot. In an election, all Party members have the unlimited right to challenge candidates and to criticise them. Each candidate shall be voted upon separately. A candidate is considered elected if more than one half of

those attending the meeting, conference or congress have voted for him.

25. The principle of systematic renewal of the composition of Party bodies and of continuity of leadership shall be observed in the election of those bodies.

At each regular election, not less than one quarter of the composition of the Central Committee of the C.P.S.U. and its Presidium shall be renewed. Members of the Presidium shall not, as a rule, be elected for more than three successive terms. Particular Party officials may, by virtue of their generally recognised prestige and high political, organisational and other qualities, be successively elected to leading bodies for a longer period. In that case, a candidate is considered elected if not less than three quarters of the votes are cast for him by secret ballot.

The composition of the Central Committees of the Communist Parties of the Union Republics, and of the territorial and regional Party committees shall be renewed by not less than one-third at each regular election; the composition of the area, city and district Party committees and of the committees or bureaus of primary Party organisations, by one half. Furthermore, members of these leading Party bodies may be elected successively for not more than three terms, and the secretaries of primary Party organisations, for not more than two terms.

A Party meeting, conference or congress may, in consideration of the political and professional qualities of an individual, elect him to a leading body for a longer period. In such cases a candidate is considered elected if not less than three quarters of the Communists attending vote for him.

Party members not re-elected to a leading Party body due to the expiration of their term may be re-elected at subsequent elections.

26. A member or alternate member of the C.C. C.P.S.U. must by his entire activity justify the great trust placed in him by the Party. A member or alternate member of the

C.C. C.P.S.U. who degrades his honour and dignity may not remain on the Central Committee. The question of the removal of a member or alternate member of the C.C. C.P.S.U. from that body shall be decided by a plenary meeting of the Central Committee by secret ballot. The decision is regarded as adopted if not less than two-thirds of the membership of the C.C. C.P.S.U. vote for it.

The question of the removal of a member or alternate member of the C.C. of the Communist Party of a Union Republic, or of a territorial, regional, area, city or district Party committee from the Party body concerned is decided by a plenary meeting of that body. The decision is regarded as adopted if not less than two-thirds of the membership of the committee in question vote for it by secret ballot.

A member of the Central Auditing Commission who does not justify the great trust placed in him by the Party shall be removed from that body. This question shall be decided by a meeting of the Central Auditing Commission. The decision is regarded as adopted if not less than two-thirds of the membership of the Central Auditing Commission vote by secret ballot for the removal of the member concerned from that body.

The question of the removal of a member from the auditing commission of a republican, territorial, regional, area, city or district Party organisation shall be decided by a meeting of the appropriate commission according to the procedure established for members and alternate members of Party committees.

27. The free and business-like discussion of questions of Party policy in individual Party organisations or in the Party as a whole is the inalienable right of every Party member and an important principle of inner-Party democracy. Only on the basis of inner-Party democracy is it possible to develop criticism and self-criticism and to strengthen Party discipline, which must be conscious and not mechanical.

Discussion of controversial or insufficiently clear issues

may be held within the framework of individual organisations or the Party as a whole.

Party-wide discussion is necessary:

(a) if the necessity is recognised by several Party organisations at regional or republican level;

(b) if there is not a sufficiently solid majority in the Central Committee on major questions of Party policy;

(c) if the C.C. C.P.S.U. considers it necessary to consult the Party as a whole on any particular question of policy.

Wide discussion, especially discussion on a country-wide scale, of questions of Party policy must be so held as to ensure for Party members the free expression of their views and preclude attempts to form factional groupings destroying Party unity, attempts to split the Party.

28. The supreme principle of Party leadership is collective leadership, which is an absolute requisite for the normal functioning of Party organisations, the proper education of cadres, and the promotion of the activity and initiative of Communists. The cult of the individual and the violations of inner-Party democracy resulting from it must not be tolerated in the Party; they are incompatible with the Leninist principles of Party life.

Collective leadership does not exempt individuals in office from personal responsibility for the job entrusted to them.

29. The Central Committees of the Communist Parties of the Union Republics, and territorial, regional, area, city and district Party committees shall systematically inform Party organisations of their work in the interim between congresses and conferences.

30. Meetings of the active of district, city, area, regional and territorial Party organisations and of the Communist Parties of the Union Republics shall be held to discuss major decisions of the Party and to work out measures for their execution, as well as to examine questions of local significance.

IV

HIGHER PARTY ORGANS

31. The supreme organ of the Communist Party of the Soviet Union is the Party Congress. Congresses are convened by the Central Committee at least once in four years. The convocation of a Party Congress and its agenda shall be announced at least six weeks before the Congress. Extraordinary congresses are convened by the Central Committee of the Party on its own initiative or on the demand of not less than one-third of the total membership represented at the preceding Party Congress. Extraordinary congresses shall be convened within two months. A congress is considered properly constituted if not less than one half of the total Party membership is represented at it.

The rates of representation at a Party Congress are determined by the Central Committee.

32. Should the Central Committee of the Party fail to convene an extraordinary congress within the period specified in Article 31, the organisations which demanded it have the right to form an Organising Committee which shall enjoy the powers of the Central Committee of the Party in respect of the convocation of the extraordinary congress.

33. The Congress:

(a) hears and approves the reports of the Central Committee, of the Central Auditing Commission, and of the other central organisations;

(b) reviews, amends and endorses the Programme and the Rules of the Party;

(c) determines the line of the Party in matters of home and foreign policy, and examines and decides the most important questions of communist construction;

(d) elects the Central Committee and the Central Auditing Commission.

34. The number of members to be elected to the Central Committee and to the Central Auditing Commission is de-

termined by the Congress. In the event of vacancies occurring in the Central Committee, they are filled from among the alternate members of the C.C. C.P.S.U. elected by the Congress.

35. Between congresses, the Central Committee of the Communist Party of the Soviet Union directs the activities of the Party, the local Party bodies, selects and appoints leading functionaries, directs the work of central government bodies and public organisations of working people through the Party groups in them, sets up various Party organs, institutions and enterprises and directs their activities, appoints the editors of the central newspapers and journals operating under its control, and distributes the funds of the Party budget and controls its execution.

The Central Committee represents the C.P.S.U. in its relations with other parties.

36. The C.C. C.P.S.U. shall keep the Party organisations regularly informed of its work.

37. The Central Auditing Commission of the C.P.S.U. supervises the expeditious and proper handling of affairs by the central bodies of the Party, and audits the accounts of the treasury and the enterprises of the Central Committee of the C.P.S.U.

38. The C.C. C.P.S.U. shall hold not less than one plenary meeting every six months. Alternate members of the Central Committee shall attend its plenary meetings with consultative voice.

39. The Central Committee of the Communist Party of the Soviet Union elects a Presidium to direct the work of the C.C. between plenary meetings and a Secretariat to direct current work, chiefly the selection of cadres and the verification of the fulfilment of Party decisions, and sets up a Bureau of the C.C. C.P.S.U. for the R.S.F.S.R.

40. The Central Committee of the Communist Party of the Soviet Union organises the Party Control Committee of the C.C.

The Party Control Committee of the C.C. C.P.S.U.:

(a) verifies the observance of Party discipline by members and candidate members of the C.P.S.U., and takes action against Communists who violate the Programme and the Rules of the Party and Party or state discipline, and against violators of Party ethics;

(b) considers appeals against decisions of Central Committees of the Communist Parties of the Union Republics or of territorial and regional Party committees to expel members from the Party or impose Party penalties upon them.

V

REPUBLICAN, TERRITORIAL, REGIONAL, AREA, CITY AND DISTRICT ORGANISATIONS OF THE PARTY

41. The republican, territorial, regional, area, city and district Party organisations and their committees take guidance in their activities from the Programme and the Rules of the C.P.S.U., conduct all work for the implementation of Party policy and organise the fulfilment of the directives of the C.C. C.P.S.U. within the republics, territories, regions, areas, cities and districts concerned.

42. The basic duties of republican, territorial, regional, area, city and district Party organisations, and of their leading bodies, are:

(a) political and organisational work among the masses, mobilisation of the masses for the fulfilment of the tasks of communist construction, for the maximum development of industrial and agricultural production, for the fulfilment and over-fulfilment of state plans; solicitude for the steady improvement of the material and cultural standards of the working people;

(b) organisation of ideological work, propaganda of Marxism-Leninism, promotion of the communist awareness of the working people, guidance of the local press, radio and television, and control over the activities of cultural and educational institutions;

(c) guidance of Soviets, trade unions, the Y.C.L., the co-operatives and other public organisations through the Party groups in them, and increasingly broader enlistment of working people in the activities of these organisations, development of the initiative and activity of the masses as an essential condition for the gradual transition from socialist statehood to public self-government under communism.

Party organisations must not act in place of government, trade union, co-operative or other public organisations of the working people; they must not allow either the merging of the functions of Party and other bodies or undue parallelism in work;

(d) selection and appointment of leading personnel, their education in the spirit of communist ideas, honesty and truthfulness, and a high sense of responsibility to the Party and the people for the work entrusted to them;

(e) large-scale enlistment of Communists in the conduct of Party activities as non-staff workers, as a form of social work;

(f) organisation of various institutions and enterprises of the Party within the bounds of their republic, territory, region, area, city or district, and guidance of their activities; distribution of Party funds within the given organisation; systematic information of the higher Party body and accountability to it for their work.

LEADING BODIES OF REPUBLICAN, TERRITORIAL AND REGIONAL PARTY ORGANISATIONS

43. The highest body of regional, territorial and republican Party organisations is the respective regional or territorial Party conference or the congress of the Communist Party of the Union Republic, and in the interim between them the regional committee, territorial committee or the Central Committee of the Communist Party of the Union Republic.

44. Regular regional and territorial Party conferences, and congresses of the Communist Parties of the Union Republics, are convened by the respective regional or territorial committees or the Central Committees of the Communist Parties of the Union Republics once every two years, and extraordinary conferences and congresses are convened by decision of regional or territorial committees, or the Central Committees of the Communist Parties of the Union Republics, or on the demand of one-third of the total membership of the organisations belonging to the regional, territorial or republican Party organisation. Congresses of Communist Parties of the Union Republics divided into regions (the Ukraine, Byelorussia, Kazakhstan and Uzbekistan) may be convened once in four years.

The rates of representation at regional and territorial conferences and at congresses of the Communist Parties of the Union Republics are determined by the respective Party committees.

Regional and territorial conferences, and congresses of the Communist Parties of the Union Republics, hear the reports of the respective regional or territorial committees, or the Central Committee of the Communist Party of the Union Republic, and of the auditing commission; discuss at their own discretion other matters of Party, economic and cultural development, and elect the regional or territorial committee, the Central Committee of the Union Republic, the auditing commission and the delegates to the Congress of the C.P.S.U.

45. The regional and territorial committees and the Central Committees of the Communist Parties of the Union Republics elect bureaus, which also include secretaries of the committees. The secretaries must have a Party standing of not less than five years. The plenary meetings of the committees also confirm the chairmen of Party commissions, heads of departments of these committees, editors of Party newspapers and journals.

Regional and territorial committees and the Central Committees of the Communist Parties of the Union Republics may set up secretariats to examine current business and verify the execution of decisions.

46. The plenary meetings of regional and territorial committees and the Central Committees of the Communist Parties of the Union Republics shall be convened at least once every four months.

47. The regional and territorial committees and the Central Committees of the Communist Parties of the Union Republics direct the area, city and district Party organisations, inspect their work and regularly hear reports of area, city and district Party committees.

Party organisations in Autonomous Republics, and in autonomous and other regions forming part of a territory or a Union Republic, function under the guidance of the respective territorial committees or Central Committees of the Communist Parties of the Union Republics.

LEADING BODIES OF AREA, CITY AND DISTRICT (URBAN AND RURAL) PARTY ORGANISATIONS

48. The highest body of an area, city or district Party organisation is the area, city and district Party conference or the general meeting of Communists convened by the area, city or district committee at least once in two years, and the extraordinary conference convened by decision of the respective committee or on the demand of one-third of the total membership of the Party organisation concerned.

The area, city or district conference (general meeting) hears reports of the committee and auditing commission, discusses at its own discretion other questions of Party, economic and cultural development, and elects the area, city and district committee, the auditing commission and delegates to the regional and territorial conference or the congress of the Communist Party of the Union Republic.

The quota of representation to the area, city or district

conference are established by the respective Party committee.

49. The area, city or district committee elects a bureau, including the committee secretaries, and confirms the appointment of heads of committee departments and newspaper editors. The secretaries of the area, city and district committees must have a Party standing of at least three years. The committee secretaries are confirmed by the respective regional or territorial committee, or the Central Committee of the Communist Party of the Union Republic.

50. The area, city and district committee organises and confirms the primary Party organisations, directs their work, regularly hears reports concerning the work of Party organisations, and keeps a register of Communists.

51. The plenary meeting of the area, city and district committee is convened at least once in three months.

52. The area, city and district committee has non-staff functionaries, sets up standing or ad hoc commissions on various aspects of Party work and uses other ways to draw Communists into the activities of the Party committee on social lines.

VI

PRIMARY PARTY ORGANISATIONS

53. The primary Party organisations are the basis of the Party.

Primary Party organisations are formed at the places of work of Party members—in factories, state farms and other enterprises, collective farms, units of the Soviet Army, offices, educational establishments, etc., wherever there are not less than three Party members. Primary Party organisations may also be organised on the residential principle in villages and at house administrations.

54. At enterprises, collective farms and institutions with over 50 Party members and candidate members, shop, sectional, farm, team, departmental, etc., Party organisations

may be formed as units of the general primary Party organisation with the sanction of the district, city or area committee.

Within shop, sectional, etc., organisations, and also within primary Party organisations having less than 50 members and candidate members, Party groups may be formed in the teams and other production units.

55. The highest organ of the primary Party organisation is the Party meeting, which is convened at least once a month.

In large Party organisations with a membership of more than 300 Communists, a general Party meeting is convened when necessary at times fixed by the Party committee or on the demand of a number of shop or departmental Party organisations.

56. For the conduct of current business the primary, shop or departmental Party organisation elects a bureau for the term of one year. The number of its members is fixed by the Party meeting. Primary, shop and departmental Party organisations with less than 15 Party members do not elect a bureau. Instead, they elect a secretary and deputy secretary of the Party organisation.

Secretaries of primary, shop and departmental Party organisations must have a Party standing of at least one year.

Primary Party organisations with less than 150 Party members shall have, as a rule, no salaried functionaries released from their regular work.

57. In large factories and offices with more than 300 members and candidate members of the Party, and in exceptional cases in factories and offices with over 100 Communists by virtue of special production conditions and territorial dispersion, subject to the approval of the regional committee, territorial committee or Central Committee of the Communist Party of the Union Republic, Party committees may be formed, the shop and departmental Party organisations at these factories and offices being granted the status of primary Party organisations.

The Party organisations of collective farms may set up Party committees if they have a minimum of 50 Communists.

The Party committees are elected for the term of one year. Their numerical composition is fixed by the general Party meeting or conference.

58. In its activities the primary Party organisation takes guidance from the Programme and the Rules of the C.P.S.U. It conducts its work directly among the working people, rallies them round the Communist Party of the Soviet Union, organises the masses to carry out the Party policy and to work for the building of communism.

The primary Party organisation:

(a) admits new members to the C.P.S.U.;

(b) educates Communists in a spirit of loyalty to the Party cause, ideological staunchness and communist ethics;

(c) organises the study by Communists of Marxist-Leninist theory in close connection with the practice of communist construction and opposes all attempts at revisionist distortions of Marxism-Leninism and its dogmatic interpretation;

(d) ensures the vanguard role of Communists in the sphere of labour and in the socio-political and economic activities of enterprises, collective farms, institutions, educational establishments, etc.;

(e) acts as the organiser of the working people for the performance of the current tasks of communist construction, heads the socialist emulation movement for the fulfilment of state plans and undertakings of the working people, rallies the masses to disclose and make the best use of untapped resources at enterprises and collective farms, and to apply in production on a broad scale the achievements of science, engineering and the experience of front-rankers; works for the strengthening of labour discipline, the steady increase of labour productivity and improvement of the quality of production, and shows concern for the protection and increase of social wealth at enterprises, state farms and collective farms;

(f) conducts agitational and propaganda work among the masses, educates them in the communist spirit, helps the working people to acquire proficiency in administering state and social affairs;

(g) on the basis of extensive criticism and self-criticism, combats cases of bureaucracy, parochialism, and violations of state discipline, thwarts attempts to deceive the state, acts against negligence, waste and extravagance at enterprises, collective farms and offices;

(h) assists the area, city and district committees in their activities and is accountable to them for its work.

The Party organisation must see to it that every Communist should observe in his own life and cultivate among working people the moral principles set forth in the Programme of the C.P.S.U., in the moral code of the builder of communism:

loyalty to the communist cause, love of his own socialist country, and of other socialist countries;

conscientious labour for the benefit of society, for he who does not work, neither shall he eat;

concern on everyone's part for the protection and increase of social wealth;

lofty sense of public duty, intolerance of violations of public interests;

collectivism and comradely mutual assistance: one for all, and all for one;

humane relations and mutual respect among people: man is to man a friend, comrade and brother;

honesty and truthfulness, moral purity unpretentiousness and modesty in public and personal life;

mutual respect in the family circle and concern for the upbringing of children;

intolerance of injustice, parasitism, dishonesty, careerism and money-grubbing;

friendship and fraternity among all peoples of the U.S.S.R., intolerance of national and racial hostility;

intolerance of the enemies of communism, the enemies of peace and those who oppose the freedom of the peoples;

fraternal solidarity with the working people of all countries, with all peoples.

59. Primary Party organisations of industrial enterprises and trading establishments, state farms, collective farms and designing organisations, drafting offices and research institutes directly related to production, enjoy the right to control the work of the administration.

The Party organisations at Ministries, State Committees, economic councils and other central and local government or economic agencies and departments which do not have the function of controlling the administration, must actively promote improvement of the apparatus, cultivate among the personnel a high sense of responsibility for work entrusted to them, promote state discipline and the better servicing of the population, firmly combat bureaucracy and red tape, inform the appropriate Party bodies in good time on shortcomings in the work of the respective offices and individuals, regardless of what posts the latter may occupy.

VII

THE PARTY AND THE Y.C.L.

60. The Leninist Young Communist League of the Soviet Union is an independently acting social organisation of young people, an active helper and reserve of the Party. The Y.C.L. helps the Party educate the youth in the communist spirit, draw it into the work of building a new society, train a rising generation of harmoniously developed people who will live and work and administer public affairs under communism.

61. Y.C.L. organisations enjoy the right of broad initiative in discussing and submitting to the appropriate Party

organisations questions related to the work of enterprises, collective farms and offices. They must be active levers in the implementation of Party directives in all spheres of communist construction, especially where there are no primary Party organisations.

62. The Y.C.L. conducts its activities under the guidance of the Communist Party of the Soviet Union. The work of the local Y.C.L. organisations is directed and controlled by the appropriate republican, territorial, regional, area, city and district Party organisations.

In their communist educational work among the youth, local Party bodies and primary Party organisations rely on the support of the Y.C.L. organisations, and uphold and promote their useful undertakings.

63. Members of the Y.C.L. who have been admitted into the C.P.S.U. cease to belong to the Y.C.L. the moment they join the Party, provided they do not hold leading posts in Y.C.L. organisations.

VIII

PARTY ORGANISATIONS IN THE SOVIET ARMY

64. Party organisations in the Soviet Army take guidance in their work from the Programme and the Rules of the C.P.S.U. and operate on the basis of instructions issued by the Central Committee.

The Party organisations of the Soviet Army carry through the policy of the Party in the Armed Forces, rally servicemen round the Communist Party, educate them in the spirit of Marxism-Leninism and boundless loyalty to the socialist homeland, actively further the unity of the army and the people, work for the strengthening of military discipline, rally servicemen to carry out the tasks of military and political training and acquire skill in the use of new technique and weapons, and to irreproachably perform their military duty and the orders and instructions of the command.

65. The guidance of Party work in the Armed Forces is exercised by the Central Committee of the C.P.S.U. through the Chief Political Administration of the Soviet Army and Navy, which functions as a department of the C.C. C.P.S.U.

The chiefs of the political administrations of military areas and fleets, and chiefs of the political administrations of armies must be Party members of five years' standing, and the chiefs of political departments of military formations must be Party members of three years' standing.

66. The Party organisations and political bodies of the Soviet Army maintain close contact with local Party committees, and keep them informed about political work in the military units. The secretaries of military Party organisations and chiefs of political bodies participate in the work of local Party committees.

IX

PARTY GROUPS IN NON-PARTY ORGANISATIONS

67. At congresses, conferences and meetings and in the elective bodies of Soviets, trade unions, co-operatives and other mass organisations of the working people, having at least three Party members, Party groups are formed for the purpose of strengthening the influence of the Party in every way and carrying out Party policy among non-Party people, strengthening Party and state discipline, combating bureaucracy, and verifying the fulfilment of Party and government directives.

68. The Party groups are subordinate to the appropriate Party bodies: the Central Committee of the Communist Party of the Soviet Union, the Central Committees of the Communist Parties of the Union Republics, territorial, regional, area, city or district Party committees.

In all matters the groups must strictly and unswervingly abide by decisions of the leading Party bodies.

X

PARTY FUNDS

69. The funds of the Party and its organisations are derived from membership dues, incomes from Party enterprises and other revenue.

70. The monthly membership dues for Party members and candidate members are as follows:

Monthly earnings	Dues	
up to 50 rubles	10 kopeks	
from 51 to 100 rubles	0.5 per cent	
from 101 to 150 rubles	1.0 per cent	of the
from 151 to 200 rubles	1.5 per cent	monthly
from 201 to 250 rubles	2.0 per cent	earnings
from 251 to 300 rubles	2.5 per cent	
over 300 rubles	3.0 per cent	

71. An entrance fee of 2 per cent of monthly earnings is paid on admission to the Party as a candidate member.

ON THE LENIN MAUSOLEUM

Decision of the 22nd Congress of the C.P.S.U.

The Twenty-Second Congress of the Communist Party of the Soviet Union has resolved:

1. The Mausoleum in Red Square beside the wall of the Kremlin, erected to perpetuate the memory of Vladimir Ilyich LENIN, the immortal founder of the Communist Party and the Soviet state, the leader and teacher of the working people of the whole world, is to be henceforth named:

THE VLADIMIR ILYICH LENIN MAUSOLEUM

2. The further maintenance in the Mausoleum of the sarcophagus with the coffin of J. V. Stalin is considered inexpedient, because the grave violations by Stalin of Lenin's behests, his abuses of power, mass repressions of honest Soviet people and other actions performed at the time of the personality cult make it impossible to leave the coffin with his body in the Lenin Mausoleum.

N. S. KHRUSHCHOV

SPEECH AT THE CLOSING SESSION
OF THE 22nd CONGRESS OF THE C.P.S.U.

October 31, 1961

Dear Comrades,

The Twenty-Second Congress has completed its work. All the items on the agenda have been dealt with. The Congress has adopted the Resolution on the Central Committee Report, it has adopted the new Party Programme and the Party Rules, endorsed the Report of the Central Inspection Committee and elected the governing organs of the Party.

There is every reason to say that the Twenty-Second Congress marks a most important stage in the life of our Party and country, in the struggle for the triumph of communism. (*Stormy applause.*)

The ways and means of building communist society were scientifically substantiated by Marx, Engels and Lenin, the great teachers of the working class. Our immortal leader, Vladimir Ilyich Lenin, founded the revolutionary Bolshevik Party, which led the working class, the working people, to victory in the Great October Socialist Revolution. After the October Revolution our Party was named the Communist Party. This signified that its goal was to build communism. The Communists, the working people as a whole, had deep confidence in Lenin, in the Party. But to many communism then seemed a dream, appealing, cherished, but very distant.

Since then we have come a long way. The Soviet people have built socialism, wrought immense transformations in the economic, political and state life of the country, and emerged on the high road of communist construction.

Having adopted the new Programme, the Twenty-Second Congress proclaimed to the whole world that the peoples of the Soviet Union headed by the Communist Party and guided by the Marxist-Leninist teaching, are raising aloft the banner of struggle for the building of a communist society in our country. The building of a communist society has become the practical task of the Party and people. *(Applause.)*

A sound material basis and an abundance of material and spiritual benefits is needed to establish communism. And that cannot be achieved by invocations and appeals. It is the labour and nothing but the labour of millions of people that can build communism. (*Prolonged applause.*)

Comrades, the Party Congress has received tens of thousands of telegrams and letters with warm greetings and wishes of fruitful work. More than ten thousand communications have been received from collectives of workers, kolkhoz farmers, state-farm workers, and scientific, cultural and art workers, reporting the fulfilment of pledges undertaken in honour of the Twenty-Second Party Congress.

Allow me on behalf of the Congress delegates to express heartfelt thanks to all the collectives and comrades who have sent greetings to the Twenty-Second Congress, and to wish them new big successes in their work. *(Stormy applause.)*

Allow me once more, on behalf of the Congress delegates, of our entire Party and the Soviet people, to express our profound gratitude to the fraternal Marxist-Leninist parties for taking part in the work of the Congress, and for their good wishes. (*Prolonged applause.*) We assure our friends that Lenin's Party will continue to hold aloft the banner of communism, the banner of proletarian internationalism. *(Prolonged applause.)*

Hearty thanks to the representatives of the democratic national parties of the independent African states for the warm greetings they expressed to our Congress. *(Stormy applause.)* We have always supported the struggle of the peoples for their freedom and independence, against colonial slavery, and will continue to do so. *(Stormy applause.)*

We shall work for friendship among all peoples, consistently carry into effect the Leninist principle of peaceful coexistence, and struggle for world peace. *(Stormy applause.)*

Equipped with the new Programme, our people will rally still more closely round the Party under the banner of Marxism-Leninism. *(Stormy, prolonged applause.)*

Our goals are clear and our tasks are set.

Let's set to work, comrades! May communism win new victories! *(Stormy, prolonged applause. Ovation. All rise.)*

* * *

Allow me to declare the Twenty-Second Congress of the Communist Party of the Soviet Union closed! *(Rousing ovation. The Congress delegates and guests sing the Party anthem, "Internationale", with immense enthusiasm. After the anthem the ovation breaks out with added force, and lasts several minutes. Salutations ring out throughout the auditorium: "Cheers for the Twenty-Second Congress of the C.P.S.U.!", "Glory to Lenin's Party!", "Long live the Leninist Party Programme! Hurrah!", "Cheers for the fraternal Marxist-Leninist parties!", "Cheers for the socialist camp!", "Long live the Leninist Central Committee! Hurrah!", "Cheers for the Soviet people!", "Viva Cuba!". The audience scans: "Leninism—communism!", "Leninism—communism, hurrah!", "Friendship of the Peoples!", "Friendship of the Peoples!", "Peace!", "Hurrah!".*

Comrade Khrushchov proposes:

"Cheers for the fraternal Marxist-Leninist parties!"

A fresh ovation bursts forth. Salutations ring out in honour of the international Communist and working-class movement, in honour of Marxism-Leninism.

"Long live the peoples fighting for their freedom and independence, against colonial and imperialist oppression! Hurrah!"

Thousands of Congress delegates and guests heartily greet the representatives of the peoples of Asia, Africa and Latin America fighting for their freedom and independence.

The foreign guests hail the Soviet Union, Lenin's great party, the unity and brotherhood of peoples in their struggle for peace and the bright future.

The demonstration of the unity and solidarity of Lenin's great party, of its determination to carry through its new Programme, the programme of communist construction, was powerful and inspiring.)

PHOTOGRAPHS

Delegates to the Twenty-Second Congress go to the Kremlin Palace of Congresses

N. Khrushchov addresses the Twenty-Second Congress

The Twenty-Second Congress in session. October 17, 1961

Delegates vote for the Resolution of the Congress by a show of Congress credentials

The Presidium of the Congress included (*left to right, front*):
L. Brezhnev, N. Khrushchov, F. Kozlov and M. Suslov

N. Khrushchov among delegates from the Moscow Party organisation

Delegates fill the lobby of the Kremlin Palace of Congresses during a break between sessions

Delegates to the Twenty-Second Congress (*left to right*): M. Prokhorov, a veteran Bolshevik, Hero of Socialist Labour S. Pereyaslavsky, Chairman of the Rodina Collective Farm of Dnepropetrovsk Region in the Ukraine, and Hero of Socialist Labour M. Keldysh, President of the Academy of Sciences of the U.S.S.R.

Delegates to the Twenty-Second Congress (*left to right*): Y. Shkolyar, foreman of the Gorodishche Sugar Refinery of Cherkassy Region in the Ukraine. Hero of Socialist Labour S. Amirkhanyan, foreman of the Kirov Works in Yerevan, the capital of Armenia, P. Leontyeva, Chairman of the Vyselki Village Soviet in Kuibyshev Region of the R.S.F.S.R., Hero of Socialist Labour A. Melkonyan, foreman of the Kafan Copper Ore Project, and S. Matshinyan, engine driver of the Leninakan Railway Depot in Armenia

Delegates to the Twenty-Second Congress: Hero of Socialist Labour Valentina Gaganova, team leader of Vyshny Volochok Textile Factory, and Y. Kutsy, team leader of Krasny Ekskavator Works in Kiev Region

Delegates to the Twenty-Second Congress (*left to right*): Hero of
Socialist Labour N. Mamai, team leader of Sukhodolskaya Coal
Mine, Hero of Socialist Labour V. Gurgal, of the Lvov Engineering
Works, and People's Artiste of the U.S.S.R. N. Okhlopkov

Delegates to the Twenty-Second Congress *(left to right)*: A. Anikhi-
movsky, fitter of the Kirov Machine-Tool Plant in Vitebsk,
L. Sorokoletova, team leader of Gomel Woodworking Plant, B. Marty-
nov, engine driver of the Ilyich Locomotive Depot, of Moscow, and
N. Moskvichova, head of a communist work team at the Gomel
Knitted Goods Factory

Delegates to the Twenty-Second Congress: Hero of the Soviet Union
Yuri Gagarin, the cosmonaut, and others

Delegates to the Twenty-Second Congress from the Party organisations of Uzbekistan (*left to right*): H. Irgashev, Chairman of the Tashkent Regional Executive Committee, U. Arifov, Director of the Institute of Nuclear Physics, of the Academy of Sciences of Uzbekistan, Hero of Socialist Labour H. Tursunkulov, Chairman of the Khrushchov Collective Farm, and N. Nugmanov, Secretary of the Uzbekistan Union of Writers

Delegates to the Twenty-Second Congress: Hero of Socialist Labour Yelena Stasova, a veteran Party member, and Hero of the Soviet Union cosmonaut Herman Titov

During break between sessions at the Kremlin Palace of Congresses

Delegates to the Twenty-Second Congress from Party organisations of Tambov Region (*left to right*): A. Zakurnayeva, team leader at dairy of the Inokovsky State Farm, T. Kondrakova, team leader of the Pamyat Ilyicha Collective Farm of Tokarevka District, and M. Plutalov, team leader of the Uvarovo Sugar Refinery

Before a session

Delegates to the Twenty-Second Congress (*left to right*): R. Sikorina, team leader at the Gorodishchensky State Farm of Mogilev Region, T. Klimashevskaya, team leader of the Yanka Kupala Collective Farm of Minsk Region in Byelorussia, and Hero of Socialist Labour T. Pereshivko, pig-breeder of the Pobeditel State Farm of Omsk Region in the R.S.F.S.R.

In the Congress Presidium (*left to right*), front row, Foreign Minister A. Gromyko and Defence Minister R. Malinovsky; back row, members of the Communist Party of China delegation to the Twenty-Second Congress of the C.P.S.U., Chou En-lai and Peng Chen, and a member of the Polish United Workers Party delegation, Władisław Gomułka

Fraternal delegations to the Twenty-Second Congress: Members of the Polish United Workers Party delegation headed by Władisław Gomułka

Fraternal delegations to the Twenty-Second Congress: Members of the Rumanian Workers Party delegation, First Secretary of the C.C. Gheorghe Gheorghiu-Dej (*extreme left*) converses with Politbureau Member Anton Yugov, of the Bulgarian Communist Party delegation (*extreme right*)

Fraternal delegations to the Twenty-Second Congress: Members of the Communist Party of Czechoslovakia delegation headed by Antonín Novotný (*extreme right*) in the Kremlin grounds

Fraternal delegations to the Twenty-Second Congress: Members of the Italian Communist Party delegation headed by Palmiro Togliatti (*second from right*) in Red Square

Fraternal delegations to the Twenty-Second Congress (*left to right*): Members of the French Communist Party delegation, Politbureau Member Jeannette Vermeersch and Maurice Thorez, General Secretary of the Party, converse with P. Voyevodin, member of the C.P.S.U. since 1899

Fraternal delegations to the Twenty-Second Congress: Members of the U.S. Communist Party delegation Elizabeth Gurley Flynn (*centre*) and Henry Winston (*right*) converse with Justas Paleckis, Chairman of the Presidium of the Supreme Soviet of the Lithuanian S.S.R.

Fraternal delegations to the Twenty-Second Congress: Members of the Cuban United Revolutionary Organisations delegation Blas Roca and Rita Díaz among Congress delegates

Members of the Sudanese Union delegation, of the Mali Republic, to the Twenty-Second Congress of the C.P.S.U.

A view of the Kremlin Palace of Congresses

Leaders of the Communist Party of the Soviet Union and members of fraternal delegations to the Twenty-Second Congress at the unveiling of the monument to Karl Marx in Moscow